The Iran–Iraq War

Impact and Implications

Edited by
Efraim Karsh
Senior Fellow at the Jaffee Center for Strategic Studies and
Lecturer in International Relations, Tel-Aviv University

M
MACMILLAN in association with the
JAFFEE CENTER FOR STRATEGIC
STUDIES, TEL-AVIV UNIVERSITY
JCSS

First published 1989

Published by
THE MACMILLAN PRESS LTD
Houndmills, Basingstoke, Hampshire RG21 2XS
and London
Companies and representatives
throughout the world

Printed in Great Britain by Billing & Sons Ltd, Worcester

British Library Cataloguing in Publication Data
The Iran–Iraq War: impact and implications.
1. Iran. Wars with Iraq, 1980
I. Karsh, Efraim   II. Merkaz le-mehkarim
estrategiyim 'al shem Yafeh.
955'.054
ISBN 0–333–48685–4 (hardcover)
ISBN 0–333–48686–2 (paperback)

In memory of Efraim Marszalkowicz

The Jaffee Center for Strategic Studies (JCSS)

The Center for Strategic Studies was established at Tel-Aviv University at the end of 1977. In 1983 it was named the Jaffee Center for Strategic Studies in honour of Mr and Mrs Mel Jaffee. The objective of the Center is to contribute to the expansion of knowledge on strategic subjects and to promote public understanding of and pluralistic thought on matters of national and international security.

The Center relates to the concept of strategy in its broadest meaning, namely, the complex of processes involved in the identification, mobilization, and application of resources in peace and war, in order to solidify and strengthen national and international security.

JCSS Publications

JCSS publications present the findings and assessments of the Center's research staff. Each paper represents the work of a single investigator or a team. Such teams may include research fellows who are not members of the Center's staff. Views expressed in the Center's publications are those of the authors and do not necessarily reflect the views of the Center, its trustees, officers, or other staff members or the organizations and individuals that support its research. Thus the publication of a work by JCSS signifies that it is deemed worthy of public consideration but does not imply endorsement of conclusions or recommendations.

Editor
AHARON YARIV

Executive Editor
JOSEPH ALPHER

Contents

List of Figures and Tables

Figures

Tables

Notes on the Contributors

Joseph Alpher is Deputy Head of the Jaffee Center for Strategic Studies, Tel-Aviv University. He is a former department head in the Israeli Prime Minister's Office. He recently served as co-ordinator and co-editor of the JCSS Study Group Report *The West Bank and Gaza: Israel's Options for Peace* (1989).

Amazia Baram is a Lecturer on Modern Middle Eastern History at the University of Haifa and the author of numerous articles on Iraqi politics. In 1988–9 he was a Visiting Scholar at the Woodrow Wilson International Center for Scholars (Washington, DC).

Henri J. Barkey is Assistant Professor in International Relations at Lehigh University, specializing in Turkish affairs. He is currently completing a book on the industrialization of Turkey.

John Chipman is Assistant-Director for Regional Security Studies at the IISS, where he directs the Institute's research and conference programme on the Middle East, Africa, Asia, and Latin America. He is the editor of *NATO's Southern Allies: Internal and External Challenges* (1988), and the author of *French Power and Africa: History of an Idea and its Post Colonial Practice* (1989), among other works.

Shahram Chubin an Iranian national is currently at the Graduate Institute of International Studies, Geneva. Formerly on the staff of the International Institute of Strategic Studies (London), his most recent publication (with Charles Tripp) is *Iran and Iraq at War* (1988). His other books include *The Persian Gulf: The Role of the Outside Powers* (1981) and *Iran's Foreign Relations* (1974).

Chaim Herzog is President of the State of Israel, and a leading commentator on military and strategic affairs. His long and distinguished career includes postings as Director of Military Intelligence, Member of the Foreign Affairs and Defence Committee of the Knesset, and Israel's Permanent Representative to the United Nations. His many publications include *The War of Atonement* (1975); *The Arab–Israeli Wars* (1982); and *Battles of the Bible* (1982), of which he is co-author.

Eliyahu Kanovsky, Professor of Economics, is Dean of the Faculty of Social Sciences at Bar-Ilan University. His recent publications include: 'Soviet-American Competition in the Middle East: The US – The Economic

Dimension', in Spiegel, Heller and Goldberg (eds), *The Soviet-American Competition in the Middle East* (1988); 'Another Oil Shock in the 1990s? A Dissenting View', Washington Institute for Near East Policy, 1987; 'Saudi Arabia's Dismal Future: Regional and Global Implications', *Middle East Contemporary Survey 1987*; 'What's Behind Syria's Current Economic Problems?' *Middle East Contemporary Survey*, 1986.

Efraim Karsh, the volume editor, is a Senior Fellow at the Jaffee Center for Strategic Studies and a Lecturer on International Relations, Tel- Aviv University. He has held teaching and/or research posts at Columbia University, the International Institute for Strategic Studies (London), and the Kennan Institute for Advanced Russian Studies (Washington DC). His most recent publications include *The Iran–Iraq War: A Military Analysis* (1987) and *The Soviet Union and Syria* (1988).

Geoffrey Kemp is a Senior Associate at the Carnegie Endowment for International Peace. He served in the White House on the National Security Council staff from 1981–4 and was Senior Director for Near East & South Asian Affairs.

Robert S. Litwak directs the International Security Studies Program at the Woodrow Wilson International Center for Scholars in Washington. He has held research fellowships at Harvard University and at the International Institute for Strategic Studies in London. He is the author of *Detente and the Nixon Doctrine* and *Security in the Persian Gulf: Sources of Interstate Conflict*, amongst other publications. Dr Litwak was a visiting scholar at the Institute of Oriental Studies (USSR Academy of Sciences) in Moscow in spring 1986 and is currently completing a book on Soviet policies in the Third World under Gorbachev.

Thomas L. McNaugher is a Senior Fellow in Foreign Policy Studies at the Brookings Institution. Formerly a policy analyst at the Rand Corporation, he is the author, *inter alia*, of *Arms and Oil: U.S. Military Strategy and the Persian Gulf*.

David Menashri is a Senior Research Fellow at the Dayan Center for Middle Eastern and African Studies, Tel Aviv-University. He has held teaching and/ or research posts at Princeton and Cornell universities, and is the author of *Iran: The Revolution and Beyond* (1989), among other works.

Itamar Rábinovich, Professor of Middle Eastern History, is Dean of the Faculty of Humanities as Head of the Dayan Center for Middle Eastern and African Studies, Tel-Aviv University. His many publications include *Syria under the Ba'th* (1972) and *The War for Lebanon* (1985).

Barry Rubin is a Fellow at the Johns Hopkins University School of Advanced International studies. He is author of *Paved with Good Intentions: The American Experience and Iran*, and *Modern Dictators: Third World Coupmakers, Strongmen, and Populist Tyrants*, among other books.

Philip A. G. Sabin is a Lecturer in Technology and Military Policy at the Department of War Studies, King's College London. He has held research fellowships at Harvard and at the International Institute for Strategic Studies in London. His publications include a book on *The Third World War Scare in Britain* (1986), an Adelphi Paper on *Perceptions and Symbolism in Nuclear Force Planning* (1987), and an edited volume on *The Future of UK Air Power* (1988), together with numerous articles on defence issues.

Charles Tripp is currently a Lecturer in Politics, with special reference to the Near and Middle East, at the School of Oriental and African Studies, University of London. In 1988 he co-authored, with Shahram Chubin, the book *Iran and Iraq at War*.

Robin Wright wrote her chapter as a Senior Associate at the Carnegie Endowment for International Peace. Formerly the Beirut correspondent of the *Sunday Times*, she is the author of *Sacred Rage: The Wrath of Militant Islam* (1986), and has recently completed another book entitled, *In the Name of God: The First Decade of the Islamic Revolution*.

Preface

Perhaps the first *post-bellum* analysis of the eight-year war between Iran and Iraq, this book evolved from papers delivered initially at an international conference convened at Tel-Aviv University in September 1988. The papers were revised and updated in early 1989.

The numerous studies of the war published so far have concentrated on limited aspects of this protracted conflict, without trying to present a comprehensive analysis. The end of the war generated a need for an updated multifaceted analysis, addressing the various dimensions of the war, from its impact on Iran and Iraq to the regional and global implications; from its social and political ramifications to the military, strategic and economic significance. In filling this research lacuna, this volume adopts an interdisciplinary approach, bringing together historians of modern Middle East affairs, political scientists, economists and military strategists.

In undertaking such a wide-ranging project, one must, naturally, draw on the support and counsel of many individuals and institutions. I am especially indebted to Maj.-General (Res.) Aharon Yariv, Head of the Jaffee Center for Strategic Studies, and Joseph Alpher, Deputy Head of JCSS, for their invaluable support and encouragement throughout the various stages of the project. Special thanks are also due to the US Naval War College Foundation which co-sponsored the conference. I am also grateful to the following guest speakers, commentators and chairmen who greatly enriched the conference discussions, thus contributing to the refinement of the essays: Richard Boidin of the French Foreign Office, Eliot Cohen of the Naval War College, Yair Evron, Azar Gat, and Aaron Klieman of the Department of Political Science, Tel-Aviv University, Gad Gilbar of the University of Haifa, Galia Golan of the Hebrew University of Jerusalem, Mark Heller, Aharon Levran and Aryeh Shalev from the JCSS, Martin Kramer of the Tel-Aviv University, Aryeh Levin of the Israeli Ministry of Foreign Affairs, Daniel Pipes of the Foreign Policy Research Institute, Philadelphia, Ze'ev Schiff of Ha'aretz newspaper, and Barry Watts of the Northrop Corporation. Finally, I am grateful to Tova Polonsky and Shulamit Reich of the JCSS for their administrative assistance, and to Alexandra Szilvassy for research and editorial assistance.

Tel-Aviv   EFRAIM KARSH

Introduction
Efraim Karsh

On 18 July, after a year of evasion and hesitation, Iran accepted Security Council Resolution 598 on a ceasefire in the Gulf war. A month later the ceasefire came into force, and in September peace talks between the two protagonists began in Geneva. Thus ended the eight-year Gulf War, the longest and bloodiest conflict between two Third World states in the post-1945 era; a war that towered over the Middle Eastern political scene for nearly a decade and reached unprecedented peaks of violence, even by the standards of this strife-torn region.

The Iran–Iraq War has often been viewed as the most recent eruption of the longstanding Persian–Arab animosity. It is not. While there is obviously little love lost between the two nations, the perception of the war along ethnic/national lines overlooks the fact that the periods of convergence and co-operation between twentieth-century Iran and Iraq have exceeded by far the spells of hostility and antagonism. If anything, the war was a relentless struggle over power and ideas between two mutually exclusive regimes. In this sense it was the most acute direct outcome of the Iranian Revolution. For, although it was Iraq, and not Iran, that resorted to armed force, the onset of the war and its persistence for eight bloody years were of the making of revolutionary Iran.

The war was one of those outstanding historical events in which the advent of a revolutionary regime in a major country triggered a violent response on the part of those powers bent on preserving the prevailing *status quo*. Hence the fortunes of the Iranian revolution show a striking similarity to its two great predecessors, the French and the Russian revolutions: each heralded a universal ideology professing the subversion of all other existing forms of government, while at the same time displaying a visible physical frailty due to the disintegration of the professional military and its replacement by ill-equipped and poorly trained popular militias. This unique combination of an extremely menacing ideology and military vulnerability provided the *status quo* powers with a 'window of opportunity' to try to deflect the perceived existential threat by resorting to armed force. Hence, the Iraqi invasion of Iran in September 1980 is not fundamentally different (though far wider in scope) from the Austro-Prussian invasion of France in 1792–3 or the Allies' military intervention in Russia between 1918 and 1920: an offensive move motivated by a defensive strategy. In the words of Shahram Chubin: 'What made war likely – even inevitable – was not simply ... [the] making [of] a conservative and satisfied Iran into a revolutionary power intent on a quasi-

1

universal mission of spreading its version of true Islam and hence destabilizing its neighbours . . . but also its neglect of, and disdain for, the (traditional)
military balance obtaining between two countries' (p. 13). The termination of
the war on the basis of the 1980 *status quo ante*, with neither victor nor
vanquished, has therefore left the core of the conflict unresolved – if not
exacerbated.

Whether the Geneva peace negotiations lead to the diminution of this
conflict and its replacement by a durable settlement, or whether it succumbs
again to the enduring sources of antagonism and slide into hostilities,
depends first and foremost on the long-range impact of the war on both
belligerents. The eight-year war has certainly done precious little to cultivate
mutual trust and benevolence between them. On the other hand, it has
exerted a sobering impact on both regimes, demonstrating in the most
devastating way the futility of armed force as a means of settling inter-state
conflicts.

In examining the impact of the war on Iran, the key motif is undoubtedly
disillusionment and moderation. To Iran, like the First French Republic and
the newly-established Bolshevik state, war was the main means for rallying
popular support behind the regime, and at once the major sobering force,
subduing messianic zeal in both the external and the domestic spheres. To be
sure, the persistence of the war for nearly a decade despite its exorbitant costs
and against tremendous odds can hardly be considered a demonstration of
moderation. This fact, nevertheless, should not blur the prolonged and
painful process of disillusionment undergone by the Iranian society and
political system during these demanding years, which culminated in the
desperate plea for a ceasefire in the summer of 1988.

Indeed, as Efraim Karsh shows in his examination of the vicissitudes in
Iran's Gulf policy during the war, Tehran's acceptance of Security Council
Resolution 598 implied the completion of a cyclic reversal in its worldview –
from the revisionist dream of shaping the Gulf along Islamic lines, to
acquiescence in the regional *status quo* established by the Shah in 1975; from
the vision of 'the permanent revolution' to the notion of 'Islam in one
country'. With Iran's ill-equipped military unable to breach the formidable
Iraqi line of defence, the civilian population severely exhausted, and the
economy largely devastated, the clerics were forced to discard their far-
reaching dream of establishing an Islamic order throughout the Gulf, and to
readopt the conventional 'rules of the game' to which they had been so
adamantly opposed.

Once 'back to its senses', Iran's return to 'normalcy' was fast and
sweeping: apart from mending the fences with its Gulf neighbours, Tehran
has embarked on a vigorous campaign aimed at breaking its international
isolation and rejoining into the mainstream of international politics. Excluding neither East nor West, this campaign has met with considerable success,
culminating in the re-establishment of diplomatic (and working) relations

with the major West European powers. True, this process has suffered a certain setback as a result of the Rushdie affair. Nevertheless, even at the height of the crisis, Iran did not fail to signal its reluctance to escalate into an irreversable breach with the West.

Nor was the process of disillusionment confined to external policy; both the regime and the public at large had to come to terms with reality in the domestic sphere as well. True, for quite some time the war fulfilled a crucial function for the regime by enabling the clerics to rally public support behind their cause. However, following the suppression of the major opposition groups in 1983–4, and in view of the mounting human toll and economic dislocation, the war ceased to serve its major domestic purpose, becoming instead the most serious challenge to the existence of the revolutionary regime. This, in turn, has injected a significant measure of pragmatism into the clerics' behaviour in their attempt to bridge the widening gap between the grim reality and their ideals of social justice and political order.

The most fundamental element of the regime's pragmatism on the domestic front, argues David Menashri, is the modification of the concept of *velayat-e faqih*, the governance of the Muslim jurisprudent. The source of legitimization for the concentration of political power in the hands of the clerics, the doctrine of *velayat-e faqih* faced a growing challenge as the issue of succession became topical, with no undisputed religious authority in sight to replace Ayatollah Ruhollah Khomeini in his capacity as *vali-e faqih*. Hence, by way of securing the survivability of the regime after his demise, in the late war years Khomeini displayed a readiness to risk a measure of erosion in the powers of *vali-e faqih* by strengthening the 'conventional' state organs (government, parliament) at the expense of the supreme religious bodies, primarily the Council of Guardians. And this clear indication of pragmatism was well expressed by the powerful Speaker of the Majlis, Ali-Akbar Hashemi-Rafsanjani: 'In our country, the law should follow Islamic doctrine. However, if necessary, priority should be given to government decision over doctrine' (p. 45).

The real test of the regime's pragmatism, though, is still ahead, as Iran faces the difficult task of post-war reconstruction. Indeed, the ceasefire was followed by a heated debate within the clerics whether to allow greater room for the private sector in the reconstruction effort and to accept foreign aid to this end. At the time of writing the pragmatists, who advocate greater openness of the Iranian economy, appear to have the upper hand over the more doctrinaire faction, though their fortunes have somewhat waned following the Rushdie affair.

In contrast to Iran's subdued reaction to the ceasefire, Iraq loudly praised this development. Baghdad's vociferous approval led not a few analysts and observers to crown Iraq as the victor of the eight-year war. At first glance, this view seems quite comprehensible: did not the ceasefire come in the wake of a long chain of Iraqi successes that brought Iran to its knees? Did not

Khomeini in person define the decision to stop fighting as worse than taking poison? Moreover, the war entailed some positive results from the standpoint of the Ba'th regime, primarily its contribution to the crystallization of Iraqi nationalism. Since the mid-1970s the Ba'th has made a sustained effort to create a new and specifically Iraqi identity out of the disparate elements of Iraq's population. Without seeking to divorce Iraq from the Arab world, it has emphasised Iraq's unique Mesopotamian heritage in order to create a 'new Iraqi man'. This approach was pursued into the war with a fairly good measure of success, as the enormous pressure placed by the Iranians on the Iraqi people reinforced its cohesiveness and created a strong sense of shared destiny.

Yet, notwithstanding the Iraqi gains – the very survivability of the Ba'th regime can be considered a real achievement in view of Tehran's determination to overthrow it – Iraq has undoubtedly paid a far higher price than Saddam Hussein had anticipated in 1980. The Ba'th regime may well rejoice in victory, but the real victim of the war was the Iraqi people which bore the consequences of the ambitions of its leaders. Hence, as Charles Tripp shows in his analysis of the implications of the war for Iraqi politics, the termination of hostilities does not necessarily augur well for Saddam Hussein: 'The removal of an unmistakable Iranian military threat, combined with the existence of the legacy of devices used to ward off that threat, are likely to present Saddam Hussein with considerable challenges in the future. In terms of Saddam Hussein's political survival, the war may have ended, but the battle may have only just begun' (p. 76).

In examining the impact of the war on Iraq's international orientation it is hard to avoid noting the irony of the fact that Baghdad has been a true disciple of the Iranian concept of 'neither East nor West'. Entering the war as a close ally of the Soviet Union (although bilateral relations at the time were at their lowest ebb), Iraq's disappointment with the level of Soviet support for its cause drove it to rehabilitate relations with the United States, with which it had severed diplomatic ties following the 1967 Six-Day War. Subsequently, the war years witnessed the (partial) unravelling of the close Iraqi-Soviet partnership and the emergence of an Iraqi-American collaboration in the political, economic, and even the military spheres.

By way of improving its bargaining position *vis-à-vis* the two superpowers and keeping both at arm's length, Iraq made skilful use of the 'power of the weak', to borrow Arnold Wolfers' term. As shown by Amazia Baram in Chapter 5, the superpowers' reluctance to see an Iranian victory, which appeared imminent on several occasions, was Iraq's main asset throughout the war. This in turn enabled Iraq, through a dispassionate and ideology-free policy, to use the frightening spectre of an Iranian victory (and Tehran's many follies) in order to harness both East and West to its war effort.

Paradoxically, and not unlike the domestic sphere, the ending of the war is not necessarily an asset for Iraq's relations with the two superpowers. While losing its major bargaining chip – vulnerability – Iraq remains highly dependent on both East and West for its survival: it needs a continued substantial influx of Soviet weaponry to counter the (however latent) Iranian threat, and it requires Western, particularly American, economic aid for its ambitious reconstruction programmes. Above all, the support of both East and West may be crucial for the extraction of a satisfactory peace agreement from Iran. Therefore, in the foreseeable future Iraq can be expected to 'continue to walk the tightrope between East and West, trying to benefit from both and making all the ideological sacrifices necessary to secure its strategic and economic needs' (p. 94). An already discernable by-product of this anxiety to placate both superpowers, is apparent Iraqi moderation on the issue of the Arab-Israeli conflict – from vehement rejection of Israel's right to exist, to implicit recognition of that country's legitimacy. Of course, this change in the Iraqi position is by no means exclusively dependent on Baghdad's relations with the superpowers; indeed it is largely a derivative of the considerable improvement in Iraq's relations with the moderate Arab countries (Jordan and Egypt in particular) throughout the war. However, the existence of an unequivocal superpower consensus regarding Israel's right to exist makes Iraqi gestures in this realm appealing at once to both East and West.

Viewed from a regional point of view, the outcome of the war is, by and large, positive. Not only did Iran fail to topple the Ba'th regime and thus set in train a fundamentalist wave throughout the Gulf, but its vision of an Islamic order was widely spurned by most Sunni and many moderate Shi'ite fundamentalists. Only in Lebanon does Iran's version of Islamic fundamentalism appear to have left a lasting impact, but even there it has been severely constrained by domestic and external factors. It would be no exaggeration to argue that with the confinement of the revolution to Iran's boundaries the Middle Eastern state-system has withstood one of the gravest ideological challenge to its existence.

And yet, though they have prevailed over a formidable force of revisionism the *status quo* powers can hardly relax. Islamic fundamentalism is subdued but not completely eradicated. As Robin Wright relates in her examination of the impact of the war on the resurgence of Islam in the region, 'just as the broader Islamic movement did not begin in the Islamic republic, it also was unlikely to die due solely to developments in Iran' (p. 117). Rooted essentially in the broader Third World trend of seeking refuge in religion from the alienating forces of modernization, Islamic fundamentalism can be expected to meet a similar fate to that which befell the other two great revolutions: in both cases the international system succeeded in containing the dissemination of the universal ideology in the short-run, yet eventually had to acquiesce in the worldwide spread of this message, though in a far more muted form than originally conceived. The fundamentalist genie is largely back inside the bottle, but for how long?

Yet, not all the countries of the Middle East have welcomed the ending of the war. Turkey, argues Henri Barkey, has hardly any reason to rejoice with the ceasefire given its substantial gains from the persistence of the war. In the economic sphere, the significant increase in Turkey's trade with both belligerents immeasurably improved the outlook of its crisis ridden economy. Strategically, Turkey's importance in the region, already boosted following the Iranian revolution and the consequent loss of Western strategic position there, was further enhanced by the war in general and by a once possible Iranian victory in particular.

Iraq's other neighbour, Syria, shared Turkey's lack of enthusiasm about the war's termination, though for different reasons. Perhaps Iran's closest ally throughout the war, maintains Itamar Rabinovich, Syria could be expected to figure prominently on Iraq's grudge list; indeed, the ceasefire in the Gulf was followed by a resurgence in Iraqi support, with money and arms, for Syria's most intransigent enemies in Lebanon.

Surprisingly to some extent, the Israeli reaction to the Iranian-Iraqi ceasefire was far less negative than that of its neighbour to the north. To be sure, by interlocking two hostile states and their allies in a deadly conflict for eight years, the war gave Israel a much needed 'strategic breather'; indeed, the ceasefire was followed by loud cautions that Iraq, now free of the Iranian pressure, would direct its energies against Israel. However, as established by Joseph Alpher, following the Irangate affair in 1985–6, and all the more so in view of Iraq's impressive chain of successes in 1988, decision makers in Jerusalem were gradually driven to the conclusion that the war had outlived its usefulness as far as Israeli interests were concerned: 'Rather than distracting Israel's enemies and eroding their strength, [the war] was perceived to be spawning a new and dangerous Middle Eastern arms race, involving missiles and chemical weapons, that affected the longterm Arab-Israeli military balance' (p. 164). This, together with the twin dangers of an Iraqi victory and friction between Israel and the United States (which at the time had become anxious to see a termination of hostilities), could not but reverse the conventional wisdom in Jerusalem regarding the desirability of the war's persistence.

In a sense, the attitude of the Gulf Arab states towards the war was much like the Israeli one. Like Israel, the conservative Arab monarchies had little reason to be deeply saddened by the mutual exhaustion of the two hegemonistic powers in the Gulf, particularly insofar Khomeini sought to deligitimize dynastic rule as un-Islamic; and like Israel, they viewed a strategic draw as the most desirable outcome to the war. Their direct stakes in the war, nevertheless, were far higher than those of Israel. Given their military weakness and proximity to the theatre of war, the conservative Gulf states would have been the first victims of either an Iranian or Iraqi victory. Although the Iranians proclaimed that a victory over Baghdad was merely the first step on the road to Jerusalem, the conservative Arab monarchies feared that the Iranians would make a short 'detour' in the Gulf before proceeding to Jerusalem. An Iraqi victory, on the other hand, unlikely as it seemed until the spring of 1988 (and even then), would have established Baghdad as the leading power in the Gulf, an equally undesirable development from the Gulf states' standpoint. Barry Rubin examines the problems posed by the war for these Gulf Arab states and the ways in which they reacted to them. As long as the war was raging in their vicinity the Gulf monarchies sought to ensure their security on all sides by simultaneously aiding Iraq, appeasing Iran, reinforcing their links with the United States and attempting to improve their defensive posture by forming the Gulf Co-operation Council (GCC). Once Iran announced its acceptance of Security Council Resolution 598, the Gulf monarchies reacted with a deep sigh of relief.

Yet this satisfaction was not completely unqualified. While removing the Sword of Damocles of the Iranian revolution that hung over the Gulf monarchies, the post-war era entails new risks for these countries in the economic sphere. True, the ceasefire may herald a measure of economic relief in the sense that Gulf financial support for Iraq is liable to cease, or at least be reduced sharply. However, as Eliyahu Kanovsky assesses, Iraq and Iran are likely to increase their oil quotas in order to revive their devastated economies, and these 'savings' for the Gulf states 'may well be offset by the deepening of the oil glut, and depressed prices which would ensue as a consequence of far higher Iraqi and Iranian production'. In short, while bringing a sense of relief, 'for those countries in the region overwhelmingly dependent on oil revenues for their survival – of which Saudi Arabia is a prime example – the aftermath of the Iran–Iraq War may be almost as burdensome, from an economic and financial point of view, as the war itself' (pp. 250–1).

The Iran–Iraq War is often portrayed as one of the most impenetrable inter-state conflicts since the Second World War. In a way it was. Despite its extraordinarily long duration and sensitive geopolitical location, the war witnessed no direct superpower intervention of the sort so common in the Arab-Israeli wars, not to mention the Korea and the Vietnam wars. Yet both superpowers were anything but indifferent to the fortunes of the war. While avoiding a direct and visible interference until the later stages of the war, this exerted a significant influence on the course of the conflict. Indeed, it is no exaggeration to argue that both superpowers saved Iraq from total collapse and enabled it to tip the scales in its favour: the USSR by providing Iraq with the necessary weapons and war material at critical times, and the United States by withholding any sustained supply of offensive arms from Iran. For, even though Iran managed to secure alternative sources of arms with which to continue to prosecute the war, it was beyond its power to reconstruct and reorganize its forces to the extent that would enable it to prevail over Iraq.

Moreover, as shown by Thomas McNaugher, when the United States

decided to discard its ostensible aloofness and thrust itself more aggressively
into the Gulf – by reflagging Kuwaiti tankers, engineering Security Council
Resolution 598, and concentrating an international arms embargo on Iran –
its policy carried a significant, though not decisive, weight in the Iranian
decision to opt for a ceasefire. Yet, cautions McNaugher, even though the
reflagging operation – the most visible facet of the US Gulf policy – must be
judged a success, 'it is a success that provides a cautionary lesson for future
US military operations in the Third World'. Though run well and with
considerable sensitivity to the dangerous political dynamics in the Gulf, the
reflagging's success owed much to good luck, as well as to Iran's rapidly
deteriorating position. For, not unlike its experience in Vietnam, the US
found itself largely reacting to developments in the Gulf rather than initiating
them. Consequently, 'notwithstanding the nation's success in reflagging ...
the prior question – is commitment necessary at all? – remains as important
as ever' (p. 194).

Whatever the lessons of the reflagging operation, it is clear that the United
States was one of the major beneficiaries of the Iran–Iraq War. If in
September 1980 US relations with both Iran and Iraq were at a very low ebb,
the war enabled Washington to rebuild relations with Iraq, obtain a potential
strategic opening to Iran, and reinforce its partnership with the conservative
Gulf states. And considering that the years of massive reconstruction
awaiting the two protagonists will require substantial Western investments
and support, the prospects for the future look rather promising. In short, a
decade after its humiliating expulsion from the Gulf following the Iranian
Revolution, the United States is back in the region, and well-poised to meet
future events.

Nor did the eight-year war damage the USSR's regional position in any
meaningful way. True, as argued earlier, the war somewhat eroded Soviet-
Iraqi relations following Moscow's objection to the Iraqi initiative in
launching it, and its subsequent avoidance of supporting the Iraqi offensive.
But it should be kept in mind that the Iraqis had never been subservient allies
and had always tried to keep their distance from Moscow. In any event, once
Iraq was forced on to the defensive the USSR provided it with the necessary
military backing to ward off Iranian pressure; this, in turn, generated a
significant improvement in Soviet-Iraqi relations. Therefore, maintains
Robert Litwak, 'in assessing the Iran–Iraq War from the perspective of
Soviet state interests, the outcome, on balance, has been positive. The war,
albeit one which the USSR did not welcome, did provide Moscow with an
opportunity to expand and further legitimise its regional role' (p. 210).

This mirror-image superpower judgement of the outcome of the war – with
both pleased and neither aggrieved – stands in sharp contradiction to the
customary Soviet-American practice in regional conflicts. Unlike previous
inter-state wars in the post-Second World War epoch (e.g., Korea, Vietnam,
Arab-Israeli wars, Ethiopia) where the two superpowers tended to adopt a

'zero-sum' approach according to which a gain for one was necessarily a loss for the other, this time the conflict was viewed as a 'mixed-motive game'. While elements of a 'zero-sum game' were also evident in this conflict, as manifested by the mutual anxiety to see the withdrawal of the opposing naval forces from the Gulf, they were undoubtedly overshadowed by shared common interests and goals which, in turn, led to the evolution of tacit co-operation. In the words of Robert Litwak, 'both emphasized the dangers of escalation; neither Washington nor Moscow desired to see a decisive victory by either combatant' (p. 212).

Interestingly enough, this communality of US–Soviet interests, however limited, was not shared by Europe. In fact, argues John Chipman, not only did the major European powers 'distinguish themselves from the US', making 'separate if not radically different definitions of "Western" interests in the region', but there was never a unified European policy towards the war, only disparate national policies motivated by the desire to reap the utmost gains from the vicissitudes of the conflict. And this divisiveness is likely to be pursued into the post-war era: 'Whatever order is established, or whatever form of anarchy prevails, individual European states will continue to pursue national interests that will only on some issues reflect a common European view and that probably more by accident than by design' (p. 226).

The Iran–Iraq War is unlikely to be studied by military historians for its strategic lessons or battlefield accomplishments, but will rather be remembered as an extremely costly exercise in futility which eroded several crucial thresholds and 'red lines' in inter-state conflicts: it is the first war since the First World War to witness the operational employment of gas at a fairly wide scale; it involved the most intensive campaign against non-belligerent shipping since the Second World War, and also, perhaps, the harshest attacks on population centres and economic targets. These escalations entail far-reaching adverse implications for regional stability. Philip Sabin shows that most of the war's escalations tended to occur in a deliberate rather than uncontrolled manner and were, by and large, a defensive move initiated by the losing side. Nevertheless, few Middle Eastern countries can maintain their coolness in the face of so many broken taboos. Hence, argues Chaim Herzog, given the exceptionally mild international reaction to the use of chemical weapons by the Iraqis during the war (only when Iraq resorted to an extremely widespread employment of gas against civilian Kurdish population in late 1988, several months after the war, did the United States take action), 'every army facing the possibility of war must now take into consideration that the international accords barring the use of chemical weapons in war are apparently of little binding value' (p. 266).

Indeed, as shown by Geoffrey Kemp, the Iran–Iraq War has accelerated the already alarming arms race in the region: 'The purchase of long-range Chinese surface-to-surface missiles by Saudi Arabia; reliable reports that Libya and Syria are developing chemical warfare capabilities in addition to their continuing interest in procuring more surface-to-surface missiles; and Israel's successful launching of a research satellite in September 1988 which conclusively demonstrates the sophistication of its own missile programmes' (p. 276).

Given this evolving combination of widespread 'less conventional' weaponry and eroding norms of employment, the implications of an all-out Arab-Israeli war appear horrendous. But has the termination of the Gulf War increased the likelihood of such a conflict? From a purely military point of view it has. Not only did the war not weaken Iraq militarily, but this country has emerged from the eight-year conflict a far stronger power: its ground forces grew from 200,000 troops (12 divisions employing 2750 tanks) in 1980 to some 955,000 (50 divisions and 6000 tanks). The Iraqi Air Force has been increased during the same period from 332 fighting aircraft to 500. This formidable force is not only far better equipped than it was in 1980, but has also acquired substantial operational experience. The sustained Iraqi campaign of 1988, for example, was a swift and well co-ordinated combined-arms operation, reflecting a fairly impressive ability to manoeuvre effectively with armoured units; the success of the Iraqi Air Force in mounting long-range raids on Iranian targets at a distance of 1000 kilometres, though performed against an exceptionally meagre air defence opposition, is something few air forces in the Middle East are capable of carrying out.

Yet, the exorbitant human and economic cost paid by Iraq during the war, its engrained hostility towards Syria, and its growing reliance on great-power support for future rehabilitation have already injected an apparent element of moderation into Baghdad's stance on the Arab-Israeli conflict. On a parallel, the Iranian threat has receded but not diminished. While emerging from the war in far less enviable shape than Iraq, the exhausted and poorly-equipped Iranian armed forces of 1988 are nevertheless far better than their proud imperial predecessors. The corrupt and incompetent military leadership of the imperial army was replaced (albeit in a brutal process) by a professional, imaginative and dedicated officer corps that gained abundant first-hand experience during lengthy years of fighting. Hence, Iraq is fully aware of the temporal nature of Iran's military inferiority: once arms supplies to Iran are restored in full and its two main military organs, the professional army and the Revolutionary Guards (*Pasdaran*) are incorporated into an effective unified command (and this may turn out to be a less remote goal than is commonly assumed), Tehran will regain its predominant regional military stature that was jeopardized by nearly a decade of material starvation. Accordingly, argues Kemp, 'neither Iran nor Iraq will be able to sweep their mutual animosity under the carpet under such bitter confrontation. Rather, one can expect both to retain a healthy scepticism of each other's intents and, for this reason, maintain significant military forces on, or near, the front line. Both sides will have to assume that at some point in the future they may have to fight again' (p. 271).

The eight-year Gulf War may be over, but the end of the Iranian-Iraqi conflict is still not in sight.

Part I

The War and the Belligerents

1 Iran and the War: From Stalemate to Ceasefire

Shahram Chubin

Among conflicts in the Third World, the Iran–Iraq War is unusual in several respects. Most commonly cited are its costs in human life and economic resources and its inordinate length. Less often remarked was the genre of conflict that it represented, being untypical of the prevailing pattern in the non-industrial areas, where the tendency has been for internal or civil wars. In contrast, this was a relatively rare case of (pure) interstate conflict. It was also in the classic mould in that it represented not simply – or principally – a dispute over territory, but rather a contest over power and ideas.

The war, which ended one month short of its eighth anniversary, had become part of the political and strategic landscape of the Middle East throughout the decade, establishing or accelerating new alignments and forcing new priorities. Because of its durability, its bouts of intense clashes alternating with seasonal lulls, and the impenetrability of the Iranian/Islamic revolution, it had by the middle of the decade given rise to a host of assumptions, *bon mots* and cliches among observers that substituted for informed analysis. The Islamic republic which challenged the prevailing international system and seemed bent on reversing it, appeared implacable in purpose and insensitive to pressures, threats and punishment. No part of the war, I believe, came as a greater surprise to this class of spectator (as well as to others) than the way the war ended, and it is on this phase in particular that this chapter is concentrated.

The *onset* of the war at least should not have come as a surprise. The relationship between revolution and war is a close one often noted in history. In this as in other cases the advent of a cataclysmic change in a major state and its replacement by a revolutionary 'order' that made claims on its neighbours, was bound to cause instability. The revolution in Iran upset the balance in two ways: first militarily, by replacing the Shah's army with what looked like a revolutionary rabble; and second politically, by making a conservative and satisfied Iran into a revolutionary power intent on a quasi-universal mission of spreading its version of true Islam and hence destabilizing its neighbours. What made war likely – even inevitable – was not simply Iran's provocations, but also its neglect of, and disdain for, the (traditional) military balance obtaining between the two countries. (It had been this balance – in Iran's favour – that had secured the 1975 Algiers Agreement and sustained the new relationship of respect and reciprocity that had followed

13

it.) Iran's rhetorical excesses and claims and inattention to the military balance were matched on the Iraqi side by a compound of fear and ambition: fear about Iran's goals if the revolution were to become entrenched, and ambition to achieve a position of regional supremacy while Iran was preoccupied and Iraq was in a relative position of unmatched military/ economic strength. From Iraq's perspective the time to strike (preventively perhaps) was unlikely to be better than in 1980, before the revolution put down its roots, while its forces were in disarray, and while its relationship with both superpowers and most regional states were at best strained.[1]

Iraq's miscalculation was nearly total in that it overestimated its own capabilities while misconstruing the nature of its adversary and the sources of power at the latter's disposal. For while revolutionary Iran was deficient in the traditional or quantitative indices of military power, it made up for this, to a certain extent, by reliance on the superior commitment of its populace to the regime and hence the war. Indeed so eagerly did the revolutionary regime embrace the war as a 'blessing', labelling it as a struggle between 'Islam and blasphemy' and defining its war aims as the overthrow of the Ba'thist regime in Baghdad, and using the war to suppress its enemies at home, that Iraq's leaders might well have wondered what Iran would have done in the absence of such an external diversion.

Iraq's inability to capitalize on surprise in the early weeks of the war to military effect was not as serious as its failure to fashion a clear political objective. It seems to have expected either a quick collapse of the regime, or a willingness to sue for peace, based on limited losses. This completely misjudged the nature of revolutionary systems which do not traditionally understand or wage limited wars (let alone a revolution based on the Shi'i emphasis on the positive value of martyrdom and sacrifice). Martin Wight noted this phenomenon common to most revolutions:

> International revolution . . . transforms the character of war. It blurs the distinction between war and peace, inernational war and civil war, war and revolution . . . International revolutions generate revolutionary wars, in the sense that their wars are tinged with a doctrinal ferocity, and have unlimited aims. They tend to be not wars for defined objectives but crusades or wars for righteousness. They aim not at a negotiated peace but at a 'Carthaginian peace' or unconditional surrender.[2]

Iran stumbled into a war which it did much to provoke and little to prepare for. Once embarked upon the 'imposed war', which it embraced with characteristic ardour and militancy, Iran used it to harness the energies of the mobilized revolutionary rank and file, settle domestic scores, consolidate power and focus on the revolution's mission abroad. The latter was less controversial than the content of the revolution at home which remained contentious. The war thus came to represent a test of the revolution, its capacity for commitment and sacrifice, as well as its ingenuity and self-reliance. It came gradually to epitomize all the themes of suffering and martyrdom which the leadership seemed determined to cultivate. In time it simply displaced any other item on the revolution's agenda. The war and the revolution had merged; support for the two had become so intertwined as to make them virtually indistinguishable.

If Iran's revolution and its claims helped to precipitate the conflict, its definition of the absolute stakes that the war represented (which brooked no compromise) helped fuel it long after it made any sense. Iran's expulsion of Iraqi forces from its territory had been effected by mid-1982, yet the momentum of war and the drive to extend the sway of the Islamic revolution throughout the region, prevailed over a more sober assessment of Iran's military capabilities. A series of costly offensives led by revolutionary guards and volunteers (Basijis) failed. The war in the next two years settled down into a pattern of reckless Iranian attacks on Iraqi forces dug in behind water and earth obstacles and defended by a network of mines, artillery and automatic weapons. Iran's attacks at Majnoun and Howeizah in the spring of 1984 and 1985 respectively, demonstrated Iran's ingenuity and tolerance for punishment but also an inability to hold territory it captured.

Iraq seemed unwilling to resort to counteroffensives or to take casualties; consequently it let Iran dictate the tempo of the war. Iraq also relied on superior weapons-systems because of its continued access to friendly governments (especially after 1982 the USSR and France), but otherwise resorted to universal conscription. The morale of its forces appeared suspect if only because it had lost three times as many POW to Iran as its adversary had lost.

Iran by contrast relied heavily on the superior commitment of its forces. It constantly affirmed and came to believe the slogan articulated by Rafsanjani in 1984 that 'The faith of the Islamic troops is stronger than Iraq's superior firepower.' As a consequence Iran's leaders really believed that they could demonstrate the vitality of the revolution and affirm its message and validity by confronting and overcoming adversity through self-reliance. They were in no mood for lessons from the West or the professional military; their war like their revolution was to be an experience unique in the annals of war, unsullied by practical considerations or constraints.

If Iran's military successes between 1982 and 1986 were ephemeral and costly, with long gaps between major offensives in 1984–6, the problem stemmed as much from deficiencies in strategy as from logistics. Alternating between frontal offensives and attrition along the length of the frontier ('defensive Jihad'), between enthusiasm for the derring-do of the revolutionary guard and the more sober appraisals of the professional military, Iran's leaders were unable to frame a strategy that tied their war aims – the overthrow of the enemy – to their military capabilities, which in terms of equipment dwindled with each offensive. To achieve their war aims which were total in Clausewitzian terms, Iran needed to either defeat the enemy's forces decisively, or to capture a major stretegic asset precipitating his surrender (e.g., for example the southern post city of Basra, which was predominantly Shi'i). The problem was that Iraq's forces would not venture out into the field to fight (or be defeated), while the capture of Basra or Baghdad remained (and even became more) difficult because of their redundant defence lines.[3] This gap between aims and capabilities was to widen (as we shall see) and precipitate the process that led to the end of the war.

Iran fought the war with both hands tied; without dependable or rich allies, without access to weapons systems compatible with those in its inventory, and without the benefit of its own best-trained minds. Iran's leadership revelled in this, insisting, as Khomeini said in 1984, that 'Those who think that the Koran does not say "war until victory" are mistaken.' If self-sufficiency was the goal, improvisation, self-reliance and a refusal to be bound by conventional approaches had to be the means. At times the war appeared to be merely a vehicle for consciousness-raising, rather than a deadly serious business. It was 'a continuation of politics with the admixture of other means' in a sense that Clausewitz had surely not meant or intended.

Even so, Iran seemed to be winning the war. The breakthrough at Fao in February 1986 only seemed to confirm that an Iranian victory was a matter of time. Jeffrey Record's analysis (to name one) was typical of this conventional wisdom.

> The longer the war lasts, the greater the prospects for a decisive Iranian victory. Iran has three times the population of Iraq, and Iranian forces though less well-equipped, appear to be much more highly motivated than those of Iraq. In February 1986 Iran launched a series of offensives that succeeded in gaining firm control of the Shatt al-Arab waterway. Iraqi counterattacks, which deliberately sought to avoid high casualty rates for fear of undermining already tepid popular support for the war, relied primarily upon artillery fire and failed to dislodge Iranian forces. According to some Western observers of the conflict, Iraqi military leadership borders on the incompetent, and Iraqi troops, especially infantry, have little motivation.[4]

By February 1986 a number of cliches had achieved wide currency. One was that peace was only possible with the removal or disappearance of one or both of the two leaders, Saddam Hussein and Ayatollah Khomeini, implying that compromise short of victory (for Iran) would be unimaginable and tantamount to political suicide. Another was that Iran could not lose the war nor Iraq win it, implying that time was on Iran's side. For the Iranian leadership the lesson drawn from Fao had been that a military solution to the war was now indeed possible, contrary to the cautious (and possibly faint-hearted) advice of the professional military. In this view one Fao followed by several others could wrap up the war quickly. What was lacking was not material for the war effort but commitment and faith. Iran's political leaders began to unlearn what had been painfully learned on the battlefield, namely, that incremental success was an inadequate basis for achieving the total victory required to attain Iran's ambitious war aims and that only a smashing, devastating defeat of the enemy could possibly achieve this, and this was still unattainable. Now, after Fao, it looked more attainable, and the Iranian leadership sought to capitalize on the success to proclaim 'a year of decision'. Naturally, it again reverted to the style of war most suited to its forces, the frontal offensive.

In fact in one of those paradoxes in which strategy abounds, [5] Fao was to be the culminating point of Iran's success, the point at which it both over-reached itself and misled itself as to the implications. Why was the prevailing wisdom on the likely outcome of the war if it continued, so wrong? In war the relative positions of the two sides is in constant flux, and the longer the war and more fluid the picture and the more delicate the assessment of the relative balances on various levels between the two adversaries. To take but one element in relative strengths – Iran's superior commitment – its principal asset, was neither indefinitely sustainable nor by itself and adequate substitute for access to weapons systems, spares, training, etc. While 'final offensives' gave at least a semblance of momentum to Iran's war effort, so necessary to stimulate the 'bandwagon effect' on the popular forces of the revolution, they also chewed up trained manpower and hard-to-replace equipment. And the prospect of breakthrough seemed to recede with each effort. Yet at the same time, recourse to a strategy of attrition held obvious drawbacks: it could not deliver the decisive victory essential for the achievement of Iran's war aims; it was uncongenial to the revolutionary spirit nurtured on elan, and it was a two-edged sword in that it could wear down Iran's will to flight as much as Iraq's and (because of the importance of commitment in Iran's limited inventory of assets) with quite devastating consequences. A casualty of attrition, or a strategy that relied on incremental progress without the dynamic momentum of battlefield success could be the superior commitment of Iran's troops, and Iran's will to continue the war.

On the other hand the instruments for prosecuting the war were dwindling; Iraqi air attacks and the sharp drop in the price of oil in 1986, made the replacement of weapons more onerous economically. At the same time, the inventroy of arms inherited from the Shah's day was a finite resource; at some point it could no longer be cannibalized and needed to be replaced. Furthermore Operation Staunch, in place since 1984, was being taken more seriously by the US which appeared in a vengeful mood after the revelations of Irangate. European governments also began to take the issue more seriously. There is also reason to suppose that Iran's suppliers from the east – China and North Korea – though perhaps for different reasons, began to limit their supplies to Iran. Thus Iran's access to arms was being curtailed at precisely the time when its strategy called for more resources and existing stocks could no longer be raided to serve as improvised replacements.

The gap between Iran's military needs and its political aims widened as the war went on. On every quantitative index of power, Iraq's position improved year by year, compared to that of Iran. To take a few illustrative examples: in terms of arms purchases (from all sources expressed in dollar terms), Iraq spent more than Iran every year between 1981 and 1985, in ratios varying between six and three to one.[6] In military expenditures Iraq consistently outspent Iran and maintained a constant rate of between $12–14 billion (1984–7), while Iran's plunged and dipped from $14 billion in 1985-6 to a $5.89 billion the next year to between $6–8 billion in the succeeding years. As the war dragged on, Iraq's access to superior sources of arms became increasingly pronounced. In 1984 Iraq could 'only' manage a 2.5:1 superiority in tanks, 4:1 in aircraft and APC and had a 3:4 inferiority in artillery.[7] This was widened by 1988 to a 4:1 superiority in tanks, 10:1 in aircraft and 3:1 in artillery. The Commander of the Revolutionary Guard, Mohsen Reza'i was to say after the war:

> They had armour and we did not. If our circumstances in the war are not taken into account when comparisons are made with classical warfare, it will be a major error on the part of analysts. We were unarmed infantrymen against the enemy's cavalry. There are few instances in the history of Islam of such a war.[8]

Even Iran's much vaunted demographic advantage of 3:1 was not much in evidence at the battlefield towards the end of the war. Whereas between 1986 and 1988 Iraq was able to increase its manpower by some 150,000 men and expand and reorganize its forces from 30 to 39 infantry divisions, Iran's manpower fell in the same period by 100,000 men.[9]

In addition to a declining pool of volunteers necessitating greater reliance on conscripts who could not match the former in zeal, Iran's war effort was clearly hampered by logistical difficulties. These stemmed partly from political decisions such as the fielding of two sets of armed forces, the regular military and Revolutionary Guard, who duplicated each other and did not always work harmoniously. They were compounded no doubt by the difficulty of supplying troops with an astonishing variety of ammunition and spare parts, part of Western origin, part Soviet bloc (bought and captured), part from third sources, and part of indigenous manufacture. It would have been surprising if under these conditions Iran could have obtained a 'teeth to tail' ratio anywhere near that of Iraq.

As Iran launched what were to be the last major offensives of the war at Basra and in the central sector between December 24 and mid-March 1986-7, the attacks took on the aspect of a last gasp – a make-or-break attempt to force a military decision. Even the limited advance towards Basra was revealing for it demonstrated not an unstoppable, dynamic force but a strenuous and costly effort barely adequate to sustain itself. As such Iran could scarcely count on Iraq's collapse even in the unlikely event of the capture of Basra.

If the war was becoming harder for Iran to prosecute militarily, demanding greater resources, it was also becoming politically more onerous as well in two ways. Iraq's strategy of internationalizing the conflict, begun in 1984, was beginning to bear fruit. In 1986 the 'tanker war' had expanded with more shipping hit and casualties than the cumulative total of the preceding years. Iraq's aircraft with new missiles and air-refuelling capabilities were not ranging as far south as the Larak and Lavan terminals, putting all Iran's oil terminals in the Persian Gulf at risk.

In response, Iran had threatened in extremis to close the Straits of Hormuz and in the meantime had targeted those Gulf states known to be actively supporting Iraq's war effort, particularly Kuwait. Iran's accusation that Kuwait served as a transhipment point for arms destined for Iraq and that the sheikhdom with its financial subsidies and anti-Iranian policies was in effect an undeclared belligerent, was not seriously contested. But neither of the superpowers (nor the GCC states) were prepared to allow Iran to target shipping destined for the Gulf sheikhdoms as a legitimate response to Iraq's attacks on Iran's shipping. This ran counter to the outside powers' policy of containing the Gulf war (as it had by now become) and defending the other Gulf states.

The more sustained Iraq's attacks on shipping serving Iran became, the more acute the pressure on Iran to submit passively or to exert pressure militarily on the Gulf states. The dilemma posed did not admit of a solution; unable to find Iraqi targets in the waterway, Iran attacked the next best thing and found itself playing into Iraq's hand by antagonizing its immediate neighbours and also the superpowers. (Iran's retaliation against third party shipping for attacks sustained from Iraq thus played into Iraqi hands by bringing in outside powers against Iran.)

By mid-1987 the result of this was seen on two levels: a virtual schism between Persian and Arab in the Gulf after the Mecca incident in July. This was symbolized by the Arab summit conference in Amman in November which, at the insistence of Saudi Arabia, for the first time gave priority to the Gulf war in Arab councils. The concerting of policies by the superpowers in the United Nations in the form of Security Council Resolution 598 was another indicator of the degree to which Iran's conduct of the war had aroused international concern and even stimulated a parallel response. For the resolution for all its apparently neutral terminology was manifestly aimed at arresting Iran's continuation of the war, threatening mandatory sanctions (in the form of an arms embargo) if a ceasefire were not accepted.

This is not the place to discuss Iran's relations with the superpowers except to note that by mid-1987 it had done little to cultivate the friendship of either and much to push the two together in order to contain and end the war.

Soviet leaders, particularly Andrei Gromyko, repeatedly counselled Iranian officials that 'three years of negotiation are better than one day of war'. In December 1987 Gromyko pointedly told the Iranian ambassador prophetically that the later Iran's leaders reach the conclusion that it needs to end the war, the less favourable it will be for Iran.[10] Iranian leaders consistently overestimated their own centrality in international affairs and the importance of oil, while being insensitive to the changing nature of relations between the superpowers. At the same time they were unable to improve their margin for manoeuvre between the superpowers simply because Iran's ideological inflexibility shackled its diplomacy and prevented it being able to offer credible threats.

If the internationalization of the war, regional isolation and the threat of a future comprehensive arms embargo increased the psychological pressure on Iran, the lack of success since Fao (February 1986) had also begun to diminish the domestic enthusiasm for the war, even among the diehard hezbollah and the mustazefin (oppressed) class. Thus in the second arena, domestic politics, the cost of continuing the war without decisive result was beginning to be felt.

There were several indications that Iranian leaders were at least reassessing their approach to the war as of mid-1987.

1. Iran's willingness to take up the gauntlet thrown down by the super-powers' decision to excort Kuwaiti shipping suggested that Iran somehow welcomed the diversion in a sideshow of the war rather than concentrate on the serious prosecution of the war on land.
2. Iran's unwillingness to reject the Security Council resolution of July 1987 outright but to seek modifications was also indicative of a change in attitude.
3. Iran's still ambiguous war aims had nonetheless been modified over previous months; the demand for the removal of Saddam Hussein still stood, but the insistence on the removal of the Ba'th Party, reparations, and the installation of an Islamic republic, had disappeared.
4. The stream of volunteers for the front had dwindled and Iran's leaders, notably Rafsanjani, had begun to talk publicly in mid-1987 of continuing the war *unless* (or until) it began to interfere with the political administration of society.[11]

Iran's leadership had begun to despair of a military solution to the conflict by the autumn of 1987, but they were still far from devising a diplomatic strategy for extrication from the war. For one thing the war, whose importance had been repeatedly and irresponsibly inflated and equated with 'Islam' and 'our life', was clearly becoming costly to continue, but who could guess what the political costs of ending it ignominiously – in failure – would be? And who would be the courageous soul willing to convince Khomeini of the necessity, and the change in the cost-calculus of protracted war versus negotiations? This was not made any easier by the fact that Iran's sense of aggrievement about the origins and hence blame for the start of the war was not shared by many permanent members of the Security Council, in part because of Iran's prolongation of the conflict since mid-1982. And the *political* collapse of Iraq now looked more remote and a less likely source of salvation. Furthermore, the US fleet (together with that of five European allies) had taken on the appearance of a permanent fixture, less vulnerable and therefore less susceptible to political intimidation, than the land presence in Lebanon (1982–3) to which Iranian leaders erroneously compared it.

However, it was one thing for Iran's war effort to be running out of steam and quite another for it to collapse outright, precipitating the difficult, if unavoidable decision to sue for peace. The elements crushing Iran's war effort left to themselves were not such as to galvanize its leaders to make such a momentous decision in favour of peace. Only a perception that the continuation of the war would threaten the very existence of the Islamic republic, Khomeini's legacy, could have done so. Simply stated, two sets of events catalyzed Iran into the decision to seek a quick ceasefire in mid-1988; first, the intensive use by Iraq of long-range missiles on cities, and chemical weapons on the front; and second (a consequence of the first), a change in the balance of power on the ground and, particularly, the shattering of the morale of Iranian forces.

Although Iran and Iraq had traded attacks on each other's city centres in the course of the war, beginning in 1984, these had not reached the intensity of the exchanges witnessed in the revived 'war of the cities' in early 1988. In earlier years Iraq had used its air superiority to bring the war home to Iran by bombing Tehran (e.g., in the spring of 1985) in order to raise the political and economic costs of continuing the war. Though this had had some political effect, it had not been sustained enough to produce more than occasional panic and resentment. Iran had responded by proclaiming a programme for building air shelters and by acquiring Soviet bloc SSMs from Syria, Libya and possibly China. These missiles together with artillery were to counter Iraq's air threat to Iran's inland cities, for Iran had the advantage of being within shelling range of Iraq's principal cities. The situation of mutual vulnerability might have been expected to produce an end to these exchanges, were it not for Iraq's perception in late 1987 of the need to intensify the war against Iran at the period of its maximum vulnerability.

Reference has already been made to the widening gap between the two adversaries' military equipment. Nowhere was this more evident than in the next phase of the war when Iraq launched 150 SCUD-B missiles (modified for extended range at the cost of reduced payload, allegedly by East German technicians)[12] in a period of five weeks starting at the end of February. Iran in the same period fired one-third the number. Less significant than the ratio was the fact that Iraq felt confident enough of the numbers at its disposal to loose off such barrages, and it was indicative also that Iraq with uncontested advantage in fixed-wing aircraft was now being supplied with apparently unlimited numbers of SSMs as well. The effect of these indiscriminate terror attacks was to instill panic in the urban populations. (It may be that Iranian leaders' attempts to publicize these attacks for propaganda advantage inadvertently led to amplification of their terror effect.) Later, after the war, Rafsanjani was to claim that of total losses in the war of 133,000 killed, 10–11,000 were attributable to air and missile attacks on cities.[13]

The effect of this was doubled by the resumption by Iraq of the use of chemical weapons at the front, notably in the attack in February 1988 on the town of Halabja in the north. Again the effects may have been greater psychologically than they were militarily. But it did not escape notice in Iran that the international outcry at documented uses of these banned substances was relatively restrained when they fell on Iranian soldiers or villages. Rafsanjani was later to tell the Revolutionary Guards that the war had shown chemical and biological weapons to be 'very decisive', and that 'all the moral teachings of the world are not very effective when war reaches a serious position'.[14]

The turning point in the war came, I believe, shortly after this in the double blow sustained by Iran on 17–18 April with the loss of Fao to Iraq and several boats to the US Navy. Fao, of course, was politically and psychologically significant, being the major tangible symbol of Iranian success in the war, whose loss would leave Iran virtually empty-handed after six years of prolonging the war. But more important still was what Iraq's recapture of Fao signalled in terms of the shift in the psychological balance that had taken place; Iraq had dumped its 'defence only' policy, of leaving the initiative to Iran, hiding behind static defences, and seeking to limit casualties in engagements. By seizing the initiative and striking out with counteroffensives, Iraq not only complicated Iran's defence planning, but served notice of new and unsuspected confidence.

Certainly Iraq's newfound confidence and belligerence on the battlefield came as a surprise to the Iranians, who were not used to reacting, but dictating the timing and place of engagements. A week before Iraq's recapture of Fao, President Khamenei was depicting the 'war of the cities' as a logical outgrowth of Iraq's incapacity to do anything else militarily: 'The Iraqi regime lacks the power even to defend itself. For years it had lost the power to mount an offensive on the battlefield. Today it does not even command defensive forces, as is evidenced by Halabja.'[15] In Iranian eyes, the double blow was suspiciously coincidental in timing to have happened accidentally. After all, it was generally known (and admitted) that the US was already providing Iraq with detailed intelligence data to aid Iraqi bombing runs on Iranian targets. Furthermore, both the range of Iraqi aircraft and the accuracy of their bombing against Iran's oil refineries and terminals had suspiciously improved of late. It was but a short step from there to seeing the actions on 17–18 April as being coordinated and even jointly planned. Rafsanjani accordingly depicted them as a plot.[16]

The fact none the less remained that Iraqi troops had wrested the initiative away from Iran (which had been unable to mount an offensive in the appropriate season for the first time since the start of the war) and forced its troops to flee. Coming on the heels of the missiles and chemical weapons, it was evident that morale had finally cracked on the Iranian side. The one asset on which Iran had relied to compensate for inferiority in every other area, had simply dissolved. This was of decisive importance because morale, commitment, zeal, dedication – whatever its label – could not, by its very nature, be reconstituted overnight. Unlike a shortage of aircraft or spare parts, it could not be made good or topped-up by outside suppliers.

Indicative of this shift in the respective motivation of the two sides were the tremours of discontent that were again emanating from within Iranian society. In May Mehdi Bazargan, the Head of the Liberation Movement of Iran, the only 'opposition' partly allowed by the Islamic republic, made public a scathing criticism of the government's policy of continuing the war. What distinguished this from earlier criticisms from the same source were the echoes it now audibly evoked in many sectors of society. For the stoical populace of the Islamic republic, economic hardship and other privations such as fuel rationing and electricity cuts were tolerable in the cause of victory, not otherwise. Now there was precious little optimism about this goal evident even among the high priests of the war.

The scene was now set for a radical rethinking of policy. What lent it urgency was the evidence that Iran's soldiers were unwilling and unable to continue the fight. Even in those cases where impending Iraqi attacks were publicized as in Majnoun, the Iranian troops' commitment to defence was a shadow of their earlier performance. (The lack of supplies and ammunition clearly aggravated the deficiency in morale.) The string of Iraqi military victories after Fao, Shalamcheh, Mehran and Majnoon among others only hastened Rafsanjani's determination to get Khomeini's approval for Iran's acceptance of a ceasefire.

The destruction of an Iran-Air airbus by a US naval vessel's missile in early July provided a convenient occasion for the announcement of this decision. It gave Iran's leader precisely the moral cover of martyrdom and suffering in the face of an unjust superior force, to camouflage the comprehensive defeat of their political goals. Khomeini, at least, could not dissemble the depth of the defeat.

If the war and the revolution had imperceptibly merged into one, and the war had proven virtually the only achievement of the revolution in nine years, what possible verdict on the revolution could now be passed? Judged from the standpoint of traditional diplomacy, Iran's war effort had been a valiant but pointless exercise. Having elevated self-reliance to an absolute goal, Iran had found through its own immoderation that it was no longer just a goal but a reality, and a constraint with which its war effort had to struggle. Self-reliance, self-sufficiency, a nation tempered and forged in war and similar such romantic notions were the most that could be salvaged from a war that should never have occurred. Iran's inattention to the military balance had made war attractive to its rival neighbour. Similar inattention to the business of making peace at the optimum time, ensured that Iran was to reach the conference table at the point of its maximum weakness.

The major casualty of the war has been the credibility of the Islamic republic among its own rank and file. It will no longer be able to effectively call upon its populace for crusades and sacrifices, but will have to act more like a normal state. It is for this reason that Hashemi-Rafsanjani has indulged in pre-emptive self-criticism of past policies. It is for this reason, too, that reconstruction policies are particularly important. A peace dividend must be found for the supporters of the revolution if the virus of discontent is not to spread and affect the very legitimacy of the revolution. Whether future generations will commemorate the war as a glorious chapter in the revolution, the present generation may be forgiven for not doing so. Indeed, the palpable sense of relief felt in Iran at the end of the war has been followed by a silence that may turn out to be a prelude to a sense of disgust at the waste and be followed by a demand for an accounting from the leadership.

The war which provided Iran's revolution with a focus and a sense of unity in which politics were submerged, has been followed by a resurfacing of contentious issues long left dormant or unresolved. The course of the revolution and its priorities is now the object of political competition, and the struggle for power sharpened by expectations of Khomeini's imminent demise is likely to exacerbate the differences among the Islamic republic's leaders. In this sense the war, by providing the Islamic leadership with a convenient alibi, postponed the very real difficulties facing the revolution which still will have to be met. Only now they must do so in the wake of an inglorious and costly war.

Notes

1. For a more detailed discussion see Chubin and Tripp, *Iran and Iraq at War* (London: Tauris, 1988).
2. Martin Wight in *Power Politics*, Hedley Bull and Carsten Holbraad (eds) (Harmondsworth: Penguin, for RIIA, 1979) pp. 89–90, 91–2.
3. See my longer discussion of this problem in 'Les Conduites des Operations Militaires', *Politique Etrangere* 2, 1987 (Special issue on Iran-Irak: La Diplomatie du Conflit) pp. 303–17.
4. Jeffrey Record, 'The Rapid Deployment Force', *Strategic Review*, Spring 1986, p. 44, fn. 4.
5. See Edward Luttwak's *Strategy: The Logic of War and Peace* (Cambridge, Mass.: Belknap Press, 1987).
6. Figures can be consulted in *World Military Expenditures and Arms Transfers 1986*, quoted in 'Overview of the Situation in the Persian Gulf', Hearings and

Markup before the Committee on Foreign Affairs, May/June 1987, pp. 230–1.

7. See 'War in the Gulf', a Staff Report prepared for US Committee on Foreign Relations, Senate (Committee Print), .Wash.: USGPO, August 1984.

8. Tehran television, 22 Sepetember in *BBC Summary of World Broadcasts* (henceforth *SWB*), ME/0267/A/3, 27 September 1988.

9. Unless otherwise stated, these figures are all derived from the annual IISS *Military Balance*, 1984–8. Saddam Hussein recently boasted about this: 'Our people who began with 12 divisions at the beginning of the war, now have about 70 divisions at the end of the war. The entire world has never seen such a development', Baghdad Home Service, 14 November, in *SWB*, ME/0311/A/9, 17, November 1988.

10. *Pravda*, 5 December 1987, *Izvestiya*, 8 December 1987.

11. Chubin and Tripp, *Iran and Iraq at War*, pp. 73–4 and citations therein.

12. See *The Independent*, 22 March 1988; and *Washington Post*, 10 March 1988.

13. See Rafsanjani's speech in Qom, 24 September, broadcast by Tehran radio on 25 September and excerpted in *SWB*, ME/0267/A/4, 27 September 1988.

14. Tehran home service, 6 October excerpted in *SWB*, ME/0277/A/2, 8 October 1988.

15. President Khamenei. Sermon, Tehran University, 8 April, excerpted in *SWB*, ME/0122/A/3, 11 April 1988.

16. See his interview with *Tehran Television*, 18 April in *SWB*, ME/0130/A/6, 20 April 1988.

2 From Ideological Zeal to Geopolitical Realism: The Islamic Republic and the Gulf

Efraim Karsh

There are probably no two political systems more antithetic than monarchic and republican Iran; the deep ideological gulf between these two regimes dating back to the millenarian cultural-religious confrontation between West and East: between the drive for modernization and the yearning for the Islamic origins; between the cultural emulation and the political alignment with the West and the perception of Western civilization as the source of all evils; between the acceptance of the modern international system based on the nation-state and the Islamic internationalist vision of the *ummah* (religious body or community) as the core political unit in international affairs.

And yet for all this polarization, the two regimes share a striking similarity in their perception of Iran's regional role: both have been hegemonic powers motivated by the unyielding determination to assert Iran's supremacy throughout the Gulf. Moreover, the means employed in the pursuit of Iran's ambitious desire under the two rules have not differed drastically, ranging from political pressures to subversion to resort to armed force.

The two major differences between monarchic and revolutionary Iran, though, revolve around both the nature of the aspired hegemony and the success to attain this goal. Whereas the Shah perceived hegemony in purely geopolitical terms, namely, assertion of Iran as the strongest power in the Gulf and attainment of general recognition of this fact, the Islamic Republic has extended its hegemonic claims from the geopolitical to the spiritual (or ideological) domain as well, envisaging Iran's supremacy as taking place within an entirely new, and hitherto unprecedented, system – that of an Islamic order. While the Shah succeeded by the mid-1970s in asserting Iran's leading role in the Gulf, changing subsequently from a revisionist into a *status quo* power, this goal has not only remained beyond the Islamic Republic's reach, but the Gulf War, the most acute direct outcome of Iran's quest for spiritual hegemony, has introduced a fundamental, though not precipitous, shift in Iran's perception of its regional role in the direction of the Shah's geopolitical worldview. Indeed, it is even arguable that with the acceptance of Security Council Resolution 598 on 18 July 1988, a year after this resolution was issued, Iran's worldview had completed a cyclic reversal – from the revisionist dream to shape the Gulf along Islamic lines to acquiescence in the *status quo* established by the Shah in the mid-1970s.

By way of substantiating this argument, the following chapter will trace the Shah's and revolutionary Iran's quest for regional hegemony, and will examine the sobering impact of the war on the revolutionary zeal of the Islamic Republic.

THE QUEST FOR GEOPOLITICAL HEGEMONY: MONARCHIC IRAN

From the mid-1960s onwards, in particular after Britain's 1968 announcement of the intention to withdraw from its military bases east of Suez, Shah Mohamad Reza Pahlavi embarked on an ambitious drive aimed at filling the vacuum left by the British withdrawal and asserting Iran's position as the leading power in the Gulf. To justify this policy, the Shah argued that the responsibility for maintaining Gulf security lay solely with the local states and that no external powers were to be allowed to interfere in the affairs of the region; and being the largest and most powerful Gulf country, Iran had a moral, historical and geopolitical obligation to ensure stability in this region, not only for the benefit of the local factors but for the benefit of the world at large as well.

Becoming a regular theme in the Shah's pronouncements in the following years, his perception of Iran as the 'guardian of the Gulf'[1] manifested itself in an impressive expansion of Iran's military capabilities during the 1970s which turned Iran into the most powerful country in the Gulf, and was highlighted by a series of Iranian actions intended to signal both to the Gulf countries and to the great powers who had the final say in the region. These included *inter alia* the occupation (on 30 November 1971) of three strategically-located islands near the Strait of Hormuz (Abu Musa, Greater and Lesser Tunbs), which were at the time under the sovereignty of the Emirates of Sharja and Ras al-Khaima respectively, as well as the military intervention in Oman from 1972 onwards, at the request of the Omani Sultan, Qabous, to suppress the Dhofari rebels then operating along Oman's border with South Yemen (and supported by the latter).

But the most salient manifestation of the Shah's mounting ambitions was the intensifying pressures on Iraq, the only potential obstacle to Iran's military supremacy in the Gulf. In July 1969 Tehran was implicated in an abortive coup attempt against the Ba'th regime,[2] and already during that same year Iran challenged the prevailing *status quo* with Iraq by unilaterally abrogating the 1937 Iraqi-Iranian agreement on the navigation regime in the

Shatt al-Arab.[3] These actions were followed by a series of Iranian moves in the early 1970s which severely exacerbated bilateral relations, ranging from attempts to isolate Iraq politically from other Arab states of the Gulf by the establishment of a regional defence organization comprising Iran, Saudi Arabia and Kuwait, to the provision of extensive economic and military assistance to the Kurdish rebels in northern Iraq. The growing Iranian-Iraqi hostility erupted into violence in the winter of 1973-4 with fierce border clashes involving tanks, heavy artillery and aircraft.

Unable to suppress an insurgency which imposed an intolerable burden on its domestic system, Iraq had no alternative but to seek some kind of agreement with Iran which would lead to the withdrawal of Iranian support for the Kurds. This took the form of the Algiers Agreement of 6 March 1975, which provided for territorial adjustments, including the demarcation of the Shatt al-Arab waterway's boundary on the basis of the *thalweg* (i.e., median) line.[4]

Reflecting the painful awareness that an effective enforcement of Iraq's internal sovereignty depended on the goodwill of its neighbour to the east, the Algiers Agreement constituted a formal Iraqi acquiescence in Iran's supremacy, thereby opening a new era in regional relations, the era of *Pax Irana*. After almost a decade, the Shah had managed to achieve his goal – the substitution of a relationship that presupposed unquestioned Iranian dominance for the old Iraq–Iran *status quo* based on the 1937 Agreement. Having attained its goals, the Shah's Iran changed naturaly from a revisionist into a *status quo* power, and began to advocate the perpetuation of stability in the Gulf. Iraq was neither in the position nor had it the inclination to undermine the newly established *status quo*. Rather the Ba'th preferred to turn inward, to put down the Kurdish insurgency, to reconstruct its armed forces and to stabilize Iraq's social, economic and political systems. Consequently the agreement was followed by a period of much-reduced tension between Iran and Iraq which lasted for four years – until the overthrow of the Shah.

The other Gulf states, for their part, while criticizing Iraq for compromising 'historical Arab rights' in signing the Algiers Agreement, did not view Iran's rise to prominence negatively, as this development bridled Iraq's ambitions in the Gulf and, in consequence, tempered its radical zeal and diminished its pressures on the conservative regimes. As a longtime observer of Iranian foreign policy put it: 'The Gulf states' inclination to seek a "free ride" from Iran's power was rather striking: They condemned Iranian "intervention" in Oman, yet were secretly relieved at Iran's assistance; critical of the Shah's tough line with Iraq, yet secretly delighted.'[5]

THE QUEST FOR SPIRITUAL HEGEMONY: THE ORIGINS OF THE GULF WAR

This apparently idyllic *status quo* was put to an abrupt end by the birth of the

Islamic Republic. For one, the very act of overthrowing the most powerful monarchy in the region and its replacement by republican regime challenged the legitimacy of the remaining dynasties in the Gulf and, moreover, exposed the fragility of these regimes and the feasibility of overthrowing them. Furthermore, the challenge of the Islamic Republic to the conservative regimes was all the more menacing given its fundamentalist ideology and its vocal commitment to the uprooting of the dynasties throughout the Gulf since 'Islam proclaims monarchy and hereditary succession wrong and invalid.'[6] And yet, like in the early 1970s it was Ba'thist Iraq, rather than the conservative Gulf dynasties, which took the brunt of Iran's revisionist aspirations.

Apart from Khomeini's personal grudge against the Ba'th regime because of the latter's acquiescence in the Shah's request to expel him from Iraq (October 1978), several factors made Iraq the primary target for the export of the revolution. With Shi'ites accounting for about 60 per cent of Iraq's total population, the revolutionary regime in Tehran could, and certainly did, entertain hopes that this community, which had always viewed itself as a deprived group, would emulate the Iranian example and rise against their 'oppressors'. These expectations were further fuelled by the secular, 'heretic' nature of the Ba'th which was adamantly opposed to the very notion of an Islamic political order, on the one hand, and the location of the holiest Shi'ite shrines (Karbala, Najaf, Kazimain) on Iraqi territory, on the other; a combination which could serve as a potentially powerful weapon in the hands of the Islamic regime. But above all, the mullahs in Tehran were confronted with the same geostrategic challenge faced by the Shah a decade earlier, namely, Iraq's position as the major obstacle to the Iranian quest for regional hegemony. And just as the Shah's road to supremacy passed through subduing Iraq, so the replacement of the *status quo* in the Persian Gulf by an Islamic order had to begin with the removal of the primary hindrance to this goal – the secular Ba'th regime. In the words of a leading Ayatollah: 'We have taken the path of true Islam and our aim in defeating Saddam lies in the fact that we consider Saddam the main obstacle to the advance of Islam in the region.'[7]

Creating both opportunities and risks for Iran, this apparently dialectical combination of Iraqi internal vulnerability and military power stands at the root of the overly hostile attitude of the mullahs towards the Ba'th regime from the outset. Rejecting Iraq's consecutive shows of goodwill during the spring and summer of 1979 which indicated Baghdad's clear interest in preserving the 1975 *status quo*,[8] from June 1979 onwards the revolutionary regime began publicly urging the Iraqi population to rise up and overthrow the Ba'th regime.[9] A few months later Iran escalated its anti-Ba'thist campaign by resuming support for the Iraqi Kurds, by providing moral and material support to Shi'ite underground movements in Iraq, and by initiating terrorist attacks against prominent Iraqi officials, the most significant of which being the failed attempt on the life of the Iraqi Deputy Premier, Tariq Aziz, on 1 April 1980.

By way of checking the Iranian pressures Iraq resorted to a variety of means; these included the suppression of Shi'ite underground organizations and the execution of some of their leaders (most notably the Iraqi Shi'i religious leader, Muhammad Baqir al-Sadr), mass expulsions of Iranian citizens from Iraq, attempts to organize a united Arab front to oppose the export of the Iranian revolution, and extension of support to Iranian separatist elements (such as the Kurds and the Arabs in Khuzestan). These Iraqi countermeasures failed to impress the revolutionary regime, and by August 1980 the Iranian-Iraqi confrontation had escalated into heavy fighting, involving tank and artillery duels and air strikes.

Iran's subversive activities in general – and the protracted and escalating border fighting in particular – drove the Iraqi leadership to the conclusion that it had no alternative but to contain the Iranian threat by resorting to arms. Faced with the growing amount of evidence that the Iranian regime was set upon destabilizing the Ba'th, and fully aware of Iraq's fundamental inferiority to Iran, the Iraqi leaders had serious doubts whether the Iraqi political system could sustain another prolonged, exhausting confrontation with Iran. Hence, they decided to exploit Iran's *temporary* weakening following the revolution and raise the stakes for both sides by resorting to armed force.

INCURRING THE REVOLUTIONARY ZEAL: THE CONSERVATIVE GULF STATES

While undoubtedly the primary victim of Iran's desire to assert its 'spiritual' hegemony throughout the Gulf, Iraq did not remain the sole target of such an ambition; the other Gulf states also experienced a measure of the Iranian ardour. True, as Shi'ites constitute a small minority on the Arab side of the Gulf (with the exception of Bahrain where they comprise about 70 per cent of the population), and given the lack of direct contiguity of these countries to Iranian territory, both the prospects for internal instability and the spectre of direct military threat from Tehran loom weaker than in the case of Iraq. Moreover, since none of these states challenged Iran's aspirations for Gulf hegemony in the way Iraq did, they occupied a lesser role in revolutionary Iran's strategy, both in terms of objectives and means.

This by no means prevented the conservative Gulf states from being shaken by the huge wave of Islamic fundamentalism attending the Iranian revolution. In November 1979 and February 1980 widespread riots erupted in the Shi'ite towns of the Saudi oil-rich province of Hasa, leading to dozens of fatal casualties and the sealing off of the Shi'ite areas. Similar disturbances occurred in Bahrain during the summer of 1979 and the spring of 1980 which, though essentially a part of the general trend of indigenous Shi'ite unrest sweeping the region in the wake of the Iranian Revolution, involved a far greater Iranian role than in the Saudi case: they were inspired and instigated by Hojat al-Islam Muhammad Hadi al-Mudarissi, a young cleric of Iranian origin exiled to Bahrain during the Shah's days, who was appointed as Khomeini's representative in Bahrain and the United Arab Emirates. Iran's hand was also visible in the far milder Shi'ite unrest in Kuwait. Here the key figure was Abbas Muhri, Khomeini's brother-in-law and a Kuwaiti citizen, who in August 1979 was nominated as the Imam's personal representative in Kuwait. Muhri's deportation from Kuwait in September 1979 stabilized the situation, but not before the outbreak of several disturbances, such as the attack on the American Embassy in Kuwait in November 1979.[10]

While becoming decisively dependent on the course of the war, Iran's policy towards the conservative Gulf states continued to reflect for quite some time the persistence of aspirations for Gulf supremacy. Carried out on three parallel planes – propaganda campaign coupled with occasional limited retaliation, manipulation of Iran's ideological appeal, and subversive and terrorist activities against the Gulf regimes – the Iranian policy sought to attain a mixture of goals, ranging from dissuading these states from support for Iraq, all the way to the overthrow of the indigenous regimes.

(a) Dissuasion and Retaliation: Kuwait

From the very outset of the war, the Iranians tirelessly and repeatedly reminded the Gulf states of the counterproductivity of their support for Iraq; the major argument being that the alienation of Iran, by far the strongest power in the Gulf, could not but entail severe risks to the security – or even the existence – of these states. The Iranian threats were occasionally accompanied by limited military action, primarily against Kuwait. The choice of Kuwait as the main target for the demonstration of the seriousness of Iran's intentions was hardly surprising given the abundance of the latter's support (however reluctant) for Iraq, on the one hand, and its military frailty and proximity to Iran, on the other. Accordingly, already in November 1980, less than two months after the outbreak of hostilities, the Kuwaiti town of Abdali was subjected to two attacks by Iranian aircraft, and witnessed another raid in June 1981. Also, in September 1981 Iran attacked for the first time a major economic target in Kuwait, Umm al-Aysh petrochemical complex and oil terminal, thereby setting a precedent which was to be repeated on several future occasions, most notably the attack (with surface-to-sea *Silkworm* missiles) on Kuwait's main oil-loading terminal for supertankers in October 1987.

(b) Islam as a Political Instrument: Pressuring the Saudis

Several factors combined to make Saudi Arabia the second most important target of Iran's ideological crusade after Iraq. Towering far above the rest of its regional counterparts, Saudi Arabia appeared to hold the key to the support for Iraq on the Arab side of the Gulf from the early stages of the war by making the prime direct contribution to Iraq's war effort and the major damage to that of Iran (e.g., by pushing oil prices down Saudi Arabia deprived Iran of important oil revenues), by rallying wide international backing for Iraq and by constituting the military axis of the newly established defence system of the Gulf, the GCC (Gulf Co-operation Council). And most importantly, just as Iraq constituted the major military obstacle to Iran's quest for Gulf hegemony, so Saudi Arabia posed the most significant challenge to Tehran's spiritual pretensions. Hence, and given Iran's limited ability to exert military pressure on Saudi Arabia due to the latter's formidable arms build-up, on the one hand, and the lack of physical contiguity between the two countries, on the other, it aimed at the Saudi *Achilles' heel* – religious legitimacy.

The tool chosen by Tehran for the assertion of its spiritual supremacy, or at least – for keeping the Iranian shadow looming large over Saudi Arabia, was the annual pilgrimage to Mecca and Medina, the Hajj. Dismissing out of hand the Saudi interpretation of the Hajj as an exclusively religious duty and viewing this event as a religio-political obligation, Khomeini urged the Iranian pilgrims to use the Hajj as an occasion 'to make their country and their revolution proud among the Muslims of the world and export their dear Islamic revolution to the Muslims of the world and other Islamic countries'.[11]

Indeed, already in October 1979 the Saudi authorities expelled an unspecified number of pilgrims, having reportedly uncovered Iranian plans for political demonstrations during the Hajj. Two years later, in 1981, an activist group among Iran's 75,000 pilgrims staged a violent demonstration in Medina, clashing with the Saudi security forces and leaving 22 Iranians and 6 Saudi soldiers injured.[12] The political importance attached by Iran to the Hajj was underlined in 1982 by both the establishment of the Permanent Committee for the Hajj and the appointment of Hojat al-Islam Muhammad Musavi-Kho'iniha, a militant cleric who had led the Iranian 'students' during the 'hostage crisis' of 1979–80, as the head of Iran's Hajj organization.[13] The result of these moves was a far more vibrant Hajj in 1982 and 1983, with thousands of Iranians involved in violent demonstrations in Mecca and Medina, and the Iranian Premier, Mir-Hussein Musavi, voicing from Tehran strong criticism on Saudi Arabia's competence to administer the holy sites. Large-scale and ferocious Iranian demonstrations which were only contained with much effort and necessitated the arrest of 113 pilgrims also took place in 1986, reaching their peak in the tragic events of 1987, when some 400 pilgrims (more than 600 in the Iranian account) were killed in a clash with the Saudi security forces on the 'Black Friday' of 31 July.

(c) Subversion and Terror

More than anything, Iran's resort to subversive and terrorist activities against its Gulf neighbours reflected a measure of disappointment with the mass-revolutionary potential of the Shi'ite minorities in the Gulf. For, while forced by the wave of Shi'ite unrest of 1979–80 and the Iranian spiritual presence throughout the Gulf to undertake, however modest, social and political strides in the direction of 'Islamization', the Gulf regimes managed, through a combination of repressive and reassuring measures, to contain the dangerous wave of Shi'ite restiveness, thereby pushing the Iranians towards a far more limited target audience – (mainly Shi'ite) subversive organizations.

As early as March 1979, having learnt of an Iranian intention to topple the Bahraini regime by means of volunteers that would be landed in the tiny sheikhdom, the British Government warned the newly established revolutionary regime to forego this idea.[14] Heeding the British warning, the Iranians postponed their premature plan, but they have never shelved it altogether: in December 1981 the Bahraini authorities exposed an Iranian plot to overthrow the regime arresting 73 terrorists, all Shi'ites. Though generating the opposite outcome of the intended one (the Gulf sheikhdoms reacted to the increasing Iranian threat by consolidating their ranks), the abortive Bahraini plot was soon followed by a series of equally alarming terrorist activities: on 12 December 1983 Kuwait was rocked by six simultaneous explosions directed against strategic and economic targets, and against the US and French embassies; on 25 May 1985 the Amir of Kuwait made a narrow escape from an attempt on his life, and in January 1987, on the eve of the opening of the Islamic Conference Organization's (ICO) summit in Kuwait and amidst Iranian claims that Kuwait was incapable of guaranteeing the security of the conference, several bombings erupted in the tiny sheikhdom. Finally, the Iranians were implicated in a long host of lower-key subversive and terrorist activities which, while less salient than the above mentioned attempts to shake the entire political systems of the sheikhdoms, kept Tehran's pressure felt along the Gulf. These included *inter alia* the hijacking of several Kuwaiti airlines (e.g., in May 1985, April 1988) as a means to pressure the Kuwaiti authorities to release Shi'ite terrorists, attacks on public places (such as cinemas, restaurants, etc.), oil installations (June 1986, January 1987) and government officials.

TEMPERING THE REVOLUTIONARY ZEAL: IRAN'S THORNY ROAD TO A CEASEFIRE

Just as the outbreak of the Iran–Iraq War constituted the most serious direct outcome of Iran's attempts to export the revolution, so did its persistence reflect Khomeini's reluctance to compromise his commitment to this concept, at least in relation to Iraq. To be sure, for quite some time the war fulfilled an important, in fact vital, internal function by enabling the clerics to consolidate their power base, suppress domestic opposition and rally public support behind the regime. However, with the crackdown in 1983 of the major oppositionary groups, the *Tudeh* and the *Mojaheddin e-Khalq*, and the consequent disappearance of internal threat to the existence of the regime, the war ceased to serve its major domestic purpose.

Moreover, the exorbitant human toll and economic dislocation of the war did not fail to breach the edifice of the Iranian national morale, turning the continuation of hostilities into the most serious threat to the survival of the revolutionary regime: already in 1983 several instances of violent parental opposition to the recruitment of their children were reported, and in early 1985 public resentment manifested itself in large-scale demonstrations of anti-war and anti-government feeling, notable for the fact that they involved elements of those poorer classes which constitute the backbone of the regime's support. The middle classes were, in any case, increasingly disillusioned with the Islamic regime, the cost and apparent futility of the war only reinforcing their discontent. Finally, from late 1984 onwards the growing war weariness was reflected in a steady and significant drop in the number of volunteers for the war fronts, which assumed alarming proportions in 1987–8.

The mounting public dissatisfaction found an echo within the ranks of the regime, leading to the evolution of a more modest definition of Iran's goals *vis-à-vis* Iraq and, in fact, the entire Gulf region. As early as mid-1982, a loose coalition of political and military figures had begun to question the logic of prosecuting the war. This first major dispute within the government revolved around the fundamental question of taking the war into Iraq. Chief among those who rejected this option was the majority of the military leadership which doubted the armed forces' ability to carry out such an enterprise. The military leaders were supported in their judgement by some leading politicians (such as the Prime Minister, Mir-Hussein Musavi and the President, Sayyed Ali Khamenei) who rejected the invasion on grounds of its high human, material and political costs.

By mid-1984, however, the voice of the moderates appeared to have carried far greater weight within Iran's decision-making elite, as could be inferred from the decision to end the first 'war of the cities' (February 1984) despite the position of the hard-liners, and all the more so by the reversal of the costly Iranian war strategy of human wave attacks in favour of a more conventional and orderly fighting. The deepening rift inside the Iranian leadership continued apace after 1984, making its way to the public at large,[15] and culminating in the summer of 1988 in reported armed clashes between the rival factions within Iran's 150,000-strong mullah community and an open defiance of Khomeini's position on the war issue by leading clergymen.[16]

Against this backdrop, Tehran's evasion of Security Council Resolution 598 for nearly a year, despite the keen awareness within the Iranian leadership of the counterproductivity of the war for the stability of the regime, was apparently related to one factor – Khomeini's dogged adherence to his vision of an Iranian-led Islamic Gulf. However, the fact that the Imam's position was widely contested and ultimately reversed, illustrates that, however temporarily, the process of a redefinition of Iran's regional role completed a full cycle. This reversal of the Iranian position is all the more evident given the fact that the advocates of war termination were not deterred from implying for quite some time their readiness to abide by the *status quo* established by the Shah in the late 1970s, to which the Islamic Republic had been so adamantly opposed in its early days. As the Speaker of the Parliament, Ali-Akbar Hashemi-Rafsanjani, perhaps the most eloquent spokesman for this approach put it in February 1986, after Iran's capture of the Fao Peninsula: 'We do accept that half of the Shatt al-Arab belongs to Iran and the other half to Iraq. We do accept the *thalweg* which is international law. *We seek nothing more than that.'*[17]

And if this view was true at one of Iran's brightest moments in the war, it is hardly surprising that it was to gain widespread support during the dark days of 1988. Indeed, the re-establishment of the 1975 *status quo* has been, perhaps, Iran's major demand in the peace talks with Iraq.

STRETCHING A HAND TO THE GULF STATES

If the Islamic Republic's revolutionary zeal showed significant fatigue with regard to Iraq, Iran's perennial enemy, it was moderated even further *vis-à-vis* the Arab states of the Gulf. Reluctant to alienate and frighten these states to the point of increasing their internal cohesion and driving them into the arms of new, and no less dangerous, protectors, Iran sought to soften its threatening image by denying any link to subversive or terrorist activities in the Gulf and by reassuring the conservative states of the lack of any Iranian aggressive or territorial designs against them. Also, Iran opted to establish working, if not cordial, relations with some of the Gulf states, most notably the UAE which, throughout the war, displayed the most friendly attitude towards Tehran, and Oman whose relations with Iran have significantly warmed from mid-1987 onwards, following the beginning of the American reflagging operation in the Gulf. Even more significant were Iran's attempts to reach a *rapprochement* with Saudi Arabia, its main spiritual rival.

In 1984, in response to a Saudi decision to allow the entry of 150,000 Iranian pilgrims, the largest number until then, Iran considerably mellowed its zealous pronouncements regarding the Hajj and in 1985 even removed the radical Musavi-Kho'ini from his post as the head of the Hajj organization, replacing him by Hojat at-Islam Mehdi Karruby.[18] Also, when in June 1984

Saudi aircraft downed an Iranian fighter plane in Saudi territorial waters, Tehran, in a demonstration of caution and circumspection, refrained from any response short of a mild pro-forma protest.

This moderation opened the door for an Iranian-Saudi reconciliation: in May 1985 the Saudi Foreign Minister, Prince Saud al-Faysal, visited Tehran for the first time since the revolution and his Iranian counterpart, Ali-Akbar Velayati, reciprocated the visit seven months later. Furthermore, even after the eclipse of bilateral relations in 1986 following Iran's military successes in Fao and Mehran which rekindled widespread fears of an Iranian victory and gave a significant boost to Iran's self-confidence, Tehran remained reluctant to rock its relations with Riyadh; the tragic events of the 1987 Hajj should, therefore, be viewed as an extremely unfortunate incident rather than the outcome of a remeditated plan. To be sure, coming against the backdrop of intensifying American naval presence in the Gulf the 1987 Hajj season was perceived by Tehran as a golden opportunity to assert Iran's position and to promote its cause; yet, fully aware of the undesirablity of any deterioration in Iranian-Saudi relations at the time, Khomeini gave strict instructions to the heads of Iran's 150,000-strong Hajj delegation to make their utmost efforts to ensure the orderly procession of the pilgrimage, so as to avoid any escalation that would 'nullify the results of the Hajj and create difficulties and restrictions for the respected pilgrims'.[119]

That Iran was disinterested in a showdown with Saudi Arabia was also borne out by its behaviour in the aftermath of the Mecca incident. Not only did Iran avoid any real political, let alone military, retaliation, but the Iranian authorities called upon the mourning demonstrators to exert restraint and to avoid both the infringement on the 'security of foreign diplomats' and the occupation of embassies – a clear indication of how far Iran had travelled since the days of the Hostage Crisis of 1979–1980.[20] No wonder therefore that the initiative for the severance of bilateral diplomatic relations in April 1988, almost a year after the Mecca incident, came from Riyadh rather than Tehran.

Iran's attempts to soothe the Gulf states were also reflected in its attitude towards the GCC. Just as the Shah had advocated the maintenance of Gulf security through a collective regional effort (in which, naturally, Iran would play the key role), so the revolutionary regime voiced strong support for the GCC from its very inception, on condition that it would serve the 'genuine' interests of the Gulf countries. Moreover, nearly a decade after discrediting the Shah's conception of regional security, revolutionary Iran has found itself voicing the same ideas: when in early 1988 the GCC signalled its willingness to warm up relations with Tehran, the Islamic Republic capitalized on the event to try to rally the regional organization behind Iran's longstanding rejection of the role of external powers in ensuring Gulf security and its insistence on the achievement of this goal through exclusive reliance on indigenous means.

Finally, Iran's gradual tilt from a purely ideological to a more 'conventional' way of thinking was manifested in its legal approach towards the issue of international navigation in the Gulf. Occupying the Shah's seat at the Third United Nations Conference on the Law of the Sea (begun in 1973), the revolutionary regime remained faithful to monarchical Iran's worldview regarding the navigation regime in the Gulf, most notably, opposition to the establishment of a special regime for straits used for international nagivation (no international treaty, such as the Montreux Convention regulating the use of the Turkish Straits, exists for the Strait of Hormuz and passage in the waterway is regulated by customary law), as well as insistence on prior authorization of warships intending to exercise innocent passage through the territorial sea.[21]

But the most important single development which led the Islamic Republic to speak and, moreover, to think along the Shah's geopolitical line has been the mounting threat to the freedom of civilian navigation in the Gulf, posed from 1984 onwards by Iraq's initiation of the so-called Tanker War.

BACK TOWARDS A GEOPOLITICAL THINKING

The beginning of the Tanker War in February 1984 constituted a major landmark in the course of the war. True, attacks on oil installations and merchant shipping were not a completely novel development in the prolonged war. However, the Tanker War differed from previous campaigns against shipping not only in its scope (53 Iraqi and 18 Iranian attacks in 1984 alone as compared to 43 and five attacks respectively between the outbreak of the war and February 1984) but also in its strategic rationale. Unlike earlier Iraqi attacks on civilian shipping, which were directed solely against Iran and aimed at convincing it of the futility of continuing the war, the Tanker War sought to draw in other states, the Western powers in particular, in the hope that they would support Iraq and help to bring about a peaceful settlement. The idea seems to have been that the intensification of anti-shipping attacks would provoke Iran into extreme reactions, such as attempting to close the Strait of Hormuz, which, in turn, would leave the Western oil consumers (and especially the US) with no other alternative but to intervene forcefully.

Yet before long Iraq realized that the Iranian response to its escalatory moves did not live up to expectations. Fully aware of the rationale behind the new Iraqi strategy,[22] Iran did its best to keep the great powers out of the Gulf. Accordingly, not only did Tehran forego any attempts to block the Strait of Hormuz, but it went to great lengths to keep its responses to the lowest level possible, avoiding public acknowledgement of attacks on civilian shipping and taking much care to alleviate international fears of the possible closure of the Strait of Hormuz by emphasizing time and again its disinterest in carrying out this act since 'the Islamic Republic of Iran would be the first to suffer as a result of the closing of this strait'.[23]

Iran's cautious response was the right one – the Western powers remained relatively aloof, and it was only in late 1986, more than two years after the beginning of the Tanker War, that the Iranian caution began to falter. Responding to the considerable exacerbation of the Iraqi campaign against Iranian economic targets and commercial shipping by intensifying its own attacks on Iraqi-bound shipping, Tehran intimidated Kuwait to the point of approaching both superpowers with the request to protect a number of its tankers against naval attacks: on 7 March 1987 the United States informed the Kuwaiti government of its willingness to escort that country's eleven tankers through the Gulf, provided that they would fly the US flag, and a month later Kuwait chartered three tankers from the USSR which were put under the Soviet flag.

Notwithstanding a measure of muscle-flexing (e.g., deployment of Chinese Silkworm surface-to-sea missiles at the Strait of Hormuz, the conduct of large-scale naval manoeuvres, etc.), Iran sought to forestall the arrival of the superpowers into the Gulf through de-escalation. Accordingly, Tehran signalled its strong interest in crisis avoidance and made intensive political and diplomatic efforts to mobilize widespread international opposition to the reflagging scheme; these included improvement of relations with the GCC states, attempts to sow discord among the Western powers on the reflagging issue, and efforts to harness Soviet support to Iran's longstanding opposition to external interference in the Gulf.

Above all, Iran's anxiety to see the Gulf free of great-power intervention was manifested in an extremely cautious and circumspect behaviour: with the exception of minor incidents Iran avoided any contact with the American-escorted convoys, preferring instead to continue the already-established pattern of intercepting merchant shipping and attacking non-escorted vessels. Also it resorted to the old-new means of retaliation of naval mining, which, due to its highly indirect and elusive nature, was apparently viewed as the best way to eat the cake and have it at the same time, to frustrate the reflagging operation while evading the perils of direct clash with the US Navy. Even when the mining operation backfired by rallying the hitherto reluctant Europeans behind the United States and bringing them into the Gulf, Iran did not abandon caution: when on 10 August 1987 an American F-14 fired on an Iranian F-4 and two weeks later a US destroyer fired on two Iranian vessels, Tehran refrained from any response. Similarly, when on 21 September US forces attacked and captured an Iranian vessel, the *Iran Ajr*, which allegedly was laying mines off the Bahraini coast, Iran limited its response to vehement denial of the American accusation of mine-laying.[24] Even during the severe escalation of October 1987 in which the US Navy sank three Iranian gunboats and destroyed two Iranian oil platforms, Tehran's retaliation was directed, by and large, against Kuwait and not the

US naval forces.[25] It was hardly surprising, therefore, that Tehran avoided any retaliation following the (mistaken) downing of an Iranian airliner by the USS Vincennes in July 1988.

All in all, not only was the Iranian reaction to the Tanker War throughout its various stages motivated by the Shah-coined concept of 'the Gulf for the Gulfers', but it also made extensive use of the argumentation, and even the terminology, used by the Shah in the early 1970s in justification of his drive for regional hegemony. Following the Shah's footsteps, the revolutionary regime argued that the maintenance of Gulf security lay with the local states and with them alone, and that all foreign powers should be kept out of the region; Iran, in its capacity as the most powerful country in the region and the one with the longest coastline had, therefore, 'every right to maintain security there'.[26] And just as the Shah had portrayed Iran's interest in Gulf supremacy as motivated by altruistic considerations, so the Islamic Republic depicted its policy as emanating from a deep sense of responsibility for the 'security of the whole world and also of humanity'.[27] In short, within less than four years after renouncing the Shah's proclaimed role as the guardian of the Gulf, Tehran had already readopted the same position: 'Three years have passed since the start of the imposed war. During all this time our country has considered itself the guardian of the Persian Gulf security and has protected it.'[28]

Notes

1. See, for example, *Tehran Domestic Service*, 6 October 1970; *Guardian*, 9 October 1971; *Financial Times*, 31 May 1973; *Christian Science Monitor*, 27 July 1973.
2. F. Halliday, *Iran: Dictatorship and Development* (Harmondsworth: Penguin, 1979) p. 274.
3. The 1937 Agreement contained two major provisions: in designating the lower water-mark on the eastern bank of the Shatt-al-Arab as the frontier, it conferred control over the waterway on Iraq with the exception of the area adjacent to the Iranian ports of Abadan, Khorramshahr and Khosrowabad where it was fixed at the *thalweg* (the deep water line); and, second, as a result of that demarcation, it provided that vessels in the Shatt should employ Iraqi pilots and fly the Iraqi flag (again with the exception of those three areas in which the boundaries were determined by the *thalweg*).
4. The Algiers Agreement stipulated for the following: a) Demarcation of the land frontier in accordance with the 1913 Protocol of Constantinopole and the verbal accord of 1914; b) Agreement to demarcate the Shatt-al-Arab water-way's boundary on the basis of the *thalweg* line; c) Agreement to 're-establish security and mutual confidence along their common frontiers' and undertake to exercise a strict and effective control with the aim of finally putting an end to 'all infiltrations of a subversive character from either side'; d) The pledge of both parties to regard the provisions negotiated at the 1975 OPEC meeting as indivisible elements of a comprehensive settlement, such that a breach of any

one would be considered a violation of the spirit of the Algiers Agreement. For the English text of the agreement see *New York Times*, 8 March 1975.

5. S. Chubin, 'The Islamic Republic's Foreign Policy in the Gulf', in M. Kramer (ed.), *Shi'ism, Resistance and Revolution* (Boulder and London: Westview and Mansell, 1987) pp. 160–1.
6. Ayatollah Khomeini, 'Islamic Government' in H. Algar (trans.), *Islam and Revolution* (Berkeley: Mizan, 1981) pp. 31, 48.
7. *Tehran Domestic Service*, 24 July 1982.
8. Thus, for example, the Iraqi government took the opportunity of Iran's withdrawal from CENTO to offer its good services in case Iran should decide to join the Non-Aligned Movement; and as late as July/August 1979 Iraqi authorities extended an invitation to the Iranian Premier, Mehdi Bazargan, to visit Iraq in order to improve relations between the two countries.
9. See, for example, *SWB*, 8 June 1979, ME/6144/A5; *SWB*, 9 June 1979, ME/6145/A7.
10. J. Kostiner, 'Shi'i Unrest in the Gulf', in Kramer (ed.), *Shi'ism, Resistance and Revolution*, pp. 178–9; R. Wright, *Sacred Rage* (New York: Simon & Schuster, 1986) p. 156.
11. *Tehran Domestic Service*, 20 September 1982.
12. Wright, *Sacred Rage*, pp. 154, 159; D. Hiro, *Iran Under the Ayatollahs* (London: Routledge & Kegan Paul, 1985) p. 337.
13. S. Bakhash, *The Reign of the Ayatollahs* (London: Counterpoint, 1986) p. 234; R. K. Ramazani, *Revolutionary Iran* (Baltimore: Johns Hopkins University Press, 1986) p. 95.
14. A. Taheri, *Holy Terror* (London: Hutchinson, 1987) p. 156.
15. For manifestations of war weariness in Iran and the regime's attempts to contain them see, for example, *Tehran Domestic Service*, 8, 16, 23 August 1983; 5 February 1985; 27 June, 22 October, 29 November 1987; 16 March 1988. See also, *Financial Times*, 23 November 1982; *Christian Science Monitor*, 11 June 1985; *Sunday Times*, 11 March 1984; *New York Times*, 7 May 1985.
16. For divisions among the clerics on the desirability of prosecuting the war see, for example, *Financial Times*, 10 July 1982; *Sunday Times*, 25 July 1982, 29 May 1988; *Guardian*, 22 June 1984; *IRNA*, 23 September 1983, *Tehran Domestic Service*, 22 September 1986; *Jerusalem Post*, 1 June 1988.
17. *Tehran Domestic Service*, 24 February 1986.
18. For denial of any moderation in the Iranian position following Musavi-Kho'ini's removal see, for example, Khomeini's address to the Assembly of Experts, *Tehran Domestic Service*, 16 July 1985.
19. Ibid., 31 July 1987. These appeals, nevertheless, failed to prevent a large demonstration in Tehran which ransacked the embassies of Saudi Arabia and Kuwait.
20. Ibid., 1 August 1987.
21. I am grateful to Inari Karsh for indicating this point to me.
22. For a succinct Iranian analysis of the causes of the Iraqi strategy see *Tehran Domestic Service in Arabic*, 3 January 1985.
23. *Tehran Domestic Service*, 17 May 1984.
24. Ibid., 16 October 1987.
25. The only exception to this pattern of Iranian caution occurred in April 1988 when a direct Iranian–American collision took place following the damaging of a US frigate by an underwater mine. Iran's exceptional readiness to clash with the US Navy should be attributed to the inopportune timing of the incident, namely, its coincidence with the dislodging of the Iranian forces from

the Fao Peninsula; this, in turn left the Iranian leadership with no choice but to retaliate in order to avoid further loss of face.

26. *Tehran Domestic Service*, 10 April 1986, 22 March 1987.
27. *IRNA*, 17 September 1983.
28. *Tehran Domestic Service*, 20 September 1983.

3 Iran: Doctrine and Reality
David Menashri

INTRODUCTION

The Islamic revolution in Iran presents a new pattern of power-seizure in the modern history of the Middle East. Typically, the many coups in the last generation in this region and in the Third World in general were carried out by small groups, led mostly by army officers, who only after their seizure of power endeavoured to gain popular support for themselves and their new ideology. The Iranian revolution was a striking exception: it was led primarily by clerics, it enjoyed mass support (from its inception), and its 'new' ideology was nothing more than the return to the glorious past of early Islam and to the ideology most familiar to Iranians – to Islam.[1]

Having come to power in 1979, the clerics concentrated in the first ten years of their rule on the following two main targets. First, the consideration, the institutionalization and – as much as possible – the perpetuation of clerical rule. Secondly, the implementation of Ayatollah Ruhollah Khoemini's ideology, which, in turn, would further promote legitimization and consolidation. For the new rulers of Iran, 'Islamic Revolution' was not just a title for their movement, it reflected their intent to concentrate all power and to bring all spheres of life in conformity with Islamic tenets and ideals. The war, running on in eight years of their first decade in power has significantly influenced all spheres of life.

This chapter is an attempt to evaluate what can be seen today as the impact of the revolutionary experience and the eight years of war on revolutionary Iran. It will concentrate on examining their impact on the implementation of Khomeini's ideology. To do this, I will examine what I believe are the four most important elements in his creed: the concept of the *velayate faqih* (the rule of the jurisconsult); improving the lot of the *mostaz'efin* (the dispossessed) and advancing Iran towards economic independence; 'exporting the revolution'; and 'Neither the East nor the West'. The concept of 'War, War until Victory' – though not an inherent tenet of Khomeini's ideology but rather a major policy line the regime has adopted – could have similarly supported the arguments raised in this chapter, but this issue is covered elsewhere in this volume and will therefore not be referred to in this context.

Two caveats seem essential: first, it is too early to evaluate the full-scale impact of the war; second, Iranian domestic and foreign policy in the last decade was fundamentally dependent on two, interrelated, developments: revolution and war. It is often difficult to separate one from the other.

THE CONCEPT OF VELAYATE FAQIH

Perhaps the most significant change brought about by the Islamic revolution was the concentration of all power, both spiritual and temporal, in the hands of the *velayate faqih*, i.e., the imam Khomeini. Yet, it was in this regard that his disciples faced their most crucial challenge. The problem was twofold, yet interrelated: doctrinal (the limits of government authority) and personal (the question of the succession).

Since the 'leader', i.e., the *velayate faqih*, is the Islamic Republic's highest authority, it was crucial for its future stability and for the posture of Iran to guarantee a smooth transfer of power from Khomeini to his successor. According to Shi'i tradition and the Iranian constitution the 'leader' must be a 'righteous *faqih*' (i.e. theologian) who apart from being the most learned *faqih* must be 'just, aware of the [requirements of the] times and courageous', and capable of 'managing the affairs [of the state] with good sense'. If no single *faqih* is recognized as such, the Council of Experts was empowered to select one of the leading contenders and introduce him to the people. Should they fail to agree on an accepted leader, they were to select three *or* five prominent theologians to form a Council of Leadership. Initial steps in this direction were taken in 1983 when a Council of Experts (*shuraye khebregan*) was elected and empowered to choose the next leader. Khomeini wrote his political testament in 1983 and in 1985 the Council nominated Ayatollah Hussein 'Ali Montazeri as Khomeini's designated successor. But his authority was not sufficiently recognized even within the narrow circle of Khomeini's disciples. Aware of the delicate nature of the question and the importance of resolving it, Khomeini took two important steps in 1987–8: he revised his will and defined more clearly his vision of the *velayate faqih*'s authority.

However, Khomeini had much more authority than comparable religious figures had had in the past. This could explain the argument within the establishment over the succession. Montazeri was promoted to the rank of *Ayatollah 'Uzma* (Grand Ayatollah) only during the revolution, and even that mainly because of his loyalty to Khomeini rather than the course of his scholarship. Thus, the very nomination of Montazeri was a retreat from Khomeini's ideology. Moreover, after his nomination, many Iranians had second thoughts about the wisdom of naming him as the sole successor. Opposition came from various circles. Some followers of the other Grand Ayatollahs had not supported the decision in the first place. Other prominent Ayatollahs (though not possessing the rank of *Ayatollah 'Uzma*) had also challenged the nomination all along. Then there were less prominent clerics, albeit politically powerful, who also resented the nomination. Some opposed Montazeri personally, others (such as the *Hujjatiyyah* movement) preferred a collective leadership. If the issue of Khomeini's succession was a major concern for the regime ever since Montazeri's nomination, the events of 1986 (the Iran-Contra affair) and 1988 (the cease-fire and later in the year the attack on his supporters) made it even more visible. In both cases Montazeri seemed to have lost power to his opponents.

It was apparently in order to spare Iran a contested succession that Khomeini revised his will in December 1987. Although it is not clear, at this point, precisely what the new will – or, for that matter, the old one – said, it is safe to assume that Khomeini wished to make his choice more explicit and to urge his disciples to unite behind the new leader (or leadership). Yet, it is arguable that in either case there is likely to be a deviation from Islamic tradition as well as from his own doctrine and the constitution.

In the past, it must be remembered, there were numerous instances of no single *faqih* being generally accepted as the sole legitimate source of religious authoritiy, and there was often a kind of collective spiritual leadership. Then, Khomeini has rightly pointed out in November 1988, there was a permanent debate within top-clerics on theological-ideological issues.[2] But then, with the acutal power in the hands of the Shah, their differences 'existed in books' only,[3] while now such differences are likely to disturb the functioning of the government. In such circumstances, many Iranians believed, the government would be paralyzed. 'If there is a leadership Council,' Majlis deputy Fakhr al-Din Hijazi claimed, 'Iran will be another Lebanon.' Rejecting the idea of the formation of a council, Ayatollah Ahmad Azari Qomi explained: 'we need a focus for people's emotions... How can the people shout [during their demonstrations] slogans like, "we are your soldiers, O Council of Leadership" [as they shout, "We are your soldiers, Khomeini"]?'[4]

Moreover, even if a Leadership Council were to be formed, tradition and the constitution would demand that it be composed of the most prominent clerics. In that case, it would no longer represent then Khomeini's ideology, since (except for Montazeri) none of the Grand Ayatollahs follow Khomeini's line. Alternatively, it could include clerics of lower rank (such as Rafsanjani or Khamenei, who are both *Hujjat ul-Islam*). Again, this would be far removed from Khomeini's vision of what the rule of the *velayate faqih* should be. If, on the other hand, Montazeri becomes the sole successor, this will still not conform with the original *velayate faqih* doctrine, since he is certainly not the most distinguished Ayatollah. The main question will then be to what degree his authority will be accepted by the other Grand Ayatollahs or by Khomeini's own disciples. These questions remain unanswered. (Late in 1988, however, dozens of Montazeri's supporters were executed and, no less important, the actual policy seemed to be in greater conformity with the views of his opponents in the domestic struggle for power.)

This is not all, however. Several times during 1987 and 1988, Khomeini intervened in domestic politics to give more authority to the 'politicians' (some of them clerics of lower rank) at the expense of the authority of the prominent clerics. In notes exchanged in late December 1987 and early January 1988 between Khomeini and Khamenei and between Khomeini and the Council of Guardians (*shuraye negahban*), one of the principal questions in Shi'i theology was discussed: the limits of government power.[5] Under the constitution the Council of Guardians has the ultimate right to review whether laws passed by the Majlis are in conformity with Islamic law and compatible with the constitution, and to veto them should they deviate from them. But now Khomeini pressured it to approve Majlis laws it had hitherto vetoed, claiming they were unIslamic (such were the laws regarding agrarian reform, nationalization of foreign trade, taxation and the labour law).[6] This was an important step in stripping the council of its constitutional authority. Until then the 12-man Council (or, more precisely the six theologians nominated by the *imam*) were the main authority empowered to confirm legislation.

A month later he went one step further. Early in February 1988, a group of prominent leaders turned to Khomeini to help bypass the Council of Guardians in case of disagreement between it and the Majlis. On his response (6 February) he laid down that such an impasse should be resolved by an assembly consisting of the six theologian-members of the Council as well as six state functionaries: Hujjat ul-Islam Khamenei (the President), Hujjat ul-Islam 'Ali-Akbar Hashemi-Rafsanjani (the Speaker), Ayatollah 'Abdul-Karim Musavi Ardebili (President of the Supreme Court), Hujjat ul-Islam Tavassoli, Hojjat ul-Islam Muhammad Musavi Kho'iniha (the Prosecutor General). The minister concerned with the proposed legislation should also be co-opted. Ahmad Khomeini, the son of the Ayatollah, will take part in the assembly 'so that reports of the meetings can be brought to me faster'. The assembly should decide by a majority vote and its decisions, the Ayatollah decreed, 'must be accepted'.[7] This was another blatant retreat from his own earlier dogma. The authority of 'ascertaining the interest [of the state]' (a phrase worked into the name of the new assembly: *shuraye tashkhise maslahat*) was thus entrusted with a mixed (i.e., 'political' and theological) assembly. The prominent clerics of the Council of Guardians found themselves dispossessed of their exclusive right to approve legislation. Instead they had to consider more seriously the views of the 'politicians' in the assembly (some of them, lower-ranking clerics). In August 1988, Khomeini ordered the formation of yet another body, a four-man concil (*shuraye ta'ine siyasathaye bazsazi*), to resolve disagreements over post-war reconstruction policy and/or ministerial appointments. Its members were the heads of the three branches of government (Rafsanjani, Khamenei and Ardebili) and the prime minister (Mir-Hussein Musavi).[8]

By means of these steps, Khomeini in fact sanctioned the supremacy of the state over the philosophy of the revolution. Rafsanjani interpreted Khomeini's guidelines early in the year saying: 'In our country, the law should follow Islamic doctrine. However, if necessary, priority will be given to government decision over doctrine.'[9] After Khomeini's August decree he added that the four-man Council will be the 'source [*marja*'] of authority for the designation of public matters'. It is, of course, unlikely that he viewed this council as the 'source' of authority in its full-Shi'i meaning (i.e., replacing the *velayate faqih*); but he nevertheless pointed to the gap already existing between Khomeini's concept of the *velayate faquih* to the realities of 1988. The doctrine has clearly been whittled down in face of the harsh realities. The State became no less important than the Revolution.

As long as Khomeini is alive, he can probably depend on his hold over the masses and the leadership alike to prevent open conflict within the establishment. But if it is permissible to speculate, one might argue that the authority of the *velayate faqih* as currently exercised by Khomeini will probably not survive him. Thus, with regard to its most basic element, the future regime – even if led by Khomeini's disciples – will not longer function in keeping with his doctrine.

The relationship between these developments and the war is only indirect. For example: the economic hardships of the war called for a more radical social and economic legislation which pragmatists, Islamic conservatives as well as the majority of the Council of Guardians were unwilling to approve (the main doctrinal-theological controversy revolved, in fact, around social and economic legislation); indeed, the formation of the four-man council was directly related to the debate on the strategy for post-war reconstruction. The need for arms and spare parts drove Rafsanjani to approach the US in 1985–6; subsequent developments of this affair appear to have harmed the position of Montazeri. Finally, the difficulties in the front led to the appointment of Rafsanjani as acting Commander-in-Chief, a position that helped him, it seems now, to reinforce his power.

THE IDEA OF SOCIAL JUSTICE

Khomeini came to power without having laid down social and economic policies. His writings stress the goals of social justice and economic independence, but contain no specific programme of action. An economic philosophy was developed in the decades preceding the revolution by other revolutionary-Islamic ideologists. Most prominent among them were Ayatollah Muhammad Baqir Sadr (from Iraq), Ayatollah Mahmud Taleqani, and Abul-Hasan Bani Sadr. In their writings, as well as in the many declarations by Khomeini upon seizing power, the main point was to improve the lot of the *mostaz'efin*. After a decade of revolution and war no material improvement has been achieved. Khamenei himself, in an attempt to justify the cease-fire admitted: 'During these ten years we have not done enough in this field.'[10]

In fact, since the advent of the revolution the economy has steadily deteriorated.[11] Several factors contributed: the rapid growth of the population and the accelerated urbanization process; the brain drain; the outflow of capital; and the virtual cessation of local and foreign investment. Exports declined, and the government found itself unable to deal with specific problems, such as the growing unemployment and rising inflation, let alone the underlying economic causes of the deterioration. Two factors further exacerbated the situation: one, the war with Iraq, which consumed vast resources,[12] cut oil exports and created additional stresses (such as the need to assist refugees and to rebuild the infrastructure in the war zones); and two, the fall in oil prices on the world market. Iraqi air raids on Iranian oil installations (which had begun in the summer of 1985 and become more intense since 1986) brought down the volume of oil exports, so that Iran was selling smaller quantities and earning much less than formerly.

Long-term economic goals, such as creating self-sufficiency, diminishing the country's dependence on oil revenue, and improving the lot of the *mostaz'efin* were almost completely neglected. Major plans to solve economic problems turned into theological-ideological controversies. Attempts to block the influx of people into the large cities, mainly to the capital, failed totally. Plans to improve basic services – such as housing, education and health care – were conspicuously unsuccessful. In fact, in many areas a change for the worse was noticeable, and soaring prices put many commodities beyond the reach of the *mostaz'efin*.

Just how delicate these problems were could be discerned from the official – often exaggerated – statistics quoted by the government. Some of the basic problems that had led to alienation from the previous regime were again evident, sometimes to a greater extent than a decade earlier.[13]

Housing was no less a problem in 1987 than it had been in 1977. According to government statistics, there was a shortage of 3.7 million housing units in the period of the first five-year plan (1983–8). Since the beginning of the plan, housing costs have risen faster than income of urban families. According to a survey carried out by the prime minister's office, up to 82 per cent of family income in Tehran was spent on rent in 1983–4. Future prospects were even gloomier – at least as long as the war went on.[14]

Education was another major field in which conditions steadily deteriorated. The rapid expansion of academic education led to a lowering of standards but even so growing numbers of high-school graduates failed to be admitted to university. The disproportionate increase in the number of those receiving a primary and secondary education created a large number of aspirants for higher education with decreasing chances of being admitted to university, let alone to a specific faculty. In each of the last three years of the Shah's rule, between 250,000 and 300,000 young people applied for university admission, the highest actual admission figure for 1977–8 was little short of 30,000. Thus, in the final years of the monarchy there were well over 200,000 young people each year who had their hopes dashed by cruel reality. This had caused much resentment and added to the ferment of the late 1970s.[15] In the 1984–5 academic year, 581,000 candidates took entrance examinations, but only 44,000 were admitted to universities and other institutions of higher learning,[16] meaning that in 1987, some half a million youngsters were turned away.

Similarly, health services – mainly for the *mostaz'efin* – remained as much a problem as they had been before the revolution. Unemployment continued to be high, most critically among high school graduates. The prime minister said there were 4 million unemployed in 1987.[17] Inflation remained high and the devaluation of the Riyal continued. The American dollar could buy 75 Riyals at the official rate, but almost 20 times more on the black market in 1988.

For constant population growth and accelerated urbanization made the Government's work more difficult. The Islamic regime, unlike the Shah's, did not encourage birth control. The 1986 census (the first under the Islamic regime) showed a population growth of 11 million since the revolution – from 37 m in1979 to 48 m in 1986. The prospect for the future was even more ominous.[18] A sociologist in one of the leading Iranian universities gave the author the following statistics of births in Iran: in 1978, there were 1,338,000 births (and 127,857 deaths); in 1981, there were 2,421,000 births (178,099 deaths); because of the war there was a temporary decrease in the number of births in 1982 (2,101,000) and since then a renewed growth was registered. Urbanization continued apace, with the government's plans to curb it clearly failing (the city of Tehran grew from about 5 million in 1978 to over 8 million ten years later).

In every sphere, signs of social and economic strain were increasingly visible and the effects of the war were undeniably imposing hardships on the people, but mainly on the *mostaz'efin*.

As always during revolution and war, hoarding and profiteering reached peak proportions. While soaring prices put many commodities beyond the reach of the *mostaz'efin*, the black market boomed and speculators prospered. A shortage of some commodities and the lack of fair distribution of what was available pressed hard on the *mostaz'efin*. They were clearly beginning to feel themselves unjustly treated. They realized that there were no real shortages and that those able to afford it could buy almost anything, in almost any quantity. It was not surprising that signs of a growing sense of alienation between the haves and the have-nots became noticeable.

Signs of growing disillusionment among the *mostaz'efin* also became increasingly evident. For the Islamic regime and for Khomeini personally, this was both painful and frustrating, considering the pledges that had been made to improve the lot of the *mostaz'efin*. The growing disillusionment was also becoming a potential threat to the regime. No less important was the fact that economic policy had become the main subject of theological-ideological controversy.

Many of the *mostaz'efin* felt that, although they had borne the main burden of the revolution and the war, the gap between the poor and the rich persisted even under the Islamic regime. The *mostaz'efin*, Montazeri said in 1984, had been the first to join the revolution; its prime supporters and the chief contributors to the war; they were 'the main owners of the revolution'.[19] He came closest to the truth in expressing what was probably a very widespread view when he said (in November 1983): 'Today, the heavy burden of the revolution, the war and the resultant shortages, is pressing far more on the lower strata'; the upper strata, who enjoy a large share of the existing services and commodities, contribute precious little at the front lines of revolution and war.[20] It is unacceptable, Khamenei added, that some people sacrified their lives while others were engaged in 'pursuing luxury'.[21]

Nevertheless, those whose children 'avoided going to the fronts' were the main beneficiaries of its fruits.[22] Hussein Kamali, the chairman of the Majlis labour committee, and that 'economic gangs and pressure groups' who were willing 'to sell the revolution for their own benefit' were acquiring fortunes, while the *mostaz'efin* remained suppressed.[23] Muhammad Khaza'i, spokesman of the Majlis Economic Committee, argued that it was unacceptable to an Islamic regime that 'one part of the population walks around with stomachs bloated with malnutrition, while the stomachs of another part are bloated from over-eating'.[24] Judge Ahmad 'Ali Burhani argued that a society with a huge gap between the rich and the poor had no right to call itself Islamic; yet, in Iran the rich were becoming richer and the poor poorer.[25] Added to the frustration was the fact that the link between the war and the economy had become blatantly obvious, and some *mostaz'efin* began to question the worth of continuing the war.

The government, for its part, set out to counter criticism, by recourse to two key words: Revolution and War. Similarly it tried to lower material expectations, urging the *mostaz'efin* not to expect quick gains and advising them against consumerism. But patience was visibly wearing thin. On several occasions, mainly since 1985, people took to the streets, demonstrating against economic hardships. But, until the end of 1988 no real challenge to the regime emerged from such discontent.

In a different vein, the war made it even more difficult for revolutionary Iran to advance towards self-sufficiency and economic independence (though it contributed to the progress of Iran's military industries).

The need for rapid economic reform was felt even more forcefully following the cease-fire, when as Khamenei has put it: 'reconstruction has become our nation's slogan'.[26] On this, all the actors on the Iranian scene are agreed. But goals, priorities and methods are being disputed, with each group fully aware of the ideological, political and personal implications of the different choices. The broad debate has become encapsulated in two distinct, but related issues: the future of the private sector, and the attitudes towards foreign aid. Two entirely different world views of the future path of revolutionary Iran – one pragmatist and conservative, the other radical and more revolutionary – compete to lay down policy on them. At the time of writing, the more pragmatic faction had the upper hand *vis-à-vis* the more doctrinaire revolutionaries.

Rafsanjani gave vent to the existing rifts saying in October 1988: 'We have differences of opinion among ourselves over these issues.' But he had also, albeit implicity, suggested that he was aware of the need to follow a more pragmatic policy. He reminded the people that the old good days of early Islam have long passed: 'today ... we live under new conditions'.[27] He advised the advancement of reconstruction in a manner which would 'maintain ideals' but also 'meet the needs of the people'.[28] He supported greater involvement of the private sector (a policy, he said, aimed at 'taking the wind out of the sails of the [radical] etatist'). He went on to blame the radicals as 'frozen in their beliefs [i.e., fanatics] ... who cannot adjust themselves to the circumstances of the day'.[29] Khamenei made clear even more explicitly, that 'in reconstruction, the public participation is the main element, just as was the case in the ... war'.[30] Late in November Rafsanjani said that 'we have [already] reached the conclusion that we should make the import of certain vital commodities free, gradually, and place them at the disposal of the private sector.'[31]

The question of the role of foreign countries (or foreign companies) in the reconstruction was clearly related to both the general issue of the private sector and to Iran's foreign relations. Here again, Rafsanjani was the most pragmatic. In mid-September Khamenei too made clear that since Iran lacked sufficient domestic resources and because time was an important factor, his country needed external support: 'We need both financial resources and technology and know-how other than our domestic resources and technology. And we shall obtain them from foreigners.'[32] He added: since 'we cannot prolong the issue [of reconstruction] for a hundred years' outside support and encouragement of the private sector were both essential.[33]

As long as Khomeini did not explicitly state his own views, both sides could legitimately claim to be loyal to him, even though the faction led by Rafsanjani carried much greater weight. Eventually, in November, Hujjat ul-Islam Muhammad 'Ali Ansari (a radical cleric from the staff of the Ayatollah's personal bureau) appealed to Khomeini to spell out his stand. In his letter he said that 'two political-ideological schools of thought ... have embarked on serious competition'.[34] Khomeini, it turned out, was unwilling to antagonize either side, and gave no clear answer.[35] Earlier, however, he said (30 August) that the government should allow greater room for private initiative, though 'under government supervision'. He said: 'the people should be free in matters of trade', including foreign trade, but 'supervision should be excercised to avoid corruption'. The priorities, he added, should be decided by the four-man council.[36] But, in fact, late in 1988 it was the more pragmatic group which seemed to be shaping the actual policy.

'EXPORTING' THE ISLAMIC REVOLUTION

The radical Islamic concepts voiced by Khomeini since the late 1960s were meant to apply far beyond the borders of Iran and were closely bound up with pan-Islamic *motifs* and aimed at the realization of Islamic unity (moral, if not political). Being united, Islam would become capable of playing its ordained role in human history. Khomeini considered the Iranian revolution a stage and an instrument in an overall Islamic revolution. He declared: 'Our movement is for an Islamic goal, not for Iran alone ... Iran has [only] been the starting point.'[37] Consistent with this approach, Khomeini rejected nationalism as an 'imperialist plot' intended to divide and weaken Islam. The notion of 'exporting the revolution' follows naturally.

Yet, even though national considerations were alien to Khomeini's own principle and to his theory of foreign relations in general, and within the Muslim world in particular, his regime none the less chose to act towards the Arab world from a perception of Iran's national interest. How else is it possible to reconcile his insistence on the irrelevance of borders between Muslim lands (and thus rejecting the demand of the United Arab Emirates for the return of the three islands captured by the Shah in 1971), with his demand for the total withdrawal of Iraq from all Iranian territories? How does his supra-national ideology and his assertion that there was no difference between Muslims anywhere, neither ethnically nor with regard to Shi'i and Sunni affiliation, accord with the article of the constitution laying down that only a Shi'i with Iranian origin can hold office as president of the Islamic Republic of Iran? How is it possible to explain that one article of the constitution asserts Muslim unity and another lays down that the government must preserve the territorial integrity of Iran? How can one reconcile his abhorrence of national divisions within Islam with his insistence that the Gulf must be called (and therefore be) Persian?[38]

Moreover, since the outbreak of the war Khomeini himself has begun to use nationalist terminology. For instance, in a speech to religious leaders a week after the war started, he vowed 'to fight until death the attackers of our beloved homeland (*mihane 'Aziz*)'.[39] In fact, the very name by which the country is now officially called – *Jumhuriyye Islamiyye Iran* – is a contradiction in terms: its first part befits a government of the Islamic *ummah*, the second limits it to a small part thereof. Being surrounded by other independent Muslim states which differ from Iran in their ethnic and sectarian affiliation, Khomeini was in fact in an awkward position 'for as the Iranian head of state he cannot disavow the idea of the nation-state, but as a revolutionary Islamic leader he cannot make his commitment to the national idea too strong or his commitment to the *ummah* too weak'.[40]

Furthermore, 'exporting the revolution' meant different things at different times in the regime's history, and it meant different things when addressed to

mankind at large, or to the Muslim *ummah* or to the Shi'i community.
Moreover, there were significant differences of opinion between more
pragmatic elements within the revolutionary establishment, headed by
Rafsanjani, and a more doctrinaire group with Montazeri, Kho'iniha,
Ayatollah 'Ali Meshkini most prominent among them.

There remained one point, however, on which all were agreed in principle:
it was the view of both, that while Muslim lands were the primary target for
exporting the revolution, it must eventually offer 'salvation' to *mostaz'efin*
the world over. The idea was powerful enough for Foreign Minister Musavi
to declare, on entering office in August 1981, that the 'objectives of Iran's
foreign policy' was to 'carry the message of Iran's Islamic revolution to the
[entire] world'.[41] Meshkini went to the length of saying that the goal of the
revolution was 'to impose the Qur'an over the entire world'.[42] But then such
statements always had a ritual rather than programmatic ring to them.

As for the perhaps more practical question of 'exporting' the revolution to
the Muslim world, the radicals had one advantage: they could point out that
the very doctrine of *velayate faqih* made it obligatory to do so – whether for
the ultimate purpose of establishing 'the government of the *imam mahdi*' or
for the more immediate need of making 'the Iranian regional environment
safe for Iran's power and for its revolutionary ideology'.[43] But, taken as a
whole, the more radical expressions regarding the 'export' of the revolution,
typical of the early days, were toned down over time. Leaders no longer
spoke of the use of force for spreading the revolution. The emphasis shifted
to cultural and ideological themes.

Khomeini himself (mainly since 1983), has consistently refrained from
implying any intention to spread the revolution by force. The course of
history, he stressed, made the spread of the revolution inevitable and
irreversible. But Iran did not need to 'worm its way' into other countries;
rather it should walk in 'like an invited guest'.[44] Until that happened, it was
Iran's primary duty to spread the word of Islamic ideology and to make the
country's 'new realities' known, so as to encourage its being 'invited'.[45] By
then, the emphasis on 'exporting' the revolution had clearly shifted to
cultural and ideological themes. Even Khomeini's messages to the *hajj*
pilgrims, to the participants in Unity Week or at *jum'ah imam* conferences –
usually the occasion for radical statements regarding the 'export of the
revolution' – revealed a gradual, if implicit, recognition of Muslims having
national affiliation with different countries. Over time the plea for unity made
room for vaguer appeals for brotherhood (*bradari*), 'unity of the word'
(*vahdate kalam*) and 'unity of purpose' (*vahdate hadaf*).

True, some of Khomeini's associates were less restrained and continued
taking Khomeini's earlier views altogether literally: for many of them
'exporting' the revolution was and still is, a principal goal to be actively and
constantly pursued by the Islamic Republic. But – more often than not – they
too disclaimed any intention to use force to spread the revolution.

Having so little success in exporting his universal ideology, Khomeini 'turned to devising and exporting a more particularistic Shi'i ideology'.[46] But even this did not have top prority. Taking a broad view, there can be no doubt that, as one observer put it, Tehran had become 'less concerned with fomenting rebellion abroad and more concerned with consolidating its own borders'.[47] Today, the *Hizbollah* in Lebanon, or the followers of *al-Da'wah* movement in Iraq seem more faithful to Khomeini's vision of world order than are the rulers of Tehran.

In practice Khomeini's policy, like that of earlier Iranian pan-Islamists turned out to be motivated in the main by tactical and pragmatic rather than by ideological considerations. Though the vision has not been abandoned, its implementation has been subordinated to practical calculations. If Iran originally expected a spontaneous and widespread acceptance of its revolutionary experience, it realized soon enough that this was not happening. This and the exigencies of war and, for that matter of the post-war, era compelled Khomeini to change his order of priorities. The 'export' of the revolution had to give way to its consolidation in Iran, in the hope of making it an attractive model for emulation elsewhere. Again Iranian national interests gained primacy over revolutionary Islamic conceptions. (Only Lebanon seems to be, to a degree at least, an exception to this rule.)

In this sense, the Iranian revolution resembles the French, American and Bolshevik ones: all initially aspired to export the revolution in one way or another, but all were compelled, sooner or later, to come to terms with realities. 'Khomeinism in one country', has not become an officially proclaimed policy, but Tehran has certainly come a long way way from the vision of an 'Islamic order' formulated upon seizing power. The war, again, was a factor in accelerating the process.

Following the cease-fire Tehran has proved even more flexible in dealing with its Muslim neighbours. The initial radical attitude towards them notwithstanding, Tehran seems to regret its former policy. Rafsanjani was openly critical of past policies towards some Arab states: 'If Iran had demonstrated a little more tactfulness' in its relations with Saudi Arabia and Kuwait', he said late in November 1988, 'they would have not supported Iraq'.[48] The same day, Deputy Foreign Minister 'Ali Muhammad Besharati spoke of Iran's desire to 'open a new page' in its relations with the Gulf littoral states. He quoted from the Koran to support his view that 'bygones are bygones. We should think of the future.' Referring specifically to Saudi Arabia, he said: 'We are prepared to sit down, talk and overcome the great misunderstanding that has been created between us.' Using arguments, which in themselves prove greater pragmatism, he reminded his people that 'neighbourhood is unchangeable' and that 'our holy shrines . . . and our Ka'bah are there. The Prophet is buried in Saudi Arabia. Can we ignore it?'[49] Such statements clearly contradict those of the early days of the revolution.

'NEITHER THE EAST NOR THE WEST'

Similarly, the notion of 'Neither the East nor the West' has undergone considerable change. In the early days of the revolution, Khomeini had declared all governments anywhere, and most particularly in the Muslim countries, to be illegitimate in principle. The Islamic Republic would ignore governments and deal directly with peoples instead. In 1981 Khomeini still had upheld isolation as a new ideal for Iran's foreign policy: only through isolation could Iran become truly independent, he then argued.[50] In terms of Iran's relations with the superpowers the view of revolutionary Iran was – as Khomeini often put it – that 'all infidels belong to the same camp'. His concept of non-alignment was: 'Neither the East, nor the West.' The US remained the 'Great Satan', but Khomeini promised that: 'America cannot do any damned thing.' This became one of the main slogans of the revolution. Gradually, the doctrinaire approach has been whittled down by realities. In October 1984, Khomeini announced that Tehran wanted 're-lations with *all countries*' (with the sole exception of the United States, Israel and South Africa). Not to do so, he said then, was 'against reason and the Islamic law'.[51]

Rafsanjani, for his part, came out with the most pragmatic declarations. In a Friday sermon on 13 May 1983 he addressed 'the Americans' directly to remind them that, in principle, Iran was ready for relations with all countries which were prepared to have 'proper (*sahih*) relations with us'. He now excluded only Israel and South Africa.[52] In fact, Rafsanjani had long been known for his appreciation of American weapons and his recognition of the necessity to buy American arms.[53] Already in April 1986 he said: 'We will buy American weapons wherever they will be available for us.'[54]

Later, in July 1988, Iran was compelled to concede that Khomeini's special version of non-alignment had harmed the country: Rafsanjani said that 'by the use of an unappropriate method ... we have created enemies for our country'. Those who could have remained indifferent were made to trans-form their indifference into hostility, and Tehran did not labour to attract the friendship of those 'who could have been our friends'. He added that the foreign ministry had already been instructed to 'tread the correct path' – the path 'we should have always followed'.[55] An editorial in *Kayhan* (2 July) wrote that, unlike past practices, 'the breaking of diplomatic ties should not be seen as a principle'. Khomeini himself, in his message to the people of 20 July 1988, made it clear that 'the support' of the super-powers for Iraq was a factor in Iran's decision to accept the cease-fire.

In this respect the impact of the war was clearly apparent. The American military presence in the Gulf and their determination to fight back in meeting the Iranian challenges (mainly in September-October 1987 and in April 1988), the difficulties in acquiring arms and spare-parts, and even the need for economic support (among others the unfreezing of Iranian assets in

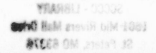

France and the US) were instrumental in producing the change in the war and forcing Iran to accept the cease-fire.

This trend was continued, even more explicitly following the cease-fire. Here too, it was Rafsanjani who came out in support of making some kind of compromise between his country's old radical ideology and the new realities. Although Tehran was as yet unwilling to admit this, the need to do so was recognized by now by many Iranians. Early in October, Khamenei set out to deny speculations that Tehran was seeking to 'compromise with the superpowers' by making 'concessions on the revolution's principles'. He made clear that his country will 'preserve its principles under all conditions'. But he himself admitted that some 'writers and orators' write and say things that may be so interpreted.[56] This trend was powerful enough to lead *Abrar* to call upon the government not to set aside the revolutionary ideology in its search for expanding foreign ties. It emphasized that the idea that Iran should 'stretch a begging arm to anyone and any country' to end its isolation must be cleansed from the minds of Iran's policy makers.[57]

Thus, while criticism of the US continues, since late 1988 there has been a clear trend of improving relations with foreign countries (thus, among others, with Britain, Canada, France, the USSR). Those who are (like Rafsanjani) more pragmatic do not altogether close all doors for rapprochement with Washington even when they set out to harshly criticise the US.[58]

CONCLUSION

By the very nature of things, revolutionary movements are often led to deviate from their radical doctrine once they have made the transition from opposition to power. The Islamic revolution was no exception. As long as he headed an opposition movement, Khomeini had depicted a 'new Iran' as being modelled on early Islam. Once in power, he knew he could not rule by means of revolutionary slogan – certainly not slogans drawn from seventh-century thought. He and his disciples were now called to manage, rather than discuss, affairs of State. Soon they had to compromise with reality, not from a new-found moderation, but from a pragmatism responsive to the exigencies of their situation. The *State* became no less important than the *Revolution*.

As far as Iran is concerned, the most momentous question is not whether the war is over, but rather to what extent the cease-fire signals a decline of Khomeini's doctrine. But one must guard against equating the fate of Khomeini's ideology with that of the Islamic regime. In ideological as well as practical terms, there have already been considerable deviations from some of the most basic elements in Khomeini's philosophy. The pragmatic interests of the *state* have clearly gained supremacy over the radical philosophy of the *revolution*. Yet this does not signal, or portend, the end of clerical rule. Paradoxically, the greater the deviations from *revolutionary dogma* (and the concomitant adaptability to new realities) the greater is the likelihood for the *Islamic regime* to continue. One way or another, Khomeini's death is bound to be the supreme challenge for Islamic rule in Iran.

Notes

1. Though fundamentally different from revolutions elsewhere in the Muslim world the Islamic revolution was entirely within the tradition of earlier Iranian protest movements. For this, and more detail on the ideology of the Islamic movement and the rule of the regime in its first decade, see my book: *Iran: The Revolution and Beyond* (New York: Holmes and Meier, 1989).
2. *Jumhuriyye Islami*, 7 November; *Kayhan* (Tehran), 26 November 1988.
3. These are the words of President 'Ali Khamenei cited in Radio Tehran, 11 November – *SWB*, 14 November 1988.
4. Both are quoted in *Tehran Times*, 29 November 1985.
5. The decrees are brought in *Ettela'at*, 7 and 12 Jaunary 1988.
6. For the constitutional right of the Council see: Menashri, *Iran: The Revolution and Beyond*, 117, 192–3; for the use of such power to block such radical legislation see, for example, pp. 173, 183, 224, 246, 327–8, 356–7, 358.
7. *Ettela'at*, 7 February 1988.
8. *Ettela'at*, 31 August 1988.
9. NHK television, Tokyo, 1 February – *SWB*, 3 February 1988.
10. *Ettela'at*, 23 July 1988.
11. For a detailed study of the economic problems in their relation with the war, see chapter by Eliyahu Kanovsky in this volume.
12. In his budget speech, on 28 December 1987, Musavi said that 41 per cent of the expenditure in the general budget and 52 per cent of the current total allocations for the government 'have been earmarked for the military and security affairs': Radio Tehran, 28 December – *SWB*, 29 December 1987. Foreign observers estimated that the country was spending as much as $5 billion on its *c.* $7 million annual budget on the war: *Times*, May 1987.
13. For a discussion of similar problems in the background to the growing opposition to the Shah, see my book *Iran: The Revolution and Beyond*, 1–4.
14. *Iran Press Digest* (Economic Bulletin), 14 July 1987. According to statistics for 1981 1,400,000 families in Tehran shared only 900,000 apartments.
15. David Menashri, *Education and the Development of Modern Iran* (forthcoming).
16. J. Behruz, *Iran Almanac, 1987* (Tehran: Echo of Iran, 1987) p. 135.
17. *Iran Press Digest* (Political Bulletin) 13 July 1987.
18. Radio Tehran, 29 October and 1 November – *SWB*, 31 October and 5 November 1986.
19. *Jumhuriyye Islami*, 21 November 1984.
20. *Kayhan*, 24 November 1983; see also his speech quoted in *Kayhan*, 7 November 1988.
21. *Kayhan*, 13 December 1983; *Ettela'at*, 19 January 1984.
22. *Kayhan Hava'i*, 22 May; *Kayhan*, 1 May 1985.
23. *Jumhuriyye Islami*, 28 November 1984.
24. *Kayhan*, 8 January 1983. See similarly words to this regard by Ayatollah Muhammad Mo'men Qomi (*Kayhan*, 10 April 1983), by Rafsanjani (*Kayhan*, 26 February and 31 March 1983) and by Khamenei (*Kayhan*, 30 March 1983).

25. *Ettela'at*, 1 November 1982.
26. Radio Tehran, 7 October – *SWB*, 10 October 1988.
27. Radio Tehran, 25 September – *SWB*, 27 September 1988.
28. Radio Tehran, 9 October – *SWB*, 11 October 1988.
29. Radio Tehran, 14 October – *SWB*, 17 October 1988.
30. IRNA (in English), 19 October – *SWB*, 20 October 1988.
31. Radio Tehran, 25 November – *SWB*, 28 November 1988.
32. *Ettela'at*, 17 September 1988.
33. Radio Tehran, 14 October – *SWB*, 17 October 1988.
34. *Kayhan* (Tehran), 16 November 1988; *The Echo of Iran*, 1 December 1988.
35. *Jumhuriyye Islami*, 7 November; *Kayhan* (Tehran), 16 November 1988.
36. *Ettela'at*, 31 August 1988.
37. Ayatollah Ruhollah Khomeini, *Islam and Revolution: Writings and Declarations of Imam Khomeini* (Berkeley: Mizan, 1981), 34–5; an interview with *al-Mustaqbal*, 13 January 1979; Radio Tehran, 7 May – *FBIS*, 8 May 1979.
38. Khomeini even rejected Ayatollah Sadiq Khalkhali's proposal to name it the 'Muslim Gulf': *Kayhan*, 29 May 1979. On 5 May 1981, Prime Minister Raja'i issued a statement saying that 'Persian Gulf' was the 'correct historical and original name'. He gave instructions for that appelation only to be used in all official documents and speech Radio Tehran, 7 May – *SWB*, 9 May 1981.
39. *Ettela'at*, 29 September 1980.
40. James Piscatori, *Islam in the World of Nation-States* (Cambridge University Press, 1986) p. 111.
41. *Ettela'at*, 23 August 1981.
42. *Kayhan*, 19 December 1982.
43. R.K. Ramazani, *Revolutionary Iran* (Baltimore: Johns Hopkins, 1986), 24–5; idem, 'Iran's Islamic Revolution and the Persian Gulf', *Current History*, January 1985, 5–6.
44. *Kayhan*, 24 October 1983.
45. *Kayhan*, 30 September 1982.
46. Marvin Zonis and Daniel Brumberg, 'Khomeini, the Islamic Republic of Iran, and the Arab World', *Harvard Middle East Papers* (no. 5, 1987), 74–5.
47. Gary Sick, 'Iran's Quest for Superpower Status', *Foreign Affairs*, Spring 1987, 714.
48. IRNA (in English), 19 November – *SWB*, 21 November 1988.
49. Radio Tehran, 19 November – *SWB*, 21 November 1988.
50. See his speech broadcast over Radio Tehran, 3 November – *SWB*, 5 November 1981.
51. *Kayhan*, 29 October 1984. For a similar view expressed a year later: *Kayhan Hava'i* 11 November 1985.
52. *Kayhan*, 14 May 1983.
53. See mainly his statements from July 1984 (*Jumhuriyye Islami* 19 July 1984), September 1985 (*Guardian*, 9 September 1985), February 1986 (*Kayhan Hava'i*, 19 February 1986) and in April 1986 (*Kayhan Hava'i*, 30 April 1986).
54. *Kayhan Hava'i*, 30 April 1986.
55. *Ettela'at*, 3 July 1988.
56. Radio Tehran, 14 October – *SWB*, 17 October 1988.
57. IRNA (in English), 21 November – *SWB*, 24 November 1988.
58. See, for example, a Friday sermon by Rafsanjani (Radio Tehran, 25 November – *SWB*, 28 November 1988) and his letter to former President Carter in November 1988 (Radio Tehran, 28 November – *SWB*, 30 November 1988).

4 The Consequences of the Iran–Iraq War for Iraqi Politics

Charles Tripp

INTRODUCTION

In the last analysis, the foundations of political power in Iraq lie in the degree of personal trust that exists amongst those who hold high office in the state. This has been both the cause of the particular nature of political developments in Iraq and has, quite naturally, been enhanced by the form of those developments since the creation of the state. Such trust is founded in the first place on the deeply rooted and highly resilient social facts of family, clan and tribal origins, expanding beyond this to those who share similar provincial origins with the clan members. It is a symptom of largely communal, parochial politics which have tended first to resist and then to move in on the apparatus of the modern state. Its practitioners have used the bonds of personal confidence to construct within the bureaucratic machinery of army, party and governing administration a network of greater indigenous social and cultural meaning. These personal links are the ones which reassure both ruler and the immediate circle of his intimates, giving substance to a mediation of power unavailable in the alien notions of collective national purpose and impersonal authority suggested by the administration of a modern state.

In Iraq for the past decade, such highly personalized and socially derived power has found its most complete expression in the figure of Saddam Hussein. He has surrounded himself with confidants and dependants who are expected to ensure and to 'deliver' the complete obedience of all sectors of state and society to the *irada* of Saddam Hussein. They are expected to give him their complete loyalty, not only because of what he does, but also because of who he is: their kinsman, the native son of their class and provincial setting, their colleague in arms from the days of Ba'thist opposition, their co-conspirator during the years of power. These factors have enabled him to achieve a supreme position, since they have granted him an effective circle of supporters and assistants who could not easily be alienated from him by the siren song of alternative ideologies, loyalties or figures of authority. He is the guarantee of their prominence, the source of their

58

benefits and, it is their earnest hope, the guardian of the order they require to secure their interests, however defined.

Saddam Hussein, as the autocrat at the centre of such a system of power, must manage this inner constituency, but he must also project himself as the rightful and effective ruler of Iraq as a state. In doing so, he must attend not only to the instruments of state power itself, but also to the associated society, ensuring that 'centres of power' do not coalesce within the former, or that autonomous collective loyalties do not gain strength within the latter. The passivity which this demands of political society can be achieved in the short term through the ruthless and ubiquitous deployment of the instruments of surveillance and repression. In the longer term and in the face of widespread crisis, other techniques must be used. It is in this respect that the war with Iran during the past eight years has required particular forms of effort and organization in the mobilization of the human resources of Iraq to withstand the evident threat to Saddam Hussein's own power and to the Iraqi state. The two endeavours are inextricably mixed. Success in war at the price of undermining his own autocracy would be worthless. The past eight years have been characterized, therefore, by political as much as military strategies on the part of Saddam Hussein. These have aimed at the reinforcement of his own power, while nevertheless seeking to marshall the Iraqi people into active and not wholly coerced participation in the war effort.

It could be argued that the outbreak of war was the result of this preoccupation with the foundations of autocratic power within Iraq. Although the implications of this may be of particular and grave relevance to the war's ending, it is more important to establish the degree to which the fact and conduct of war have significantly affected the loci of social and political power in Iraq. In a system so relentlessly and publicly based on the will of one man, Saddam Hussein, the implications of such changes for his position and the political system which he has constructed to amplify the dictates of his will are clearly of significance. In this respect, it will be instructive to examine the ways in which the need to mobilize for war has affected the structural aspects of the Iraqi state and society and their relationship with the figure of Saddam Hussein, as well as to assess the moral climate of Iraqi politics, affecting the assessment of Saddam Hussein's worth and ultimately his right to rule.

SADDAM HUSSEIN AS NATIONAL LEADER

One of the most notable features of Iraqi politics during the war has been the cohesion and survival of the small group of men who constitute Saddam Hussein's immediate circle of associates in the upper echelons of the party and state administration. Kinsmen (Gen. Adnan Khairallah Tulfah, Ali

Hassan al-Majid and Hussein Yassin Kamil), fellow Takritis and clansmen (Gen. Hamid Shaaban al-Takriti, Gen. Hussein Rashid al-Takriti, and Fadil Barak Hussein), long-time associates (Izzat Ibrahim al-Duri, Taha Yasin Ramadhan al-Jazrawi and Gen. Abd al-Jabar Shanshal), and prominent dependants (Tariq Mikhail Aziz and Latif Nussayif Jasim) have remained in their posts or have witnesses their fortunes rise during the war. One or two, such as Saddam Hussein's half-brother, Barzan al-Takriti, and Saadoun Shakir have seen their fortunes wane. By and large, however, the inner circle of *dirigeants* has remained constant.

This consistency seems to have been due to two particular causes. First, all these men had been closely associated with Saddam Hussein's inexorable rise to power. They had been tested, therefore, not simply in the Ba'th's opposition struggles prior to 1968, but also, and perhaps more crucially, in the gradual subordination of party and state to Saddam Hussein following the coups of 1968. They formed the pillars of the regime which Saddam Hussein had sought to put in place in order to allow him to seize absolute power in 1979 and were thus intimately linked to his own fate. The second reason was that they were as much implicated in the decision to go to war in 1980 as was Saddam Hussein himself, and were, as a result, equally targets of Iranian enmity. This created a sense of beleaguered solidarity among Saddam Hussein's associates both in the field of domestic politics and in the prosecution of the war effort.

Unlike less prudent and less fortunate colleagues, they kept their nerve in the summer and autumn of 1982 and reinforced thereby the intimate nature of their links with Saddam Hussein. Whilst there may have been differences from time to time within this group about the most effective strategies to be pursued in the prosecution of the war, there was no doubt among them of the need to continue fighting, nor of the importance of rallying around the figure of Saddam Hussein in order to guarantee not simply their own power, but also their survival. Precisely because of their position as the instruments of Saddam Hussein's will and the figures closest to the centre of power, they are in a position to affect drastically his chances of survival. However, even should the inclination have existed, the lessons of the short-lived 1963 Ba'thist regime and of the end of the Arif regime in 1968 were likely to deter thoughts of this kind. The Iranian enemy was only too obviously poised to exploit rifts of this kind in the Iraqi leadership. Even when Saddam Hussein himself appeared to pose something of an obstacle to the effective conduct of the war, and when mutterings of dissatisfaction were heard in this connection, it was clear that their inclination was to rally round him, rather than to think of replacing him, since the risks of the latter course of action were far too great. Quite apart from the gains for their own interests inherent in maintaining, rather than undermining the authority of Saddam Hussein, the unmistakable hostility of Iran could be calculated to create a sense of common purpose among the elite.

In order to organize a war effort commensurate with the threat faced by Iraq, however, it was imperative that Saddam Hussein try to instill a similar sense of common purpose among the inhabitants of Iraq. As he was later to acknowledge, the failure to do so had caused severe problems and had impaired Iraq's military capacity in the early years of the war.[1] Forced into the defensive in 1982, it was important that Saddam Hussein be able to impress upon the Iraqis the fact that they had something worth defending both in the state and society of Iraq, as well as in his own leadership. From his point of view, these were inextricable, since it was by no means his intention that the obligation of defending the former should lead to the possibility of ending the latter.

Prior to the war, the establishment of the National Assembly had been part of this endeavour to legitimize his hold on power, by apparently granting to Iraqis the opportunity to decide, for the first time in their history, the nature of their collective interests, under the guidance of their enlightened leader. During the war, this charade was continued, with Saddam Hussein periodically proclaiming that all political decisions would be open and collective, repeating his promise of 1980 that the fate of the people would no longer be decided in the 'dark labyrinths' of power.[2] As further disguise for the real nature of the dispensation of power, he would go out of his way to state that he saw himself as a true son of 'the people', favouring no particular group, not even his family, members of whom were not immune to punishment if they infringed the rule of law that existed in Iraq for the benefit of all citizens.[3] These symbolic gestures in the direction of open, participatory government were accompanied by the relentless propagation of the myth of Iraq's continuous history as a great and unique national community. Instilling in the people the sense that they belonged to a particular and valued civilization under threat from Iran was thought to be a necessary adjunct to the effort to defend Iraq as a territorial state. It went further in stressing Iraqi patriotism and, indeed, nationalism, then the claim that the Iranian armies represented a threat to the Arab nation or indeed to the Muslim community.[4] The latter themes were used, but the idea of Great Iraq and its people was evidently thought to be more efficacious: it allowed the regime to stress the emotive themes of family, hearth and home under threat. Above all, perhaps, it allowed Saddam Hussein to represent himself as the authentic personification of this putative Iraqi identity. The indissoluble link between the leader and 'his' people, as well as the uniqueness and inevitability of his appearance at this particular juncture of this people's history, allowed him to control and to dominate the myth of collective identity and power in a way which the other images of the Arab nation and the Islamic *ummah* did not. The latter, after all, might suggest other, more authoritative interpreters of the obligations of all Iraqis. The existence of the imperative, necessary and indispensable leader of the people did not permit this, but focused all eyes on Saddam Hussein, making his pronouncements an obligation for all.[5]

THE BA'TH PARTY

Nowhere has this determination to dominate and to set the ideological agenda been more in evidence than in Saddam Hussein's handling of the Ba'th itself. Prior to the war, it had become clear that Saddam Hussein was determined that the Ba'th should not represent a potential threat to his own absolutism, in the sense of constituting a vehicle for the propagation of an ideology to which he himself would be beholden. The war has allowed him, and may even have required him, to assert his own primacy in all matters of ideological obligation. As he was to state in 1987, addressing provincial party officials:

> When you say that the people now argue with you and take my speeches and statements as evidence in their arguments, I would say that I mean it to be this way. In fact, I had meant it to be this way since the early days of the July 1968 revolution ... I wanted to get the help of the people against you. I wanted the people to make use of my words and my conduct so that nobody would come and tell them the opposite or act in a contradictory manner, claiming that this is the line adopted by the party.[6]

In making such a statement, he was merely spelling out for the assembled officials the implications of the position of 'imperative leader' which the Regional Command of the Ba'th had accorded him in the 9th Congress of 1982. It was then, faced not simply by serious military reverses at the front, but also by the consequent questioning of his role in launching the war in 1980, that Saddam Hussein moved rapidly and ruthlessly to neutralize the party as a potential forum for his future indictment. The purges of that year, the exemplary execution of the Minister of Health, the repeated and extraordinary endorsement of Saddam Hussein's leadership in the proceedings of the congress, and the submission to his ideological direction signalled the suppression of any alternative interpretation of Ba'thist mission.

This was now to be subordinated to the need to mobilize the people for war. It is in this respect that Saddam Hussein's claim to 'use the people' against the officials of the Ba'th is significant. It not only gives him pride of place, but also founds his own authority to occupy such a position on the direct link he is claimed to have established between himself and the people of Iraq. The massive and elaborate personality cult woven around Saddam Hussein was intended not simply to win the allegiance of the mass of Iraqis, but also, in appearing to do so, to pre-empt anyone else, be they in the Revolutionary Command Council, the Cabinet or the Regional Command of the Ba'th, from believing that they had a better claim than he to a popular mandate.

In a country at war, Saddam Hussein found that the party was not the single most important constituency for the assertion of his own authority. On the contrary, 'the people', as an undifferentiated mass whose approval conferred legitimacy, were to be cultivated and mobilized by the leader. The authority of the party itself could then be portrayed as depending upon the ability of the leader to maintain national cohesion and participation in the war effort, as Saddam Hussein was keen to remind the Ba'thist faithful: 'We have not asked the people whether they want the Ba'th party or not, but the people's referendum has taken place as a result of what we see and sense.'[7] This 'referendum' referred to both the massive demonstrations of acclaim for Saddam Hussein organized in 1982, and to the defence effort to prevent the Iranian forces from invading Iraq.

Before the outbreak of war, the organizational groundwork had been laid for the transformation of the Ba'th from a vanguard party of difficult access to one of mass recruitment and mobilization. While advancement through the Ba'th to positions of responsibility was to be as selective, hierarchical and controlled as ever, during the war mass membership was encouraged and, in many spheres of life, became obligatory. The public rationale for this was claimed by Saddam Hussein to be the fact that all Iraqis who had demonstrated their steadfastness and loyalty in the struggle with Iran, should be considered on a par with the Ba'thists who had been associated with the struggle of the party within Iraq since its earliest days. In an explicit warning to the old guard of the party, Saddam Hussein stated that 'the people have now demonstrated their allegiance [to the leadership] by spilling their blood in the battle of Qadisiyya', and it was possible as a result to abandon the previous idea of a 'Police state' [Dawlat al-Mukhabirat] in favour of a 'state of the people' [Dawlat al-Sha'b]. In this, the party may have a leading role, but it must remember that it needed to rely on 'numerous foundations' – it could not, in short, come to believe that it was independent either of the society which it directed, or of the will of the leader who formed the crucial link with that society.[8]

Personal domination by Saddam Hussein of the party's agenda allowed him to steer it in the direction he believed would best help the war effort, even if it meant playing down, or abandoning, the previous ideological absolutes of the Ba'th. Quite apart from the decimation of their ranks during the previous years and the personal risk involved in trying to advocate any line that did not conform with Saddam Hussein's dictates, such ideologues as the Ba'th still contained were undoubtedly persuaded to stifle any protest at the line being followed by the overwhelming fact of the Iranian military menace. In the face of this, the greatest threat to their collective existence, they would have been hard pressed to find allies within the state apparatus who would be willing to challenge the leadership of Saddam Hussein, whatever disquiet or distaste may have been felt about the autocratic nature of his power. Equally, it may well have felt that in order to mobilize the Iraqis for war, Saddam Hussein was right to stress the themes he did, even if they seemed to go against the Ba'thist ideological grain.

Thus, the increasing deference to the symbolic trappings of Islam and to its role in creating a collective consciousness, may have sat oddly with the Ba'th's commitment to secularism, but was no doubt thought to be a more popular and emotive theme than the ever-suspect 'secularism', especially when fighting the self-proclaimed champions of a specifically Islamic dispensation. Equally, the stress on Iraqi national identity, albeit within the framework of the Arab nation, and the commitment to Iraqi national interests at the expense of purely pan-Arab interests may have been looked upon askance by the champions of Arab unity. However, it was undoubtedly thought to be a more effective, popular message if all Iraqis, including the non-Arabs, were to be mobilized for war. Lastly, the increasing denigration of the record of socialist argiculture and industrialization, and the accompanying encouragement of private capital and entrepreneurship may have started those who still thought of the Ba'th as a socialist party. However, it was undoubtedly a popular measure among those well placed to profit from the opportunities it offered – many of whom were, in any case, members of the party hierarchy.

THE 'NATIONAL BOURGEOISIE'

In the same speech to party officials as that in which Saddam Hussein asserted the complete subordination of the party to his will and, by association, to 'the people's will', he said that 'the state should not embark on any uneconomic activity – excluding the police and Army, etc. Any activity that does not make a return should be ignored.'[9] This had been preceded, earlier in the year, by the deregulation of prices for most agricultural goods, as well as the abolition of quota systems and the encouragement of private investment. It was to be followed by a decree instructing the police and security forces not to interfere with traders and shopkeepers, as well as by moves to privatize a large number of hitherto state-owned industries, epecially in the transport, distribution and agricultural sectors.[10] Although this led to a raising of prices, the shortages of foodstuffs and consumer goods that had been very evident since 1982, began to disappear. Equally important, this official encouragement for private enterprise and initiative was clearly welcomed by a burgeoning 'class' of agricultural, commercial and manufacturing entrepreneurs.

Given the problems of empirical research in Iraq and the relatively recent open official encouragement of private economic activity, one cannot be very precise about the scale, or indeed the true nature of this apparent cultivation of a 'national bourgeoisie'. The latter term has always been somewhat suspect in Ba'thist terminology and it was noticeable that, although permitted to stand for election to the National Assembly in 1980, none were apparently elected.[11] That, in itself, may be testimony to Saddam Hussein's determination that there be no coalition of economic and political interests, independent of his own direction. Nevertheless, there appear to be two war-related motives at work in this encouragement of private enterprise.

The first is undoubtedly the fact that, given the massive financial allocations which the government has been forced to make to the war effort, it was in its interest to encourage the release and productive utilization of private capital. Despite the dominance of the Iraqi economy by the state since the Arif 'Nasserist' measures of the 1960s, there had existed, as in Nasser's Egypt, a substantial stratum of entrepreneurs who had worked in alliance with the state organizations. With the massive increase of state expenditure and development projects after the oil price rises of the 1970s, not only were many private fortunes made, but also the number of those able to benefit from the state's desperate need for entrepreneurial expertise greatly increased.[12]

This fact suggests the second reason why Saddam Hussein saw political utility in encouraging such a class to expand their activities during the war: they constitute a group of people defined both by their intimate links to the system of favour and patronage of the present regime, as well as by their economic status. This makes them unlikely to be swayed by sectarian or communal feeling since, as far as one can gather, rewards and economic opportunities – while they heavily favour those of state apparatus – have not been confined to this particular community. On the contrary, just as the Ba'th itself once seemed to hold out the possibility of equality for all Arab Iraqis, regardless of origin, so the new economic opportunities can and do cut across the traditionally divisive lines of Iraqi society. Even where this is less easy to perceive, the very creation of 'class' divisions within particular communities has not been without its use in preventing the formation of communal and collective feeling.[13] At the same time, in a way analogous to developments in Sadat's Egypt, the interests of such a 'class' lie chiefly in the guarantee of order which the regime can provide, as much as in its promise of opportunity. Thus, whatever their individual feelings about Saddam Hussein or others in the leadership, the tendency will be to rally behind the principle of 'strong government' – whether that strength is manifested in the internal arena, or on the battlefront. The war effort, despite its costs, is seen as a valid means of staving off the chaos that would follow defeat.

THE SHI'I AND THE KURDS

The idea of chaos as the alternative to continued successful resistance to the Iranian armed forces during the war, whatever the price exacted by the personal dictatorship of Saddam Hussein, has been a powerful motive in the war effort. The pre-existing nature of Iraqi society would suggest that while there may be little true approbation for Saddam Hussein and his style of leadership, and while the idea of an Iraqi nation may be hazy at best, nevertheless the possibility of being subjected to an Iranian invading army was apprehended as a direct misfortune which could be avoided through active participation in the war effort. This seems to have applied, in differing degrees, both to the Shi'i and to the Kurdish inhabitants of Iraq. Since they are by definition excluded from that inner circle of trust on which the power of Saddam Hussein ultimately rests, it was believed at the outset of the war that they would constitute an internal opposition so widespread and effective that the Iraqi war effort would be seriously, and possibly fatally impaired. Instead, it has been noticeable that the Iraqi government has been able to mobilize substantial and significant numbers of the Shi'i and Kurds to fight with some effect their 'fellow' Shi'i in the Iranian armed forces, or their 'fellow' Kurds in the Democratic Party of Kurdistan (KDP) or the Patriotic Union of Kurdistan (PUK). The reason for this, and for the differences of the responses of those identified as Shi'i and Kurd to the war with Iran, lie in the nature of their communities, as well as in their past and present relations with the governments in Baghdad and Tehran.

As far as the Shi'i Iraqis are concerned, the divisions among them have always been more important determinants of their social organization and political behaviour than the fact that they were all nominally adherents of the Shi'i sect of Islam. The major division has been between the inhabitants of the cities, especially of Najaf and Karbala, and the rural Shi'i of southern Iraq. Within the urban and rural communities, further significant divisions exist. In Najaf and Karbala, prominent clerical families, linked doctrinally and through kinship to similar families in Iran, have tended to dominate urban society. Increasingly, however, their status has been contested during the twentieth century by a growing class of educated lay people. The latter resented the monopoly of education and opportunity by the clerics and saw in the secular educational system, the administration of the state and in the Communist and Ba'th parties greater chances for advancement – chances which they tended to exploit by moving to the more rapidly modernizing cities of Basrah and Baghdad. In the countryside, the social units of clan and tribe predominated, customary law prevailed and clerics were few. With the transformation of many tribal shaikhs into large landowners under the monarchy, Communists and Ba'thists found fertile terrain for their message of land reform and social justice.

Those who advocated a specifically Islamic political order were, therefore, in a minority. Although the fate of the Communist Party in Iraq and disillusionment with the reality of Ba'thist rule undoubtedly won new adherents for the message of Islamic renewal of the state, this was a message which seems to have left the bulk of the Shi'i population untouched. The revolution in Iran and the subsequent propagation of a Shi'i Islamic call for revolt caused grave concern for the government in Baghdad and was evidently greeted enthusiastically by those in Iraq already prone to welcome such a development. However, the ruthless and forceful actions of the Iraqi government in 1978–80 not only decapitated the movement and suppressed its organization, but also ensured the expulsion or liquidation of large numbers of its potential adherents. The government's physical control of the urban centres of such dissent – Najaf, Karbala, and al-Thawra townships in Baghdad – ensured that no real resistance could be offered. In the country-side, there did not appear to be even the beginnings of such resistance.

Consequently, with the outbreak of war, the bulk of the Shi'i conscripts fought as well, or as badly, as their fellow soldiers. There may have been some cases of dissent, significantly among Shi'i officers, but this was not sufficient to make an impact on the Iraqi war effort, or to act as a focus for communal or sectarian refusal to fight their Iranian co-religionists. There-after, the centre of specifically Shi'i Iraqi resistance lay in Iran, where the more prominent dissidents had already found refuge. They enjoyed the protection and finance of the Iranian government and sought to recruit a fighting force from among both the Iraqi Shi'i refugees and the Iraqi prisoners of war in Iranian hands after 1982. This allowed formation of the Supreme Assembly of the Islamic Revolution in Iraq (SAIRI) in November of that year. Under the chairmanship of Sayyid Muhammad Baqir al-Hakim, it brought together a number of shadowy and often far from harmonious groups of Iraqi Shi'i, united only by a common desire to see the establish-ment of some form of Islamic order in Iraq. However, like all exile movements, they suffered the disability of being dependent on and identified with the fortunes of their hosts, as well as being cut off from the very people who should, in theory, have formed their principal constituency. This weakened their political effectiveness within Iraq, although they compen-sated for this by sporadic bombing and assassination campaigns, some of which came close to eliminating senior figures in the regime. Given the political systems, the assassination of someone such as Saddam Hussein himself would clearly have a dramatic impact. However, there is no evidence that SAIRI or its member organizations have the capacity to exploit such an event to their own political advantage. Although irksome to the government, the activities of adherents of SAIRI have not posed a serious threat, and have been met with ferocious exercises in collective reprisal, mass arrests and the systematic elimination of members of the al–Hakim family.[14]

Quite apart from the divisions among the Iraqi Shi'i, few of them had a tradition of seeing conflict between Baghdad and Tehran as an opportunity to further their own diverse interests. War, when it came, found them ill-prepared, both perceptually and organizationally. On the contrary, the majority seem to have seen it as a catastrophe, the effects of which they sought to avoid by blocking the Iranian advance or by deserting. It is impossible to establish whether the Shi'i rate of desertion was significantly higher than that of their Sunni compatriots. Given the personal risks involved and the retribution visited on the families of deserters, service in the armed forces and participation in the defence of Iraqi territory seemed to be the more prudent course of action, whatever the individual's feelings towards the government of the Iraqi state. Service at the front naturally brought with it risks of its own, but at least the families of those who fought could be assured of security.

The rather different reactions among the Kurds to the outbreaks of war with Iran is testimony to a different set of attitudes towards the government in Baghdad and the opportunities offered by conflict with Iran. Here too, however, it would be a mistake to see the Kurds as a single cohesive community, working in union towards a common end, or even sharing a common hostility towards the government in Baghdad. On the contrary, linguistic, tribal, geographical and political divisions have been as notoriously destructive of Kurdish unity, as of Iraqi unity in general. This gave the Iraqi government considerable respite in its dealing with the Kurds. It was not until 1982-3, when Iraqi forces were on the defensive in the south, and when the Iranian forces had made their first incursions into Iraqi Kurdistan, that effective reistance was organized. Even then, Saddam Hussein discovered that he could negotiate with both of the principal Kurdish politico-military organizations, the KDP and the PUK, promising them concessions of one kind or another in return for their support for the war effort. It took the PUK marginally longer to be disillusioned on this score than its rivals in the KDP. Nevertheless they, too, eventually discovered that Saddam Hussein might wish to buy their quiescence, but was as unwilling as ever to make any real concessions in order to do so.[15]

The eventual alliance of the KDP and the PUK in 1986, when they came together in order to devote themselves to a common struggle against the forces of the Baghdad government, led to a number of military successes, sometimes with the co-operation of the Iranian armed forces and sometimes alone. However, despite the fact that they could command roughly 18,000 *peshmerga*, and although the rate of desertion from the Kurdish irregular forces of the Iraqi government was high, it was clear that all they could realistically hope to achieve was a kind of *de facto* autonomy in certain limited areas of Kurdistan. Whether they could use this as a base for future negotiation for a more substantial and guaranteed form of autonomy from the government in Baghdad would depend ultimately on three factors over which they have no control: first, the seriousness of Iraq's military plight in the face of the major threat of the Iranian armed forces; secondly, the worth of any guarantees given by the Baghdad government, once the latter felt that it had a free hand once more in Kurdistan; and lastly, the degree of sympathy these organizations could evoke, not only among the bulk of the Kurdish population, but among the most influential circles of Iraqi political society. In none of these spheres did it seem likely that the gains made by the KDP and the PUK at any particular moment in the war could be transformed into lasting political achievements; indeed, the ceasefire was followed by a massive Iraqi massacre of the Kurds.

The indivisibility of political power under the regime of Saddam Hussein has made it clear that, however much the circumstances of the war may have raised hopes in Kurdistan, the Kurds are unlikely to realize their goals without a collapse or transformation of the regime in Baghdad. For all their local military prowess, they are clearly unable to bring about such a collapse.

THE ARMED FORCES

The armed forces, as the instrument of the state primarily concerned with war, but also as the repository of massive coercive power in the state, have justifiably been regarded with mixed feelings by Saddam Hussein. On the one hand, success in war required that he expand and develop the armed forces to a point where they could thwart and overcome the forces of Iran. On the other hand, it was equally imperative that such expansion should not be at the expense of his own personal control and that their conduct of operations, successful or otherwise, should not erode his own authority. This process had been in train since the Ba'thist coup of 1968, mindful as the leadership was of the dangers of an officer corps whose loyalty to the personnel of the regime could not be guaranteed. With the great expansion of the armed forces after the mid-1970s, it could be said that ensuring political loyalty was as much a preoccupation as professional competence. Since Iraq did not face an existential threat during the 1970s, there seemed to be little to be lost, and much to be gained, in expanding the various techniques whereby, if not loyalty, then absence of effective conspiracy could be ensured. As the first years of the war with Iran made plain, however, these techniques were highly destructive of the armed forces' capacity to operate effectively in the field, despite the relatively ill-equipped nature of the enemy.

With the turning of the tide of the war, it became clear that all would be lost if the armed forces could not carry out their professional functions in blocking an Iranian invasion. Equally imperative was the need to expand the size of the army in order to man the massive defensive lines along the border. The result was that the close and confining supervision of officers' political loyalties could not be carried out as diligently as in the past.

All might declare themselves to be Ba'thists, but in the equally expanded Ba'th party, that was no longer any indication of political commitment. As even Saddam Hussein was to admit, in order to transform the army into a more effective fighting force, new principles of administrative and professional organization were introduced.[16] Such things as encouraging unit solidarity, granting independent initiative to field commanders, relying on technical competence to master the new technologies of warfare – all of these had hitherto clearly been regarded with some suspicion, since they seemed to suggest that criteria other than those of political loyalty should determine seniority in the armed forces. In the face of Iranian attack, the government of Iraq could no longer afford to employ non-professional criteria.

At the same time, as a means of boosting morale, the corporate identity and continuity of the armed forces was underlined. Army Day was celebrated each January with increasing fanfare, proclaiming not only the present prowess of the armed forces, but also its past glories and its contribution to the economic, political and social development of Iraq. In 1986, on the 65th anniversary of the foundation of the Iraqi army, Saddam Hussein was moved to proclaim that:

> The standard which the Iraqi army has now achieved was the dream of those sincere men who contributed to the building of this army sixty five years ago and who served in it throughout these long years.[17]

Although understandable in the circumstances, this was nevertheless a significant change from the pre-war glorification of the Ba'th's role in transforming the armed forces from a preserve of a 'military aristocracy' into an 'ideological army'. In addition, Saddam Hussein was increasingly assiduous in decorating individual army officers, the state media gave generous air time to the activities of the military, and the armed forces' newspaper, *Al-Qadisiyya*, provided a forum for soldiers to be held up as examples of bravery and patriotism, as well as allowing them to express themselves, within closely controlled limits.

These measures aimed at reinforcing the professional effectiveness and the institutional coherence of the armed forces have not meant that Saddam Hussein has relaxed his efforts to maintain a large degree of personal control. In symbolic terms, he has taken the trouble to identify himself with the armed forces: the use of self-conferred rank of Field-Marshal and the ubiquitous battledress; the references in the party press to the army as 'the army of Saddam Hussein', especially at moments of military success; the many claims that military strategies are examples of Saddam Hussein's 'military genius' and the public glorification of his role in making major military decisions. All of these have transformed the image of Saddam Hussein, the civilian President, into the great war leader. More practically, Saddam Hussein has ensured control by drawing senior commanders into a form of collegial decision-making on the National Defence Council, as well as in the armed forces General Command, which he frequently chairs as Commander-in-Chief; key posts are filled by relatives and clansmen, such as the Minister of Defence, the commanding officer of the Air Force and the commander of the Presidential Guard. The latter is now claimed by Saddam Hussein to be the largest corps in the Iraqi army. After its decimation in Fao in 1986 it was greatly expanded, re-equipped and acquitted itself well in the recapture of Fao in 1988.[18] In addition, the old methods of party supervision continue to be employed.

There is little doubt that the nature of the enemy and the effect of the war have allowed Saddam Hussein considerable latitude in his dealings with the armed forces. That is, the dilution of the close political vetting that was necessary in peacetime has not caused any marked divergence between Saddam Hussein and his senior officers. In fact, it is unlikely that any who were actually suspect could hope to achieve general staff status, however competent they were as field commanders. Nevertheless, the war's objectives were scarcely controversial, once Iraq was thrown onto the defensive after 1982. Controversy has, however, arisen from time to time when Saddam Hussein's personal intervention has been believed to make it difficult to attain given objectives or to lead to military débâcles.

This may well have been the case in 1982 itself, although it seems that the units which were forced to bear the brunt of the sudden retreat of Iraqi forces belonged to the poorly-trained and badly led units of the Popular Army. It seems equally to have been the case in 1986, when the loss of Fao and the subsequent ill-advised offensive to capture Mehran led to a spate of mutual recrimination and possibly also to an assertion by the general staff that it must thenceforth conduct military operations without interference from the political leadership.[19] In the nature of the Iraqi regime, it is difficult to verify such developments. Nevertheless, it was interesting that some trouble was taken during that year to remind the Iraqi people and the armed forces of the very centrality of Saddam Hussein to the successful prosecution of the national war effort. These suggested that he alone could maintain the national cohesion, economic development and international diplomatic effort required to supply the armed forces with all that they needed in order to perform their professional task at the front.[20]

This is a point which Saddam Hussein has clearly felt it necessary to drive home, even at the moment of apparent military victory. After the recapture of the Fao peninsula in April 1988, the scene was set when Gen. Adnan Khairallah Tulfah made a broadcast, praising:

> The great leader, the triumphant President Saddam Hussein, who planned this battle, provided the requirements for its success and led it in a unique way, thus achieving victory for Iraq and the Arab nation under his triumphant leadership.[21]

A few days later, at a medal ceremony for those involved in the Fao victory, Saddam Hussein was rather more explicit about the need for the military to keep a sense of proportion and due modesty: 'The commander should remain level-headed when he is honoured, when he deals with the authorities, when he deals with money and when he is confronted by worldly temptations.'[22]

A month later, following further successes on the battlefield, Saddam Hussein was to remind the military in forceful, if rather opaque terms, of the fact that they owed much of their success not simply to their proficiency with modern weapons, but also to the political leadership's ability both to give the men under their command something to fight for and to grant to the armed forces all the resources they had requested. Saddam Hussein ended the speech on a curious note for the celebration of a military victory:

> When we make plans, we do not allow anybody to amend these plans – by presenting justifications which are not relevant and which are impermissible – as a means of changing the plans in order to retreat from implementing them.[23]

This may be seen as evidence of some professional opposition in the armed forces to Saddam Hussein's determination to take the initiative, by ordering the recapture of the Fao peninsula and the launching of offensives to recapture Iraqi territory lost east of Basra. Taken together, however, these speeches to the armed forces seem to be warnings not to allow success to go to their heads, leading them to question the absolute authority of the central leadership.

CONSEQUENCES AND CONCLUSIONS

The war with Iran has had the effect of reinforcing Saddam Hussein's autocracy in Iraq, by allowing him to demand complete submission to his will, as the means of ensuring effective mass mobilization to prevent an Iranian invasion. Although coercion has played a part in the organization of this country-wide war effort, the willingness with which large numbers of Iraqis have submitted to the directives of their President has not been wholly coerced. From the inner circles of power to the conscripted infantryman, the nature of the Iranian threat was unmistakable.

For those concerned with preserving their own political and economic interests under the present dispensation of power, there could be no compromise and little hope of mercy from the government of revolutionary Iran, or from those the latter once hoped to install as the governors of an Islamic Republic of Iraq. For the mass of subjects of the Iraqi state, the possibility of invasion and conquest by the Iranians held little attraction. On the contrary, it threatened to bring chaos and devastation into their country and, with it, the spectre of sectarian strife and civil war which had erupted in moments of political breakdown at other periods of Iraq's recent history. Defensive warfare against an alien army was, therefore, seen to be necessary in order to preserve a minimum of social order, whatever particular reservations may have been entertained about the nature of those who commanded the political structure that seemed to guarantee that order. This expedient community of purpose could be said to have conferred upon those leaders a functional legitimacy, a right to command obedience in defence of social order.

Saddam Hussein has capitalized upon this perception of common threat to extend his own personal control and to assert his right to absolute obedience.

At the same time, he has found it both expedient and necessary to reinforce the mechanisms whereby an effective war effort can be sustained. Apart from the ever possible danger of his personal elimination through assassination, his major problem is how to maintain such a degree of control in the absence of so pressing, immediate and relatively uncontroversial a task as the defence of Iraq against the Iranian armed forces. This is, to some extent, the problem facing all autocrats. In the endeavour to free himself from being beholden to institutions beyond his immediate reach, he has done his best to ensure that few, if any relatively autonomous bodies exist, either within the state machinery or in society at large. However, whilst this may free him in the immediate present, it makes his future as uncertain as his past, since with the elimination of institutions, goes the potential asset of 'institutional memory'. Present authority and political advantage cannot easily be translated into future gains.

Saddam Hussein is condemned, therefore, to continue his constant assertion of personal control. Whilst Saddam Hussein has demonstrated that he is unlikely to be daunted by such a task, the question which hangs over the enterprise is whether, with the war's ending, he will be able to rely on the same degree of acquiescence to his absolutism and to his policies as was the case during the war. It was clearly too soon to state with any certainty what the consequences of this war will be in the long-term for the shape of the Iraqi polity. However, it is worth speculating upon the ways in which some of the developments, described in the preceding pages as stemming from the need to organize for war, may affect the post-war political dispensation in Iraq.

Quite apart from the problems faced by a Ba'thist leader in asserting and propagating the myth of Iraqi 'nationalism', there has always been a difficulty inherent in such an attempt for any leader of Iraq. The reality of power and the predominantly Sunni Arab nature of those surrounding the leader would suggest that there are many among them who would look with genuine disquiet upon the equality of opportunity suggested by the notion of 'Iraqism'. It is by no means in their interest that their clan leader should dismantle a system of inequality which has served them so well since the founding of the state. According to the Shi'i, Kurds, Turcomans and others treatment on a par with that accorded to those who regard it as their natural right to dominate the state is a risky business for an Iraqi ruler. Although other factors were also involved, the overthrow of Qasim in 1963 could be seen to be in part due to the force of this mounting unease. On a more parochial and, luckily for Saddam Hussein, more limited scale, the confrontation with his own half-brothers in 1983 could also be interpreted as a symptom of their resentment that they were not receiving the benefits which they believed were their due.

Saddam Hussein still relies on such a system of communal support to cement his power and has been careful to ensure that the idea of 'Iraqism' also grants him primacy, as the 'historic leader'. However, he is also, in a sense, a hostage to such a system. Should he be tempted to give concrete expression to a myth which has been so relentlessly propagated during the war, he may face opposition from the very constituency he can least afford to alienate. Much will depend, therefore, upon the degree to which he can maintain control of the principles through which he has attempted to rally all Iraqis into a common war effort. When such an effort is no longer required, the idea behind the assertion of a collective Iraqi identity may cause problems beyond the narrow circle of his intimates, if it is generally perceived that the internal dispensation of power bears no resemblance to the principles by which its tenure has been justified.

One of the means by which Sunni Arab fears about a ruler's intentions have been expressed, has been in the reassertion of Iraq's Arab identity and the call that its government commit itself to the goal of pan-Arab unity in one form or other. This not only reassures the Sunni Arabs of their pre-eminence, but has frequently been used as the public justification for the displacement of one provincial or clan group by another. In this respect, it will be interesting to see whether Saddam Hussein's domination of the Ba'th, organizationally and ideologically, has been as complete as it has appeared during the war. Ba'thism, after all, offers a menu of policy prescriptions from which a programme of obligations can be constructed that might be interpreted as running directly counter to Saddam Hussein's direction. This has, after all, formed the core of the specifically Ba'thist indictment of the Iraqi regime that continues to emanate from Damascus, however much the latter, in fact, resembles its counterpart in Baghdad. It is unknown whether the terms of that indictment find much sympathy among the Ba'thists in Iraq. Nevertheless, understandable resentment of the position of absolutism which Saddam Hussein has created for himself may yet coincide with the unease felt about the Iraq's party's stance on such issues as Islam vs. secularism, private enterprise vs. socialism and Iraqi national interests vs. pan-Arab obligations.

These are the outlines of possible future ideological conflicts. However, in order for them to be transformed into or used as a cover for political action aimed at remedying the situation, social and structural features need also to be taken into account. One of these, as outlined above, may lie in the patterns of clan and communal politics that have always characterized the Sunni Arabs of Iraq.[24] Two further features, more closely associated with the effects of the war, should also be taken into account. The first lies in the degree to which the present encouragement of a 'class' or private entrepreneurs is in fact leading to the formation of collective interests associated with the development of such a class. Given the place of oil revenues in the Iraqi economy, it is clear that the state will remain for the foreseeable future the dominant actor in that economy. There is little danger, therefore, that, however much they are permitted to expand, a private capitalist interest will be able to set the agenda for government. Nevertheless, it is possible that its members will come to resent the somewhat arbitrary treatment accorded to them under a political system that is best described as a 'populist autocracy'.

Saddam Hussein has never ceased to remind those whom his government favours at present of the precariousness of their position.[25] During the war, this might be accepted because the external Iranian threat was regarded as making that position even more precarious. After the war, however, the major threat to the stability, order and predictability of the conditions which they require in order to exploit economic opportunity may be seen to lie in the very autocratic nature of Saddam Hussein's rule. This would be particularly the case if it were combined with growing resentment at the disproportionate favour enjoyed by members of the presidential clan. Furthermore, relations between Saddam Hussein and the private capitalists might be soured by mutual suspicion. Saddam Hussein might fear that this 'class' had established close personal and financial links with external financial sources, especially in the Gulf states, to which Iraq would be nominally heavily in debt, due to the 'loans' of the war years. For their part, the private capitalists may fear that Saddam Hussein, in order to shore up his authority in other spheres, or simply in order to demonstrate his power, might be tempted to reassert the socialist principles of the Ba'th and to curb their activities. These developments are all hypothetical. However, it is already possible to see the lines along which they may develop.

The second feature of the Iraqi state affected by the war is, of course, the armed forces. Again, one can only suggest potential sources of friction, stemming from their development during the war years, their relationship with Saddam Hussein and their possible uses after the end of the war with Iran. The ending of the war is unlikely to end the mistrust with which the Iraqi government will regard the intentions of the government of Tehran, or the effort required to guard the eastern borders of Iraq. However, the conduct of future relations with Iran, the nature of future operations in and settlement of Kurdistan and the role assigned therein to the professional advice of the armed forces are likely to raise more potential differences on the conduct of strategy than the unambiguous defence of Iraq during the years of war.

Equally, the very determination of Saddam Hussein to retain absolute control of such a process, and the means by which he seeks to enforce such control, may well be sources of friction with the officer corps. They have enjoyed a degree of corporate identity, of relative independence to pursue their professional functions and of access to the major decision making government unmatched by other organizations in Iraq. They may, therefore, come to resent their complete subordination and political 'purification' which are likely to follow the ending of hostilities with Iran. It has been hinted that operations in Kurdistan and Saddam Hussein's methods of handling them have raised issues of precisely such an awkward and damaging nature during 1987–8.[26] It would, of course, be unwise to predict the exact nature or direction of conspiracy. Nevertheless, one might hypothesize that, combined with the re-emergence of controversy in domestic politics, there lies in the officer corps both a potential for both corporate and personal grievance, as well as an awareness of their own coercive strength, that may make some of them receptive to the idea that their interests would be better served by an alternative leader. The very suspicion that this might be the case on the part of the ever-wary Saddam Hussein might equally reinforce existing tensions.

Saddam Hussein's endeavour to deal with the consequences of the structural developments which he has encouraged during the war and the continued operation of some of the constants of Iraqi politics will form the nexus within which the policies of the Iraqi state, as well as the nature of its regime, will be decided. These are by no means as free of structural tensions or of the potential for social and political conflict as may have been suggested by the years during which the attention and energies of most were focused on the war effort. The crucial question for Saddam Hussein remains the extent to which his ability to suppress these conflicts, and to curb the ambitions associated with them, has been due simply to a common perception of the imminent danger of Iranian invasion, or whether more lasting foundations for his own role as supreme arbiter have been laid down in the process. The foregoing would suggest that the latter is unlikely to be the case. Rather, the removal of an unmistakable Iranian military threat, combined with the existence of the legacy of devices used to ward off that threat, are likely to present Saddam Hussein with considerable challenges in the future. In terms of Saddam Hussein's political survival, the war may have ended, but the battle may have only just begun.

Notes

1. See the speech by Saddam Hussein to the 2nd Army Corps in September 1987, *SWB*, ME/A/3–4, 7 September 1987.
2. *SWB*, ME/A/7–9, 2 July 1980.
3. *Al-Thawra*, 23 August 1986, p. 5.
4. This could be happily combined in the charge that the Iranian hostility was simply the latest manifestation of Shu'ubiyya – that is, the rejection by non-Arabs of the Arabs' special role in and understanding of Islam. *Al-Anwar*, 19 May 1987, pp. 2–4.
5. *Al-Thawra*, 19 June 1986, p. 3: 'Saddam Hussein: Historic Leader and National Symbol'.
6. *SWB*, ME/A/11–12, 16 July 1987.
7. *SWB*, ME/A/8–9, 13 November 1982.
8. *Al-Thawra*, 23 August 1986, pp. 4–5: 'I am the Son of the People – they are my Inspiration and my Guide'.
9. *SWB*, ME/A/8–10, 16 July 1987.
10. *The Times*, 29 April 1988.
11. A. Baram, 'The June 1980 Elections to the National Assembly in Iraq: an experiment in controlled democracy', *Orient*, September 1981, pp. 395–6, 405–6.

12. See M. Farouk-Sluglett, '"Socialist" Iraq 1963–1978 – towards a reappraisal', *Orient*, June 1982, pp. 207–18.
13. See Isam al-Khafaji, 'State Incubation of Iraqi Capitalism', *MERIP Report*, 142 September/October 1986, pp. 8–9; but also, R. Springborg, 'Infitah, Agrarian Transformation and Elite Consolidation in Contemporary Iraq', *Middle East Journal*, Winter 1986, pp. 38–51.
14. *Guardian*, 28 June 1983; *Middle East Reporter*, 9 March 1985; *The Times*, 19 January 1988.
15. D. McDowall, *The Kurds* (London: MRG Report 23, 1985) pp. 24–5; *Internnational Herald Tribune*, 28 March 1984.
16. Saddam Hussein, *Two Letters to the Iranian People* (Baghdad: Dar al-Ma'mun, 1983) pp. 98–109.
17. *FBIS/MEA*, 6 January 1986, El.
18. *SWB*, ME/A/3, 23 April 1988. It seems quite probable that those recruited for the Presidential Guard are more carefully vetted than for any other unit in the armed forces. For that reason, it is believed to be largely, if not exclusively, filled by recruits from Saddam Hussein's tribal or provincial background.
19. *Middle East Economic Digest*, 9 August 1986; *Le Monde*, 15 October 1986.
20. See, for example, *Al-Thawra*, 21 November 1986, p. 3.
21. *SWB*, ME/A/6–7, 21 April 1988.
22. *SWB*, ME/A/3, 23 April 1988.
23. *SWB*, ME/A/1–2, 30 May 1988.
24. It has been suggested that the rather different configuration of clans and tribes centred on Mosul may form a future base of active disaffection with the personnel of Saddam Hussein's regime – made more effective by the prominence of some of their number within that regime and within the armed forces. See, *Le Monde*, 15 October 1986.
25. See for instance the revealing remarks made by Saddam Hussein to groups of entrepreneurs in 1983, when he suggested that if they did not conform to his wishes, he would have to unleash 'the anger of the masses' on them. Al-Khafaji, *State Incubation*, p. 4; see also H. Batatu, 'State Capitalism in Iraq: a comment', *MERIP Report*, 142, September/October 1986, pp. 11–12.
26. See 'Document: La Nomenklatura Irakienne', *Les Cahiers de l'Orient* 8/9, 1987/8, pp. 346–7. A more suspect source of such hints is the 'Voice of Iraq' (based in Damascus), see *SWB*, ME/A/1, 25 March 1988.

5 Iraq: Between East and West

Amazia Baram

INTRODUCTION

Soviet-Ba'th relations in Iraq saw extreme ups and downs from the very outset. When the Ba'th Party came to power in February 1963, they initiated a campaign of mass arrests and killed thousands of members of the Iraqi Communist Party (ICP). The Soviet Union reacted by stopping all arms shipments to Iraq as well as freezing all economic co-operation, and the Soviet media severely criticized Baghdad. When the Ba'th came to power for the second time in July 1968, the Soviet Union was very reserved and cautious in its attitude towards the new regime, despite the Ba'th's staunch anti-Western (particularly anti-American) stance. Indeed, besides attacking the West and praising the USSR as leader of the world progressive revolution, the Ba'th persecuted the ICP, jailed many of its members and executed a few of them.

Improving relations with the USSR was, however, essential for Iraq. Due to the anti-American public mood in Baghdad following the Six-Day War, and to Ba'th unpopularity as a result of its factionalism and brutality in 1963, the new regime could not afford to turn to the West for arms or even meaningful economic aid, as this would have entailed total alienation from the army and the civilian intelligentsia elite. Yet Iraq was in a desperate need for both arms (against the Kurds, Israel and Iran) and economic support, due to difficulties with the oil companies that resulted in low oil revenues. Thus, between 1970 and 1972 relations with the USSR improved markedly until in April of that year the two countries signed a Treaty of Friendship and Co-operation. In return for economic, technological and military aid, Iraq allowed the Soviets to use its harbour at Umm Qasr and a few airfields. Also, in July 1973 the communists joined a 'National Front' with the Ba'th which allowed them some freedom of expression (though not any hold over political or economic decision making). Even beforehand, in 1972, two communists were given minor government portfolios, and these portfolios remained in communist hands until 1979.

As Iraq's dependence on Soviet economic aid decreased substantially following the October 1973 war and the sharp rise in oil prices and revenues, it turned to the West for capital and consumer goods as well as for technological knowhow. Following the 1975 Algiers Agreement with Iran and the consequent victory over the Mustafa al-Barzanis Kurds in the north, Iraq's dependence on Soviet military aid diminished further. In 1978–9 the regime felt secure enough to clamp down again on the ICP and effectively put an end to the National Front. In December 1979, in marked contrast to its twin in Damascus, the Iraqi Ba'th openly and vociferously criticized the Soviet invasion of Afghanistan (as well as Soviet involvement in South Yemen, where a pro-Soviet regime was replaced in 1978 by a through-and-through Marxist one). Clearly, its reduced dependence on the Soviet Union allowed the Ba'th to give full expression to its old haunting fear of a Soviet-ICP collusion to replace the existing regime with a communist one. Thus when the Gulf war started, Iraqi-Soviet relations were at their lowest ebb since 1968.

RELATIONS WITH THE USSR: 1980–2

The Iraqi invasion of Iran in September 1980 rocked the fragile edifice of Soviet-Iraqi relations. Not only did the USSR declare its neutrality and called for a negotiated settlement for the conflict, but the Soviet media were not deterred from occasionally pointing to Iraq as the aggressor.[1] Moreover, while praising 'the historical role of the Iranian revolution',[2] the Soviet leadership allowed the first secretary of the ICP to launch a harsh attack on the Ba'th regime during the 26th Congress of the Soviet Communist Party (1981), and gave it due publicity.[3]

On the more practical issue of military aid, the Soviets denied that they were supplying either side; but they were particularly adamant in denying arms deliveries to Iraq.[4] No wonder, then, that Iraq's President replied with obvious frustration to his interviewer's remark that 'no support is coming from the USSR' to wit: 'By God, the USSR adopts a neutral position!'.[5]

Furthermore, the fact that Soviet weaponry was reaching Iran – via Syria, Libya, and even some socialist states – at the time when the USSR was withholding arms from Iraq was received with deep exasperation by the Iraqi leadership which believed Moscow to be fully aware of these deliveries.[6] Subsequently, although the Soviet arms embargo had no immediate impact on Iraq (until the spring of 1982 Iraqi forces were deep inside Iranian territory and their superiority in military hardware was overwhelming), and even though Iraq could hardly invoke the 1972 Soviet-Iraqi Treaty of Friendship and Co-operation, especially since it initiated the war, Baghdad perceived Soviet behaviour as a breach of faith, and, at the most distinguished forum – the 9th Regional Congress of the Ba'th Party in June 1982 – it accused the Soviet Union indirectly of trying 'to put shackles on our free national will by blockading these [arms] supplies'.[7]

In addition to a near-complete halt of military supplies (some shipments were still arriving from Eastern Bloc countries), Soviet-Iraqi economic ties, too, underwent a slump: imports from the USA during the years 1980–2 were roughly six-fold those from the USSR. Also, even though the number of economic, technological and scientific agreements signed with Eastern Bloc and Western countries between 1977 and 1982 was roughly equal, the more important agreements were those concluded with the latter.[8]

TRYING THE AMERICAN TACK: 1980–6

Iraq's disappointment with the Soviet behaviour drove it towards an accommodation with the United States, with which the previous regime had cut diplomatic relations following the 1967 Six-Day War. Indeed, the war years witnessed a steady improvement in Iraqi-American relations. Economically, Iraqi imports from the US increased substantially since 1974, and they remained higher than those from the Soviet Union throughout the rest of the 1970s.

In the early 1980s an American source reported the presence of a very large American interest section in the Belgian Embassy in Baghdad (including 15 officials) with 'better access to Iraqi officials than that of many communist diplomats', as well as the presence of 200 American businessmen in the Iraqi capital. In 1980 the consular staff issued 2000 visas for Iraqi students to study in the USA – triple the number of three years earlier. In March 1981 the US State Department lifted a freeze of five Boeing planes to Iraq that could easily be fitted to carry troops.[9] In December 1982 it was announced that American helicopters would be sold to Iraq, and in July 1985 Iraq reportedly took delivery of 48 civilian Bell helicopters and fitted them with rocket launchers.[10]

Between 1979 and 1985 Iraqi imports from the US were fairly substantial – between 5 and 7.5 per cent of all Iraqi imports. Also, between mid-1982 and mid-1985, Iraq bought American agricultural commodities on one-year credit for 1.5 billion dollars.[11] All these credits and transactions were made possible when, in February 1982, Iraq was excluded from the list of terrorism supporting states.

On the diplomatic level, Iraq made it known that the US asked 'from time to time' to re-establish full diplomatic relations. 'We made it clear to them,' Iraqi sources explained, 'that the American policy in regard to the Arab nations and Iraq is still preventing it.'[12] More specifically, the Iraqi side demanded that the US 'reduce its support for Israel' and change its position *vis-à-vis* 'the pan-Arab causes'.[13]

Yet Saddam Hussein took care to ensure that unofficial relations would indeed be special ones, disclosing in 1981 that 'we shall work together with their representatives . . . in a political, not just a professional way'. It was promised that the US chargé d'affaires would be treated like an ambassador, American politicians would be welcome in Baghdad, and the American staff there would be allowed to establish a communications system equal to that of proper embassies.[14] Also, apparently in return for American readiness to get Iraq off the list of terrorism-supporting states, in October 1983 Iraq banished the notorious international terrorist Abu Nidal.

Finally, in December 1983 Baghdad hosted Donald Rampsfeld, the most senior American official to visit the Iraqi capital since the visit of Philip Habib in 1976. Details about the discussions were not released, but from future developments it may be deduced that the American guest informed his hosts of the imposition of limitations on American civilian trade with Iran, and US consent to increase American economic aid to Iraq. In exchange, the resumption of full diplomatic relations was apparently discussed, as by November 1984 diplomatic relations had indeed been resumed after a lapse of 17 years.[15] Since the US Embassy in Baghdad began providing Iraq with military intelligence in December 1984, it may be inferred that this, too, was part of the deal.[16]

Following the resumption of diplomatic relations, American credits for foodstuffs and agricultural equipment were nearly doubled, from $345 million in 1984 to $635 million (and according to some sources $675 million) in 1985. In 1987 it was $680 million and in late 1987 Iraq was promised nearly $1 billion credit for the fiscal year 1988, the largest such credit given to any single country in the world.[17]

In 1985 a number of US delegations, official and private, visited Iraq, and the two countries concluded a few economic and technological agreements. In October 1985 some private companies established an Iraqi-American centre for the development of mutual trade. In August 1987 the two countries signed a five-year agreement to promote trade, but already in the first half of 1987 the volume of Iraqi-American trade increased by some 30 per cent over the previous six months.[18]

The Iraqi press reported the resumption of diplomatic relations without comment. In the few places where the regime tried to explain its decision, it sounded very apologetic. Iraq, it was argued, was the last Arab country to do so; more interestingly, it was implied that this move was an essential step to end the war, as both superpowers were necessary to achieve this goal.[19] Thus the regime admitted, however implicitly, that it preferred Iraq's interests to those of the Palestinians or the revolutionary movements of the Third World. A few months later, when Iraq started to reap the fruits of its pragmatism, its leadership was emboldened enough to declare that : 'We are getting closer to or further from any state according to our interests'.[20] Indeed, a far cry from the traditional Ba'thi stance that Iraq's international relations were 'entirely' dictated by the needs of the struggle for Palestine.

Ever since November 1984, Iraqi-American diplomatic relations underwent a few crises. One followed the Israeli raid on the PLO headquarters in Tunis in October 1985, which the Iraqi political analysts saw as a result of American-Israeli collusion. Another, albeit a minor one, followed the

American air raid against Libya (in view of Libya's support for Iran, Iraq's protest was muffled and entailed no action). Yet the most trying crisis came in the wake of the exposure of the American-Israeli-Iranian arms deal in late 1986. The most extreme condemnation of the deal was issued by the Iraqi parliament, apparently in order to distance the main policymakers from direct confrontation with the US. In a very strongly worded communique the deal was defined as 'a very contemptible and dirty game', deserving 'to be strongly condemned by all peace loving peoples of the world'. The communique ended by condemning 'the dubious contacts between Israel and Iran' but, most importantly, it did not call for any political measures to be adopted against the US.[21]

Even more revealing was the line adopted by the Iraqi daily press between December 1986 and late spring 1987: defining the arms deal as a 'fiasco', the front pages carried almost daily reports from the US about widespread public and congressional criticism of President Reagan and his mavericks. This clarified to the Iraqi reader that the American people and lawmakers strongly denounced the arms deal. Such media coverage made it relatively easy for the Iraqi leadership to retain American-Iraqi diplomatic relations and dismiss the whole affair as an error in judgement that resulted from the bad advice the American president had received from some of his advisers and from the influential Zionist circles in Washington. As put magnanimously by Iraq's Foreign Minister, Tariq Aziz, this whole affair was 'contrary to official American policy'.[22]

Paradoxically to some extent, a most unusual crisis between the two countries resulted from co-operation rather than from in-built antagonistic interests. After the Popular Army lost the Fao Peninsula in February 1986, Taha Yasin Ramadan, Commander of the Popular Army, accused the US of providing Iraq with false information 'in order to prolong the war'. Later on, Ramadan was to argue that following the 'Irangate' fiasco, Iraq could no longer trust the intelligence data provided by the US.[23] Tariq Aziz, for his part, further explained that the US had informed Iraq that the attack on Fao was a secondary thrust, with the intention that the Iraqi preparations would be insufficient and this, indeed, was precisely what happened.

These incredible accusations created a strange situation: even though in 1987 the US was ready to provide Iraq with military intelligence, Iraq refused to use it.[24]

Ideologically, the early 1980s witnessed the diminution of explicit denunciation of the US as an 'imperialist' power, let alone 'the leader of the world imperialism', as it had been traditionally defined in party doctrine.

Moreover, except for special occasions like those described above, the United States was no longer attacked for its support for and special relations with 'the Zionist entity'. Indeed, too many attacks of this sort could have embarrassed the regime itself after it had waived its reservations and resumed full diplomatic relations with the US. This does not mean that the US was not occasionally criticized as was the USSR, and even more severely (see below), but the old zest and the sweeping ideological condemnation were gone altogether, and the attitude towards the two superpowers became less differentiated. Alongside echoes from the past praising the special relationship with the USSR, one could hear more and more expressions of disillusionment, even bitterness with regard to both. Thus for example, in 1983, when Iraq's relations with the two superpowers were already improving, Saddam Hussein poured out his heart to a Kuwaiti reporter: 'The war has taught us that the superpowers do not respect the small [nations] . . . and that the sentimental in international relations should give way to the professional . . . we learnt from Abd al-Nasser that we should not rely on any foreign country, either on what it says or on documents it signs with us [sic!].'[25]

As Iraq had never pinned high expectations on, or signed a Treaty of Friendship and Co-operation with the US, these words should be understood as aimed primarily against the USSR.

Finally, while being the result of the predicament imposed by the war (and before the war by the growing estrangement from Syria since the mid-1970s), rather than a conscious intention to woo the United States, Iraq drew closer than ever to the moderate and the staunchest pro-American Arab countries such as Jordan, Saudi Arabia, Egypt and Morocco. As part of this process, Iraq has shed its old rejectionist radicalism and began to voice, however limited, public support for peace negotiations between the Arabs and Israel.

MENDING THE FENCES WITH MOSCOW: 1982–6

While doing its best to improve relations with the US, and thereby win economic and technological aid, military intelligence and semi-military supplies, Iraq also endeavoured to rehabilitate relations with the Soviet Union: by 1981 Baghdad had realized that it was facing a long war of attrition in which superior firepower was the only answer to Iran's superiority in manpower and morale. In the summer of 1982 the situation worsened substantially as Iraq was compelled to evacuate its forces from Iran and to defend its own territory against consecutive Iranian incursions.

Yet there were not many immediate returns that Iraq was willing or able to offer the USSR for the resumption of full-scale arms supplies. At least as long as the war was raging Iraq refused to change its attitude towards the ICP, and even if it was willing to offer the Soviet Union military bases, the Soviets could not use them during the war. True, the Iraqi leaders began referring to the Soviet Union much more positively than before once arms shipments were resumed, but this could hardly be regarded as a substantial political concession.

Indeed, the Soviet decision to resume arms shipments appears to have stemmed from external reasons, namely, the fundamental reversal in the fortunes of the war in the summer of 1982 which threatened the very existence of Iraq. Withholding military aid under such circumstances could have been considered by all a clear-cut Soviet betrayal of an ally and breach of a Treaty. In addition, the Soviets had no reason to desire an Iranian victory in view of their difficulties in Afghanistan and because of the Muslim problem inside the Soviet Union. In short, Iraq's perceptible weakness has become the main asset in its dealings with the USSR.[26]

A significant improvement in Iraqi-Soviet relations took place in early 1983, and again – not due to any immediate Iraqi concession to the USSR, following the Iranian clampdown on the *Tudeh* party. By that time, Iraq had come to be praised by the Soviet media for its willingness to end hostilities, whereas Iran was criticized for its refusal to do so. This refusal, the Soviets asserted, served the imperialists by giving the US a pretext to increase its military presence in the Gulf.[27]

Also, since late 1983 Iraq and the USSR began to exchange high-level visits every few months. These visits generated a visible improvement in the bilateral relationship which, in turn, was reflected in an increase in arms shipments. In mid-1985, without any previous warning, Saddam Hussein in person landed in Moscow at the head of a delegation which included the Minister of State for military affairs. According to Arab diplomatic sources, the visit produced a Soviet agreement to give Iraq enough arms to 'tip the military scale' in its favour; the Iraqi president and the RCC expressed 'full satisfaction' with the results of the visit.[28] It cannot be ruled out that, in return, Hussein promised the Soviets to re-legalize the Communist Party once the war was over; this to avoid the impression that Iraq buckled under Soviet pressure.

And indeed, following Saddam Hussein's visit to Moscow on the one hand, and the loss of the Fao peninsula in February 1986 on the other, arms shipments to Iraq were intensified in 1986 despite the decrease in Soviet arms transfers to the Middle East during that year. Arms supplies were stepped up again following heavy Iraqi losses in tanks and jet fighters (up to 50, that is almost ten per cent of the Iraqi air force) in the battle for Basra in December 1986–February 1987. Supplies between early 1983 and early 1987 consisted of over 800 T–72 tanks, as well as other, less modern tanks, and a few score jet fighters and bombers, including at least 20 ultra-modern MiG-29s fitted with the latest radar systems.[29]

Iraq's old grievance seemed to have disappeared, as Iraqi officials made it known that the USSR had promised them military supplies and economic aid 'even if the war ends tomorrow'.[30]

In the economic sphere, Soviet credits became yet again of paramount importance due to Iraq's shrinking foreign currency reserves (from some $30–35 billion in 1980 to less than $5 billion in late 1982). Thus, for example, in 1984 Tariq Aziz revealed that Iraq had received a long-term $2 billion loan from the USSR (apparently for civilian purposes). He further informed his interviewer that all political, military and economic ties with the USSR were back to normal, and new oil, industrial and dam-building agreements had been signed.[31]

In the following years further economic, scientific and technological agreements, with a heavy emphasis on gas, oil and irrigation, were signed as a matter of routine; they were supervised in the annual meetings of the Joint Committee for Economic, Scientific and Technological Co-operation.[32]

Due to Iraq's worsening balance of payments, there was no wonder that its civilian trade with the USSR increased by the year. Thus for example, according to well-informed sources, it reached $1.2 billion in 1987 – a 46 per cent increase over 1986.[33]

To mark the rekindled love, the two sides celebrated in Baghdad in April 1987 the 15th anniversary of the Iraqi-Soviet treaty and its renewal for an additional five years.[34]

All in all, then, since late 1982 Iraq had no meaningful complaints with regard to arms supplies or economic aid from the USSR.

THE CRUCIAL YEARS: 1987–8

On 20 July 1987 Iraq achieved a major success in the international arena when the Security Council unanimously adopted Resolution 598. True, the resolution gave some satisfaction to the Iranian side as well, by promising to work towards the establishment of a committee that would investigate the question of the responsibility for the outbreak of the war: however, this promise was placed low in the order of priorities and was phrased in somewhat vague terms, while the Iraqi demands were given high priority and were very clearly phrased. These were mainly: a ceasefire that would be linked to a withdrawal (primarily Iranian, as Iraq occupied very limited territories within Iran) to internationally recognized borders, exchange of prisoners of war, and a call to the two countries to co-operate with the UN Secretary General in his efforts to achieve a mutually acceptable comprehensive and just agreement. Last but not least, the resolution stipulated for the reconvening of the Security Council, should the need arise, to consider further steps for the implementation of the resolution. This last clause was nothing short of a promise to consider an arms embargo on the side that would reject the resolution. Iraq accepted the resolution immediately, and the Iraqi press described it, justly, as a major diplomatic victory. Iran did not reject it, but did not accept it either.

Resolution 598 was the result of nine months of intensive negotiations in New York, and there was no doubt in Iraq's mind that the US was the main driving force behind both the resolution and the efforts to implement it.[35] But then, the US contributed much more towards the Iraqi war effort than mere diplomatic support: in March 1987, in response to a Kuwaiti appeal, the US Administration decided to reflag eleven Kuwaiti tankers and escort them to the Gulf. The immediate Iraqi reaction to this development was something surprising, although it had its own logic: Iraq protested to the US and claimed that it was opposed to any foreign military presence in the Gulf.[36]

This objection was, in fact, an exposition of Iraq's traditional policy of nonalignment that was phrased very cogently in an Eight Point Programme by Saddam Hussein to the Gulf Arabs on 8 February 1980. Yet Iraq's opposition to the American move melted away within days when it became clear that the US military presence in the Gulf would not constrain Iraqi operations against shipping in Iranian territorial (as different from international) waters, and that in fact it was exclusively aimed at the Iranian navy and air force.

On 17 May 1987, an Iraqi aircraft hit the USS *Stark* with a missile. At first Iraq tried to blame the incident on Iran, but two days after the tragedy the Iraqi President and Foreign Minister admitted their country's responsibility. In a rather unusual gesture, they expressed 'deep sorrow' and apologized.[37]

There was some reason for the Americans to regard the attack as deliberate: occurring only a few months after the exposure of the clandestine American-Israeli-Iranian arms deal, the incident could be viewed as an Iraqi reprisal. Then again, the fact that the Iraqis tried at first to blame the Iranians for the incident did not contribute much to mutual trust. Also, in his message to President Reagan, Saddam Hussein's conclusion was that the *Stark* tragedy should serve as a further incentive to force the Iranians to agree to peace. When coming from the guilty party, this conclusion sounded callous. Finally, with hindsight it looked as if the *Stark* tragedy consolidated the Administration's resolve to send naval units to the Gulf; however, had the Iraqi leadership had any understanding of both the capabilities of US intelligence and the American political process, it should have known that: a) there could be no mistake in identifying the true source of the lethal missile and, b) that American casualties in the Gulf, before the US Navy was deployed there in force, could only make it more difficult for the administration to proceed with its plan in the face of public reservations.[38]

Whether or not the US believed the Iraqi version, it decided to accept President Hussein's exceptional gesture at face value.

Following the adoption of Resolution 598, the Iraqis refrained from further attacks on shipping for forty days; during this period, however, Iran declined to accept the resolution.[39] Hence, on 30 August, after a few warnings that Iraq could not allow Iran to export its oil with impunity through the Gulf for much longer, while it was blocking Iraq's oil sea route, the Iraqis renewed their attacks on ships in Iranian territorial waters. The American reaction was quite peculiar: while expressing concern at the renewed attacks, the Department of State also made clear that Iraq's frustration in the face of Iran's reluctance to accept Resolution 598 was understandable. Furthermore, its spokeswoman clarified that the solution to the renewed hostilities on the Gulf was a new resolution (of arms embargo on Iran) to be adopted by the Security Council,[40] namely, that Iraq should be rewarded for its fighting spirit.

In view of this stance it was quite clear that the US attempts to convince Iraq to stop its attacks, genuine as they may have been, had no chance of success whatsoever.[41] The Soviets, for their part, accused Iraq of acting upon an American dictate designed to provide the US with a pretext to enter the Gulf in force.[42]

Iraq achieved two goals by rekindling the Tanker War. Firstly, it limited Iran's capacity to export oil. Secondly, it pitted the Iranian and the American navies against each other without any risk to itself. Under the best of circumstances, Iraq could hope that Iranian attacks on Kuwaiti or on international shipping would provoke an angry American response, possibly the decimation of the Iranian navy and much of the remaining air force. Under worse conditions, the US was safeguarding much of the oil export of Iraq's closest ally and causing the Iranian supreme command a major headache by forcing it to divert its energies from the Iraqi to the Gulf front. In the end, both things happened: the Iranian navy suffered meaningful losses as did the Iranian economy due to US attacks on Iranian oil rigs and, at the same time, Kuwait was encouraged not to succumb to Iranian pressures to become truly neutral.

What did the US get from Iraq in return for its services? Apparently not much. For one, the American insistence on retaining its official neutrality (the reflagging operation was arguably intended to 'protect . . . Kuwaiti ships registered in the US')[43] constrained its ability to ask for returns from Iraq.

This does not mean, however, that Iraq was totally thankless.[44] To start with, in a number of closed meetings in the US since 1985, Tariq Aziz was reported to have promised that once the war was over, Iraq would immerse itself in the quest for an Arab-Israeli peace settlement. More tangibly, after a period of noncommittal remarks, the Iraqi leadership came out of the bush and made it crystal clear that the presence of the American Navy in the Gulf was essential to Iraq. Thus, for example, Taha Yasin Ramadan, told a United Arab Emirates newspaper that the presence of the American navy was a part of the war and a result of its continuation. Only when the war was over, he explained, would the American Navy evacuate the Gulf, as its presence was essential to safeguard the freedom of navigation against Iranian aggression. Then, in a barely veiled hint at the Soviet Union, he announced that anyone who called for the separation between the US presence in the Gulf and the end of the war 'harbours ill intentions towards Iraq'.[45] On other instances, he and other leaders attacked the USSR explicitly.

The Iraqi media also praised the US for its special efforts to bring about an arms embargo against Iran, while criticizing the Soviet Union for attempting to benefit from the American-Iranian estrangement.[46]

Indeed, the Iraqi–American honeymoon during the second half of 1987 was paralleled by a deterioration in Soviet–Iraqi relations. Even though the Soviet Union held the same view as Iraq over the desirable solution to the Gulf War, tactical differences between the two sufficed to sour their relations. In principle, the Soviets resented the continuation of the war because they felt it wasted the resources of both nations and turned them against one another, rather than uniting them against imperialist penetration. Indeed, the Soviets claimed that the 'imperialist' presence even increased since the beginning of the war, and that its continuation gave the US a pretext to establish itself in the Gulf on a more permanent basis.[47]

In accordance with this position, after mid-1982 Moscow's main criticism was directed against Iran for obstructing peace negotiations. Thus, for example, in his speech in honour of Saddam Hussein's visit to Moscow, Gromyko stated that 'those who call, contrary to reason, for a continuation of the war "till victory," and see the war as a way of settling their accounts with their enemy and a way of imposing [on him] their political will act in an irrational way'.[48]

In June, a senior Soviet official declared in Baghdad that the Soviet Union accepted Saddam Hussein's Five Point Programme for ending the war.[49] Moreover, while dragging its feet for fear of damaging its fledgling relations with Iran, the Soviet Union eventually supported Resolution 598; still the Soviets refused to commit themselves to a United Nations-sponsored arms embargo on Iran.[50]

Iraq reacted to this feet dragging with growing impatience. Thus, for example, by the end of 1987 the Iraqi Foreign Minister defined the Soviet Union as 'the only obstacle on the way of progress towards implementation of the UN Resolution for a ceasefire'.[51]

An anonymous senior Iraqi official confided to a Saudi newspaper: 'if the Soviets believe that their well-established relations with us allow them to develop close ties with our enemies, they are very wrong. Iraq will not be able to turn a blind eye to this Soviet–Iranian flirtation' which enables Iran to continue the war. The Soviets, he added, often talk of internationalism, but 'they are experts in manipulating the internationalist principles for their own security'.[52] On 20 August the Iraqi Television stopped its usual broadcast and instead read an extreme anti-Soviet article in the Kuwaiti press, referring to the issue of an unofficial ceasefire that would not necessarily be linked to withdrawal, exchange of prisoners of war, and peace talks. This new plan seemed to be a variation of an earlier Soviet proposal that sought to convene peace talks in Moscow after a ceasefire that would apply only to the Tanker War. Though aimed at denying the US a pretext to interfere, the Soviet plan threatened to deny Iraq a major tool of economic warfare against Iran. Indeed, a major bone of contention was the Soviet attempts to persuade Iraq to stop its attacks against Iranian shipping. But much like the US, the USSR was also unable to force Iraq into submission. All it received in return for its efforts was an angry Iraqi growl.[53]

Finally, on a great number of occasions Iraqi politicians expressed various degrees of displeasure with the fact that despite its awareness of arms shipments from communist countries to Iran, and repeated pledges 'to make greater efforts in the future' to prevent this 'leak', the Soviet Union did not do 'everything that they ought to do about it'.[54]

To sum up, notwithstanding Moscow's declared support for an early end to the war and its efforts to guarantee Iraq's survival without getting directly involved in the conflict, the Soviets did precious little to actually bring the war to an end.

They did not do much to stop arms 'leaks' from Eastern Bloc countries to Iran, and they rejected all American efforts aimed at a new Security Council Resolution on arms embargo on Iran. It is hardly surprising therefore that while never bringing up direct accusations against the USSR, the tone of Iraq's official references to the political behaviour of the USSR reflects the belief in a Soviet interest in the persistence of the war.

Another important point of divergence between the USSR and Iraq was the latter's attitude towards its Communist Party. Even though this issue did not come out into the open during 1987–8, there are indications that the Soviets resent the Iraqi resolve to keep the Communist Party outlawed; Iraq, for its part, has not failed to remind its Soviet ally that both sides should uphold 'mutual respect and non-interference in internal affairs'.[55]

In November 1987 Iraq and the Soviet Union decided to work out a programme for exchanging diplomatic delegations to relieve the tension. By early 1988 the diplomatic crises had subsided; moreover, Iraq made it abundantly clear that even though the Soviets did not change their position on any of the disputed issues (and most importantly, on the arms embargo), as long as the war was going on it could not allow the dispute to spill over from the diplomatic into the more tangible spheres of arms supplies and economic and technological aid: Baghdad certainly learnt its lesson after the confrontation with the USSR in 1978 and 1982. The Soviet contribution towards the ceasefire was reportedly a new airlift in December 1987 which delivered to Iraq SCUD-B surface-to-surface missiles, T-72 tanks, SU-25 bombers, MI-24 helicopters, artillery, ground-to-air missiles.[56]

In early 1988 Iraq seemed to be tilting on the diplomatic level towards the US, as demonstrated *inter-alia* by its attitude to the American peace initiative (the 'Shultz Plan'). Unlike the PLO, Syria, or the USSR, Iraq did not reject it, and on one occasion even gave it implicit support.[57]

In view of the fact that since the early 1980s the Iraqi official stance on the Arab-Israeli conflict has held that Iraq would acquiesce in any solution acceptable to the PLO, and given the US preference not to use its military presence in the Gulf or its effective *de facto* arms embargo on Iran as political leverage to get Iraqi concessions over the Arab–Israeli conflict, all Iraq had to do was to refrain from a clash with the US over the Shultz Plan. Sticking their precious head out for Shultz required very different political circumstances.

If one adds this, however, to the fact that on an issue much closer to home, like the presence of the American Navy in the Gulf, Iraq stood firmly alongside the US against a joint Soviet–Iranian front, and that the Soviet Union became a target for angry attacks from Baghdad, then the overall picture as seen from Washington looked promising.

In these circumstances it was only natural that Iraq would be deeply disappointed with the radical change in the American position over Resolution 598 in May 1988: in a visit to the Gulf, US Ambassador to the UN, Vernon Walters, declared in Bahrain: 'Washington is seeking to persuade Iran and Iraq to soften their position on UN Resolution [598] . . . Everybody has got to give something.' Walters added that he spoke about it to the Iraqis when in Baghdad.[58] If this indeed was the subject of his talks with the Iraqi officials, then no wonder that his scheduled meeting with Saddam Hussein was cancelled.

A day later it was reported that in his visit to Saudi Arabia Walters discussed a new American plan according to which the first step towards resolving the Gulf conflict would be the establishment of a committee to investigate the issue of responsibility for outbreak of the war. This would be followed by a ceasefire.[59] If true, then this new American plan was nothing short of accepting the Iranian proposal. Yet, even the more conservative announcement in Manama implied that the US was no longer willing to uphold and fight for the implementation of Resolution 598.

In June 1988 American–Iraqi estrangement was deepening. In his visit to the US, Tariq Aziz cancelled a scheduled meeting with Secretary of State Shultz on the pretext that American officials met with the Kurdish rebel (whom the Iraqi sources described as a 'terrorist') Jalal Talabani. A few days later President Hussein said he was too busy to meet Assistant Secretary of State Murphy, who arrived in Baghdad with a message from President Reagan.[60]

Then, in late June, in a colourful ceremony in which Hussein decorated his pilots for their impressive successes in the battle for the Majnoun Islands, the Iraqi President disclosed that 'the Americans informed the Iranians about our concentrations and provided them with intelligence from their satellites'. This way the Iraqi victory could be presented as a major independent achievement in the face of great odds.[61]

Apart from the obvious wish to present Iraq's military exploits in the best light, there may hardly be any doubt that these accusations were aimed at warning the US against introducing any changes in Resolution 598. This could easily be inferred from an interview given by Ramadan to a Tunisian newspaper in which he confided that in Iraq's view, the Soviet position over

Resolution 598 was closer to the Iraqi view than that of the US. He added that there was considerable co-operation between Iraq and the USSR, while the US was in fact co-operating with Iran [sic!]. To prove his point, Ramadan invoked, if somewhat belatedly, the 'Irangate' affair.[62]

The termination of the war could be expected to ease the tension between Iraq and the US, as it removed the main bone of contention. However, very soon another bone of contention emerged. During the war, the US (and the West in general) turned a blind eye to the Iraqi use of chemical weapons and reacted very feebly even when such weapons were used against the Kurdish town of Halabja in March 1988. As soon as the war was over and Iraq no longer faced the spectre of defeat, the Western attitude has changed. Completely unaware of this change, Iraq made a fairly lavish use of chemical weapons against Kurdish villages in the hope that this way it could end, once and for all, the simmering revolt in the north. The American response this time was swift. As soon as the use of chemical weapons was corroborated, the US Congress voted in September 1988 to impose economic sanctions against Iraq, and criticism of Iraq in the American press was prevalent and severe.[63] Eventually, the sanctions Bill did not get through due to technical obstacles and, as believed by 'some Congressmen', due to the 'unseen hands of the US Administration and its oil companies'.[64] Yet the Iraqi response was an angry and offended one, denying the allegations and accusing the US of duplicity, of trying to placate the Iranians, etc.[65] This did not mean that insofar as Iraq was concerned, Iraqi–American relations were back to square one. Despite the diplomatic thunderstorm, Baghdad took much care (as it did in its relations with the USSR) not to precipitate a crisis that would be difficult to undo. It even promised to forego the employment of chemical weapons, thus implicitly admitting that it had used such weapons. Indeed, amidst all the commotions, the Department of Agriculture allocated to Iraq $1.05 billion in credits for 1989.[66] Iraq, for its part, reciprocated the American move by lauding the US presence in the Gulf as 'keeping the Iranians under some check'; it also sought to allay American fears for the safety of their regional allies by pointing out that after the war Iraq would remain close to Jordan, Egypt, Saudi Arabia and Kuwait.

CONCLUSIONS

If before the war it was Iraq's strength which enabled it to extract support from both superpowers, since 1981–2 it was primarily its apparent (or real) weakness which enabled it to harness both East and West to its war effort. The superpowers' reluctance to see an Iranian victory or a spillover of the war into the Gulf, together with Iran's hostility towards both, were Iraq's main assets in the international arena. But then, it must also be pointed out that Iraq contributed in a meaningful way to its own success. It assessed correctly its own value in the eyes of the superpowers and refrained from unnecessary concessions. At the same time, however, it showed remarkable readiness to waive ideological considerations when it was essential in order to get tangible support. The former characteristic was revealed, particularly in Iraq's relations with the USSR; the latter, in its relations with the US and its Arab allies.

As for the Soviets, it seems that Iraq's only immediate concession (if, indeed, a concession it was) was to remain non-aligned and not to join the Western camp, as Egypt had done in the mid-1970s. And it is possible that the Ba'th gave assurances regarding the ICP's future in Iraq after the war. In return, Iraq received massive arms shipments and meaningful economic aid. This, in addition to the USSR's decision to support Resolution 598, despite the possible adverse implications of this decision on Soviet–Iranian relations.

Iraq's main direct concessions to the US were the resumption of diplomatic relations and the explicit support for the American naval presence in the Gulf. Indirect, but far-reaching ideological concessions included the endorsement for peace talks between Israel and its Arab neighbours (including the PLO) and the resumption of diplomatic relations with Cairo. Even though the latter gestures were primarily made to reciprocate services accorded by the Arab states themselves, rather than to please the United States, they were conducive to the improvement of Iraqi–American relations.[67] The returns for these concessions were, indeed, formidable. Chiefly, they included massive credits, an effective Western arms embargo on Iran, ushering in Resolution 598 and pushing for its implementation, the protection of Kuwaiti tankers, and finally: American-Iranian military clashes that diverted much of Iran's attention from the Iraqi front.

It is true that neither the reflagging operation, nor the *de facto* arms embargo may be ascribed primarily to Iraqi diplomacy. The first was a combination of the need to uphold the sagging credibility of the US in the Gulf following the arms deal with Iran, the fear that the war would spill over, and the apprehension that Iraq's Arab allies would abandon it and thus enable Iran to win the war. The second was designed primarily to end the war in order to enable the US to extract its enlarged Naval Force from the dangers of the Gulf. Yet Iraq's unequivocal support for the American presence in the Gulf and Baghdad's attacks on the USSR in that context made it diplomatically easier for the US to carry it out. Furthermore, the Iraqi-American honeymoon from July 1987 through May 1988 and Iraq's relative moderation over the Arab–Israeli conflict were conducive to the US efforts to enforce an arms embargo, which involved the unpleasant need to pressure allies like Israel and West European countries.

Having persuaded the superpowers to give them diplomatic backing (through Resolution 598), massive military support (Soviet supplies and American embargo and naval presence) and economic aid, the Iraqis turned to patrol the frontiers of the diplomatic and strategic status quo and prevent 'defection' on the part of either the USSR or the USA. This they achieved very successfully through diplomatic fine tuning, namely, a series of gestures of approval or, alternatively, angry warning growls. They were far less successful in their efforts to extract more from the USSR in the way of UN-sponsored or Eastern Bloc arms embargo, but they did not allow it to undermine the deeper foundations of Iraqi–Soviet relations, as they did not allow their differences with the US to stand in the way of a relationship that was extremely beneficial to Iraq. It may be summed up, then, that at the time that Khomeini's Iran was conducting highly emotional and ideology-oriented foreign policy, and busily turning friends and potential allies into foes, Iraq conducted its foreign policy in a calculated, dispassionate and ideology-free manner. Using Iran's folly to its own advantage, Iraq managed to manipulate the superpowers and harness them to its war effort.

With the war over, the tasks facing Iraqi foreign policymakers are even more trying than those faced during the war. Iraq needs the support of both East and West for its efforts to wrest from Iran a satisfactory peace agreement. This will be more difficult than before if Iran's foreign policy shows more flexibility and sophistication due to the great attraction that a more pragmatic Iran holds to the superpowers. Iraq will also have to make sure that neither of the superpowers provides Iran with a new arsenal of modern weaponry before the political situation in the Gulf is stabilized. During that interim period, which may last a long time, Iraq will depend on fairly massive Soviet arms supplies, and Soviet civilian credits will be essential due to Iraq's huge foreign debt (some $60 billion, half of which Iraq owes to Western countries and banks). In the same way, American credits and technology will be of great value for Iraq's reconstruction. Iraq will also need the continued support of America's Arab allies, the Gulf states, in the case of renewed hostilities. In the same way Jordan, Saudi Arabia and Kuwait will be needed for strategic routes; Egypt for strategic support; and all, to take Iraq's side in the peace negotiations with Iran and in its struggle against Syria or, at least, to remain neutral. This state of affairs means that, if Iraq's past *modus operandi* may serve as a guideline, then Iraq would remain essentially non-aligned. Yet, in trying to repeat its diplomatic success of benefiting from both sides during the war, it may be expected to go further towards the two superpowers. It may legalize the ICP, probably as part of a wider 'democratization' scheme of introducing a multi-party system (to avoid the impression that Iraq succumbed to Soviet pressure) and, at the same time, to placate Western criticism;[68] after all, the US cannot object to democratization. Allowing Soviet military use of Iraqi ports and airfields again is less likely as it may conflict with the wish to cultivate the US as well, although the USSR may expect such a return as part of the renewed Treaty. In any case, Iraq may be expected to give its sponsorship, jointly with Egypt, to the peace process between Jordan, the PLO and Israel, thus isolating Syria, the USSR's staunchest supporter in the Middle East. And it will very possibly appeal to the American, as well as the conservative Arab business communities to step up investments in Iraq. In short, it seems that Iraq will, in the foreseeable future, continue to walk the tightrope between East and West, trying to benefit from both and making all the ideological sacrifices necessary to secure its strategic and economic needs. And even if it snarls occasionally at either of the two, and in particular at the US, for criticism over human rights or for real or perceived contacts with Iran, it is not likely to allow this to turn into a real political crisis and thus return to square one: complete dependence on the USSR. Furthermore, if the present movement towards private enterprise points in any direction at all, then Iraq, while retaining a communist-style political system, is moving, insofar as its socio-economic system is concerned, towards the capitalist model. This, in turn, though only in the long run, may serve as yet another link to the West.

Notes

1. *The Soviet Union and the Middle East*, The Centre of Soviet and East European Research, vol. 5, no. 9 (1980), pp. 2–3; no. 11, p. 2; vol. 6, no. 3, pp. 4–5.
2. *Keesings*, 7 August 1981, pp. 31012, 30149; 1982, p. 31522.
3. *Pravda*, 2 March 1981, in *Keesings*, 7 August 1981, p. 31012.
4. *The Soviet Union and the Middle East*, vol. 5, no. 10, p. 3; vol. 6, no. 1 (1981), p. 4. Describing such deliveries as 'absurd', see *Krasnaya Zvezda*, quoted ibid., vol. 6, no. 1 (1981), p. 4.
5. *Al-Siyasa* (Kuwait), 17 January 1981. And for an Iraqi confirmation that they received no arms from the USSR, see *Keesings*, ibid. See also Taha Yasin Ramadan in an interview with *al-Siyasa* (Kuwait), as quoted by *FBIS*, 14 July 1981.
6. President Saddam Hussein, interviewed by Jordan Press (Baghdad, 17 November 1980), p. 20. Also Hussein to *Der Spiegel*, 31 May 1981.
7. *The Central Report of the 9th Regional Congress*, June 1982 (Baghdad, January 1983), pp. 187, 190.
8. Based on International Monetary Fund, *Direction of Trade Yearbook, 1979*, pp. 158–9; *1985*, pp. 227–8; *Weekly Gazette* (The Official Iraqi government gazette in the English Language), 1977–82.
9. *International Herald Tribune*, 30 November 1982; *Middle East International*, 28 September 1979; Barry Rubin, 'US–Iraqi Relations: A Spring of Thaw?' in Tim Niblok (ed.), *Iraq: The Contemporary State* (London, 1982) pp. 114–19.
10. *Keesings*, July 1986, p. 34515.
11. *The Washington Post Magazine*, 12 August 1985, p. 42.
12. Saddam Hussein, *al-Alam wa surat al-ahdath al-jariya* (The World and the Shape of Present Events) (Baghdad, 1981) p. 17.
13. First Deputy Prime Minister Taha Yasin Ramadan in *al-Siyasa* (Kuwait), 12 July 1981; Saddam Hussein in wa'i al-Ummal, 17 February 1979.
14. Saddam Hussein, *al-Alam wa surat al-ahdath*, ibid.
15. US Information Service, *Official Text: Iraq Resumed Diplomatic Relations*, Tel Aviv, 26 November 1984.
16. *Keesings*, March 1985, p. 33497. See also pp. 32689, 33495; *Ha'aretz*, 16 December 1986, p. 1.

17. For example, *Reuter* from Washington, 17 October 1987.
18. *Reuter* from Washington, 26 August 1987; *Iraq al-Ghad* (London), 22 October, 1987.
19. See, for example, *al-Iraq*, 24 November 1984, p. 3.
20. Ramadan to *al-Ahrar*, 1 July 1985.
21. *Baghdad Observer* and *al-Thawra*, 1 December 1986; for articles in the same spirit see Salah al-Mukhtar, *al-Iraq*, 30 November 1986; Hasan Tawahba, Alif Ba, 10 December 1986.
22. *Al-Usbu al-Arabi*, 9 March 1987; *al-Sayyad*, 6 March 1987. For news analysis that blames everything on Israel, see Shafiq *al-Samarrai al-Iraq*, 2 December; Sam Jawad, ibid., 3 December 1986.
23. Ramadan, as reported by *Reuter* from Amman, 18 January 1987; Aziz to *al-Sayyad* (Beirut), 6 March 1987.
24. Interview, Fall 1987.
25. Saddam Hussein to *al Anba*, 27 April 1983.
26. *Facts on File*, 1984, p. 261; *The Middle East and Africa*, 1986, p. 426; *Keesings*, 2 March 1985, p. 33497. According to a number of interviews with Western diplomats, the first shipments of arms started to pour in during the spring of 1981.
27. *The Soviet Union and the Middle East*, vol. 6, nos. 1, 3 (1981); vol. 7, nos. 4, 10 (1982); vol. 8, nos. 2, 4, 6–8, 11, 12 (1983); vol. 9, nos. 1–4, 7–9, 11, 12 (1984; vol. 10, nos. 2, 3, 10 (1985).
28. *Associated Press (AP)*, 18 December 1981; Tariq Azia to *Arab Times* (Kuwait), 5 January 1986; *The Soviet Union in the Middle East*, vol. 10, no. 12, pp. 10–11.
29. *Al Tadamun* (London), 2 May 1987; *Jane's Defence Weekly*, 25 March 1987; *al-Qabas* (Kuwait), 2 March 1987; *Kuwait News Agency* (KUNA), 6 June 1987; *al-Alam* (London), 22 March; 8 September 1986.
30. *Al-Sayyad* (Beirut), 31 July 1987.
31. *Al-Anba* (Kuwait), 14 July 1984.
32. See, for example, *al-Iraq*, 18 September 1985; *TASS*, 3 October 1984; *OPEC News Agency*, 16 February 1985; *Iraqi News Agency* (INA), 21 May 1986; *Baghdad Radio*, 16 September 1987; *Middle East News Agency (MENA)* (Cairo), 17 July 1987; *al-Tali'a al-Arabiyya* (Paris), 25 February 1985.
33. The Soviet commercial attaché in Amman to *AP*, 17 February 1988.
34. See, for example, *TASS*, 8 April 1987; *INA*, 10 April 1987.
35. See, for example, editorial, *al-Thawra*, 20 July 1987.
36. Interviews, Fall 1987.
37. See *INA*, 19 May 1987.
38. For evidence that the administration was, indeed, under pressure from American public opinion to abandon the reflagging, see the United States Department of State Special Report No. 166, *US Policy in the Persian Gulf* (Washington), July 1987, p. 5.
39. See *Tehran Radio*, 26 August 1987, an interview with Rajai Khorasani, Iran's ambassador to the UN. In his interview, however, the Iranian official provoked the Iraqis by claiming that their abstention from attacks in the Gulf was nothing other than an acceptance of an American dictate.
40. *Reuter*, from Washington, 31 August 1987. For similar American views see *Associated Press* from Washington, 30 August 1987.
41. See report of a discussion between the American and the Iraqi ambassadors to the UN, *Reuters* from London, 6 September 1987.
42. *US Policy in the Persian Gulf*, ibid.
43. On 'Operation Staunch', a 'Diplomatic Program to Prevent Military Supplies from Reaching Iran', see *US Policy in the Persian Gulf*, p. 3. See also, Richard

Murphy in a press conference in Baghdad *INA*, 1 May 1987. According to interviews, this American pressure that extended not only to Western states but also to private arms dealers became particularly effective from the summer of 1987, namely: from the moment the reflagging operation and the risks it involved went into full gear.

44. *Al-Ittihad*, 12 September 1987.
45. *al-Thawra*, 20 July 1987. And see a typical report on the American initiative to enforce Resolution 598 on the 'refusing side', ibid., 4 November 1987; Tariq Aziz in London, *SWB*, 30 November 1987.
46. *TASS*, 20 February, 26 September 1986; 28, 29 April 1987; *Moscow Radio*, 9 April 1986; *INA*, 25 April 1987.
47. *TASS*, 16 December 1985.
48. These were brought up in August 1986 and included withdrawal to internationally recognized borders; an exchange of prisoners of war; the signing of a peace agreement; non-interference in the internal affairs of others; and safeguarding the stability and security of the Gulf area. *TASS*, 20 February; *al-Qabas*, 2 March; *INA*, 17 June; *al-Jumhuriyya*, 19 June 1987.
49. See, for example, Vladimir Petrovski in the UAE, *al-Ittihad*, 6 October 1987. See also the Soviet ambassador to the UAE, *al-Khalij*, 11 November 1987.
50. *Iraq al-Ghad*, 8 December 1987. Also in a press conference in London, *SWB*, 30 November 1987.
51. *Al-Qabas al-Duwali* (Kuwait), 24 August 1987. See also Ramadan in *al-Itihad*, 12 September 1987; and *al-Thawra* and *al-Jumhuriyya*, 4 October 1987, accusing the USSR of preventing implementation of Resolution 598.
52. *Al-Jumhuriyya*, 5 September 1987 as quoted by the French News Agency, ibid. In diplomatic circles in the UN it was rumoured, since mid-1987, that the Soviets were trying to put an end to the tanker war alone (in contrast to a total ceasefire) and to arrange for peace talks in Moscow (interviews in Washington, Fall 1987). This would have denied Iraq a potent means to force Iran to halt the land war, withdraw to its borders, and avoid lengthy peace talks.
53. Taha Yasin Ramadan, to *al-Akhbar*, 1 July 1985; Aziz to *al-Siyasa*, 5 January 1986.
54. For example: Tariz Aziz to *al-Sharq al-Awsat* (London), 7 December, 1985. Also an Iraqi diplomat to *al-Usbu' al-'Arabi* (Lebanon), 31 December 1985, stressing that Iraq will not allow interference in her internal affairs nor will it ever become 'a Soviet State'.
55. *Foreign Report*, 11 December 1987; *al-Alam*, 26 December 1987.
56. In the daily press, it was usually reported without a comment. See, for example, *al-Thawra*, 27 February 1988, pp. 1, 11. And implied support, see an interview to *al-Ahram*, by its president, that was broadcast on Iraqi TV.
57. *Associated Press* from Manama, 28 May 1988.
58. *Israeli Television*, 29 May 1988.
59. *Wall Street Journal*, 1 July 1988.
60. *INA*, 28 June 1988. See also, report in the Iraqi press that the US is resuming arms shipments to Iran. *WSJ*, ibid.
61. *Al-Sabah*, 24 June 1988, as reported by the *French News Agency* from Tunis, ibid. This accusation was based on unsubstantiated reports in some news agencies that the *Washington Post* warned Iran four days in advance of the Iraqi attack on Majnoun. No such warning was ever made.
62. *The Boston Globe*, 26 July 1988, p. 6.
63. See, for example, *Middle East Economic Survey* (Cyprus), 19 September, 3 October 1988.
64. *The Observer* (London), 23 October 1983.

65.   See, for example, the Minister of Information, Jasim, *The Jerusalem Post*, 11 September 1988.
66.   *Al-Tadamun* (London), 28 November 1988, p. 39.
67.   Iraq, however, refrained from any concessions that were not absolutely necessary. Thus, for example, Iraq made it clear that it would not take part directly in Arab–Israeli peace negotiations, and Iraqi spokesmen occasionally reminded their home audience that Iraq has not given up hopes of eliminating Israel.
68.   For an indication that this is being considered in Baghdad, see Saddam Hussein's speech, *Baghdad Radio*, 27 November 1988.

Part II

Regional Implications

6 The Impact on the Arab World

Itamar Rábinovich

The eight-year war between Iran and Iraq was in several respects an unprecedented event in the modern history of the Middle East. Wars had, of course, been fought in the region in earlier decades, but not a long full blown, albeit not total, war between two important regional powers. Arab–Israeli wars tended to be intensive but brief. The civil wars in Yemen and Lebanon developed into protracted crises involving other states but not into sustained inter-state wars.

No war is a mere military conflict, but the Gulf War was particularly rich in political and ideological significance – a political and territorial conflict between two states, an Iranian–Arab conflict and a Shi'i–Sunni one, an Iraqi effort to quash the revolutionary wave emanating from Iran and the spectre of that wave swelling in the event of a potential Iranian victory. The war, furthermore, could conceivably develop into a major international crisis affecting the superpowers and the supply and price of oil.

In the event the Gulf War did not produce a major international crisis but its impact on the regional politics of the Middle East was considerable and manifold.

For one thing, the original conflict between Iran and Iraq assumed new proportions and seems to have acquired the characteristics of a profound long-term conflict comparable to the Arab–Israeli dispute. The Iranian–Iraqi conflict, whose roots go back to earlier centuries, was transformed by the war. For some twenty years, since the overthrow of the Iraqi monarchy in 1958 it was a conflict between a pro-Western Iranian nationalist monarchy, reforming but conservative, and a succession of Arab nationalist regimes, most of them radical and anti-Western in republican Iraq. Subversion and the encouragement of dissident elements across the border were common practices in this conflict. The Algiers Agreement of 1975 signed between the governments of the Shah and Saddam Hussein was an apparently successful attempt to end the conflict. It led to the Iranian abandonment of the Iraqi Kurds and to the Iraqi eviction of the exiled Ayatollah Khomeini to France (with some unforeseen consequences). The Ayatollah's return to Iran at the head of an Islamic Revolution destroyed the Algiers Accord. The ramifications of the Islamic Revolution for Iraq and the Islamic Republic's political offensive were seen by Saddam Hussein as too dangerous. They threatened not only the regime but the very foundations of a state with an underprivileged Shi'i majority. The combined perception of a severe danger and a great opportunity led Saddam Hussein to launch war.

Once the Pandora's Box of war was opened there was no closing it. Not only did the conflict become deeper and more bitter, but a precedent was established that an agreement settling the conflict between the two rival states could be broken four or five years later. Iran's military potential is far greater than Iraq's and while it had to accept an unsatisfactory agreement in the summer of 1988 its leaders may well decide several years later that the time has come to use that potential in order to redress the balance. Iraq's leaders certainly regard this as a likely possibility and are preparing for a possible renewal of the fighting. The Iran–Iraq conflict may well become a series of armed conflicts punctuated by periods of precarious peace. These fears or expectations may not materialize but the assumption shared by most states in the region that this is going to be the case is a significant fact in itself.

The prospect of a long-term conflict in the Gulf lends added significance to changes in the geo-politics that were induced by the war. One was the laying of an Iraqi oil pipeline through Turkey to the Mediterranean to replace the pipeline which crosses Syrian territory to Tripoli in Lebanon. the flow of Iraqi oil through the Syrian pipeline had been interrupted several times since the late 1960s and most recently in 1982 when Syria shut the pipeline down as a strategic move designed to help its ally, Iran, in its war effort.

It was significant that Iraq came to the conclusion that Turkey, a non-Arab state, provided a more reliable outlet for Iraq's oil than did Syria. Furthermore, an important element in the geo-political patterns of the Middle East as it had emerged from the post-First World War settlement was altered. Iraq's view of its geo-political environment changed in other ways as well. At the height of the war, when its own ports and Baghdad's airport were not secure, Iraq was supplied through the Jordanian port of Aqaba and Amman's airport became a temporary substitute for Baghdad's. Jordan's territory provided strategic depth in the confrontation with Iraq and is probably seen as likely to provide it again should the fighting be resumed.

At some point the Iraqis examined the idea of laying an oil pipeline through Jordanian territory from southern Iraq to the port of Aqaba in the Red Sea. This would have provided an alternative to the unsafe route leading through the Gulf. This pipeline would have been laid very close to the Jordan–Israeli border and would have placed the pipeline at Israel's mercy. The notion of an Israeli undertaking to the US not to interface with the pipeline and an American guarantee to Iraq was explored in the mid-1980s. The plan did not materialize but it must have left its imprint on Iraq's strategic thinking. Iraq did not become a 'confrontation state' in the Arab conflict with Israel but now that its lifeline could potentially pass along the Jordan–Israel border it could no longer view Arab–Israeli relations from the perspective afforded by a safe distance.

The threat to the export of oil through the Gulf had its influence on Saudi shipping as well. Saudi Arabia built new terminals on its Red Sea coast and laid new pipelines in that direction. One result of this development was a further rise in the strategic importance of the Red Sea.

In marked contrast to earlier centuries, Turkey and Iran played a relatively marginal role in Middle Eastern politics in the post-First World War twentieth century. After four centuries of Ottoman domination of the region the Turkish republic made a sharp break with the past and looked more to Europe than to the Middle East. Its interest and involvement in Middle Eastern affairs were sporadic and not very deep. The growing importance of the Islamic factor in Turkish politics and Turkish expectations of Arab financial support to an impoverished Turkey brought about a change and a greater interest. The Islamic revolution in Iran and the Gulf War contributed in the same direction. First the message of the Islamic revolution had an impact on Turkish Muslims. Later the Turkish government found ways of taking advantage of the war. As has already been mentioned an Iraqi oil pipeline was laid through Turkish territory and brought with it additional income and a strategic asset. Turkey also afforded both combatants use of its territory and roads for supply by trucks which turned out to have been another important source of income. This did not turn Turkey into a full participant in Middle Eastern politics but it did serve to enhance its interest and role.

In Iran's case the change was far more dramatic and significant. Unlike the Ottoman Empire, Iran had not played an important role in the early and modern Middle East. This changed in the 1950s when the Shah formulated a foreign policy which led his country to play a particularly active role in its immediate Middle Eastern environment and in shaping oil policies but to be active also in other Middle Eastern issues. But this role was overshadowed by the new position of the Islamic Republic. By seeking to export the revolution, by intervening in the affairs of other Middle Eastern states and by offering new ideas and a new model to other Muslims, Iran acquired a position in the region that it had not held since the Middle Ages. Iran was no longer a large Muslim state on the periphery of the Middle East but part of a different Middle East, with altered notions of core and periphery. The Iranian 'revolutionary guards' stationed in the Beqa Valley in Lebanon were perhaps the most vivid illustration of the change. The Gulf War and the prospect of an Iranian victory and expansion gave added significance to that change.

Iran's assumption of a new and active role in Middle Eastern politics had an immediate and disruptive effect on the Arab system. This effect derived in part from the very thrust of Iran's new orientation. The Islamic Republic's foreign policy was conceived and couched in Islamic terms (though in practice it often ended up being an Iranian nationalist policy). Iraq, Syria and Lebanon, for instance, were not seen as Arab states but as Muslim lands, the natural arena for exporting the revolution and conducting Iran's foreign policy.

This can be well illustrated through the case of *Hizballah*, the radical Shi'ite Lebanese party that can legitimately be characterized not as a pro-Iranian party but as an instrument of the Iranian government. *Hizballah*'s rival within the Lebanese Shi'i community, *Amal*, is a secular Lebanese party which operates within the framework of the Lebanese political system and seeks a greater share of power for the Shi'i community. *Hizballah*'s platform rejects the legitimacy of the present Lebanese state and political system and seeks to transform Lebanon into another Islamic Republic.

Lebanon, due to the unusual circumstances produced by the protracted crisis and the existence of a large, effervescent and accessible Shi'i community became the showcase of Iranian activism in the Arab world, but it has certainly not represented the only effort to export the Iranian Revolution. Other attempts failed, but the doctrine has not been abandoned.

It was also natural for revolutionary Iran to forge alliances and partnerships with Arab states, first and foremost with Syria. The result was the formation of an Iranian–Syrian–Libyan axis, the backbone of one of the two rival coalitions into which the Arab system has been divided since the late 1970s. Such bifurcation had become the pattern of inter-Arab relations earlier; the novel element was the role played in inter-Arab relations by a non-Arab state. Still more significant was the fact that this non-Arab state was at war with an Arab state. The paradoxical outcome was that Syria, a paragon of pan-Arab nationalism and the self-styled keeper of the pan-Arab flame was the active ally of a non-Arab state at war with an Arab one. Furthermore, as of 1982 Iran was in possession of captured Arab land and threatening to capture more. And yet, while Syria was criticized for playing this role, it was not really taken to task for its conduct and the Ba'th regime did not pay a substantial political price in earlier domestic or Arab terms for such radical deviation from the erstwhile norms of proper Arab nationalist beheviour. A decade earlier it would have been inconceivable for a regime dominated by the pan-Arab party *par excellence* to go for such a long period of time and in such a strident fashion against the grain of Arab nationalism and solidarity and to emerge unpunished. Asad's ability to do so was clearly a product of pan-Arabism's decline but it also contributed to the acceleration of the process of which it was a symptom.

Support of either Iran or Iraq in the Gulf War assumed such importance that alongside attitudes towards the United States and the Israeli-Arab peace process it became a governing issue in inter-Arab relations. The two rival coalitions in the Arab system consisted of Syria, Libya and the PDRY on the one hand and of Saudi Arabia, Iraq, Jordan, Egypt and their allies on the other. The former coalition supported Iran, was hostile to the United States and opposed the efforts to promote a 'Jordanian-Palestinian option' for a settlement with Israel. The latter group was considered pro-American, supported Iraq against Iran, and supported Eygpt's unconditional readmission into Arab ranks and a continuation of the Arab-Israeli peace process.

Not only were the disagreements between the two coalitions sharp and acrimonious but Syria, the leader of the radical coalition, chose and was able to prevent, an Arab summit from meeting for a period of more than five years. A full fledged Arab summit conference could not be convened between September 1982 and November 1987 primarily because Syria did not wish to be outnumbered and embarrassed over these issues. Indeed when Syria was weakened and agreed to come to the Amman meeting in November 1987 it had to endorse resolutions censuring Iran and permitting Arab states to renew diplomatic relations with Egypt.

In addition to its impact on the Arab system as a whole the Gulf War had a far-reaching effect on the particular positions and policies of the principal Arab states.

At the end of 1978 Iraq was at the height of its regional influence. It rested on a durable and effective regime, a medium-sized population, large enough to support ambitious foreign and defence policies and yet sufficiently small so as not to consume the state's considerable oil revenues. The settlement made with Iran in 1975 and the subsequent capitulation of the Kurdish rebels made fresh resources available for the pursuit of Arab leadership. In October 1978 Iraq hosted the Baghdad conference in which Arab opposition to the Camp David Accords was formalized. The venue of the conference, Saudi participation and the concomitant reconciliation with Syria all seemed to indicate that Iraq was well poised to claim the title of Arab leadership.

The coming to power of a hostile regime in Iran was chiefly responsible for reversing this trend. And when it transpired several months after September 1980 that an Iraqi victory, let alone a swift one, was not in the offing, an entirely new configuration was established. Iraq became dependent on its Arab allies, particularly the conservative oil producers of the Gulf, Jordan and Egypt for financial and strategic support. It had to cultivate their friendship and to moderate its own policies so as to bring them into line with those of its new partners. Its resources and attention had to be focused on the war effort and it could not be active in other Middle Eastern arenas, the Lebanese one for instance. A vacuum was created that others could exploit. In the event the war ended in Iraqi victory. This left the Ba'th regime in possession of a huge army which could potentially become once more the instrument of an ambitious regional policy. But, as will be seen later, Iraq's will and ability to pursue such a policy remain a matter of speculation.

Syria was the main beneficiary of Iraq's predicament. In the late 1970s Hafez al-Asad's Ba'th regime was hard put to overcome a severe crisis which shook its very foundations and threatened to bring it down. The challenge came from several quarters, most significantly from the radical Islamic opposition in Syria, but Iraq's role in precipitating and perpetuating the crisis was considerable. The rival Ba'th regime in Baghdad exerted direct military pressure on Syria, lent support to several opposition groups, encouraged Syria's rivals in Lebanon, and in the ideological competition between the two branches of the Ba'th seemed to outflank its rival and embarrass it. When the two Ba'th regimes seemed in October 1978 to have effected a reconciliation Iraq appeared as the stronger party while Asad and his regime were clearly uncomfortable.

Iraq's preoccupation with Iran from 1979 on, its subsequent weaking by the war, and the new alliance with Iran all played a role in Syria's recovery. A close scrutiny of the Asad regime's crisis will clearly show that it was during the final months of 1980 that the transition from the height of the crisis to the process of recovery took place. Syria had yet to ward off the Israeli and American challenges in Lebanon, but when it did, Iraq's absence from the scene and the close alliance with Iran were crucial elements in its spectacular successes of the 1982–5 period.

But the Syrian–Iranian alliance had its limitations. It was cemented primarily by mutual interests defined by common enemies. But the co-operation was limited by lack of real closeness and trust and by mutual reservations and occasional divergence of interests. The Ayatollah's regime was embarrassed by partnership with a regime perceived as sectarian, secularist and the oppressor of orthodox Islam in Syria. The Ba'th regime did overcome the Arab nationalist criticism of the alliance with Iran but it could not be oblivious to it. In the latter part of the 1980s the Syrian–Iranian alliance was running out of steam. In Lebanon co-operation was transformed into competition. Iran and its instrumental *Hizballah* vied with Syria and its protege, *Amal*, for control of the Shi'i community and of the western and southern parts of Beirut. In 1987 Asad reached the conclusion that the threat posed to Syria's hegemony in Lebanon was such that he reversed an earlier decision and dispatched a Syrian army division into Beirut. In 1988 he had to go further into the *Dahya*, *Hizballah*'s stronghold in southern Beirut. But *Hizballah* continued to challenge Syria's position in Lebanon and to co-operate with Syria's other opponents in the country. It was an important factor in transforming the Lebanese arena from the foundation of Syria's regional influence in the 1982–5 period to a source of weakness and embarrassment in the late 1980s.

Asad's growing ambivalence about the value of the Iranian alliance was reflected in 1986 and 1987 by his receptiveness to Arab pressures and financial inducements to meet with Saddam Hussein and to authorize additional (and in the event abortive) efforts at a Syrian–Iraqi reconciliation. The same trends were further accentuated by Syria's participation in the Amman Arab Summit in November 1987. When the fighting in the Gulf War stopped in the summer of 1988 the Syrian–Iranian alliance had clearly ceased to be a major factor in the region's politics.

As if to show that the bitter Syrian–Eyptian rivalry is not a zero sum game, Egypt, too, was an important beneficiary of the Gulf War. On the eve of the war's outbreak Egypt's regional position was at its lowest ebb. Sadat had signed the peace treaty with Israel and had been ostracized by the other

Arabs but had yet to regain the whole Sinai. The Shah's fall had eliminated an important regional ally who was, furthermore, replaced by a particularly hostile regime.

The war's outbreak transformed the perspective from which several important Arab countries viewed Egypt. Particularly after 1982, when the war had been transferred to Iraqi soil, Egypt loomed as the only Arab military power capable of stopping the Iranians should the latter defeat the Iraqis. Egypt should therefore be wooed and not rejected. Its peace treaty with Israel which freed the Egyptian army for other potential duties and guaranteed peace and quiet in the Red Sea, appeared less injurious. The killing of Sadat and the completion of Israel's withdrawal from the Sinai facilitated, in different ways, Egypt's return to the Arab fold without having to abrogate the peace treaty with Israel. It was achieved in phases beginning with a de facto reconciliation with a few Arab states, proceeding to a renewal of diplomatic relations with most, and leading to the threshold of formal readmission to the Arab League.

Israel's outlook on these developments was more complex. In several respects it was another beneficiary from the war. As has been shown above the war contributed to the consolidation of peace between Israel and Eygpt. By pinning Iraq down to the Iranian front it neutralized it as a potential participant in an Eastern Front and virtually eliminated the possibility of a major Arab–Israeli war during that period. Iraq's outlook on the conflict with Israel changed at least temporarily. A traditional Israeli argument, that Israel's presence was not the source of all tension in the Middle East, was reinforced by a war that had nothing to do with the Arab–Israeli dispute.

But there were other considerations as well. The Islamic Revolution in Iran created and propagated new standards of struggle against the West and Israel. Their impact was felt in Lebanon and then more directly through such groups as the Islamic Jihad in the Palestinian context. In the Gulf War, lower thresholds were established for such practices as chemical warfare, air raids on cities and the use of missiles against civilian targets. The Iraqi army was increased dramatically and while it is still preoccupied with the Iranian threat, it, or parts of its, could conceivably be directed against Israel.

The Gulf War contributed also to an interesting policy debate inside Israel. In the late 1950s a strategy was formulated by David Ben Gurion for Israel in the region that applied for twenty years. It was dubbed 'the orientation towards the periphery' and consisted of an alliance maintained in practice but without fanfare with Turkey, Iran and Ethiopia. The rationale from Israel's point of view was simple. Israel's immediate environment was hostile while the three non-Arab pro-Western states of the region's external rim were willing to co-operate in practice against the Soviet Union and Arab nationalism's radical wing.

In the 1970s as a result of the Ethiopian revolution and Turkey's turn towards the Arab world there remained of the policy a close and wide ranging Israeli–Iranian co-operation. At the decade's end two simultaneous developments took place. Iran was transformed from ally to enemy and peace was made with Egypt. In theory at least the 'orientation towards the periphery' could be laid to rest and a policy based on a more normal relationship with Israel's immediate Arab neighbours could be launched.

Some in Israel argued that the principles of such a new policy should be immediately applied to the Gulf War. Israel should refrain from supplying and supporting Iran, should seek to open bridges to beleaguered Iraq and, in general, be attentive to Egyptian and conservative Arab suspicions that, underneath the facade of bitter rivalry, Israel and Khomeini's Iran were conducting a dialogue. Others argued that these were persuasive theoretical arguments but ill suited to Middle East realities. Peace with Egypt was precarious and certainly did not afford a basis for a new Israeli regional policy; the geopolitics of Iran were such that after Khomeini's departure Iranian–Israeli co-operation was likely to be renewed, and, finally, in the best tradition of demonstrating Israel's value as a strategic asset it was important for Israel to open the door for a new American–Iranian dialogue.

The debate was not conducted in public and it was not decided; its importance may lie primarily in airing issues that will still have to be debated in Israel in the 1990s.

One of the Gulf War's most significant repercussions for the Middle East had less to do with geopolitics and power politics but rather with ideas. As has already been pointed out elsewhere, the Islamic Revolution of 1978–9 was a major historical event, reminiscent of the French and Russian revolutions. Not only did it result in a far-reaching restructuring of the political and social systems in Iran but it also had a message directed at the larger (Muslim) world. The message itself was not particularly novel; other fundamentalist movements had propagated similar ideas in the world of Islam. But this was the first time in the region's modern history that a fundamentalist movement seized power. The message resonated because the Islamic Revolution defeated the Shah and the United States and then succeeded also in humiliating the United States.

As in the case of the French and Russian revolutions an external invasion followed the domestic convulsion. The invasion and the ensuing war underlined the questions raised by the original revolution. Iran's ability to repel the invasion and then to shift the war to Iraq's own territory was impressive. The Iranian army had disintegrated under the impact of the 1978–9 revolution; indeed the assumption that Iran had no military capacity to speak of was one of the important considerations underlying Iraq's decision to invade. The revolutionary regime's ability to rally against a superior Iraqi army was rightly seen as an index of its power and vitality. To Muslims observing the evolution of the Islamic Revolution its military exploits reinforced the message relayed by the earlier successes scored against the Shah and the United States. For six years, between 1982 and 1988, Iran's offensive in Iraq thus carried with it the promise or the threat of its revolutionary message on two levels. An impressive victory over Iraq would provide the victorious Iranians with new opportunities to export their revolution. It would also amplify their call far beyond their actual reach. Their admission of defeat in the summer of 1988 thus represented an important gain for the defenders of the status quo in the region. Their sense of relief should, furthermore, have been reinforced by the absence of a decisive Iraqi victory; the conservative Arab states have yet to be persuaded that Iraq has abandoned its own visions of hegemony.

Mention should finally be made of two *motifs* raised by the war: the Persian–Arab dispute and the Sunni–Shi'i conflict. The first clearly failed to assume a great importance. Iraq's propaganda for obvious reasons tried to emphasize it, depicting Iraq as a lonely bastion of Arabism standing up to the Persian danger. Iran for its own good reasons tried to minimize it and was, on the whole, successful. The Arab world was intimidated by the message of the Islamic Revolution rather than by the threat of Iranian nationalism.

The denominational aspect of the conflict was more complex. The Ayatollah Khomeini and his regime have sought to blunt the Shi'i edge of their revolution and to endow it with a universal Islamic appeal. To some extent they were successful. But it remained a fact that when it came to practical politics as distinct from the broader appeal of an ideology, they were most successful with Shi'i groups – the alliance with an Alawi dominated regime in Syria, the following they cultivated in Lebanon and the echoes of the revolution among Shi'i communities in the Arab states of the Gulf. The one prominent exception to this rule was the failure of the Iraqi Shi'i to rally to Iran's side. Arabism and the Iraqi state proved to be more powerful in that case. The view of the Gulf War as part of a larger Shi'i-rural rebellion against the dominant Sunni-urban order remains tantalizing, but has yet to be vindicated.

7 The War and the Spread of Islamic Fundamentalism

Robin Wright

One of the underlying themes of the eight-year Gulf War was the issue of fundamentalist Islam as a political alternative in the Middle East. The fiery new brand of Islam that grew up around the Iranian revolution played a crucial role in the war's origins, in its evolution and in the conditions that contributed to its finale.

ORIGINS[1]

For Iraq, the perceived threat of Muslim zealotry was a primary catalyst in President Saddam Hussein's decision to invade Iran. Indeed, the spectre of a powerful Shi'ite theocracy inspiring Muslim constituencies elsewhere in the region, notably Iraq's Shi'ite majority, was arguably a more critical factor than was Baghdad's share of the Shatt-al Arab waterway. Repeated calls by Iran's mullahs for Iraqi Shi'a to rise up against the Ba'thist regime provoked both anger and alarm in Baghdad at a time that militant Islam was gaining momentum throughout the Middle East, notable during such events as the 1979 seizure of Saudi Arabia's Grand Mosque in Mecca by Sunni extremists, the Shi'ite uprisings in Saudia's eastern Hasa province in 1979 and 1980, and the challenge of Afghanistan's Mujahedeen after the Soviet Union's 1979 invasion. Baghdad was anxious to defuse the potential of a fundamentalist threat at home.

For Iran's theocrats, the conflict from the beginning was defined in part along religious lines. Just six days before Iran agreed to accept United Nations Resolution 598, Tehran Radio broadcast a communique from the Armed Forces General Command. 'This war is not about territory,' it said. 'It is a continuous confrontation between the righteous and the wicked which today has turned into a bloody conflict between two systems of values and countervalues. And what is at stake here is the all around defence of Islam and the Moslems.'[2] For the ruling mullahs, it really was a jihad, or holy war, elevated to a cosmic plain of good versus evil in which, even during the six years when Tehran gradually regained its own territory and ate away at Iraqi land, Iran was still always perceived at home as being on the defensive, fighting to protect the pure and total Islamic vision against injustice.

Although Tehran always referred to the conflict as 'the imposed war', it in fact fit in with Ayatollah Rouhollah Khomeini's broader vision in many ways. Six months after the revolution and more than a year before the war began, the imam declared, 'The governments of the world should know that Islam cannot be defeated. Islam will be victorious in all the countries of the world, and Islam and the teachings of the Koran will prevail all over the world.'[3] He also specified, 'We have in reality, then, no choice but to destroy those systems of government that are corrupt in themselves and also entail the corruption of others, and to overthrow all treacherous, corrupt, oppressive and criminal regimes. This is the duty that all Muslims must fulfill, in every one of the Muslim countries, in order to achieve the triumphant political revolution of Islam.'[4] Saddam Hussein's secular, socialist and Sunni-ruled Iraq perfectly fit these criteria.

EVOLUTION

As Iran built up its own war machine after the conflict started, it also began to train and aid Muslim fanatics from other countries, most notably Lebanon. Because of the war, the Revolutionary Guards were converted from a paramilitary prop for the mullahs into a conventional military unit to supplement the regular armed forces, which had been weakened by a series of purges, executions and early retirements after the Shah's ouster. In keeping with Khomeini's vision of an Islamic world without national boundaries, the Pasdaran trainers also provided rudimentary instruction in camps scattered throughout Iran for hundreds of youths from Arab states as well as Afghanistan.[5] Among the recruits were Hamza akl Hamieh, a Lebanese Shi'ite who hijacked six planes between 1979 and 1982 and who later became a military commander of a Lebanese Shi'ite militia, and the suicide bomber who drove into the American marine compound in Beirut in 1983 and killed 241 US military personnel. Others suspected by Arab and Western intelligence of receiving Iranian training and backing were members of a group who attempted a *coup d'état* in Bahrain in 1981 and the seventeen Iraqis and Lebanese who were convicted and imprisoned in Kuwait for the 1983 bombings of the US and French embassies and four other strategic installations.[6] (The imprisonment of the Kuwaiti seventeen, in turn, became the motivation for Lebanon's Islamic Jihad to kidnap American hostages, showing how the emergence of new extremist movements also often created a new cycle of political activism and violence in the region.)

The campaign to export the revolution was, in the initial stages, often haphazard and clumsy. This was particularly evident after the arrest of 73 Shi'a from several Gulf Arab states for the 1981 plot in Bahrain, one of the few cases in which Iran's role was traceable; although no Iranians were arrested, Bahraini intelligence claimed the plotters had used the Iranian Embassy's diplomatic pouch to bring in equipment. In March 1982, however, the campaign began to take more specific form. The turning point was symbolized by a seminar held in Tehran that was hosted by the Association of Combatant Clerics and the Revolutionary Guards; the meeting brought together more than 350 men with various religious and revolutionary credentials from several Middle East and Islamic nations to discuss 'the ideal Islamic government'. The talk, however, centred on Islam as 'a weapon in revolutionary wars against the rich and the corrupt'. An Iranian diplomat in a Gulf state later outlined the seminar's conclusions. 'They agreed, first, that religion should not be separated from politics. Second, the only way to achieve true independence was to return to Islamic roots. Third, there should be no reliance on superpowers or other outsiders, and the region should be rid of them. Fourth, they recommended that the Shi'a should be more active in getting rid of foreign powers.'[7]

The timing of the seminar was not an accident. The seminar coincided with a turn in the tide of the war and the consolidation of the mullahs' control over the government. The same month, Iran launched Operation Fath, or conquest, along the southwestern front in Khuzestan province. Fath was the bloodiest and most effective Iranian campaign since the war began; Iran's regular army and the Revolutionary Guards forced the better-armed and better-trained Iraqis into a major retreat and regained a total of about 8500 square miles in the oil-rich area. The outbreak of war had also provided a pretext for the clergy's clampdown on the opposition as well as on their co-partners in the revolution. During the 18 months between Iraq's invasion and Operation Fath, Khomeini loyalists removed most of the leftists and Islamic secularists, the latter being those who favoured imposition of Islamic law but daily rule of state by technocrats.[8] The two moves together gave Iran's theocrats new confidence and provided the grounds and mechanism for the revolution to go on the offensive.

After the seminar, between 1982 and 1985, pro-Iranian Shi'ite groups throughout the region became decidedly more assertive, evident during Iranian demonstrations at the annual Hajj pilgrimage in Saudi Arabia, and more aggressive, notably in the suicide bombings against American, French and Israeli compounds in Lebanon in 1983–4 as well as against foreign and Arab offices and personnel in Kuwait between 1983 and 1985. The expanded campaign to promote militant Islam paralleled Iran's offensives in the war – at a time President Hussein had begun to call for mediation to end the conflict. Iran had, however, become less interested in a mediated settlement; ousting President Hussein had become intertwined with specific objectives of its Islamic crusade and with the broader goal of proving that Islam was an effective vehicle for fighting political impurities and injustice.

The Islamic Republic's boldest step during this period was the deployment of Revolutionary Guards in Lebanon shortly after Israel invaded Lebanon in June 1982. Tehran boasted that its military would join the Lebanese and Palestinian counteroffensive. But, in fact, the guards were missionaries more than fighters throughout Israel's three-year occupation of the southern quarter of Lebanon, even though they were at some junctures only twenty-five miles from Israeli outposts. They converted the eastern Beka Valley into a stronghold of Shi'ite fanaticism, helping reinforce the pro-Iranian militias such as Islamic Amal and Hizballah, or the Party of God. As of 1983, the emerging Shi'ite militias played the leading role in attacking Israeli Defence Force positions. On the third anniversary of its invasion in 1985, Israel did the unprecedented: it unilaterally withdrew from all but a small enclave of an occupied Arab territory without a single security guarantee for the volatile border or vulnerable northern Galilee – largely due to the Shi'ite campaign. This was a high point for Iran, for Lebanon's Shi'a accomplished in three years what the Palestine Liberation Organization had been unable to do for two decades.

As with its presence in Lebanon, Tehran was careful about the level and appearance of its involvement in propagating Islamic extremism. Iran had carried out its own revolution and, as its leaders' policies and tactics seemed to indicate, other Shi'ite communities should be the ones to act on their own – if, perhaps, with assistance. During a 1988 interview with Minister of the Revolutionary Guards Mohsen Rafiqdoost, he conceded that Iran had trained various foreigners but denied that Iran had masterminded the subsequent acts they undertook. He referred specifically to the Lebanese bomber of American Marine contingent in the Multinational Force deployed in Beirut who, he acknowledged, had been trained in Iran. Rafiqdoost added that while the Iranian government had been 'happy' about the mission, Tehran had neither ordered it nor planned it. He then pointedly asked how many Iranians had been arrested for various acts of violence in the Middle East.[9]

Iranians were, however, detained by Saudi security forces during the 1985, 1986 and 1987 Hajj pilgrimages for carrying weapons and inflammatory literature intended to incite demonstrations. But Tehran's most ambitious effort to spread the word during the assemblage of the world's Muslims backfired. In July 1987, the demonstrations led to confrontations between Iranian pilgrims and Saudi National Guard in which more than four hundred were killed, an event that contributed to Riyadh's 1988 decision to break relations with Tehran. The clashes took place just a few months after Iran's equally disastrous Karbala offensives, which Iran had publicly boasted would be the final offensive. In the end, however, Iran managed to make only marginal headway around Iraq's southern port city of Basra at an enormous expenditure of human life and military resources. For Iran, it was the most important turning point in the war. Two of its boldest initiatives in seven years, one on the battlefield and the other in exporting the revolution, in effect failed, again underscoring how the progress or problems on both fronts often coincided.

FINALE

The final years of the war were defined in large part by all sides in terms of the spread of revolutionary Islam. From Iran's side, even the 1987 deployment of the Western war fleet from the United States, France, Britain, Holland, Italy and Belgium was perceived as an attempt to create a barrier not simply around Iran, but also around Islam, just as the outside world had attempted to block the path of the prophet Muhammad in the seventh century. At a Friday prayer sermon in October 1987, Parliamentary Speaker Ali-Akbar Hashemi-Rafsanjani told an assemblage of the faithful at Tehran University, 'The main problem of the revolution is that our enemies intend to create a barrier across the course of the revolution's movement – they intend to stop the spread of its message. We want to remove this barrier and, therefore, a clash occurs. Our enemies will resort to any means. This was true in the early Islamic era too. They used to spread a rumour that the prophet was a wizard, a magician, a liar, an ignorant person, an illiterate, etc. Now we see them making similar accusations about this revolution. We can interpret the accusations in the same way.'[10]

From the West's viewpoint, the potential consequences of an Iranian victory – which began to seem possible after Iran took the oil-rich Majnoun islands in 1985 and the Fao peninsula in 1986 – contributed to the 1987 decision by the United States and some European nations to pressure Iran, through deployment in the Persian Gulf, the threat of an arms embargo and either boycotts of or decreases in oil purchases, and to assist Baghdad, through intelligence and military advice. The mobilization of outside forces on Baghdad's behalf was due less, indeed far less, to admiration for Saddam Hussein's regime than to the implications of an Iranian victory on the future spread of Islamic fundamentalism and extremism. In other words, Iran's campaign to export the revolution elsewhere contributed greatly to its undoing on the domestic warfront. If, even while fighting the war, the Islamic Republic had otherwise focused only inward and if its foreign policy had been less aggressive, particularly in aiding and abetting extremists who engaged in suicide bombings, hostage seizures and hijackings, Western nations would arguably not have been as alarmed about the emergence of Islam as a political medium or as a threat to their own national security.

FUTURE

Iran's agreement in July 1988 to accept the terms of the United Nations ceasefire did not, however, necessarily signal the end of the Islamic movement in Iran – or in the region. In his message to the nation formally accepting the ceasefire on 20 July 1988 Khomeini stressed that an end to the war did not mean an end to Iran's ambitious effort to export the revolution.

'I openly announce that Iran will work with all its might for the revival of the Islamic identity of Muslims throughout the world,' he said. 'Our war is one of ideology and does not recognize borders or geography. We must ensure the vast mobilization of the soldiers of Islam around the world in our ideological war. God willing, the great Iranian nation, through its material and moral support for the revolution, will compensate for the hardships of the war with the sweetness of the defeat of God's enemies in the world.'[11]

Iran's ruling mullahs even used Islamic paradigms to justify their stunning turnabout on the war. In the immediate aftermath of the announcement, parallels were drawn with two early events in Islamic history: the prophet Muhammad's peace with the Meccans and Hussein's death at Karbala in AD 680.[12] At a Friday prayer sermon on 29 July 1988, Rafsanjani acknowledged Iran's acceptance of the ceasefire, 'No one here in our own nation or abroad expected it. The holy prophet was faced with the same reaction of disbelief when he decided to sign an agreement with the infidels at Hudaybiyah. Even the closest friends of the prophet were shocked while serious objections were rife, but they very soon realized that they were wrong when the Koran provided their reply.'[13] Later, addressing the issue of whether the martyrs' blood had been sacrificed unnecessarily, the daily *Resaalat* countered, 'The martyr is one who has fought in God's path and against the enemies of God and attained the sublime position of martyrdom, whether the Islamic army wins a superficial victory or not. Besides, victory is not confined to a military victory, just like the martyrs of Karbala who achieved no military victory but went down as the greatest martyrs of Islam.'[14]

Tehran did, however, apparently recognize the failure and costs of its campaign to foment Islamic fanaticism elsewhere. By the time the UN ceasefire was accepted in mid-1988, Iran's tangible successes in exporting militant Islam were limited to Lebanon – even there, it led to a clash with Syria; its most blatant failure was in Iraq, where it had become clear that the local Shi'ite allegiance was defined more on ethnic Arab and national Iraqi lines than on their religious identity. Although Khomeini always claimed that Iran's Islamic revolution had been carried out in the name of all Islam and that there were no distinctions between the Sunni, Islam's mainstream sect, and the Shi'a, the revolution during its first decade had increasingly appeared distinctly Shi'ite and, in the end, peculiarly Khomeini-ist in ideology and implementation.

Growing awareness of this factor, coinciding with Iran's losses during the Karbala offensives and in Mecca, helped to reignite a fundamental debate that had raged since the 1979 revolution. Although no leading Iranian theologian or politician had ever disagreed over entrenchment of Islamic rule, the revolution since its inception has been troubled by rival visions over how this should be accomplished. Iran's political spectrum is a labyrinth, but the two poles in this debate generally follow the pattern of other post-revolution periods. On one end are those who have argued that Iran should be a 'redeemer state', championing the cause of the world's oppressed in much the same way revolutionary Russians viewed themselves as champions of the proletariat. They advocate restoring Islamic purity and rule in the seventy-nation Dar al-Islam, or abode of Islam, through perpetual revolution and through an ongoing challenge to a bipolar world by creating and leading a new power bloc capable of defying both East and West. Their ambitious agenda endorses fundamentalist extremism to pure the region and eventually the world, in the same way that Iran was cleansed of the shah's domestic tyranny, his alliances with foreign imperialist and corrupting influences, and his betrayal of Islam. In other words, violence could often be condoned to achieve these ends.

The other end of the spectrum is represented by those who have argued that Iran should seek legitimacy by institutionalizing the revolution and creating a model Islamic government. Their priorities have been, first, to create a new political system that attends to indigenous goals rather than the priorities imposed by foreign development schemes and advice; second, to found a new social order that restores dignity and independence from outside intervention and ideologies; and third to establish a new economic structure that ensures 'social justice', the catchall term around which the reform debate has centred, and that redistributes wealth, particularly for the mostazefin, or disinherited, in whose name the revolution was conducted. This agenda envisions the Islamic Republic winning converts and supporters by example, not force.[15]

Iran's decision to accept Resolution 598 indicated that, at least for the time being, the pragmatists and the exigencies of the state had won out over the purists and their lofty ideals. At a Friday prayer sermon just a week before the UN ceasefire was implemented, President Ali Khamenei outlined Iran's postwar priorities to the assembled faithful, 'We should build our country as a model and exemplary Islam country and should place it before the eyes of the world and say this is the kind of society Islam builds. This is our duty.'[16] This decision also implied a major shift in the focus of the theocracy from the war to internal issues, specifically reviving Iran's deeply troubled economy and debating reforms put on hold since the war erupted just twenty months after the revolution.

The beginning of this shift in mid-1988, in turn, set off a chain reaction that ultimately also affected Iran's campaign to spread its brand of Islamic extremism. First, to revive the economy, the biggest domestic problem, Iran needed to improve its standing in the international community in order to develop trading partners. Tehran's announcement of the resumption of relations with Canada, on the same day that it accepted the terms of the UN ceasefire, was not a coincidence. After a tense year in 1987, marked by a downgrading of or a break in relations with France, Britain and Saudi Arabia as well as by the Western deployment in the Gulf, Iran in mid-1988 initiated a new effort to repair its diplomatic problems, beginning with restoring ties with France in June, Canada in July and Britain in December. The deal with Ottawa involved dropping Iran's eight-year demand for a formal apology for Canada's assistance in hiding and then sneaking out six American diplomats in Tehran during the 1979–81 hostage episode.

Second, a meaningful breakthrough also hinged on Iran's position on terrorism, most immediately the hostages held by pro-Iranian groups in Lebanon. Tehran helped free the final three French hostages in May 1988 as part of a 'no-deal deal' that culminated in June in the restoration of diplomatic relations with Paris; talks with British envoys about restoring ties included movement on an Irish and two British hostages held in Lebanon. In the aftermath of the US's disastrous arms-for-hostage swap in 1985–6 however, other Western nations were reluctant to deal with Iran without, at minimum, an informal understanding that the hostage phenomenon in general, not only the specific cases of hostages, would end. Key Iranian officials appeared to be aware of the increasing costs of Islamic zealotry. In several speeches shortly before and after the ceasefire, Parliamentary Speaker Rafsanjani referred to Tehran's need to 'stop making enemies' and to rectify past foreign policy mistakes.[17]

In other words, the ceasefire did not signal an end to Iran's crusade to spread Islamic rule throughout the region; instead, it indicated a change in its means. The 1982 seminar had been in the words of a Gulf cabinet minister, 'a change of tactics, not policy'.[18] The ceasefire marked the beginning of a further shift due to the recognition, at least among certain quarters in Tehran, that the original momentum created at the time of the revolution had been lost because of two factors: First, the theocracy's initial excesses, particularly mass executions and ruthless suppression of the opposition. Second, Iran's refusal, after the war turned in its favour, to negotiate peace with Arab Iraq, which further alienated fundamentalist elements in the Arab world.

REGIONAL IMPACT

The circumstances surrounding Iran's acceptance of the ceasefire may have signalled the failure of Tehran's militant tactics, which would amount to a major turning point in the movement. But just as the broader Islamic movement did not begin in the Islamic republic, it also was unlikely to die due solely to developments in Iran for at least three reasons. Most basic was the fact that the various movements never constituted a monolithic force. While Islam did indeed become the most energetic single new political vehicle in the region in the 1980s, the various groups in each nation had diverse strengths, disparate goals, and different tactics.

Second, the original impetus for Islam's emergence as a political alternative in the Middle East remained valid. The conventional ideologies of the late twentieth century – variations of Marxism and capitalism – were still perceived to have failed to address basic political and economic problems in the region. Muslims were actively searching for a more compatible political idiom that would also allow them to establish an independent identity for both the individual and the state and to restore cultural dignity at a time modernization had become synonymous with westernization.

Third, the roots of the religious resurgence in the Middle East were not in Iran, nor were they limited to Islam. In general terms, the broader movement of religion in politics in the Third World – including Sikh extremists in India, Liberation Theologians in Latin and Central America, Buddhist monks in Burma, the anti-apartheid protestant clergy in South Africa – has usually been related to one or more of three factors: First, politicized religions emerge to provide a leadership alternative in repressive or dictatorial nations where opposition figures have been banned, exiled or eliminated. Second, religious movements provide refuge during identity crises common to newly developing countries that gained independence since the Second World War. Third, politicized religions provide a vehicle through which to sort out the difference between westernization and modernization, which have become synonymous in the second half of the twentieth century. Modernization was clearly a priority in most Third World nations, but it often simultaneously challenged historic values and customs, triggering a backlash. This was evident in Iran, where the Shah seemed to 'sell out' his ancient culture faster and at a greater price than did other regional powers in the race to modernize – in turn eliciting a greater response: a revolution. One of the reasons Islam became attractive was that it offered an authentic source of identity that did not force the population to look or act contrary to tradition or to their own priorities.

Events on the ground, however, also played a role in accelerating a process and an idea that were already taking hold. Both the more moderate forms of Islamic fundamentalism and the zealous, violence-prone Islamic fanaticism can be traced back to the 1967 Arab-Israeli war. Many Arabs, humiliated by the devastating losses of large chunks of Egypt, Jordan and Syria, began to feel something more basic than military capability was wrong. The movement became visible during the 1973 Yom Kippur War. The rallying cry of the Arab offensive, which was code-named 'Badr' after the prophet Muhammad's first victory in AD 624, had shifted from pan-Arabism to Islam. The Arabs lost militarily, but they achieved key political objectives that helped to establish the precedent of Islam's effectiveness. Iran's 1979 revolution marked a third juncture, for it proved that Islam could be a successful political idiom against a government that had appeared to be both politically and militarily entrenched. Subsequent events elsewhere, however, such as the emergence of the Egyptian Muslim Brotherhood in 1987 elections as the largest opposition force in parliament, the use of Islam by one of the five factions involved in the Palestinian uprising, and the fundamentalist role in the 1988 Algerian riots had begun to take the limelight away from Iran.

CONCLUSION

The Iranian revolution and Iran's position on the Persian Gulf war had a major impact on the Islamic revival. In the early stages of both, Iran served as an inspiration throughout the seventy-nation House of Islam. But during the latter stages, particularly the final eighteen months, the fanatic Iranian model was widely spurned by most Sunni and many moderate Shi'ite fundamentalists in the Middle East as a dogmatic formula that did not redress political and societal wrongs and that ultimately endangered military and economic survival. Ultimately, the recognition of these weaknesses within the Islamic Republic played a leading role in forcing Tehran's theocrats to change course.

Notes

1. For a similar view regarding the origins of the war, see E. Karsh, 'From Ideological Zeal to Geopolitical Realism: the Islamic Republic and the Gulf", pp. 26–41 in this volume.
2. Translation from *Akhbaar News Service*. 'General Command issues communique', on *Radio Tehran*, 12 July 1988.
3. V. S. Naipaul, *Among the Believers: An Islamic Journey* (New York: Vintage Books, 1981) p. 82.
4. *Islam and Revolution: Writing and Declarations of Imam Khomeini*, trans. by Hamid Algar (Berkeley: Mizan Press, 1981).
5. R. Wright, *Sacred Rage: The Wrath of Militant Islam* (New York: Simon & Schuster, 1986). An interview with Minister of the Revolutionary Guards Mohsen Rafiqdoost in Tehran, 14 June 1988.
6. Wright, *Sacred Rage*. An interview with Minister of the Revolutionary Guards Mohsen Rafiqdoost on 14 June 1988.
7. Wright, *Sacred Rage*, pp. 26–31.
8. S. Bakhash, *The Reign of the Ayatollahs: Iran and the Islamic Revolution* (New York: Basic Books, 1984).
9. Author's interview with Rafiqdoost, 14 June 1988.
10. *FBIS*, 'Hashemi-Rafsanjani Delivers Friday Sermon', 5 October 1987, pp. 53–8
11. *FBIS*, 'Khomeini's Message of Haj, UN Resolution 598', 21 July 1988, pp. 41–52.
12. Karabala, now a city in southern Iraq, was the site where Hussein and a small group of seventy-two followers took on thousands of troops from the Umayyad dynasty over the issue of leadership of the then still new Islamic empire. Hussein was a grandson of the prophet Muhammad and the son of Ali, after whom the Shi'a took their name. The Shi'a believed the line of succession

should descend through the prophet's family, specifically his son-in-law and cousin Ali. Ali did eventually become the third caliph, or God's representative on earth, but power then diverted to the Umayyads. Hussein knew he and his band would be massacred, but he believed it was better to die fighting injustice than to live with injustice. This act established the precedent of martyrdom that has become part of the Shi'ite legacy, commemorated each year in the re-enactment of his death in the Shi'ite passion play during the celebration of Ashura.

13.	*FBIS*, 'Second Sermon on Ceasefire', 1 August 1988, pp. 56–60.
14.	Translation from *Akhbaar News Service*, Tehran, 21 July 1988. 'Noah is always the helmsman', editorial by A. Azari Qomi, *Resaalat*, 20 July 1988.
15.	R. Wright, 'Iran Looks Beyond Khomeini', *The Nation*, 7 February 1987.
16.	*FBIS* 15 August 1988, 'Khamenei Delivers Friday Prayer Sermons: Postwar Piety Urged', from local broadcast on 12 August 1988, pp. 58–9.
17.	*FBIS*, 'Second Sermon on Ceasefire', ibid.
18.	Wright, *Sacred Rage*, p. 30.

8 The Gulf States and the Iran–Iraq War

Barry Rubin

The Gulf Arab monarchies have been, simultaneously, the front-row observers, financiers, victims, prizes, and would-be mediators of the Iran–Iraq war. Simply to inventory the threats posed by the conflicts for these states – Saudi Arabia, Kuwait, the United Arab Emirates (UAE), Qatar, Bahrain, and Oman – reveals the intensity and variety of dangers. Their ability to handle this situation was sharply limited by a lack of power.

Four themes should be kept particularly in mind: First, the Gulf Arab monarchies most benefited by an end to the war under conditions where both belligerents were neither victors nor vanquished. These countries' main fear was that Iran would win the war, and they therefore supported Iraq. But they did not want Iraq to dominate the post-war Gulf. Some type of balance – in which an exhausted, deadlocked Tehran and Baghdad might deter each other's ambitions – was the favoured outcome.

Second, while the Gulf Arab monarchies preferred that Iran's Islamic fundamentalist regime be replaced by one more consistent with their tastes, they knew that they must be prepared to coexist with the Tehran government. Since they could not topple Khomeini's government, these rulers were willing to appease Iran if possible, but Tehran denied them that option.

Third, these weak, rich states are vulnerable to internal subversion or external attack. Yet there are also good reasons why fundamentalists do not appear likely to topple them. Conscious of the threat, the regimes parade their piety while clamping down on dissidents. Large oil earnings spread over relatively small populations finance benefits to buy loyalty. Iran's Persian, Shi'ite revolution has limited appeal for Sunni and Arab Moslems. There are Shi'ite minorities in eastern Saudi Arabia (including perhaps half the oilfield workers) and Kuwait. The majority in Bahrain and roughly half of Iraq's population are Shi'ites. But Arab nationalism, material benefits, and repression have so far kept no more than a handful of such people from actively supporting Iran. Moreover, despite its militant rhetoric and efforts to export its revolution, the Khomeini regime has essentially followed a policy of Islamic revolution in one country except in Lebanon, the only place it has won a significant following.

Finally, to provide help against Iraq and Iran (and, more subtly, against internal threats), the Gulf Arab monarchs sought US assistance. Yet to avoid provoking Baghdad, Tehran, and internal public opinion, these rulers also sought to limit the scope and visibility of US involvement unless the threat from Iran seemed too great to allow such diffidence. In any case, while seeking and accepting US arms and protection, the monarchs tried to minimize logistical support for the United States or concessions to American political objectives.

Cautiously seeking to ensure their security on all sides, the Arab monarchies simultaneously aided Iraq, tried to appease Iran, and reinforced links with the United States. For defence, they formed the Gulf Co-operation Council (GCC) and bought huge arsenals of US arms, although they remain far from self-sufficient in protecting their borders against any serious Iranian attack. Their behaviour during the past decade gives important clues for their likely post-war policies.

This chapter will analyze the problems posed by the war for these Gulf Arab states and the ways in which they reacted to fighting (and to Islamic Iran). It will also suggest the implications of their interests, history, and policy for the shape of Gulf politics in the post-war period. Since all six of these countries are members of the Gulf Co-operation Council, they will be referred to collectively herein as the GCC states, even when reference is not specifically being made to that organization.

WILLINGNESS TO CO-EXIST WITH IRAN: THE PRE-WAR PERIOD

Iran's revolution was a vivid nightmare for every Gulf government, revealing the possibility of its own demise at the hands of newly aroused fundamentalists. As King Fahd of Saudi Arabia put it in August 1978: 'The Arab states will have to support Iran and the shah, because the stability of that country is important to the [entire] region ... and any radical change will upset its security balance.'[1] Of course, Iranian ambitions even under the shah had worried Gulf rulers, but his self-appointed role as their protector did fulfill a useful role for them. The shah's fall forced them to take more responsibility for their own security, even more so as the Islamic Republic of Iran emerged as a threat.

The Gulf Arab states sought to avoid friction with the new Islamic Republic. The Kuwaiti newspaper, *Al-Ra'i al-Amm*, for example, said the Iranian revolution 'calls for admiration' and advocated better Arab-Iranian relations in June 1979, claiming, 'It is obviously clear that Iran has no claims against the Arabs and Tehran knows well that the Arabs have no claims against Iran.'[2] The problem was that Iran's new regime – by its revolutionary Islamic internationalism and Ayatollah Khomeini's belief that the revolution must be spread – chose to be a threat to the Gulf Arab states.

Some events – pro-Khomeini rallies in Kuwait and Bahrain in February 1979; the November 1979 attack on the Mecca mosque – were spontaneous but showed the potential appeal of Iran's doctrine and example. There was understandable fear that Shi'ites – the majority in Bahrain and a significant minority in Saudi Arabia and Kuwait – might form a natural constituency for Iranian influence and rise up against the Sunni rulers.

Other Iranian propaganda and actions were of a directly threatening nature. In January 1980, for example, Tehran sponsored a Conference of World Liberation Movements which included an Islamic Revolutionary Organization in Saudi Arabia. These groups were small, if they existed at all, but such deeds were taken in the Gulf as important indications of Iran's intentions. That same month, Tehran Radio broadcast a programme claiming that the Saudi regime was the 'opposite of Islam', merely 'another example of the domination of shahs [kings] and their corruption' which would be overthrown.[3]

Even when Iran tried to be conciliatory, the revolution's ideology got in the way. Hassan Ayat, a high-ranking Islamic Republican Party official, stated in February 1980 that Iran wanted cordial relations with all its neighbours and was committed to non-interference in their affairs. But he could not refrain from adding that those countries were led by unpopular, minority, and pro-imperialist governments. 'Such a situation . . . is not going to last for long because the people are no more ready to be exploited.' Iran would help the masses in their battle against their rulers, Ayat concluded.[4]

Given the open calls for spreading Islamic revolution from Tehran's highest leaders – one of them even renewed Iran's old claim to Bahrain – it was logical for the Gulf Arab states to conclude that they were a target for the new regime. The Iran–Iraq War may have deflected part of the immediate threat, but the possibility of an Iranian victory or that fighting might spread to engulf their countries seemed to enhance the danger.

The smaller states closed ranks, created the GCC in February 1981, and made policy changes designed to appease domestic Islamic sentiment while repressing any would-be revolutionaries. In addition to their traditional bases of legitimacy, the rulers' large oil earnings allowed extensive subsidies and other programmes to win subjects' loyalty. Although falling far short of hopes that the GCC would co-ordinate members' defence, intelligence, and economic policies, the group did provide a basis for co-operation which enhanced their security.

THREATS POSED BY THE WAR

The war posed five particular dangers to GCC states:

1. The conflict itself might spread and engulf them. Although the land war was restricted to the areas along the Iran–Iraq border, it was always possible that Iran might attack GCC countries. Kuwait's frontier was

only a few miles from the heaviest fighting and on several occasions, by error or as a warning, Iranian planes hit targets there. Iraqi demands might also pull the Gulf states into the fighting. Out of frustration or as a result of overconfidence in the wake of a military victory, Tehran could strike directly at regimes it saw as Iraqi allies, friends of the United States, and reactionary monarchies not governed by a proper Islamic system.

2. Iraq's declaration of a blockade against Iran led to a 'tanker war' in which ships carrying the freight and oil of GCC states came under retaliatory Iranian attacks. Although these strikes did not slow the GCC states' export of oil, they damaged ships, killed many crew members, and created a situation of high tension in the region. Iran increased attacks on GCC-flag vessels when it sought to exercise leverage over those countries. Saudi Arabia built a new pipeline to the Red Sea as an alternative oil export route to the Gulf. In 1987, faced with escalating Iranian attacks, Kuwait put its tankers under US flags, instituting the convoying of ships by the United States and several West European navies as well. While the material damage to the GCC states was limited, the tanker war was an extremely worrisome threat to their sole source of income.

3. The Iran–Iraq War was a battle over hegemony in the Persian Gulf region. After all, the conflict's underlying reasons were geostrategic and imperial ones. Both Baghdad and Tehran sought to be the dominant power in the area; the GCC states were the prizes to be dominated. A victory by either side would establish a heavily armed, ambitious regime in a position of great influence over the half-dozen other small, weak, and wealthy countries.

4. The ideologies and political systems of both Iraq and Iran are incompatible with those of the GCC states and have, at times, openly aimed at overthrowing the monarchies. Iraq has been a radical, Arab nationalist regime which opposed the monarchies on a basis of 'class', sought Arab unity by force if necessary, and supported revolutionary movements in the GCC states. Iran is an Islamic fundamentalist state which opposes the monarchies on a religio-political basis, demands Islamic unity behind its own leadership, and has supported revolutionary and terrorist groups in the GCC states.

There are, however, three significant differences between the two stronger regional powers. First, Iraq has become more moderate and 'local nationalist', explicitly dropping much of its old militancy and pan-Arabism. Second, the war made Baghdad far more dependent on GCC money and logistical support, a relationship almost certain to continue into the postwar period when Iraq needs reconstruction aid. While Iraq used some intimidation to guarantee GCC help, Iranian obduracy and Gulf Arab fear were the main factors involved. Third, Iraq is – like the GCC states – ruled by a Sunni, Arab regime. In comparison, Iran was still extremely militant; rhetorically extremist towards the GCC countries;

opposed to their stand on the war and their alliance with the United States; and Persian, Shi'ite regime.

While putting forth its own claim to Gulf hegemony – 'Iraq has become the greatest power in the Arab arena, especially in the eastern part,' proclaimed one radio broadcast – Baghdad also credibly portrayed itself as defender of the Gulf Arabs from a Persian invasion. As President Saddam Hussein put it, in frequently repeated slogans, Iraq was the 'shield of the Arabs ... defending the Arab nation ... in the face of enemies'.[5]

5. An Iranian victory would have increased Tehran's ambitions and ability to overthrow the GCC rulers. Also, it would have inspired local fundamentalist movements towards greater efforts to launch revolutions. In contrast, Iraq favoured the status quo. Iran's then-President Abol-Hassan Bani Sadr expressed this problem when he said the Gulf Arab states 'imagine that we are a serious disease and that if they open their doors to us then everybody will be infected'.[6]

Responding to Bani Sadr's statement, the Kuwaiti newspaper *al-Qabas*, which earlier had praised Iran's revolution, concluded, 'It clearly emerges that to don the garb of tolerant Islam, [Iran] cannot mask imperialist and expansionist intentions.' Gulf Arabs preferred good relations with Iran, but Tehran's policies made it impossible to 'enjoy naïve dreams' to that effect.[7]

Both Iraq and Iran had several ways of exercising leverage on the Gulf monarchies, the former to gain their support, the latter to press them towards neutrality. Both of them had the option of using indirect violence; both of them merited deference for their ruthlessness.

Iran bombed Kuwaiti targets on several occasions in 1980–1 and 1986; organized an abortive armed uprising in Bahrain in 1981; and launched terrorist attacks on the ground. Tehran also kept up the pressure on Saudi Arabia through organizing demonstrations during the Islamic pilgrimage to Mecca, culminating in the July 1987 riots and the deaths of several hundred Iranians at the hands of Saudi police. These actions, however, were ultimately counterproductive. By convincing Kuwait and Saudi Arabia that Tehran was bent on their destruction, the Khomeini regime only reinforced their support for its enemy. In other words, Iran destroyed, at least for Saudi Arabia and Kuwait, hope – and thus their incentive – for appeasing it.

Iran's direct violence and propaganda against the Gulf monarchies had a similar result. The former category included Iranian attacks against ships and tankers servicing the GCC states. For Tehran, of course, these actions were partly the result of frustration: it knew that Saudi Arabia and Kuwait were earmarking some of their oil to sell for Iraq's benefit and that Kuwait's port was used to deliver war material to Iraq. Yet Iranian pressure had no effect in stopping – though it may have succeeded in limiting – these activities. Similarly, the rhetoric and practical support for Islamic revolutionaries in GCC states had no success in subverting those regimes though it did undermine Iran's relations with them.

Iran was more successful in exploiting trade and historical connections with the UAE (particularly Dubai) and Oman. The large ethnic Persian mercantile interests in the former and the shah's past help to the latter made them more amenable to Iran compared to militantly Sunni Saudi Arabia.

OTHER FACTORS SHAPING GCC STATES' POLICIES

In facing this range of threats, a set of constraints and assets shaped the GCC states' position on the war. The most important limitations was a consciousness of their own military weakness and their difficulties in seeking outside help. Put simply, Saudi Arabia and its smaller neighbours knew that they could not hope to stand up against any direct attack from Iran or Iraq. Therefore, they must avoid, at almost any cost, a direct confrontation.

The issue of outside help is more complex. On one hand, their societies' Arab nationalism and Islamic conservatism made it difficult for them to depend too openly on American aid. On the other hand, however, this helplessness made them need US help. The Saudis used a large number of US advisers and bought mostly US weapons, while Kuwait, hitherto the GCC state most critical of the United States, sought US military equipment and reflagging. Due to Egypt's banishment from the Arab world over its Camp David Accords with Israel, the GCC had earlier co-operated fully in the anti-Egypt boycott. Ironically, Iran's pressure pushed the Gulf Arab states even closer to the United States and Egypt, making possible a level of strategic co-operation ridiculed as impossible when US Secretary of State Alexander Haig proposed it in the early 1980s. As if this were not enough, the Iranian threat also accelerated the trend in which Gulf Arab states demoted the importance of the Arab–Israeli conflict in their policy and delinked it from their relations with the United States.

The GCC's main, and not inconsiderable, asset was its billions of dollars in oil earnings. The combination of factors led to a characteristic style of GCC, particularly Saudi, diplomacy. These states were conciliatory, eager to avoid offence to any larger power. Within the Arab world, they tried to play the role of mediators, urging unity on a least common denominator basis. While giving lip service and financial contributions to Arab causes – including the Palestinian one – they were careful to avoid being drawn into military confrontations. Their timidity and willingness to appease potential threats cancelled out the apparent leverage provided by their wealth. The money was used to pacify other states, not pressure them into taking some kind of action. A limited, rule-proving, exception was the Saudi role in obtaining the 1987 Amman Arab summit resolution criticizing Iran for refusing to end the war. The key contribution was in persuading Syria to support the proposal.

But this also mean that only a general, toothless motion was passed even though Damascus desperately needed continuation of its Saudi subsidies. And Syria continued to support Iran against Iraq.

Given these factors, the GCC states chose to be as neutral as possible – fearing both local 'superpowers' and the risks of direct involvement in the war. They wanted the fighting over as soon as possible, but without there being a clear victor who could consolidate hegemony and mark them as victims for conquest, subversion, or intimidation. The GCC governments were willing to appease Iran, particularly if this could be done cheaply and without risk to their rule, but Tehran denied them that option. Hoping Iraq would stop Iranian expansionism – and preferring Baghdad's moderating Arab nationalism to Iran's increasingly militant Shi'ite fundamentalism – they elected to help the Iraqi regime to some extent.

As Iran increased the pressure on Saudi Arabia and Kuwait in 1987–8, those two states generally concluded that they had an even greater stake in denying Iran a victory and had no choice but to protect themselves. Certainly, their help to Iraq was limited by caution. As Kuwait's Foreign Minister explained, 'He who stands too close to the blacksmith gets hurt by flying sparks.'[8] Yet this assistance was still the critical margin that Baghdad needed to survive.

In addition to the $30 billion in loans (in practice, grants), Saudi Arabia and Kuwait sold some of their oil on Iraq's behalf. Kuwait allowed its port facilities to be used to import supplies and material for Iraq while the Saudis built a connector line permitting Iraqi oil to flow through their pipeline to the Red Sea. The Saudi and Kuwaiti governments also lobbied on behalf of Iraq – and the anti-Iran cause – with the United States.

On the other hand, the GCC states were willing to deal with Iran. There were frequent meetings at a high level between the two sides. For example, in October 1985 alone, Iran's deputy foreign minister led a delegation to Bahrain, the UAE, and Qatar, and Kuwait's foreign minister met with his Iranian counterpart; the Saudi and Iranian foreign ministers exchanged visits in May and December. The UAE in particular broke the US sanctions imposed during the 1979–81 hostage crisis by transhipping American-made goods to Iran. As late as April–May 1988, not long after Saudi Arabia broke relations with Iran, UAE President Zayd ibn Sultan al-Nuhayyan proclaimed, 'The UAE enjoys close ties with Islamic Iran' while Oman's Sultan Qabous told Iran's visiting foreign minister that Oman was ready to 'cooperate with Iran'.[9] Saudi billionaire Adnan Kashoggi, with apparent permission from the royal family, was involved in the secret dealings that led to the sale of US arms to Tehran in 1985–6.

In analyzing all of these developments, it is necessary to note that the GCC states did, after all, largely attain their goals. Iran did not attack them. The Tehran government knew that such a step would be counterproductive to the war effort, isolating Iran even further and bringing a strong US reaction. The

Islamic Republic was more cautious in practice about spreading revolution than in rhetoric; the Gulf Arab states were careful not to overheat antagonisms.

The pattern, then, was that the Gulf Arab states criticized Iran within limits, urged it to end the war, and kept the door open to post-war reconciliation.

ENDGAME

On 3 July 1988, a fortnight before accepting a ceasefire in the Iran–Iraq War, the powerful speaker of parliament and military Commander-in-Chief Hashemi-Rafsanjani, said that Iran's new priority was to break out of international isolation: 'One of the wrong things we did in the revolutionary atmosphere was to constantly make enemies. We pushed those who could be neutral into hostility and did not do anything to attract those who could become friends. It is part of the new plan that in foreign policy we should behave in a way not to needlessly leave ground to the enemy.'[10]

Rafsanjani spoke from experience. During 1987, Iran exerted the highest level of pressure on the Gulf Arab states since the beginning of the war. Yet while these threats were potent enough to antagonize the GCC states, they did not suffice to compel them to change policy. The situation then shifted drastically in 1988. As prospects for Iranian victory declined and the pressures on Tehran grew, Iran's leaders realized that they had undermined their own position in the Gulf. If Iran wanted to emerge from its isolation or to stop the growing US presence, it had to reconcile the GCC countries.

In late 1986, Iran stepped up assaults against Kuwaiti ships in response to an increase in the number and effectiveness of Iraqi attacks. According to some sources, Iran suggested that it would stop targeting Kuwaiti ships if that country did not put them under the US flag. None the less, on 1 November 1986, Kuwait told the Gulf Co-operation Council that it was seeking international protection for its tankers. The Kuwaitis inquired about the technical requirements for re-registering tankers as US-flag ships on 10 December; on 29 January the State Department told Kuwait that it could re-register the ships and, on 6 February, that the United States would protect them. Kuwait applied for reflagging on 2 March, and was offered protection five days later. Kuwait agreed on 10 March and the administration informed Congress of the offer which Kuwait formally accepted on 2 April.

Although the US decision shored up Kuwait, it was also the result of that country's manipulation of the threat to ask help from Moscow. Even the Kuwaitis seemed amused. 'The United States' problem,' commented Sulayman Majid al-Shahin, undersecretary at the Kuwaiti Foreign Ministry, 'is that the mentality of Hollywood tends to influence it sometimes. As for Soviet tankers, these have been quietly sailing in the Gulf for some time. So what has changed?'[11]

Iran responded by mining Kuwait's harbours and the open Gulf waters, used Silkworm missiles to strike at Kuwait, and the Revolutionary Guards used hundreds of small speedboats for stepped-up attacks on tankers flying the flags of countries not participating in the convoys.

Publicly, the GCC states demanded more US action. A leader stated, 'The whole issue is out of focus when one talks about accompanying or escorting ships. The issue is the war and how to end it.' A Saudi official complained that the United States was merely 'administering pinpricks'. 'Hitting small boats doesn't matter. What matters is that the American military presence, in order to be justified by us, must ensure our total security by ensuring Iran to total paralysis.'[12]

These countries also reiterated the urgency of ending the war, in the words of *Al Wahdah* (UAE), 'to ensure that the Gulf is not converted into a US and Soviet arsenal under the pretext of protecting their military presence and strategic interests'. Kuwait's ambassador to Washington complained that 'Iran is now settling its score with America at the expense of Kuwait'. In fact, Bahrain's monarch, Isa ibn Salman al-Khalifa, whose country was probably the most co-operative with the United States in practice, blamed the 'presence of foreign forces in the Persian Gulf' as a factor escalating tensions in the region and stressed the need for better co-operation with Iran. The GCC states were reluctant to offer the United States even minimal military facilities even in cases where the US Defence Department said assistance was forthcoming. Kuwait, for example, would not allow minesweeping helicopters to take off from its territory.[13]

The revision of the traditional GCC position opposing the presence of any US warships in the Gulf was, indeed, a dramatic change brought about by the war and the fear of Iran. The Amman Arab summit supported the measures Kuwait was taking in its defence, an implicit endorsement of the US presence. AWACS surveillance planes based in Saudi Arabia and P-3 reconnaissance aircraft taking off from Kuwait provided vital intelligence for the convoys. But the need to base US Sea Stallion mine-hunting helicopters on ships made it harder to clear the obstacles, particularly in the upper Gulf. In private conversations, American officials indicated their dissatisfaction with the level of GCC assistance.

Iran only stepped up its efforts. In July 1987, demonstrations during the pilgrimage in Mecca led to riots in which Saudi forces killed about 400 Iranians. The Saudi Embassy was attacked and sacked in Tehran and one Saudi diplomat was killed. Iranian boats also focused attacks on tankers carrying Saudi oil. Iranian diplomatic delegations visited the GCC states, pressing for the removal of Western warships from the Gulf. Instead, they argued, the area's security should be solely the responsibility of the local states.

But the GCC was in no mood to put its fate into Iran's hands. The December 1987 GCC summit meeting in Riyadh called for implementation of UN Resolution 598, criticized Iran for 'aggression' against Kuwait and

Saudi Arabia, but also asked Tehran to 'commit itself to the principles of good neighbourliness and mutual respect to keep the Gulf free from international conflict'.[14]

Even when Saudi Arabia did break relations, it did not want to make the conflict irrevocable, knowing it would have to live with Iran in the future. The official Saudi statement said, 'In spite of Iran's hostile stands towards the Kingdom of Saudi Arabia ... such as its attempt to smuggle explosives into the Kingdom during the 1986 pilgrimage season,' the 1987 riots, 'obstruction of the freedom of navigation', terrorism, and sabotage, 'the Kingdom resorted to self-restraint ... [and] tried to make the Iranian authorities understand the Kingdom's eagerness to normalize its relations with Islamic Iran on the basis of mutal respect.' King Fahd told the pilgrims that he regretted Iran's absence from the 1988 rites and hoped they would soon be back.[15]

Iran's acceptance of a ceasefire in the war and statements that it would seek a peace settlement, were received very positively in the GCC states. In fact, the monarchies were far more enthusiastic than Iraq, which worried that its own allies would force concessions on it in order to bring the war to a conclusion as quickly as possible. Still, the GCC states had to worry whether the new development would lead to peace or only a truce. Much of Ayatollah Khomeini's speech announcing his support for the ceasefire was spent attacking the Gulf states and warning the region's governments, 'particularly [Saudi] Arabia and Kuwait', that 'all of you will be partners in the adventurism and crimes created by the United States. We have not yet engaged in any action that would engulf the entire region in blood and fire, making it totally unstable. ... You ... can be sure you will be the losers in this new chapter.'[16]

In addition to the radical ideology still embodied in the Iranian regime, there were a number of material difficulties and disagreements between the belligerents that stood in the way of real peace. How could the GCC make sure that the peace would last and that Khomeini's threats remain unfulfilled?

The answer of the GCC states seems to be that Iraq must be pressed towards compromise while Iran must be reintegrated into the region. First, money is, once again, a key ingredient in Gulf monarchies diplomacy. If Iran demands huge reparations as part of a settlement, Saudi Arabia and Kuwait would be asked to pay billions of dollars. They were less able to do so in the late 1980s than at any time since the petrodollar boom that began in 1973. Low oil prices – likely to be further pressed by expanding Iranian and Iraqi production in the post-war era – was reducing their income and in 1988, for the first time, Saudi Arabia had to borrow abroad to balance its budget. Yet the GCC oil exporters had to be willing to finance large amounts of the belligerents' reconstruction in order to buy themselves peace. In addition, when Iran and Iraq seek to expand their OPEC quotas, Saudi Arabia and

Kuwait would have to cut their own production levels and, therefore, their incomes.

Second, for years to come, Iran and Iraq will dedicate most of their military and political power to countering each other. Iran, in particular, will seek expensive high-technology planes and tanks as soon as the war ends. China, North Korea, and European suppliers will be willing to sell them. The greater the arms race, the more elements on both sides will expect a new round of fighting. These may prove self-fulfilling prophecies. And the GCC states will also buy more arms, despite their falling revenues, to keep up. The Saudi purchase of missiles and British-built Tornado warplanes in 1988 and Kuwait's efforts to buy US-built F-18 planes was only the first step.

Third, they will try hard to rebuild relations with Iran. On a political level, however, it is not clear what they will offer Tehran. Even if Iran's ambitions are somewhat moderated, it will probably continue its traditional policy of seeking hegemony in the Gulf. Acting by peaceful means, including pressure, Iran will try to divide the GCC states among themselves and away from co-operation with the United States and Iraq. This could pose a greater threat to the Gulf Arab monarchies than Iran's more openly aggressive strategy of the revolution's first decade.

What will the GCC give Iran? These states might become even more outwardly pious, try to persuade the Islamic regime that they are distancing themselves from the United States, or restrict themselves about kind words for Iran's system and declarations about the peaceful coexistence of different kinds of governments. They could be more timid or a bit more assertive. This is, perhaps, the hardest point to estimate for the future.

Fourth, they will, though, continue to use the United States as a counter to Iranian ambitions. The GCC states will probably keep many elements of the closer co-operation built with the United States during the war – prepositioning of equipment, AWACS flights, plans for joint operations – while trying to reduce or eliminate the most high-profile aspects. Reducing the presence of US naval forces is the most obvious area where the GCC could appear to accede to Iranian demands.

Fifth, the end of the war will bring new GCC concerns about Iraq, a state which seemed to pose the main threat to the Gulf Arab states in the 1960s and 1970s at a time when the shah's Iran was their protector. A number of factors counteract or, at least, limit the likelihood of Iraqi imperialism. Most important, a high level of Iraq–Iran tension and military competition is likely to continue for a long time to come. Baghdad's enmity with Syria and Iran are likely to continue, money from the GCC states and access to secure pipelines through Saudi Arabia will be a necessity for the reconstruction effort as will Western technology and investment, and Iraq will want international support and guarantees to keep Iran from attacking it.

Finally, the GCC states will probably enter in the 1990s a period in which there is serious danger of internal instability. They are still reasonably stable.

Danger may intensify, however, as a new generation sees oil-wealth as its birthright, may be more influenced by fundamentalism, and faces relatively lower petroleum revenues. Rising groups (army, intellectuals, middle class) may demand more power through reforms or eventually may seek to seize power. Among the masses, social change has weakened traditional bonds of authority. These opposition forces could obtain help from Iraq, Iran, or even the Soviet Union.

Nevertheless, the GCC states have good reasons for being pleased and confident at the end of the Iran–Iraq War. They have successfully weathered the Iranian revolution, eight years of Iran–Iraq fighting, and a whole range of direct or covert Iranian efforts to undermine them. They can reasonably argue that the future cannot be worse than the recent past.

Notes

1. Quoted in D. Menashri, 'Iran', in Colin Legum (ed.), *Middle East Contemporary Survey*, vol. 2 (1977–8) (New York: Meier, 1979), p. 493.
2. *Al-Ra'i Al-Amm*, 13 February and 4 June 1974, in *FBIS*, 16 February and 6 June 1979.
3. *Radio Tehran*, 7 January 1980, in *FBIS*, 8 January 1980.
4. *Tehran Times*, 19 February 1980, in *FBIS*, 12 March 1980.
5. *Voice of the Masses Radio* (Baghdad), 4 March 1980, in *FBIS*, 6 March 1980: Saddam Hussein quoted by the *Iraqi News Agency*, 26 March 1980, in *FBIS*, 25 April 1980.
6. *Al-Nahar al Arabi wa-al-duwali*, 24–30 March 1980, in *FBIS*, 26 March 1980.
7. *Al-Qabas*, 23 March 1980, in *FBIS*, 25 March 1980.
8. *FBIS*, 12 April 1980, p. 27.
9. Ibid., 13 May 1988, p. 13; 11 April 1988, p. 25.
10. *New York Times*, 4 July 1988.
11. *FBIS*, 30 June 1987, p. J2.
12. *Washington Post*, 11 October 1987; *New York Times*, 16 October 1987.
13. *FBIS*, 20 May 1987, p. C6. See also, *Washington Post*, 25 June 1987, p. A25. Ambassador Sa'ud Nasser al-Sabah, *Kuwait News Agency*, 26 October 1987, in *FBIS*, 27 October 1987, pp. 16–17; see also *FBIS*, 23 June 1987, p. J2; 16 May 1988.
14. Quoted in *Christian Science Monitor*, 20 December 1987.
15. *Riyadh Television*, 26 April 1988, in *FBIS*, 27 April 1988.
16. *FBIS*, 21 July 1988, pp. 44 and 48.

9 The Silent Victor: Turkey's Role in the Gulf War

Henri J. Barkey

The Iraqi invasion of Iran on 22 September 1980 found the new Turkish military regime barely ten days old. Notwithstanding its declared neutrality and pronounced readiness to mediate between the belligerents, Turkey was to benefit – both politically and economically – from the persistence of the war at a time when it was facing one of the most critical challenges of its modern history.

This chapter addresses two facets in which the Gulf War impacted Turkey. On the one hand, Turkey by dramatically increasing its exports to both Iran and Iraq immeasurably improved the outlook of its crisis ridden economy. On the other hand, Turkey's strategic importance in the region was clearly enhanced by the war in general and specifically by a once possible Iranian victory. As a result, its military origins notwithstanding, the Turkish regime derived considerable support from abroad. These two repercussions more than adequately compensated for some of the adverse effects of the war; primarily the resumption of the Kurdish insurrection in border regions in southeastern Turkey. Therefore, Turkey has emerged from this prolonged conflict as a major beneficiary and is now also poised to take advantage of the declared cease-fire.

THE WAR'S ECONOMIC IMPACT ON TURKEY

As Turkey entered 1980, its economy was in shambles. The mismanagement of the preceding years, paired with a severe political crisis, had resulted in a desperate situation. Since February 1977, with the exception of some military needs, the Turkish Central Bank had been unable to transfer a single cent abroad to pay for necessary imports. With inflation looming around 100 per cent and industrial production on the decline, the minority government of Demirel and his conservative Justice Party were forced to resort to radical economic stabilization measures.

Introduced on 24 January 1980, the new policies were designed to take the economy from its existing inefficient and inward looking system, and transform it into a dynamic and outwardly oriented one. The authors of the programme (principally State Planning Organization Director Turgut Özal, who would later ride the success of these measures to become Prime Minister) believed that years of import substitution, which had been the main engine of Turkish industrialization, were responsible for the economy's lacklustre performance. The future in their view rested on seeking export markets and on developing an industry which would, unlike the present structure, be able to compete in international markets. Hence, the programme's success depended on the creation, development and maintenance of export markets.

While various international financial organizations supported Turkey by reopening aid and loan flows, the task facing the administration was an ambitious one. In the first place, because it had been protected for more than thirty years, Turkish industry had limited experience in exporting. And because they were competing with well established firms from developed countries, most Turkish industrialists were reluctant to pursue such opportunities abroad. The lure of the domestic market, where profit rates were higher and such issues as packaging were less important to consumers also mitigated against exports. Second, because the government's existence depended on the support of two extremist and unpredictable political parties, the measures' political success were also in doubt. Under conditions of general political unrest, parliamentary deadlock and polarized atmosphere where some twenty people lost their lives daily in acts of terrorism the likelihood of effectively implementing radical economic measures was remote.

With such prevailing political and economic conditions, the military's 12 September 1980 overthrow of Demirel's government surprised no one. If the new regime and its rulers were determined to transform the political landscape of Turkey, they were also willing to continue the economic transformation initiated by the Demirel government. In view of this, they not only chose to retain the services of Turgut Özal in their new administration, but also increased his powers and rendered him the 'czar' of economic policy. The army commanders' decision to continue the 24 January 1980 measures demonstrated their own conviction of the need to give the new programme a chance. In turn, one can attribute such attitudes to Özal's careful nurturing of the officers long before the advent of the coup.[1]

Turkey's Gains

Since the programme's success still depended on an expected improvement in the country's export performance, the start of the Iran–Iraq War could not have come at a more opportune moment for Turkey. Both Iran and Iraq increasingly turned to Turkey to satisfy their import needs. Turkey's proximity made its goods easier and faster to buy and transport. Furthermore, as the war increasingly damaged both countries' industrial capacity, their needs also diversified. The Iranian and Iraqi markets provided Turkish exporters with an unusual opportunity. These markets were not only less sophisticated than their European counterparts, but because of its own severe recession, Turkish industry had excess capacity and inventory to get rid of – often at very low prices.[2] When faced with foreign exchange shortfalls, Iran and Iraq found Turkish products to be less expensive substitutes for European or Japanese imports. Consequently, trade between Turkey and these two countries flourished.

As Figure 9.1 shows, exports to OECD countries, the main outlet for Turkish products, mirrored the rate of increase for total exports and demonstrated gradual and steady increase from 1978–87. By contrast, exports to the two warring nations rose dramatically. By 1983, not only had the level of exports to Iran increased to 25 times what it had been during the last year of the Shah's reign, but that country had, for the second year running, supplanted West Germany as Turkey's most important customer (see Tables 9.1 and 9.2). Similarly, Iraq also turned to its northern neighbour, and though the increase in exports to that country were not as dramatic as those to Iran, Turkey could hardly complain. By 1984, Germany had regained its leading role, but exports to Iraq had also reached an all time high.

As Figure 9.2 demonstrates, the combination of the Iranian and Iraqi markets for Turkish exports almost rivalled that of the European community

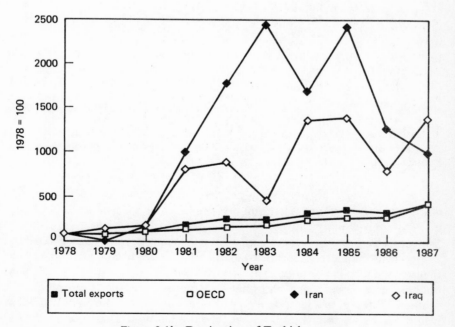

Figure 9.1[3]   Destination of Turkish exports

Table 9.1   Turkish exports 1978–87 (in millions of dollars)

Year	Total exports	Exports to Iraq	Exports to Iran	Exports to OECD	Exports to Germany
1978	$2288.20	$69.50	$44.70	$1507.00	$507.00
1979	$2261.10	$113.40	$12.00	$1446.00	$495.00
1980	$2910.00	$135.00	$85.00	$1680.00	$604.00
1981	$4703.00	$559.00	$442.00	$2264.00	$643.00
1982	$5746.00	$610.00	$791.00	$2556.00	$707.00
1983	$5728.00	$320.00	$1088.00	$2760.00	$838.00
1984	$7134.00	$934.00	$751.00	$3740.00	$1280.00
1985	$7958.00	$961.00	$1079.00	$4106.00	$1391.00
1986	$7457.00	$553.00	$564.00	$4292.00	$1444.00
1987	$10190.00	$945.00	$440.00	$6444.00	$2184.00

Source: OECD Surveys (various years) and State Institute of Statistics, Monthly Bulletin of Statistics (selected).

Table 9.2   Turkish imports 1978–87 (in millions of dollars)

Year	Total imports	Imports from Iraq	Imports from Iran	Oil imports	Imports from OECD	Imports from EC
1978	$4599.00	$260.00	$489.00	$1396.00	$2791.00	$1873.00
1979	$5069.40	$578.80	$176.00	$1712.00	$3064.00	$1828.00
1980	$7909.00	$1237.00	$803.00	$3862.00	$3583.00	$2268.00
1981	$8911.00	$1564.00	$515.00	$3878.00	$4280.00	$2520.00
1982	$8734.00	$1039.00	$748.00	$3749.00	$4434.00	$2466.00
1983	$9235.00	$947.00	$1222.00	$3665.00	$4481.00	$2596.00
1984	$10757.00	$943.00	$1548.00	$3637.00	$5561.00	$2974.00
1985	$11344.00	$1137.00	$1265.00	$3612.00	$6361.00	$3547.00
1986	$11199.00	$769.00	$221.00	$2008.00	$7303.00	$4565.00
1987	$14163.00	$1154.00	$948.00	$3154.00	$9032.00	$5666.00

Source: OECD Surveys (various years) and State Institute of Statistics, Monthly Bulletin of Statistics (selected).

in 1983. This was an impressive change from 1978 when Iran and Iraq accounted for only 2 and 3 per cent of Turkish exports respectively. Whereas in 1980 approximately 40 per cent of exports to the Middle East and the European Community overlapped, by 1984 this proportion had declined to 28 per cent, indicating a trend towards complementary of markets rather than each becoming an alternative for the other.[4] Specifically, the Iranians bought wheat, semolina, phosphates, various iron and steel products, synthetic fibres, yarn, glass, cement, sheet iron and aluminium products. The Iraqis purchased foodstuffs, plastics, chemical products, cars, automobile tyres, clothing and iron and steel products.[5] Such diversity is a goal that

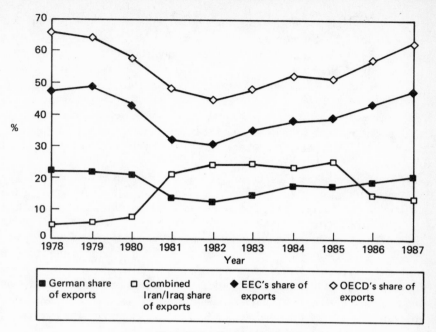

Figure 9.2   Export shares

Turkey would like to encourage and maintain as it would ensure a certain degree of stability in foreign exchange earnings.[6]

The successful export drive bought the Turkish economy and its leaders critical time to execute the transformation they were seeking. A demonstrable increase in foreign exchange earnings allowed the Turkish leadership, both civilian and military, to claim immediate and rapid results for its programme. Foreigners even started to talk about 'a Turkish miracle' and, in the IMF's view, Turkey represented an exemplary model where stabilization measures produced a rapid expansion of exports. The improved export performance enabled it to gain credibility and hence better access to international financial markets. A great deal of Turgut Özal's success in the first elections following the military takeover can be attributed to the economic upturn. After 1983, obsessed with the notion of increased trade, Özal's government undertook a determined campaign among Middle Eastern countries, and specifically with Iran and Iraq, to build on these burgeoning commercial relations. When short of foreign currency, and thus unable to make payments, Iraq, for instance, was offered generous credit terms. Admittedly, the Gulf War was not the sole contributor to this improved performance. None the less, both belligerents had been previously reluctant to buy from Turkey. Moreover, one of the complaints and worries of Turkish officials and businessmen has been the fact that, unless compelled by circumstances, Iran would rather not seek Turkish products.[7]

On the invisible side, transit trade and construction projects provided Turkey with additional sources of foreign currency. Transit trade picked up with the difficulties involved in shipping through the Gulf, and during the early years of the war, with large truck fleets, Turkish transportation companies were quick to take advantage of the situation.[8] However, as the war dragged on, both Iran and Iraq increasingly substituted trucks owned by their own nationals, and the general decline in trade reduced the transport volume.

Turkish imports from these countries are almost exclusively oil driven. The destruction of Iraqi ports on the Persian Gulf, and later the closure of the pipeline through Syria to the Mediterranean, left Iraq with a single oil outlet: a pipeline from Kirkuk to the Dortyol terminal at the Iskenderun port in Turkey. This pipeline, which initially could carry only 0.65 million b/d, was quickly upgraded to transport a million. Iraq also used land routes to ship out its oil. By August 1987, a second pipeline, roughly capable of 0.5 million b/d, connected the Kirkuk fields to the Yumurtalík terminal in Iskenderun, bringing the combined capacity of the two pipelines to 1.5 million b/d.[9] Furthermore, a third oil pipeline is being planned between the two countries.[10]

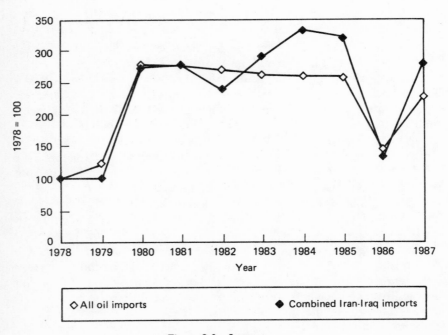

Figure 9.3   Imports

Turkey derives one third of its oil needs, or 6 million tons, from the Iraqi pipeline. The rest is marketed by Iraq. In 1985, the Turkish government made arrangements to buy another 6 million tons of crude oil from Iran.[11] The Turks also proposed the construction of a $4 billion oil pipeline linking Ahwaz to the Mediterranean,[12] with the apparent aim to cement the economic bonds between Iran and Turkey. This proposal has not, however, been received with enthusiasm by Tehran and opposition on technical grounds from such leaders as Prime Minister Musavi indicates a tough road ahead for the project.[13]

As shown in Figure 9.3, Turkish imports from Iran and Iraq are closely linked to fluctuations in oil imports since, apart from oil Turkey only imports small quantities of zinc from Iran and leather from Iraq. This accounts for Ankara's desire to secure its oil purchases from Iran by building a pipeline. The pipeline's importance was enhanced by two factors. First, all Turkish oil imports from Iran came from Kharg Island, where Turkish owned and registered tankers were often attacked by the Iraqi air force; and second, as a result of the erratic history of Turkish commercial relations with Libya, the other major supplier of crude petroleum.[14]

The Decline in Fortunes

While it has derived great commercial and financial benefits from the war, Turkey's fortunes have not remained steady. In fact, its initial gains have been slowly eroded as both Iran and Iraq had to curtail their imports as the war dragged on sapping their foreign exchange reserves.

Despite the advantagous credit terms offered by the Turkish government, and heavy loans from the Gulf countries, the Iraqis found themselves increasingly unable to pay for their purchases. As a result in 1983 the Turkish government had to agree to a two-year deferment of Iraqi payments to Turkish contractors. Since then this agreement has been renewed yearly and, in 1985, to further delay payment, Iraq issued promissory notes payable in two years at 1 per cent below the London interbank exchange rate (LIBOR).[15] By 1988, Iraqi debts to Turkey had reached $3 billion. For the Özal government, Iraq's inability to pay has become a major source of embarrassment and a potential political problem. As the payment in Turkish lira of part of the money owed to Turkish exporters in advance of Iraq's transfer of foreign exchange fuelled existing inflationary trends, the government had to curtail this practice, thereby infuriating exporters.[16] Özal's attempts to induce the Iraqis to be more forthcoming in their payments have not borne any fruits. In April 1988, Özal visited Baghdad to discuss these issues and ask Iraq to be more understanding of Turkey's economic problems. But these efforts failed. Not only did the Iraqi response consist of a 'no', but it also contained a not so veiled threat to seek other countries whose export credit policies were more advantageous than Turkey's.[17] Already, in 1985 Japan had supplanted Turkey as Iraq's main supplier.[18] Still, In June 1988, the Turkish government was compelled to suspend all new credits to Iraq and requested payment for at least $557 million of the $3 billion it was owed.[19] These measures have come too late for exporters, who are predicting that the real impact of the Iraqi non-payment will be felt in 1989 when large numbers of companies may simply collapse. To them the solution is for the government to force the Iraqis to pay,[20] although they themselves have no specific suggestion to offer. On the other hand, the decision to suspend credits to Iraq may yet prove to have been a costly mistake since it was announced a month before the cease-fire.

While the Iranians have generally been better at paying for their purchases, with the continuation of the war, as shown in Figure 9.2, Turkey has experienced a perceptible decline in its exports to both belligerents. By 1986, therefore, the war could no longer provide as much benefit to Turkey as it used to. Additional problems which emerged included the harassment of oil tanker traffic by Kurdish rebels in northern Iraq, often resulting in the death of Turkish drivers and the destruction of their equipment. More alarming than these attacks was the possibility that oil pipelines could be damaged by the same groups, thus threatening the flow of oil.

From a commercial perspective, Turkey can now hope to gain a great deal more from the war's resolution. Given the extent of the destruction on both sides, it can reasonably expect to obtain a fair share of construction contracts, especially in Iraq. If Turkish firms obtain sufficient backing from the government, it is expected that, in the medium run, some 10 to 15 billion dollars in reconstruction contracts could be won by them.[21] Conceivably, even Iran – where Turkish construction firms had made no inroads until 1983, and then only one such company established a presence – could award some contracts to Turks. Thus, from an economic point of view, Turkey is likely to benefit more from the cessation of hostilities than continuation of the war, though one casualty of a peace treaty may be the new oil pipeline the Turks would like the Iranians to undertake: given the mammoth reconstruction task ahead, Iran will probably be more interested in concentrating on rebuilding existing facilities than on constructing a new pipeline.

POLITICS AND THE WAR

Unlike its economic goals, Turkey's political objectives are not as easily discerned. And, while the economic costs associated with the conflict were negligible, the political balance sheet has been a mixed one.

The emergence of an Islamic revolutionary regime on Turkey's borders, at a time when Turkey was wrestling with a domestic upheaval of its own, was not a welcomed development. The Shi'ite fundamentalism of the Khomeini regime was an obvious danger to the Turkish state, where nearly 10 million inhabitants are of Shi'ite (or Alevi in Turkish) origin. Although, for historical reasons, this minority has been scrupulous in its embrace of the state's official doctrine of secularism, Sunni-Shi'ite antagonisms have been rekindled in recent years. Hence it was feared that, in the long run, a revolutionary regime determined to export its ideology would have a significant influence on them. And indeed, soon after his victory and before the September 1980 military coup in Turkey, Khomeini stated that the Turkish regime rested on the force of bayonets and 'suggested that Turkey's leaders were headed for the same fate as the Shah'.[22]

The Costs to Turkey

1. The Kurdish Insurrection: From the Turkish perspective, the renewal of the Kurdish insurgency in southeastern Turkey is the single most detrimental by-product of the Gulf War.[23] To be sure, the Kurdish problem is not new to Turkey. Since the inception of the Republic in 1923, there have been periodic rebellions in the East in support of Kurdish demands, either for autonomy or self-determination. The state's response has almost always been the same: the use of the armed forces to subdue.

The Gulf War's contribution to Turkey's problem was a direct result of Iraq's loss of control of its own border areas following the transfer of Iraqi troops from Kurdish areas in the north to the Iranian front. This enabled the Kurds to operate with much greater impunity and freedom of action. Most importantly, it has enabled anti-Turkish groups to penetrate the Turkish frontier to carry out operations and return to the relative security of the Iraqi side. Principal among these groups is the Workers' Party of Kurdistan (PKK).

Since the resumption of large scale PKK activity in 1984, the Turkish security forces have been unable to cope with the problem. For the most part, the PKK has managed to infiltrate at will, attacking civilian as well as military targets and inflicting heavy casualties on both groups. It has also had some local support, enabling it to sustain groups in the countryside.[24] But all infiltration does not come from Iraq. There have been charges of infiltration from Iran as well,[25] and Iranians have repeatedly tried to reassure Turkish authorities that their links extend to Iraqi Kurds and not the PKK.[26] Groups have also entered from Syria, either directly or through Iraq, although the government denies any knowledge of it.[27] In fact, not only does the PKK's leader Abdullah Ocalan reside in Syrian controlled Lebanon's Beka Valley,[28] but Syrian intelligence has reportedly had a hand in helping this group stage attacks across the border.[29]

The Iran–Iraq War not only resulted in a loosening of border controls, but it also created a fundamental change in the Kurds' strategic position.

Although both sides have used their respective enemy's Kurdish populations and groups as pawns,[30] as an anti-Iranian Kurdish leader was reported to have said: 'The Kurds never had the chance they have now. Never before have there been armed uprisings in all three countries.'[31] Adding to the woes of Turkey and Iraq, rival Iraqi Kurdish groups, such as the Democratic Party of Kurdistan (KDP) and the Patriotic Union of Kurdistan (PUK), have reconciled some of their differences.[32] In addition, the PUK has concluded an agreement of co-operation with the PKK.[33]

By 1988, the perceived improvement in their position led Jalal Talabani, the leader of the PUK, to argue that the issue was not whether or not the Kurds would have their own republic, but rather, 'whether that republic will be an equal member in a confederal set-up or whether it will go its own way'.[34] This confident view was expressed before the ceasefire and the subsequent ruthless Iraqi campaign launched against the Kurds on 15 August 1988. And this optimism was quite pervasive; his second in command had already envisioned a divided Iraq between its Sunni, Shi'ite and Kurdish populations. More importantly from a Turkish standpoint, he thought that ultimately fighting Turkey would be easier since, in this case, the Kurds could expect united support from the Arab countries.[35]

Alarmed at the changing strategic situation to its south and the rejuvenation of Kurdish organizations within its borders after a four year hiatus following the army takeover, the Turkish government responded by seeking to make up for Iraqi deficiencies.[36] In 1984, Iraq agreed to permit Turkey to engage in 'hot pursuit' operations against Kurds. On at least two occasions (14 August 1986 and 4 March 1987), the Turkish air force, carried out raids into suspected Kurdish strongholds in Iraqi territory. While it is not clear whether the Turks benefited from accurate intelligence, the raids – which probably killed more civilians than peshmerga (Kurdish fighters) – were primarily aimed at intimidating the Iraqi Kurdish organizations.[37]

The Kurdish insurrection in Turkey does not yet threaten the regime. But by engaging it militarily, scoring limited successes and keeping the issue alive, the Kurds have managed to shake the regime's foundations. The insurrection had also forced the authorities to finally acknowledge the existence of the Kurds.[38] This, in itself, is an important victory for a people hereto referred to only as 'mountain Turks'. Moreover, despite the best efforts of Turkish diplomacy, the Kurdish question has crept into the international discourse. A variety of institutions, including the European Parliament in 1987 and the State Department in 1986 and 1987, have condemned the Turkish treatment of its Kurds. In Europe, Kurdish emigre organizations have also become very visible and active in their campaigns against Turkey.

With the end of the war, the PKK is likely to face increasing difficulties in mounting cross-border operations. On the other hand, in its anxiety to demonstrate control of its own territory, Iraq is unlikely to permit the Turkish government to conduct cross-border raids. If its behaviour towards

Syria is indicative, Turkey, for its part, can be expected to avoid any unilateral action against the Kurds for fear of alienating the larger Arab masses.

A problem bothering Turkey during the war years was the prospect of getting drawn into the conflict,[39] which would have set back Turkey both economically and politically. After all, Turkey had paid dearly, on both of these fronts, for its 1974 invasion of Cyprus.

2. The Iranian Refugee Problem: One by-product of the revolution in Iran had been a surge in the number of people fleeing the new theocratic regime and its capricious dispensation of justice. This flow was further enhanced by those seeking to avoid going to the front. In addition to the sheer numbers, the Iranian refugee population in Turkey, which had swelled to 1.5 million,[40] presents two distinct, yet related, sets of security challenges. On the one hand it is feared that, with the influx of refugees, the Iranians have managed to infiltrate agents of their security service, SAVAMA, for purposes of destabilization. Some reports have even claimed that 10,000 Khomeini supporters have been sent into Turkey as part of a secret army.[41] The potential dangers posed by Iranian agents can be seen in the elimination of regime opponents and, as the investigation of the massacre at Istanbul's largest synagogue in September 1986 revealed,[42] in terror attacks.

At another level, the Iranians have gotten involved in the domestic debate on the role of religion. Alarmed at the resurgence of fundamentalism in Turkey, authorities – especially the military ones – were already combating the influence of all types of religious fundamentalist groups. The Iranian involvement in Turkish domestic politics was manifested not only in Teheran Radio's denunciations of the Turkish state for preventing religious students who wore kerchiefs from attending university, but also, for instance, in the arrest of Iranians demonstrating along with Turks in favour of a pro-fundamentalist politician.[43] In addition, the Khomeini regime provided support to Cemalettin Kaplan, a fundamentalist anti-regime preacher in Germany who had a sizeable following among Turkish workers in Europe.[44] At times, the Iranian radio or government officials have been even more hostile in their attacks on Turkey and especially its president, Evren, going so far as to telling the Turkish Shi'ite community that 'the time had come to take up arms'.[45]

Anxious not to disrupt its trade relationship, the Turkish government, for the most part, ignored such obvious insults. Özal even went out of his way to dispel fears of a fundamentalist threat from Iran when he said, 'I swear (!) to you, [religious] reaction does not come from Iran', a statement widely interpreted as implying that Turkey's mostly Sunni population was immune to Khomeini's brand of fundamentalism.[46]

Yet Özal found himself in a difficult situation with President Evren who was clearly concerned about these attacks and the opposition and the press, on the other hand, which made it a major issue. In these circumstances, he managed to negotiate an agreement with the Iranians on his visit to Tehran in June 1987 which stipulated the following: 1) no interference in each other's domestic matters, 2) avoidance of official statements against each other, 3) avoidance by state-owned radio and TV stations of broadcasting anti-Turkish or Iranian statements, 4) co-operation on border security, and 5) prevention of opposition groups from operating in their respective territories.[47]

This agreement notwithstanding, the problem for Turkey is that the conflict's end will not reduce its Iranian exile population. Already the government was trying to deter those still intent on seeking entry into Turkey by quietly publicizing cases of forcible repatriation.

Turkey's Gains

If on the domestic front both military and civilian regimes benefited politically from the improved economic performance discussed above, Turkey's major gains in the external sphere were due to the enhanced strategic position it derived from the Iranian Revolution and the War. The 'loss' of Iran, with its strategic position and US installations, had raised the obvious concerns within Western defence establishments. Of no less concern was Turkey's precarious situation on the eve of the Iran–Iraq War, when economic and political paralysis fostered an atmosphere of an imminent civil war that risked removing the second largest army from the NATO umbrella. The civil war did not materialize, primarily because the Turkish military intervened and in three years of draconian rule reshaped both the political and economic structures of Turkish society.

American-Turkish relations improved considerably in the aftermath of the Iranian Revolution and especially after the onset of the Reagan Administration which viewed Turkey as a vital strategic ally.[48] This improvement was all the more significant since Turkey's European allies were clearly disconcerted by the generals' rule and the demise of Turkish democracy. Hence, as the Europeans (even the Germans) were reducing aid levels, the US provided critical support to the regime. Visits by both Secretary of State Alexander Haig and Secretary of Defence Weinberger in 1981 were designed to reduce the military leaders' sense of isolation. In fact, military co-operation agreements were signed, and even tacit support was given to Turkey's position in its dispute with Greece by Secretary Weinberger.[49] Yet, while US administration has increased American aid to Turkey, it did not manage to delink the aid level from Greece's.[50]

Turkey's critical position was further enhanced when, in 1982, Iranian forces took the initiative and carried the war into Iraq. An imminent collapse of the Iraqi regime, with all its entailing implications, did not escape the notice of both Turkish and Western strategists. From 1982 and until early

1988, when Iraq managed to turn the tables on Iran, a great deal of speculation focused on Turkey's potential role in a débâcle of Iraqi armies. Most of the speculation emphasized the annexation of the oil-rich northern (Kirkuk) provinces of Iraq, where some of the inhabitants claimed Turkish lineage, in order to prevent the oil from falling into Iranian or an Iranian-sponsored Iraqi Islamic regime. In addition, such a move would also forestall the creation of a Kurdish state, a factor which has, since 1984, become a major irritant for Turkey. Some reports had Turkey directly warning Iran of its intentions to seize Kirkuk in the event of an Iraqi collapse.[51] While Turkish authorities have denied many of these scenarios, which have involved a Turkish 'dash to oil fields',[52] their persistence has contributed to an atmosphere of mutual suspicion between Turkey and Iraq, and especially between Turkey and Iran.[53] To some extent, this persistence can be attributed to a desire of some segment among the population to repossess territories lost during the demise of the Ottoman Empire to the British. Today, Turks allege that Iraqi citizens of Turkish origin are routinely harassed and discriminated against by the Ba'thist regime. Despite the civilian leadership's denials, the Turkish military added fuel to the speculations when, ostensibly to fight the Kurdish insurgency, it strengthened its troop deployment near the Iraqi border.[54] In any case, these moves at the military and diplomatic levels indicate that Turkey would not allow the Kirkuk fields to fall into 'hostile' hands.

For Europeans, who were uneasy with the military regime and the period of restricted democracy following the return to civilian rule in 1983, the strategic value of Turkey served to limit the criticism, especially since the latter had applied for admission into the European Community. Another factor that helped Turkey in this respect was the election of Prime Minister Papandreu in Greece, whose anti-Nato rhetoric worried the US and the allies.

Turkey tried to solidify its links with Middle Eastern countries and enhance its prestige in the area. It undertook a concerted diplomatic initiative as evidenced by the numerous trips taken to such countries by not only Prime Minister Özal and President Evren. Within the space of four years, Özal visited such countries, as Iraq three times. Similarly, a large number of dignitaries came to Ankara. This contrasts markedly with the pre-1980 situation when the elected governments' relations with these countries were cordial at best. The search for markets was a prime motivation for the improved relations on the Turkish side, whereas the respect countries such as Egypt and Saudi Arabia have viewed the Turks as a stabilizing factor. Following the Iranian Revolution, Turkey felt that it had clearly become the most powerful Muslim nation in the region.[55] This is an obvious source of satisfaction for the Turks, who often feel slighted by Westerners. For example, on the eve of Egypt's President Mubarak's visit, one weekly claimed that the Turkish President did not mind changing his plans since

Mubarak and King Hussein of Jordan 'always show him [Evren] the respect deserving of an elder'.[56]

With a large population and a Western orientation, Turkey has traditionally been regarded economically and militarily one of the strongest countries in the region. But considering that both Iraq and Iran, benefiting from oil, were acquiring wealth and resources far in excess of Turkey's abilities, the latter's relative position in the long run *vis-à-vis* its two neighbours was by no means assured. For instance, in 1982, at the peak of its capability, with a population one third of Turkey's, Iraq was able to import goods worth $20.5 billion, whereas Turkey's import bill for that year amounted to only $8.8 billion. Such acquisition of resources gave Iraq a tremendous edge over its neighbours, including Turkey.

The war had put an end to this state of affairs and forced the Iraqi regime, a vigorous opponent of NATO and the Western alliance system, towards moderation. Similarly, if the Iranian Revolution diminished Iran's economic and military power significantly, and eliminated the Shah's grandiose plan of making his country a 'regional superpower', the war has knocked it out of contention for a long time to come, thereby anchoring and solidifying Turkey's short-term position in the region. In addition, it has helped divert Iranian energies away from Turkey which, with its links to the US,[57] its sizeable Shi'ite community, budding Islamic fundamentalist movement, and a military seeking to consolidate its position in the country by eliminating all

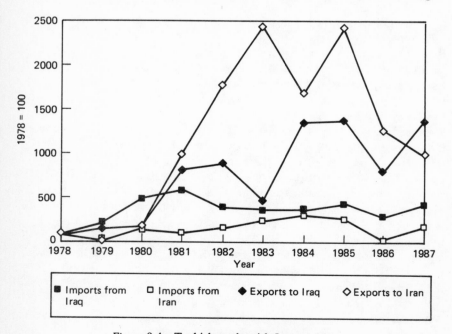

Figure 9.4   Turkish trade with Iraq and Iran

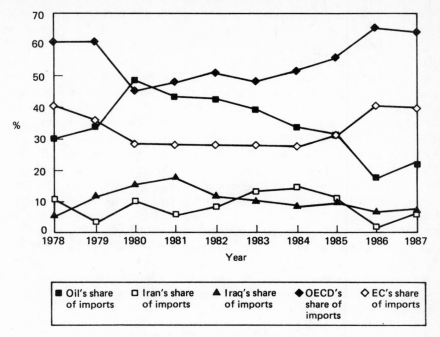

Figure 9.5   Imports as a percentage share of the total

existing and perceived internal threats, was particularly vulnerable. Thus, from a political and strategic standpoint, despite the problem associated with the Kurdish insurgency, Turkey did derive considerable gains from the Gulf War.

CONCLUSIONS AND FUTURE PROSPECTS

From the outset, Turkey declared its strict neutrality in the conflict between its two neighbours and offered its good offices to mediate, a suggestion welcomed by Iraq but refused by Iran. But, now that the war is coming to a close with the start of peace talks, what are the prospects for Turkish–Iranian and Turkish–Iraqi relations?

Despite the increased trade relationship, Iran's attitude towards Turkey has displayed a great deal of misgiving about its Western secular neighbour. Even during the Shah's reign, when both nations were members of the CENTO pact, Turkish–Iranian relations were not warm. Tensions and suspicions always existed between the two regarding the Turkish-speaking population of Azerbaijan.[58] The Iranian Revolution did not help matters much as the Islamic character of the new regime was diametrically opposed to that of the Turkish state and its military guardians' secular Kemalist doctrine. Recurrent Iranian criticisms of the Turkish government's internal policies, such as the arrest of Islamic militants or warnings against the influence of secular circles,[59] helped exacerbate already existing tensions. At one point, Iranian Prime Minister Musavi said that 'relations between Tehran and Ankara could improve only if Turkey pays respect to Muslim beliefs and values'.[60] Iranians have also shown little interest in supporting Turkish positions in international settings. For instance, much to the discomfort of Ankara, they have not prosecuted the Armenians who were caught attacking the Turkish Embassy in Tehran.

From an Iranian perspective, Turkish military collaboration with Iraq against rebel Kurds, who, in turn, were allied with Iran, helped create deep suspicions as to the real preferences of Ankara's government.[61] Turkey's increasingly active role in Kurdish areas was seen as potentially hampering the Iranian war effort which sought to accomplish a breakthrough in the north.[62] Thus, Turkey's declaration of its Kirkuk–Iskenderun pipeline as a vital economic zone did not deter Iranians from trying to attack it, either through Kurdish surrogates or their own revolutionary guards. For example, two months after the signing of a Turkish–Iranian agreement in June 1987, 100 Iranian Pasdarans were arrested crossing into Turkey on their way to sabotage oil pipeline installations.[63]

With the war coming to an end, some of these irritants are bound to disappear and the improved relations with Iran that have been developing since 1987 ought to continue. However, the post-war relationship between the Kurds and Iran has yet to be defined. Despite numerous reports to the contrary, Iranians have always denied having links with the PKK, although they readily acknowledge their support for the KDP and the Barzani faction. And unlike Iraq, Iran refused to sign a security arrangement with Turkey. Therefore, the issue of the Kurds will undoubtedly affect relations.[64] Ultimately, however, given Turkey's predominant interest in maximizing trade connections, it will focus on what it can gain from post-war Iran.

Iraq, on the other hand, has had a more cordial relationship with Turkey and two issues will dominate post-war Turkey's attitude towards its neighbour. The most immediate one will undoubtedly be the trade question and Iraqi debt to Turkish exporters and the Central Bank. At stake here is whether or not Turkey can consolidate the new relationship between the two countries, established during the war. If Turkey manages to maintain its level of exports to Iraq, and also obtain a sizeable share of construction contracts, then the war will not only have been very beneficial to it, but its end will also have come at a very opportune time.[65]

The second – and potentially difficult – issue that may have to be resolved relates to Iraqi–Turkish co-operation on the Kurdish question. With more resources at its disposal, Iraq will be better able to handle the insurrection in its own country as evidenced by the new campaign against the Kurds launched on 15 August 1988. This onslaught, in which the Iraqis have been accused by many, including the US, of using chemical weapons, has caused some 100,000 Kurds to flee into Turkey. Although Turkish authorities were reluctant to allow them in at first, they were forced by press reports to admit that the refugees had indeed crossed into their territory and needed help.[66] Though slight, there is also the possibility that Iraqi rulers may conclude an agreement with the now weakened Kurdish leadership. Such a possibility would be worrisome to Turkish officials given the potential for co-operation among the different Kurdish groups against Turkey, something that the PUK has advocated in the recent past.

While the Kurdish insurrection in Turkey remains the single most unwelcome consequence of the Iran–Iraq War, it has yet to reach a scale that is capable of threatening the regime. It should also be remembered that Kurdish rebellions are not new to this country. In fact, their re-emergence in many ways is also the result of a process of politicization and polarization which started in the 1960s and 1970s. It was after all Marshal Favzi Akmak, a long-time friend and military collaborator of Ataturk during the 1920s and 1930s, who predicted then that 'bringing roads, schools and civilization to the East will make these people [the Kurds] more aware. Then they will want their independence.'[67] Hence, the war may have merely accelerated and facilitated a longstanding process and cannot be seen as the cause for the rebellion.

Even if Turkey's political balance sheet may have been a mixed one, its overall balance sheet for the Gulf conflict shows that the economic and political benefits clearly outweighed the negatives. As argued above, the resurrection of the Kurdish problem may have been unavoidable. Were it not for the war, Turkey would probably not have been able to escape the economic morass it had created for itself at the end of the 1970s. The conflict provided it with critical breathing space to restructure its economic relations. It unquestionably was one of the major winners in the conflict and now stands poised to add to its gains once the hostilities are definitely ended.

But the future depends very much on the Turks' ability to exploit their advantages. On this matter one observation needs to be made. The war opened up many more opportunities than Turkey took advantage of. This is true with respect to both its relations with Western as well as Middle Eastern countries. Too much of its diplomats' energies were expended pursuing issues that ultimately were of little consequence to ongoings in the region. At a time when Turkey seemed the most secure of the nations in the area, and when its traditional rival, Greece, was led by a party and leader not known for their great sympathy for the Western alliance, one would have expected Turkish diplomacy to maximize its country's importance. This was not done. Despite efforts in Washington, aid levels actually declined with time and quotas on Turkish goods, specifically textiles, remained in place in both the US and Western Europe. In the Middle East, many of the Islamic countries have tended to take Turkey for granted. Despite its crucial value to Iran and Iraq, none of these ever expressed any sympathy for Turkish positions. The danger is that these gains achieved by Turkey may prove to be temporary and its wish to portray itself as a 'physical and moral bridge between the Islamic Middle East and the West',[68] will remain an unrealized potential.

Notes

1.   Indeed, before the measures were announced in January, Özal met with the high command of the armed forces in order to get their approval, Emin Cölaşan, *24 Ocak: Bir Dönemin Perde Arkasí* (24 January: Behind the Scenes of an Era) (Istanbul: Milliyet Yayínlarí, 1983, p. 317).
2.   In part because of the laws regarding lay-offs and in part because of the tense political situation, employers were reluctant to dismiss as many workers as they would have liked to. Also, in the past, government industrial policies had encouraged the acquisition of large plants leading to excess capacity in manufacturing. For both of these reasons, some industries were awash in stocks. For example, it was estimated that in 1981 OYAK–Renault, the joint venture firm manufacturing Renault cars in Turkey, was losing some $2000 on each car exported to the Middle East.
3.   All figures are tabulated from Appendix Tables 9.1 and 9.2.
4.   Halis Akder, 'Turkey's Export Expansion in the Middle East', *Middle East Journal*, vol. 41, no. 4 (Autumn 1987), p. 556.
5.   *Yankí*, 5–11 January 1987.
6.   Akder, *Turkey's Exports*, p. 562.
7.   *Yankí*, 5–11 January 1987.
8.   Compared to the Bulgarians, however, they were not quick enough. In 1985 and 1986, Bulgarian share of transit trade stood at 42.4 per cent and 34.3 per cent respectively, while the figures for Turkey during the same period were 13.3 per cent and 20.5 per cent (*Yankí*, 12–18 January 1987).
9.   Economist Intelligence Unit, *Country Report: Iraq*, No. 4 (London, 1987).
10.   *Middle East Economic Digest* (MEED), 24 June 1988.
11.   *MEED*, 8 February 1985.
12.   Economist Intelligence Unit, *Country Report Iran*, No. 1 (London, 1988).
13.   *Cumhuriyet*, 27 February 1988.
14.   As the price of oil declined, and Libya increasingly faced payment difficulties, it bartered its oil in exchange for imports of goods and services from Turkey, while at the same time refusing to pay for past obligations.
15.   *MEED*, 8 February 1985. Typically, countries borrow money at rates above LIBOR.
16.   *Ekonomik Panorama*, 22 May 1988.
17.   *Yankí*, 9–15 April 1988.
18.   Economist Intelligence Unit, *Iraq: Country Profile* (London, 1987).
19.   *MEED*, 24 June 1988.
20.   *Ekonomik Panorama*, 22 May 1988.
21.   Ibid., 28 August 1988, p. 46. Also see Ralph King, 'The Iran–Iraq War: The Political Implications', *Adelphi Papers*, no. 219 (London: The International Institute of Strategic Studies, 1987) p. 44.
22.   *New York Times*, 17 February 1980.
23.   Turkey's Kurdish population is estimated to be around 20 per cent, or roughly 10 million. However, as is the case with most statistics dealing with sensitive minority populations, these numbers have often been misinterpreted. This is

especially likely here since, until very recently, the distinctiveness of the Kurdish minority was not even acknowledged in Turkey. Turkey has the largest single Kurdish community of all its neighbours. Kurdish populations in Iraq, Iran and Syria number 4, 6 and 0.8 million, respectively.

24.   In late 1987, the Turkish authorities themselves finally admitted this fact as well (see *New York Times*, 22 October 1987).
25.   *FBIS-WE*, 12 May 1987.
26.   Ibid., 7 May 1987; *Cumhuriyet*, 17 April 1987.
27.   Unlike the Iraqi border, the Syrian–Turkish one is flat and has been sealed with barbed wire and mine fields, Martin van Bruinessen, 'Between Guerilla War and Political Murder: The Workers' Party of Kurdistan', *Middle East Report*, July–August 1988, p. 44.
28.   The PKK has also staged its last two general congresses in Damascus.
29.   Interview with a former governor of Mardin, *Yanki*, 31 March–6 April 1986. In brochures distributed to the population of the affected areas, the security forces claimed that the PKK was financed by Moscow, encouraged by Bulgaria and protected by Syria (*Yanki*, 31 March–6 April 1986).
30.   For further details on the Iranian and Iraqi manipulations of the Kurds during the Gulf War, see Borovalí, Ali-Fuat, 'Kurdish Insurgencies, the Gulf War and Turkey's Changing Role', *Conflict Quarterly*, vol. 7, Fall 1987.
31.   Quoted in Ali Fuat Borovalí, 'Kurdish Insurgencies', p. 39.
32.   Ibid.; see also *The Middle East*, April 1988.
33.   *Cumhuriyet*, 4 June 1988.
34.   *The Middle East*, April 1988.
35.   *Le Monde*, 16 April 1987.
36.   By razing villages during the war, the Iraqis have continuously tried to maintain a campaign of pacification of Kurds (*Wall Street Journal*, 13 July 1987). Ultimately, in 1988, the Iraqis used chemical weapons in the Kurdish town of Halabja, killing, by some reports, thousands of villagers, in order to dislodge pro-Iranian Kurdish rebels.
37.   *2000'e Doğru*, 8–14 March 1987. In fact, the 1986 raid had been directed at PUK villages and not PKK camps, while in the 1987 raid, the latter were the target (van Bruinessen, *Between Guerilla War and Political Murder*, p. 46).
38.   None the less, Turkish authorities are still uneasy about the whole issue and it is not clear what their level of tolerance is on this question. See interview with Mehmet Ali Birand, a Turkish journalist who has interviewed the PKK leader Ocalan in the Beka Valley there and whose daily was seized in Turkey when the interview apeared (*Nokta*, 26 June 1988).
39.   When surveyed, most of the members of Parliament of the ruling Motherland Party expressed reservations. A significant minority did, however, indicate that they would be in favour of an incursion into Kirkuk if necessary (*Nokta*, 10 April 1988), presumably to prevent an Iranian victory and/or the establishment of a Kurdish state.
40.   *Yanki*, 19–25 January 1987. Official estimates of Iranian exiles living in Turkey are deliberately understated for fear of upsetting the Iranian government who may want their repatriation also, because most of the Iranians have come illegally, the Turkish authorities themselves do not know the exact numbers. Some estimates put the number at 2 million.
41.   *Yanki*, 19–25 January 1987 and 27 July–2 August 1987.
42.   Judith Miller, 'The Istanbul Synagogue Massacre: An Investigation', *New York Times*, 4 January 1987. Accordingly, the Iranians were just one component of an operation that included Palestinians, Syrians and Libyans.
43.   *Yanki*, 2–8 February 1987.

44.   Ugur Mumcu, *Rabíta* (The Connection) (Istanbul: Tekin Yayinevi, 1987).
45.   *Yanki*, 26 January–1 February 1987.
46.   *Yanki*, 26 January–1 February 1987. Özal may be quite wrong on this issue since there has been very little movement towards fundamentalism among the Turkish Shi'ite community (*2000'e Doğru*, 14–21 March 1987). On the other hand, those who, like Cemalettin Kaplan, have embraced the Iranian-style fundamentalist beliefs are Sunnis.
47.   *Yanki*, 28 February–4 March 1988.
48.   Turkey's importance has never been in doubt. As Dankwart Rustow argues in *Turkey: America's Forgotten Ally*, 'it is Turkey's firm alliance with the West that makes possible Moscow's recurrent setback in Cairo, Baghdad, and other Arab capitals' (New York: Council of Foreign Relations, 1987) p. 109. But as the name of his book suggests, some think that Turkey has not had the attention it has deserved. Whether the fault lies with the US and its allies, or with Turkey, is open to discussion. However, as this chapter will also suggest, Turkish diplomacy has not always been quick to take advantage of opportunities presented to itself, no matter what the handicaps were.
49.   *New York Times*, 6 December 1981.
50.   At the US Congress' insistence, for every dollar given to Turkey 70 cents are allocated to Greece.
51.   *Wall Street Journal*, 11 September 1986.
52.   William Pfaff, 'Istanbul Scenario: A U.S. Dash to the Oilfields', *International Herald Tribune*, 1–2 November 1986. Also see, Eric Margolis, 'Turkey: Hot Seat Above the Gulf War', *Los Angeles Times*, 23 August 1987.
53.   See, for instance, *Cumhuriyet*, 5 April 1988, and *2000'e Doğru*, 6–12 March 1988 for extensive discussions of the scenarios, as well as the events that served as a foundation for these operations.
54.   *Yanki*, 9–15 April 1988 and *Economist*, 13 June 1987.
55.   From a military perspective, despite its NATO connections, the Turkish armed forces are not as well equipped as some of its neighbours, such as Iraq and Syria. The latter also have the added advantage of battle-tested divisions. Turkey's last major military engagement, excluding the Kurdish insurrection, was the Cyprus invasion of 1974 when, despite Turkish reports to the contrary, the armed forces did not perform well.
56.   *Yanki*, 13–19 February 1988. There are those in Egypt, such as Hassanayn Haykal, who claim that Turkey should not be trusted because it is pursuing a policy leadership in the region (ibid.).
57.   The Iranian ambassador in Ankara once called Turkey 'a lackey of the Great Satan', (*Yanki*, 1–6 December 1986) and Iranian radio claimed that Turkish plans to evacuate Kurdish villagers away from Tunceli were initiated at the US's suggestion to increase RDF capabilities (*FBIS-SA*, May 1987).
58.   Seyfi Taşhan, 'Contemporary Turkish Policies in the Middle East: Prospects and Constraints', *Middle East Review*, Spring 1985, p. 19; *Yanki*, 5–11 January 1987.
59.   *FBIS-MEA*, 24 June 1987.
60.   *Wall Street Journal*, 10 February 1987.
61.   Iran's anger over the Turkish military action against Kurdish bases in Iraq can be seen in accusations such as, the Turks had 'massacred innocent Muslim Kurds' (*Yanki*, 9–15 March 1987).
62.   Economist Intelligence Unit, *Iran: Country Report*, No. 1 (London: 1988).
63.   William Burgess, 'Iranian Special Operations in the Iran–Iraq War: Implications for the United States', *Conflict*, vol. 8, 1988, p. 28.

64. Recently, the Iranians have also refused entry to Kurds, who fleeing Iraqi attacks, sought refuge in Turkey (*New York Times*, 16 October 1988).

65. Already, with the ceasefire not yet in effect, estimates are being drawn suggesting that Turkey will obtain as much as $4 billion in construction contracts from both countries (*Cumhuriyet*, 20 July 1988).

66. Presumably worried by potential of PKK and PUK guerilla infiltration and collaboration with the PKK, the Turks have been anxious to repatriate the refugees quickly. Having failed to achieve this goal, starting in early October 1988, they sent smaller groups of 1000 Kurds back to Iraq.

67. Quoted in *Yankí*, 3 January 1988.

68. Interview with Turgut Özal, *Wall Street Journal*, 5 December 1983.

10 Israel and the Iran–Iraq War

Joseph Alpher

The Iran–Iraq War appears to have affected Israel strategically in a number of significant ways. Perhaps most critically, by pitting two hostile states and their allies against one another for eight years, the war gave Israel a 'strategic breather'. Here it juxtaposed favourably with additional regional events, such as the peace with Egypt, in reducing the regional threat to Israel. But this window of opportunity, and the fact that Israel did not exploit it in order to prepare both for war and for peace, are beyond the scope of this inquiry. Here we shall focus only on the direct relationship between Israel and the Gulf War.[1]

In the broadest sense the war contributed to a reassessment by Israel of its periphery doctrine – one of the foundations of its overall strategic approach to its role in the region and the world. The reassessment was motivated by additional factors as well – the Islamic Revolution in Iran, which in many ways generated the war, but also the largely unrelated peace with Egypt and the failure of Israel's alliance with the Lebanese Maronites. Yet without the Iran–Iraq War, this reassessment almost certainly would not have taken place. The war also provided the backdrop for a dramatic episode in Israeli–US strategic co-operation of the most intimate nature – the Iran–Contra affair; the denouement of that affair witnessed a period of sharp contention between Jerusalem and Washington. It juxtaposed with a number of additional issues to cast a shadow over the strategic relationship.

This chapter seeks to describe and assess the evolution of Israel's approach to the Iran–Iraq War throughout its duration, as Israel moved from a long period of open support for Iran and satisfaction with the persistence of the war, through a posture of neutrality, and finally to hints of a tilt towards Iraq and expressions of gratification that the war was ending. In discussing the foundations of Israel's strategic approach to the war, we shall argue that it was a mistake for Israel to support Iran after 1982, though a number of factors related to Israel's strategic status mitigated the consequences of that mistake; that Israeli strategists derived valuable lessons from the very healthy public debate generated by the recognition of this mistake; and that, as the war ends, Israel must be careful not to repeat its early strategic error.

ISRAEL'S ATTITUDE: AN OVERVIEW

The outbreak of the Iran–Iraq War found Israel holding to a traditional pattern of relations with the belligerents. Iraq was viewed with continued apprehension. The Iraqi record of having participated in all main Arab wars with Israel was reinforced in the late 1970s and early 1980s by the perception of Saddam Hussein's apparent megalomaniacal behaviour, his military nuclear ambitions, and his support for anti-Israeli terrorism. In contrast, Israel's attitude towards Iran in late 1980, when the war broke out, was characterized by attempts to pick up the pieces following the Shah's downfall: Israel was looking for inroads to the new regime, while simultaneously exploring the opposition's chances. Its approach was based on the assumption that, despite (or, indeed, perhaps because of) Khomeini's ideology and the vicissitudes of the revolution, Iran and Israel would continue to need one another as they faced a hostile Arab world.

During the early months of the war, initial fears for Iran's possible collapse, and a desire to exploit the opportunity offered to destroy the Iraqi nuclear potential, reinforced this attitude. Nor did Iran's move to the offensive in 1982 alter the Israeli approach. The negative ramifications of a possible Iranian victory over Iraq appeared to be lost on the Israeli decision-making elite. Thus Israel's overall attitude towards the Gulf conflict was until 1987 perceived as one of support, to varying degrees, for Iran, satisfaction with the inter-Arab split generated by the war, and rejoicing at the plight of the Arab world in general and of one of Israel's most intractable Arab opponents, Iraq, in particular.

It was only during 1987 that the Israeli perception of the Gulf War was modified, as Israeli national security policy makers took stock of the mistakes of Iran–Contra, grew to appreciate the link between Iran and their own difficulties with fundamentalist elements in Lebanon and Gaza, and adjusted to the ramifications of the American reflagging operation. With allowances for variations within the policy-making elite of Israel's broad coalition government of the years 1984–8, by early 1988 Israel's approach may be said to have reached a point whereby it was effectively neutral in the war itself. Indeed, it now perceived Iran as presenting a triple threat: militarily, in the event that worst case scenarios of an Iranian victory over Iraq were to prove true; ideologically, insofar as Iran served as a role model for Islamic fundamentalism in Lebanon and among Palestinian Arabs; and as an exporter of anti-Israeli terrorism, particularly terrorism emanating from Lebanon. By 1988 Israel increasingly understood that continuation of the Gulf conflict enhanced Iran's chances for success in all three spheres.

By early 1988, too, Israel had become fully supportive of American strategic aims in the region, and was prepared to explore a dialogue with the large coalition of Arab states allied with the United States in the Gulf. Even the most diehard Israeli proponents of support for Iran now felt obliged to desist aiding Tehran, if only in order to avoid a sharp US–Israeli conflict of interests in a key strategic zone. Indeed, if the American effort in the Gulf acted to improve Iraq's chances in the war then here was another reason even for supporters of Iran to seek an end to the conflict.

Finally, during the first half of 1988 it became increasingly clear that the war had spawned a regional arms race of worrisome proportions: more and more Arab states felt it necessary to acquire medium range ballistic missiles, and chemical warfare became increasingly legitimized. Here, then, was another reason for Israelis to want an end to the war.

THE BACKDROP: THE PERIPHERY DOCTRINE

As the evolution of the Israeli-Iranian relationship can only be understood within the confines of Israel's 'periphery doctrine', we must briefly digress to an exposition of Israel's core attitudes towards the surrounding Middle East. Only through an understanding of the periphery doctrine can we appreciate the reasons for Israel first supporting Iran, then abandoning its support.

Enunciated by David Ben-Gurion in the early 1950s, the periphery doctrine as a strategic approach to the Middle East derived from the perception – essentially correct at the time – that Israel was surrounded by a wall of militant Arab states, led by Nasser's Egypt, that sought its total destruction. Accordingly, Israel set out to establish relationships with countries on the periphery of the Arab Middle East that shared its fears of the Arab mainstream. These states sometimes also offered the additional attractions of pro-western regimes and large Jewish minorities anxious to emigrate.

Ben-Gurion conceived the periphery doctrine in rather subtle terms not always recalled by his disciples of recent years. Thus, the notion of alliances with the periphery was linked to the expectation that these would eventually generate a desire on the part of the Arab mainstream to enter into similar alliances with Israel – once the Arabs recognized how valuable an ally Israel could be. Additionally, the periphery alliances were seen as a means of attracting the interest of a great power, the United States – by demonstrating that Israel could be helpful in collaborating with key states in which the United States had a considerable strategic interest.[2] In this sense, the periphery doctrine interacted with a second strategic tenet enunciated by Ben-Gurion early in Israel's history as a modern state: the need for close military association with a great power.

The periphery doctrine led Israel into strategic relationships with Turkey, Iran, Ethiopia and Morocco, as well as the emerging Sahel states of Africa that feared Arab meddling with their Muslim populations. As a corollary, Israel also fostered ties with an 'ethnic periphery' of non-Arab or non-Muslim minorities within the Arab Middle East – e.g., the Maronites in

Lebanon, the Kurds in Northern Iraq – that shared its fears of Arab nationalist encroachment.[3]

Almost inevitably, strategic decisions concerning periphery interests came to be seen in Israel as operational matters, to be judged by the senior decision-making echelon (that usually knew periphery leaders intimately through clandestine contacts), without any need for the significant intelligence input considered requisite for decisions concerning the Arab countries. This perception was reinforced by the existence of an intimate military strategic relationship with some of the periphery states. In the case of Iran, this involved, in the 1950s and 1960s, primarily co-ordination in planning and intelligence, followed during the 1970s by expansion of Israeli arms sales. The latter factor, in turn, created a vested economic interest inside Israel in maintaining the relationship.

The periphery doctrine was one of the pillars of Israeli foreign and defence policy for about three decades. Viewed in retrospect, by the late 1970s its foundations had become considerably less viable, as the Arab core and the non-Arab periphery of the Middle East in many ways exchanged roles. On the one hand, the Sunni Arab heartland was becoming more stable, more moderate and more amenable to the need to deal with Israel politically rather than militarily. The Sadat peace initiative, and the emerging *de facto* coexistence between Israel and Jordan, were the principal expressions of this change.[4] On the other hand, the periphery itself was either becoming radical – Marxist in Ethiopia, Islamic fundamentalist in Iran – with sharp anti-western and anti-Israeli positions; or was abandoning Israel in favour of the Arabs – the Sahel and other African states; or, as in the case of the Maronites of Lebanon, it was simply proving itself unsuitable and unable to support a strategic alliance with Israel.

Nor, in retrospect, could Israel take its periphery relationships for granted even at their zenith. After all, periphery ruling elites had their own agenda in terms of exploiting the Israeli 'card' in dealing with the Arab world. Note, for example, the Shah's prescience in a remarkably candid interview given to Muhammad Hassanein Haykal in April 1975 – shortly after the conclusion of the Algiers Agreement, and at the height of the Israeli-Iranian alliance:

> We followed the principle 'my enemy's enemy is my friend,' and our relations with Israel began to develop. But now the situation has changed ... I think occasionally of a new equilibrium in the region ... Perhaps [it] could be integrated into an Islamic framework.[5]

In many ways, Israel's ongoing arms supply relationship during the 1980s with Islamic Revolutionary Iran, insignificant as it was in terms of Iran's needs, symbolized a lack of recognition on the part of the Israeli leadership that a major change had indeed taken place in periphery-core relationships in the Middle East.[6] Indeed, Israeli policymakers of all political persuasions – there is nothing partisan about adherence to the periphery policy – viewed the Gulf War as a manifestation of the ultimate logic of the periphery policy: by tying down Iraq's legions around the Shatt al-Arab, Iran effectively paralysed the Arab eastern front against Israel and kept a prime Arab belligerent out of mischief. Thus Iran appeared to be fulfilling its ultimate destiny as a periphery state.

IN THE AFTERMATH OF IRAN–CONTRA

The anachronism of support for Iran, and indeed, of strict adherence to the periphery doctrine, should have begun to be apparent to the Israeli policy-making elite after 1982, when support for Iran could no longer be justified in terms of preventing an Iraqi victory that would turn Iraq into a dangerous Middle East superpower, and, indeed, when it implied Israeli backing for Khomeini's long-term objective of exporting his revolution all the way to Israel's borders. Again, after 1983, repeated declarations of relative moderation regarding the Arab–Israel conflict on the part of the Iraqi leadership (albeit intended largely for American ears, as a means of encouraging a renewal of relations with Washington) appeared at least to justify a reappraisal by Israel of its support for Iran. Even the emergence in the mid-1980s of Iran as prime instigator and supporter of a radical Shi'ite movement in Lebanon dedicated to Israel's destruction, failed to bring out an immediate reassessment. Israeli fears of Arab designs, and belief that the periphery harboured similar fears, were by now so thoroughly ingrained, so instinctive, that it would take the shock of Iran–Contra to begin to dislodge them.[7]

Here it must be noted that damage to Israeli–Egyptian and other Israeli–Arab relations from Israel's support for Iran, and specifically from Iran–Contra, was relatively slight, for a number of reasons. For one, Adnan Khashoggi's revelations made it plain that pro-western Arab states and personalities had themselves been dealing with Iran, or were aware of Khashoggi's dealings. Indeed, insofar as they involved business arrangements between Saudi and Israeli businessmen, these deals themselves reflected the continued vitality of the Arab–Israel rapprochement. Further, one may speculate that pro-western Arabs were not a little envious of Israel's acumen in wheeling and dealing across the Middle East with no less than the American policy-making elite, a Saudi billionaire, and Khomeini's Iran. This image of Middle East power broker and even manipulator of American Mideast policy, was presumably one that other pro-western states in the region could not afford to ignore.

Then too, recent revelations indicate that even as Israel was selling arms to Iran, its decision-making elite was prepared to entertain ideas that might encourage Iraqi moderation and even tacit Iraqi–Israeli co-operation. Thus in early 1988, amidst the American media expose of possible impropriety by US government officials in 1985 regarding a deal to lay an oil pipeline from

Iraq to the Jordanian port of Aqaba, near the Jordan–Israel border, Shimon Peres claimed 'that the matter was discussed by the relevant Cabinet ministers [including Shamir and Rabin] and that all of them agreed not to object to the project . . . Peres and some of his top aides had feared an Iranian victory . . . and thus supported the pipeline proposal.'[8] Even earlier, in 1984 and 1985, Prime Minister Shamir encouraged American officials to suggest to Iraq that it reopen the long-defunct IPC pipeline linking Kirkuk to Haifa as a means of solving its oil-export difficulties.[9] There are indications that even earlier, Israeli officials collaborated with members of the US administration in plotting to overthrow the Khomeini regime in favour of a moderate Iranian leadership.[10]

True, these instances of flexibility on Israel's part were exceptions. As Aharon Yariv remarked, 'the concept of periphery is very deeply imbedded in the minds' of Israel's national security policy makers.[11] But the final mitigating factor is the simple fact that Israel – whether due to its own hesitations, or Iran's, or both – never became a major supplier of front-line weapons systems to Islamic Revolutionary Iran.

For Israelis, one strategic lesson of the Iran–Contra affair embodied recognition of the paradox of Israel's having indirectly assisted pro-terrorist elements centred in Lebanon – by arming their Iranian patrons – at a time when Israel was becoming locked in an increasingly ferocious struggle with these same elements. A second jolt to the periphery thesis was played out in the immediate aftermath of the exposure of the affair, as anti-Iranian sentiment and recriminations in the United States, Egypt and elsewhere made it painfully plain to Israelis that they were aligned with 'the wrong camp' in the eyes of their friends, and that they had abused their preferential status among American security circles. Then too, a rising tide of Islamic fundamentalism that was clearly inspired by Iran – in Egypt, Jordan and the Israeli-controlled Gaza Strip – began to bring home the consequences of having tolerated Iran's increasingly hostile stance.[12]

Finally, a number of veterans of Israel's defence/intelligence establishment, along with experts on Iran, sought to correct the flawed conceptual underpinnings of the Israeli (and American) decision makers who had entered into the Iran–Contra affair in the first place. We recall that the instinctive attitude of these decision makers towards questions concerning periphery states like Iran had been to treat them as operational issues, and to rely for assessments on their own experience rather than intelligence input. Coming as it did at a time when Israel's intelligence community was recommending that Israel explore contacts with Iraq,[13] the Israeli decision to enter into the Iran–Contra affair was based on a number of flawed assumptions:

—that the Iran of the 1970s so familiar to Israeli decision makers was the true, inevitable Iran that would be restored in the near future; as a corollary, that Iran's leadership was unstable and would be shortlived, while alternative, moderate leaders were waiting in the wings and were capable of returning soon to power (and this, for reasons never elicited, required that Israel defer to the present regime in Tehran);

—that Iraq remained intractably hostile, while Iran was never liable to threaten Israel militarily; indeed, that alliance with Iran might ultimately be better for Israel than the doubtful vicissitudes of a vague detente with Iraq;

—that Shi'ite terrorism in Lebanon could be dealt with through appeasement in Tehran (a supposition thoroughly clouded by the satisfaction of having 'discovered' that Tehran indeed pulled the strings within Hizballah/Islamic Jihad);

—and finally, that Iran genuinely faced the dual dangers of losing the war on its west and being overwhelmed by the Soviets from the north (these assumptions appear to have held sway primarily among the American partners to Iran–Contra).

Now, in the course of an extended and intensive debate within Israeli academic circles and in the media, the decision making echelon was largely disabused of most of these notions.[14]

THE FINAL STAGES OF THE WAR: ISRAELI REACTIONS

The most salient influence on the change in Israeli perceptions of the Gulf War, however, was the advent of the American reflagging operation. Now Israeli national security policy makers, whatever their predilections, had to digest the prospect that any lingering Israeli arms support for Iran would be perceived by their strategic ally, the United States, as directly contradicting American policy in the Gulf. In the summer and fall of 1987, American officials issued explicit warnings to Israel to desist from supporting the Iranian war effort in any way; the US even took the unprecedented step of exploiting a state visit by Israeli President Chaim Herzog to warn him that Israel 'must not shoot across our bow' in the Gulf.[15] Indeed, if the American public were to regard Israel as continuing to supply arms to Iran, then Israel could conceivably be held responsible for the death of American soldiers. It soon became apparent that the Arab press was intent on creating precisely such an impression,[16] and that the Israeli leadership would have to speak out in order to avoid the prospect of major damage to its strategic relationship with the United States, which was in any event still shaken by the reverberations of the Pollard Affair, aspects of Israel's ties to South Africa, the Lavi controversy, and the Iran–Contra affair itself.

Thus it was that during the period October–December 1987, in the immediate aftermath of the American reflagging operation in the Gulf, the Israeli policy making elite informally delineated a new policy on the Iran–

Iraq conflict. This comprised a firm consensus position condemning the war itself and supporting the American intervention in the Gulf, but considerable nuance and variation regarding attitudes towards either or both of the belligerents.

Thus, concerning the war and the American presence in the Gulf, Prime Minister Shamir stated on 20 November 1987 that

> the war between Iraq and Iran is nothing less than crazy. . . . We are not involved. . . . We have no reason to be involved. Iraq and Iran, both of them, are extreme enemies of our country. . . . We strongly support American action to prevent this ugly war from spilling over. . . . [it] is very useful and important for the security and stability of this region. We can see that all the countries, mainly the Arab countries, living in this area have the feeling that they cannot rely solely on themselves for their security, stability and existence. They can rely only on the United States.[17]

Defence Minister Rabin stated on 26 November, 'This war must not end in victory for one of the sides, certainly not Iran, which has the better chance of winning. Therefore what is required of us is noninvolvement and sensitivity.'[18] Earlier, on 16 November (in response to the US protest to Israel's President Herzog), the Defence Ministry had issued 'a renewed and firm directive . . . ordering that the ban on selling weapons to Iran, even indirectly, be scrupulously observed'.[19]

And Alternate Prime Minister and Foreign Minister Shimon Peres stated, together with Shamir, at a Cabinet meeting on 15 November, that 'Israel is not involved in the conflict between Iraq and Iran and has no interest in becoming involved.'[20]

On a more specific, semi-operational level, there were now differences of opinion among the three senior policy makers and others within the policy-making elite, over the advisability of a possible 'tilt' towards Iraq or its supporters. Peres, and to some extent Shamir – whose earlier readiness to deal with Iraq has already been noted – as well as such Peres cohorts as Minister Without Portfolio Ezer Weizmann, Minister of Energy Moshe Shahal, the Foreign Ministry Co-Director General Abraham Tamir, favoured exploring avenues of limited rapprochement with Iraq. Their efforts apparently reflected certain initial contacts with Iraqi officials. Rabin, supported by Minister of Commerce and Industry Ariel Sharon, opposed such overtures, preferring instead to remain neutral until such time (which he apparently assessed to be fairly imminent) when Khomeini passed from the scene and Israel's traditional friends returned to power in Tehran; meanwhile, as Iran was the strategic prize for Israel and the West, nothing should be done to overly antagonize it. Both sides to this debate made frequent use of prominent newspaper columnists to give free voice to their views, preferring to say little that was directly quotable.

Thus, a reliable report of 13 November in *Hadashot* quoted 'senior political sources in Jerusalem' to the effect that the Amman summit had

opened new political possibilities to Israel, one of which is identification with the moderate Arab bloc, headed by Egypt, Jordan, and Saudi Arabia, in their support of Iraq in the Gulf War.... A senior Israeli political source told *Hadashot*: 'We should develop a pro-Iraqi orientation, which may bear political fruit in the long run. In recent months senior Iraqi officials have indicated a willingness to examine the possibility of changing the policy towards Israel if the latter supports Iraq in the Gulf War.'[21]

Two days later the paper cited Foreign Ministry Co-Director General Tamir, along with Energy Minister Moshe Shahal, as being identified with this assessment.[22] *Davar* noted on 12 November that Economics and Planning Minister Gad Ya'aqobi, a Peres stalwart, had returned to Israel from a trip to New York, bearing Iraqi signals that Baghdad was seeking ties.[23] And Peres told former Egyptian Prime Minister Mustafa Khalil on 17 November (apparently in reply to messages of protest from Cairo delivered by Khalil and others, and generated by the perception that Israel was still aiding Iran), 'This is the message you must take back ... There is not a single Israeli that I am aware of who could compromise with Khomeyni ... We cannot imagine ourselves as an island of democracy and progress in an ocean of fundamentalism.'[24] Peres added in comments to journalists that such statements were to be seen as signals to Iraq and the US administration.[25] Minister of Energy Moshe Shahal (Labour) was also cited in the fall of 1987 as a prominent supporter of 'adopting the American direction and trying to approach Iraq'.[26]

Rabin and those of a similar persuasion usually confined themselves to comments that emphasized the greater danger to Israel presented by Iraq, thereby at least raising the implications that Israel should prefer Iran. Rabin's most publicized remarks on the issue at the time were made on 28 October to foreign correspondents in Jerusalem. They were summarized as indicating 'that the United States had been manipulated by Iraq into attacking Iran in the Persian Gulf war, and ... that Israel had not changed its own longstanding tilt towards Iran'.[27] Later clarifications issued by the Defence Ministry portrayed Rabin as distinguishing sharply between present-day Iran, which he strongly castigated, and the Iran that 'was a friend of this country ... during 28 out of Israel's 39 years of existence. ... why can't this situation exist again, when the idea of insane, Islamic Shi'ite fundamentalism passes away?'[28] At a minimum, Rabin's remarks appeared to reflect a rejection of any pro-Iraqi tilt by Israel (or, for that matter, by the United States), and a belief, common among those in Israel who still adhered closely to the periphery doctrine, that Khomeini's regime was but a shortlived aberration. However there was nothing in Rabin's nostalgic view of Iran, which he voiced frequently in private conversations as well, to indicate a pro-Iranian tilt by Israel at the time.

The remarks of those who favoured a pro-Iraqi tilt apparently reflect at least a few words of encouragement from the pro-western Arab camp, Iraq included. Iraqi Ambassador to Washington Nizar Hamdoon directed moderate remarks towards Israel when he told a pro-Israel newsletter in August 1987, 'I don't see the Arabs motivated by hatred . . . Iraq would be satisfied with any formula for a homeland acceptable to the Palestinian Arabs.'[29] This was followed by remarks made in Baghdad by Iraqi Vice President Taha Yasin Ramadan and Education Minister Latif Jasem, to the effect that Iraq now considered Iran to be a greater danger than Israel to the Arab World.[30] Iraq's ambassador to London remarked to *The Jerusalem Post* on 25 November 1987, that he saw no prospect of any warming of relations 'as long as Israel continues to arm Iran to the teeth'[31] – thereby implying that the perception of a change in Israeli policy towards Iran might be reciprocated by Iraq. Egypt consistently pressured Israel to develop a more positive approach towards Iraq, and the Egyptian newspaper *Al-Akhbar* reported in November that such a change was indeed taking place.[32] And while there was no concrete evidence of Israeli–Iraqi negotiations or contacts, Aharon Yariv revealed in December 1987 that 'there have been contacts, but according to the people who should know, they were non-productive' – Iraq refusing to reduce its anti-Israel propaganda or its support for terrorism. He added that Iraq had still not convincingly shown Israel that its protestations of moderation were 'a strategy and not a strategem'.[33]

Clearly, the legacy of enmity between Iraq and Israel – Iraqi participation in three major Arab wars with Israel, the exodus of some 200,000 Jews from Iraq in the early 1950s, most of whom endured considerable hardship, Israel's extended aid to Iran – runs deeper than that between, say, Israel and the GCC states. Israelis were also deeply troubled by Iraq's apparent ambitions to develop and use unconventional weaponry: first, the Osiraq weapons-grade nuclear reactor; more recently, chemical warfare. This had sharply escalatory ramifications for any future Arab-Israeli war. But Iraqi fatigue from the war with Iran appeared to have generated a more pragmatic Iraqi approach to the entire Arab–Israel issue. In any event, in view of the ambiguity of the evidence on both the Israeli and the Iraqi side, one may assert, at a minimum, that the Israeli policy-making elite, on a bipartisan basis, had by early 1988 distanced itself from any association with a pro-Iranian stand (though, in Rabin's case, only for the present), that it was supportive of American efforts in the Gulf, that most of it was receptive to the notion of exploring greater Israeli integration into Arab efforts to contain Iran, and that parts of it even contemplated efforts to support Iraq.

On a broader scale, the extensive internal Israeli debate over the issue of aid to Iran – which, in the course of 1987, spanned academic and national security circles as well as the policy elite and the media – reflected a growing perception in Israel that its own role in the region was changing: that it was increasingly recognized as a viable political entity by the Sunni Arab core of the Middle East, and that it must pursue inroads into the Sunni heartland with increased vigour, while carefully weighing its links with the geographic and ethnic periphery. The communal emphasis, however harsh, of the Palestinian uprising of late 1987 and the Israeli reaction to it complemented this assessment: all parties were increasingly aware that the issue at stake was less one of resolving outstanding differences between Israel and Arab states, and more one of finding a Jewish–Palestinian *modus vivendi*.

This brings us to the final phase of the war, from March to July 1988, leading up to the ceasefire. Here a number of additional developments helped generate a new assessment in Israel that the war had outlived its usefulness. For now the war, rather than distracting Israel's enemies and eroding their strength, was perceived to be spawning a new and dangerous Middle East arms race, involving missiles and chemical weapons, that affected the longterm Arab–Israel military balance. Moreover, the American 'tilt' towards Iraq, coupled with growing signs of Iranian fatigue and Iraqi battlefield superiority, caused even fervent supporters of aid to Iran to recognize that prolongation of the war implied the twin dangers of an Iraqi triumph, and of US–Israeli friction. Finally, the *intifada* emphasized for many Israelis the primary importance that should be attached to the Arab–Israeli peace process, for which Israel would require the goodwill of the US, Egypt and Jordan – all of whom were friendly, if not actually allied, with Iraq.

Thus Defence Minister Rabin told US Secretary of Defence Carlucci in late June 1988 that the war served no Israeli interest and had already generated a new phase in the Middle East arms race.[34] Indeed, in private remarks made in early September Rabin appeared to have placed the periphery policy in perspective in favour of an overall strategic emphasis on an Arab–Israeli settlement.[35] And new moderate feelers from Iraq spurred Shamir, Peres and Rabin to make remarks intended to emphasize Israel's desire for an end to the war without an Iranian victory.[36] Shamir, for example, stated in early July:

> I don't think [Iran and Iraq] will rush into battle again once that terrible war ends. They will want, quite naturally, to rest and enjoy peace. There have been rumours, moreover, that in Iraq there is some thinking in a different direction [regarding a more moderate line on Israel].[37]

This provides the backdrop for a brief look at initial Israeli reactions to the ceasefire. Many adherents of the periphery theory were quick to revert to form: Iraq, they argued loudly, would soon lead a new and fearsome eastern front against Israel, while, as one commentator put it,

> Tehran has begun slowly to return to prescience and a strategic approach. ... Iran's long term interest is to find non-Arab allies in the Middle East.

... Iran is almost isolated in the region and is therefore more likely than Iraq to appreciate the opportunities deriving from a renewed link with Israel.[38]

In marked contrast, those who had been pointing for several years to signs of Iraqi moderation, now felt reinforced. 'Iraq is an inseparable part of the large pragmatic Arab camp deployed to block the Iranian fundamentalist danger. ... Syria will [now] find a large, capable Iraqi army at its rear, and the IDF at its front,' noted Foreign Ministry Director-General Tamir.[39] Still others wavered between optimism and pessimism. On the one hand they pointed to the twin opportunities now presented to Israel to seek inroads to both war-weary Tehran and Baghdad. On the other they emphasized the new twin dangers of unfettered Iraqi military power and unrestrained Iranian subversion from Lebanon. Many also argued that Israel had reached the end of an era, lasting eight long years, in which the danger of attack by an Arab coalition had been effectively nil.

The most obvious fault to be found in these early assessments was that they were based on only half the classic intelligence equation that seeks to match capabilities with intentions. Iraq's and Iran's end-of-war *capabilities vis-à-vis* Israel were fairly easy to assess. Iraq had emerged from the conflict with a vastly enhanced military; its strategic air arm and armoured mobility were particularly worrisome to Israel. As for Iran, the war left it with little coherent military power, but it retained a revolutionary subversive base in Lebanon that might now be augmented radically, to Israel's extreme detriment. Yet the *intentions* of neither regime were clear. These depended largely on their evolving domestic and leadership situations, over which Israel had no influence, and which no one in the region even pretended to be able to foresee.

Nevertheless, Iraq's capabilities rendered it, again, a significant potential strategic threat to Israel, while the near-term Iranian threat was, at best, tactical. Further, Iran's capacity to pin down or preoccupy the Iraqi military was suddenly also salient for Israel.

Moreover, a fourth Middle East country, Syria, had now become the common denominator for almost any scenario offered. For Iraq to launch or join any new eastern front initiative it would have to patch up its relations with Syria. Iran's plans for Lebanon also required Syrian concurrence; would Iran's and Syria's strange strategic alliance withstand the end of the war? Could it constrain any new aggressive Iraqi intentions against Israel?

CONCLUSION

By the autumn of 1988, Israel faced the need to develop a new policy towards Iran and Iraq, based on new assessments. It was essential that this be done in an atmosphere free of cant and doctrine. The possibilities of an opening to either Iran or Iraq – or both – or, in contrast, continued enmity with one or both, would have to be weighed against an objective assessment of Israel's regional strategic interests. Certainly, Israel's growing capacity to dialogue with a large number of Middle East actors rendered it essential that that assessment not be distorted by anachronistic perceptions of a friendly Middle East periphery vs. a hostile core.

In assessing its future relations with Iran, Israel would have to take into account a large number of strategic interests: Iran's interaction with the moderate Arab states and its effect on the Arab–Israel peace process; the American factor; the fate of the Iranian Jewish community; Iran's activities in Lebanon; and its regional status – not as a 'periphery' asset, but as a potential major regional power that enjoys a crucial geostrategic location. Economic considerations would, for the near future, be relatively minor, if for no other reason than no Iranian regime would wish to be seen trading with Israel.

Looking to Iraq, two strategic factors would be paramount for Israel: the peace process, and war prevention.

Clearly, evolving Iranian and Iraqi attitudes, and their interaction, could soon provide surprises for Israel and the Arab states together.

Notes

1. I am indebted to The Washington Institute for Near East Policy, and its Executive Director, Martin Indyk, for having given me the opportunity in 1988 to collect many of the themes that find expression in this essay.
2. I am grateful to my colleague at the Jaffee Centre, Dr Shai Feldman, for drawing my attention to these aspects of Ben-Gurion's approach to the periphery.
3. The notion that the Palestinian Jewish *Yishuv* was a Middle East national minority that should seek alliance with similar minorities, was current in Zionist thinking long before the State of Israel was established. Thus, for example, in the 1920s a 'covenant of minorities' was proposed as a basis for Jewish security in the region. Other early formulations sought alliances with none other than the Shi'ites in Lebanon and the Alawites in Syria (both thoroughly anti-Israeli today). After the 1967 Six-Day War Labour Party Leader Yigal Allon proposed that Israel form an alliance with the Druze of Jabel Druze in Syria as a means of driving an ethno-geographic wedge between Syria and Jordan.
4. In this sense, the periphery doctrine may conceivably have succeeded in stimulating mainstream Arab interest in peaceful relations with Israel, and American interest in furthering this process – but it is difficult to substantiate this claim.
5. *Kayhan International*, 16 September 1975.
6. One significant but little noticed exception to this trend was apparently provided by the late Foreign Minister Moshe Dayan. Dayan indeed appears to have understood Ben-Gurion's ultimate goals in pursuing periphery relation-

ships. We must depend somewhat on surmise in order to illucidate this instance, as Dayan never recorded his motives in writing.

In 1977 and 1978 Dayan, newly appointed foreign minister in the first Begin government, attempted repeatedly to torpedo Israel's lingering clandestine ties with the Mengistu regime of Ethiopia, ultimately succeeding through the device of a 'slip of the tongue' in an interview with a Swiss newspaper. The parallels to the Iran–Israel relationship are illustrative: Ethiopia, a periphery state with a Jewish minority and a tradition of friendship with Israel, had recently fallen under an extremely radical regime, was fighting invasion by an Arab League member (Somalia), and generated fear and distrust among nearby pro-western Arab states like Egypt and Saudi Arabia. Egypt in particular was sensitive to events in Ethiopia, as that country controls the sources of the Blue Nile. Most of the Israeli decision-making elite was angry with Dayan over his attempts to end the link with Ethiopia, and advocated maintaining it even at the cost of angering the United States, which was pressuring Jerusalem to make the break.

Only later did it become apparent that, during 1977, Dayan had been deeply engrossed in laying the foundations for the Israeli–Egyptian peace initiative. In retrospect, one may surmise that Dayan judged the highly problematic Ethiopian tie to be an unnecessary risk for Israel to bear on the 'periphery' insofar as it could hinder far more important progress at the 'core' – progress for which Egyptian and American goodwill were obviously paramount.

7. For a more extensive exposition of the periphery theory and its effects on Israeli strategy see the author's 'Arms for the Ayatollahs', *Moment*, May 1987.
8. *The Washington Post*, 31 January 1988.
9. Private communication.
10. See Samuel Segev, *The Iranian Triangle* (New York: Free Press, 1988).
11. Major General (res.) Aharon Yariv, *Iraq and Iran: Imperatives for the US and Israel*, a speech sponsored by the Washington Institute for Near East Policy, Washington D.C., 10 December 1987.
12. For a discussion, somewhat behind the pace of events, of some of these arguments as they were circulated in Israel, see Thomas L. Friedman, 'Israelis, Wary of Islam's Rise, Question Tilt to Iran in War', *New York Times*, 31 October 1987.
13. See Akiva Eldar's citations from Israeli intelligence assessments of late March 1985: *Ha'aretz*, 4 August 1988.
14. For example, Israeli Defence Force Chief of Intelligence General Amnon Shachak noted shortly after the Iran–Contra revelations that Tehran, if victorious, planned 'to export the Islamic revolution to all states in the region, and to destabilize their regimes', with disastrous consequences for Israel. Abba Eban, Knesset Defence and Foreign Affairs Committee chairman, added that 'The greatest danger to Israel is the Khomeinist threat; I wouldn't sell Iran a broken typewriter.' Quoted in Alpher, *Arms for the Ayatollahs*.

Israeli officials who dealt with Lebanon, and who had intimate knowledge of Iran and had previously supported arms supply to Iran, also altered their views in light of the growing Iranian-proxy threat to Israel from Lebanon. Thus Uri Lubrani, Co-ordinator of Policy in Lebanon and a former ambassador to Tehran and ardent advocate of arms sales to Iran as late as 1987, declared in March 1988 that Israel should 'strike back at the Khomeini regime in every way possible'. JCSS seminar on 'Scenarios for the End/Continuation of the Iran–Iraq War', Tel-Aviv University, 30 March 1988.
15. Personal communication.

16.   For reports – spurious, to the best of this author's knowledge – of ongoing Israeli–Iranian arms and intelligence collaboration even in the aftermath of reflagging, see for example: *Al-Ra'i Al-'Amm* (Kuwait), 26, 27, 29 September and 17 October 1987; *INA* (Baghdad), 28 November 1987; and *Al-Nah'dah* (Kuwait), 14 January 1988. These and similar reports, including 'Jews for arms' stories, eventually found their way into the western press. See for example the *Observer* (London), 14 September 1987; *Washington Post*, 3 October 1987; and Evans and Novak's syndicated column, 'Is Israel Selling Arms to Iran Again', *Washington Post*, 9 October 1987.

17.   Yitzhak Shamir, *On the Eve of the Summit: A View from Israel*, address sponsored by The Washington Institute for Near East Policy, Washington, D.C., 20 November 1987.

18.   *Ma'ariv*, 26 November 1987, p. A6.

19.   *Ha'aretz*, 16 November 1987, pp. 1, 7.

20.   *Jerusalem Post*, 16 November 1987, report by Asher Wallfish.

21.   *Hadashot*, 13 November 1987, report by Ilan Kfir.

22.   *Hadashot*, 15 November 1987, report by Ilan Kfir.

23.   *Davar*, 12 November 1987, report by Yosi Melman.

24.   *The Jerusalem Post*, 18 November 1987, report by David Landau.

25.   *Hadashot*, 16 November 1987, report by Ilan Kfir.

26.   *Al HaMishmar*, 7 October 1987.

27.   *Washington Post*, 29 October 1987, report by Glenn Frankel.

28.   *IDF Radio*, 29 October 1987.

29.   *Near East Report*, 17 August 1987.

30.   *Ma'ariv*, 19 October 1987.

31.   *FBIS-NES*, 27 November 1987.

32.   Reported in *Hadashot*, 20 November 1987.

33.   Aharon Yariv, *Iraq and Iran*.

34.   *Ha'aretz*, 28 June 1988; see also *Jerusalem Post*, 20 July 1988.

35.   Private communication.

36.   *Ha'aretz*, 1 July 1988.

37.   *Jerusalem Post*, 12 July 1988, David Landau interview with Shamir.

38.   Moshe Zak, *Ma'ariv*, 1 August 1988.

39.   *Ha'aretz*, 22 July 1988. It is interesting to note that Tamir himself appears here to be developing a new variant on the periphery policy, with Iraq distracting Syria away from Israel.

Part III

The War and the World

11 Walking Tightropes in the Gulf

Thomas L. McNaugher

Despite the importance of Persian Gulf oil to American interests, the United States remained surprisingly aloof from the Iran–Iraq War for most of the war's duration. It supported the oil sheikhdoms of the Arabian Peninsula with formal rhetoric and occasional arms transfers. After 1983 it 'tilted' towards Iraq, but only marginally. And starting in 1984 it sought to choke the flow of arms to Iran, albeit with the notable exception of 'Iranscam', in which members of the Reagan administration secretly sold arms to Iran in return for the release of US hostages held in Lebanon. The Iranscam débâcle aside, US policies made sense in terms of the nation's overriding interest in preventing either of the Gulf's big powers from achieving hegemony. But they were minimalist policies that reflected lack of means rather than a lack of interest.

All of this changed in 1987, as the United States thrust itself more aggressively into the Gulf and diplomatic efforts to end the war. By far the more visible and controversial component of the new approach was the reflagging and subsequent protection of 11 Kuwaiti oil tankers, roughly half of Kuwait's tanker fleet, which prompted a sharp increase in the US naval presence in the Gulf and brought US and Iranian military forces into direct conflict. But the approach had a diplomatic component as well, focused principally on bringing international pressure to bear on Iran by means of United Nations Resolution 598, passed in July 1987, and the so-called 'second resolution', which called for a UN-enforced embargo of arms shipments to Iran for its failure to accept the cease-fire.

These policies called for an unusual degree of subtlety, balance, and co-ordination in US policymaking. On the military side in particular, US policy makers had to balance the need to support and thus reassure Kuwait, on the one hand, with the danger of stumbling into a widening military confrontation with Iran, on the other. All the while, of course, they had to maintain domestic political support for the operation while at the same time avoiding congressional efforts to invoke the War Powers Resolution. Recent history did not suggest that the nation could easily produce a sustained balancing act amidst these conflicting pressures. Indeed, with memories of the nation's Lebanon experience painfully in mind, even those who saw policy wisdom in reflagging worried that in the actual implementation it could produce a similar disaster.

171

Yet in practice US policy, reflagging in particular, never produced disaster. To the contrary, roughly a year after the United States launched its more aggressive approach to the Gulf war, Iran did what no one had expected it to do – on 17 July 1988 it signed the cease-fire document that US policy makers had helped shape. Not surprisingly, perhaps, the administration took some credit for this turn of events. Some in the defence department began to tout reflagging as a model for future US military operations in the Third World. Others have claimed that reflagging was the decisive element that brought Iran to the bargaining table.[1]

If the last argument is a bit extreme, reflagging must none the less be judged a success. But it is a success that provides a cautionary lesson for future US military operations in the Third World. US officials ran reflagging well, demonstrating considerable sensitivity to dangerous political dynamics in the Gulf. Yet they were never completely in control of the operation, for reasons likely to obtain in most such conflicts. If US forces are to be committed to such conflicts in the future, a similar degree of political sensitivity will be essential. But the history of reflagging suggests that policy makers should be careful indeed in agreeing to make the initial commitment.

ORIGINS

Because both tracks of America's Gulf policy originated in the months immediately after the world became aware that the United States had been selling arms to Iran, both appear to have been a reaction – an overreaction, to many critics – to the embarrassment associated with what came to be called Iranscam. But the administration was not as embarrassed by Iranscam as many of its critics felt it should be. Thus it sought merely to return to the status quo ante, reaffirming US neutrality in the war, asserting more vigorously its desire to see the war end, and re-emphasizing Operation Staunch. If there was a major new thrust to US policy, it was the effort to generate a new UN initiative towards ending the war. The impetus to reflag Kuwaiti tankers came from Kuwait rather than the administration, which accepted it with Kuwait and the Soviet Union, rather than Iran, foremost in mind.

The Mouse that Roared

Reflagging was born during the fall of 1986, when Iran, buoyed by victories at Fao and Mehran earlier in the year, stepped up its pressure on Kuwait, one of Iraq's principle financial backers. Partly in response to a sustained and damaging Iraqi bombing campaign against Iranian tankers and economic targets, Iranian attacks on ships trading with Kuwait increased substantially after September 1987.[2] To make matters worse, new tactics and technologies appeared for the first time, allowing the Iranians to attack at night, when ship captains had previously been able to move with relative impunity.[3] All of this occurred in the context of repeated Iranian calls for an 'offensive to end all offensives', which earlier Iranian successes made all too worrisome.

Thus, after notifying its GCC colleagues of its intent, Kuwait began to approach all permanent members of the UN Security Council in search of help. The Kuwaitis started with the Soviet Union, partly on grounds that the Soviets 'could act more quickly than the Americans' and partly because Iranscam made them suspicious of American intentions in the Gulf.[4] Whatever their misgivings, however, on 10 December 1986 representatives of the Kuwait Oil Tanker Company (KOTC) also approached the US Coast Guard with a request for information on the technical requirements for placing US flags on their tankers.[5]

Having informed themselves about the technical requirements for reflagging, the Kuwaitis officially approached the US ambassador in Kuwait on 13 January with the question whether Kuwaiti tankers flying the US flag would be given the same protection as other American flagships. The request apparently also indicated that Kuwait had approached the Soviet Union with a similar question. Significantly, Kuwait never asked for US protection, a point they made much of later. Instead, it left the question of protection entirely in US hands.

Official US rhetoric at this time gave little indication of what was afoot. In statements on 23 January and 25 February 1987, President Reagan expressed his fear that the Iran–Iraq War might spill over and threaten the security of other Gulf states. He reaffirmed that the United States remained 'determined to ensure the free flow of oil through the Strait of Hormuz'. But he also referred explicitly to his commitment 'to supporting the self-defence of our friends in the region'.[6] Taken together with the President's reference in February to his interest in 'an international effort to bring Iran into negotiations', these two statements suggested that the United States wished to express its growing concern with the war diplomatically rather than through more active involvement in the Gulf itself.

Yet policy decisions were at the same moment ensuring that the US Navy would become more intimately involved in Kuwait's defence. At the end of January, aware of Kuwaiti-Soviet dealings but unaware of any Soviet agreement to reflag, the United States gave Kuwait the answer it was seeking, and in so doing laid the groundwork for what was to follow: it informed Kuwait that it would protect reflagged Kuwaiti tankers as it protected all US flagships.

The tension between public rhetoric and key policy decisions is best explained by the 'business as usual' perspective on the operation that seems to have prevailed among US decision makers. Up to that point the US Navy had found intermittent convoys an effective deterrent to Iranian action.

Indeed, Iran refrained from harassing ships carrying other flags when they sailed in the vicinity of US warships. Even the CIA's risk assessment, made much of by members of congress who later claimed that the administration had underestimated the risks of an Iranian response to reflagging, apparently agreed that if the Iranians responded to reflagging it would be with terrorism rather than direct attacks on US warships.[7] Initial briefings suggested that reflagging would require little if any increase in the size of MIDEASTFOR,[8] while defence department military planners had little to do with the initial reflagging decision.[9] And although the allies were briefed on US planning in April, no one felt that they could be expected to help protect US flagships, hence no help was requested.

These initial and very low-key plans soon underwent two substantial changes, both in response to events and 'enemies' outside the Gulf itself. The first came late in February 1987, when the Kuwaitis formally asked the United States to reflag six of their tankers, noting in passing that the Soviet Union had agreed to reflag five. US officials reacted vigorously, urging Kuwait to give the Soviets a much smaller role on Kuwait's behalf, in return for which the United States would reflag all 11 Kuwait tankers. Interviews suggest that no one expected Kuwait to eliminate Moscow's participation entirely, and in this these officials were correct. None the less, in the final Kuwaiti-Soviet agreement, Moscow was reduced to chartering three of their smaller tankers to Kuwait. Having begun life as a low-key move to reassure Kuwait, reflagging thus became a much larger and more formidable vehicle for keeping the Soviets out of the Gulf.[10]

The second change to the original reflagging plan came on 17 May when an Iraqi Mirage fired two Exocet missiles into the side of the *USS Stark*, killing 37 American sailors. At this point the US naval presence in the Gulf, and with it ongoing plans to reflag Kuwaiti tankers, burst into public view. The need to justify the policy publicly, and especially on Capitol Hill, changed the scope of the operation. What had begun, as 'business as usual' quickly became a full-time protection operation. Within three days of the *Stark* attack Admiral William Crowe, the Chairman of the Joint Chiefs of Staff, was given presidential approval to increase MIDEASTFOR's size from six ships to nine.[11] With the congress pressing to ensure that the administration had covered all possible contingencies, the defence department raised the ante still further in the weeks that followed. By the end of June the battleship Missouri and its escorts had been ordered into the Arabian Sea, making it the first US battleship to deploy to the Indian Ocean. By the time the first convoy of reflagged Kuwaiti tankers began the two-day journey up the Gulf on 17 July, the US fleet in or near the Gulf had grown to roughly 33 vessels, largely in response to domestic political pressure.

Significantly, domestic politics also made it harder to define the overall purpose of reflagging and the mission of the US Gulf fleet. Iran began to figure more prominently in official US rhetoric after the *Stark* incident.

Partly this reflected a general understanding that Iranian power had prompted Kuwait's invitation; were the US to fail to exercise its power in this case the resulting vacuum would be filled by the Soviet Union or Iran. But the emphasis on Iran also seems to have been forced by domestic political expedients. Although the *USS Stark* had been hit by an Iraqi missile, the president was quick to blame Iran and its failure to end the war. And the need to 'sell' the policy also raised Iran's prominence, if only because of Kuwait's unpopularity with pro-Israeli members of congress.[12]

Carried to their extreme, however, these arguments risked suggesting that the United States and Iran were headed for a showdown, threatening the administration's continuing protestations of neutrality and risking a congressional move to invoke the War Powers Resolution. Thus, while the administration spoke ominously of the general problem of Iranian power in the Gulf, it continued to downplay the Iranian threat to US naval vessels. In his statement before congress in June, for example, Mr Weinberger held that the 'Iranian threat to US forces is primarily based on potential identification errors or a unilateral decision of a local commander'. The assumption remained that 'Iran has generally not attacked merchant ships associated with superpowers and avoids confrontation with warships of any nation.' Weinberger mentioned the possibility of mines, but suggested that Iran would use these against Kuwaiti ports as part of a 'non-attributable ... attack against Kuwait'.[13] When remarks by Assistant Secretary of State Richard Murphy suggested that an Iranian attack on a US naval vessel could provoke a US–Iranian war, White House spokesman Marlin Fitzwater quickly contradicted him.[14]

These cross-pressures help explain prominent ambiguities in the official mission statement for the reflagging operation, as reflected in public testimony by Casper Weinberger and Undersecretary of State Michael Armacost.[15] Armacost's testimony, for example, stated that reflagging's principle purpose was 'to help Kuwait counter immediate intimidation and thereby discourage Iran from similar attempts against the other moderate Gulf states' – implying either that defending Kuwaiti vessels flying US flags would somehow deter Iranian attacks on other vessels, or that the United States might reflag the vessels of other friendly Arab states if Iran sought to coerce them as it had Kuwait.[16] Weinberger was clearer in asserting that 'MIDEASTFOR is tasked with providing protection to US-flagged vessels including the reflagged Kuwaiti vessels sailing within or transiting through the international waters of the Gulf of Oman, Strait of Hormuz, and the Persian Gulf.'[17] But the defence secretary who had argued so vociferously in the years before that US military forces should only be committed with a concise statement of objectives also gave MIDEASTFOR the mission of 'assisting friendly regional states' – whatever that meant. And he went on to argue that 'the continued presence of US forces in the Persian Gulf . . . acts as a moderating element with regard to the Iran–Iraq War'.[18] These statements made sense only if one made the questionable assumption that reflagging operations would deter Iran from attacks on other Gulf shipping. The door was being left open either for embarrassment should the Iranians misbehave, or for an expansion of the Navy's mission that might have anything but a 'moderating' effect with regard to the Iran–Iraq War.

Meanwhile the president, presumably in the interest of reinforcing the appearance of neutrality, consistently referred to reflagging as a commitment to 'freedom of navigation' and 'preserving the free flow of oil through the Strait of Hormuz'. But the tanker war had never seriously threatened the flow of oil from the Gulf. And official policy statements made clear that reflagging 'was not ... an open-ended unilateral American commitment to defend all non-billigerent shipping in the Persian Gulf'.[19] Although Iran quickly violated official expectations, the president's insistence on US neutrality, combined with increasingly effective consultations with key members of congress, effectively mooted the War Powers issue. But it did nothing to provide either the public or military planners with a realistic view of what was going on.

War powers considerations thus make it difficult to judge Iran's actual place in US military planning. Still, it seems clear that reflagging's principle goal was not to pressure Iran but to reassure Kuwait, hopefully in a way that would avoid conflict with Iran. Beyond this, reflagging was meant to keep the Soviet navy out of the Gulf. Whether or not reflagging was ultimately decisive in bringing Iran to the bargaining table, this was not the policy's original intent.[20]

A Resolution 'With Teeth In It'

If the United States seemed to be reacting to events in shaping military policy towards the Gulf, it took the initiative on the diplomatic track. And while the initiative here may have been partly a response to revelations about US arms sales to Iran, there were independent grounds for optimism about the prospects for yet another UN resolution on the Iran–Iraq War. By December 1986 the tanker war had reached levels that had most countries and shipping firms more alarmed than ever before; Iran's silkworms were particularly worrisome. Iran's successful ground offensives in 1986, especially the seizure of Fao in February, raised the spectre of an Iran on the verge of victory. Partly for this reason, but partly for reasons of their own, both superpowers were coming to see increasing danger in the war's continuance. Indeed, by bringing both superpower navies more fully into the Gulf, Kuwait gave each superpower another reason to seek an end to the war.

US diplomats saw in these events an opportunity to fashion a UN resolution 'with teeth in it'. From the start, they sought not simply to table another ceasefire resolution, but to fashion sanctions that would automatically be levied on belligerents that refused to agree to a ceasefire – namely Iran. In this sense it is fair to say that the diplomatic track of US Gulf policy was aimed directly at pressuring Iran. As one US official put it, the aim was to 'internationalize Operation Staunch'. Significantly, in US public rhetoric, the twin notions of a ceasefire resolution and an arms embargo were never separated; from the start they were two sides of the same coin.

Launched in January, the UN initiative produced no working consensus until June. Two major bones of contention account for the delay. One involved Iraq's insistence on wording that called for a withdrawal to international borders immediately after a ceasefire went into effect. The ploy was understandable, a cheap way for Iraq to regain territory it was either unable or unwilling to reconquer. Precisely for that reason, however, Iraq's wording guaranteed an Iranian rejection. European diplomats tried to soften the proposed wording by allowing for a delay between the ceasefire and any troop withdrawals, but the United States, 'after an Iraqi intervention in Washington', rejected the effort.[21] The rejection held, and UN Resolution 598 as it was ultimately passed demanded that:

> as a first step towards a negotiated settlement, Iran and Iraq observe an immediate ceasefire, discontinue all military actions on land, at sea and in the air, and withdraw all forces to the internationally recognized boundaries without delay.[22]

However much it professed neutrality, the United States seems clearly to have sided with Iraq at the United Nations. It remains unclear, however, whether this was the result of a high level agreement between Iraqi President Saddam Hussein and Deputy Secretary of State Richard Murphy.[23] Iraq participated in UN discussions, while Iran generally remained aloof; it was probably natural under these circumstances that a ceasefire resolution would be biased in Iraq's favour. Moreover, Iraqi diplomats, buoyed and confident after their military and successfully defeated Iran's 'offensive to end all offensives' in January, made it plain that they would reject any resolution lacking the proper wording.[24] Theoretically, the Security Council could have probed Iraq's intentions, holding out the threat that Iraq, too, would be subjected to an arms embargo if it failed to agree with the ceasefire resolution. But that would have placed the whole diplomatic initiative at risk. Instead, US diplomats supported Iraq's demands while seeking to mollify Iran with references to an impartial body to determine responsibility for starting the war, and to the 'need for reconstruction efforts, with appropriate international assistance, once the conflict is ended'.[25]

The second source of delay in forging the new diplomatic initiatives centred on the substance and place of the 'teeth' US diplomats wished to imbed in the resolution. With the British in particular balking at economic sanctions on grounds that they would not work, agreement was reached on an arms embargo. This sat well with US officials, since it echoed their efforts to reinvigorate 'Operation Staunch' in the wake of Iranscam. Still, enough debate remained on the issue to stall Security Council agreement until late June, when the sanctions portion of the original resolution was split off to become the 'Second Resolution'. Resolution 598 was passed unanimously on 20 July 1987, but the sanctions US diplomats had sought became a matter of continuing diplomacy for some months to come.[26]

Resolution 598 was passed, of course, with Soviet help. Indeed, while US policy in the Gulf itself was designed largely to prevent Soviet co-operation, the diplomatic track of US Gulf policy depended on it. Official US policy declarations were in fact quite explicit in separating the two theatres of US action:

> The United States ... does not want to legitimize the Soviet naval presence in the Gulf as a participant in an international shipping protection plan, but we are not adverse to working with the USSR in multilateral efforts to end the war.[27]

If anyone had considered the proposition that Moscow might not care for such a deal – that in the absence of US willingness to co-operate in the Gulf the Soviets might withhold their co-operation in the United Nations – it was certainly not reflected in public documents.

THE SUMMER OF IRAN'S DISCONTENT

Reflagging caught Iran at a bad time. After the military successes of 1986 came the winter offensive of 1987, an 'offensive to end all offensives' that ended in costly failure.[28] Waning military fortunes left Iran's revolutionary regime boxed-in by its own fierce rhetoric, which for six years had promised the fall of Iraq's president, Saddam Hussein. Pragmatic leaders in Tehran faced the immediate problem of placating radical elements unwilling to give up hope of victory. That effort was not helped by revelations that key leaders like Majlis speaker Hashemi-Rafsanjani had been dealing with the Americans and the Israelis. Although the Ayatollah Khomeini backed Rafsanjani, calling US embarrassment in the affair 'a great victory for the revolution', the fact that Khomeini had to intervene in the dispute at all suggests that factionalism was on the rise.

Reflagging only made things worse. It presented radical elements in Iran with the opportunity to reinvigorate sagging revolutionary elan, possibly to isolate and weaken more pragmatic leaders, by angling to pick a fight with the 'Great Satan'. Politics in Tehran thus was likely to become more contentious and personally risky for those participating. After a year in which Iran had opened new political relationships, including a covert one with the Great Satan itself, reflagging signalled a serious reversal. Although it was unclear how far the United States would succeed in reinvigorating

Operation Staunch, no one in Tehran could have welcomed the prospect of more troubles and expense in obtaining arms. Finally, save for the few who welcomed it, an escalating conflict in the Gulf with US naval forces could all too easily bring destruction: who knew how far the Americans would go?

To be sure, no one in Tehran was willing to shrink from the prospect of a confrontation with the United States – at least in public. In fact, from April, when Iranians first heard about reflagging, through July, when US reflagging operations began, Iranians of all stripes echoed Hashemi-Rafsanjani in stating that they would not refrain from striking 'just because some countries' oil is moved on an American or Soviet ship'.[29] True to their word, the Iranians confronted Soviet warships in the Gulf twice in May, once with mines, and once with speedboats whose crews fired machine guns and grenade launchers.[30]

Notwithstanding such minor skirmishes, Iran tended towards caution in its approach to the superpowers, its leaders arguing generally that reflagging would raise tensions in the area, which, indeed, it would. Meanwhile, pressure was directed towards Kuwait. This involved direct threats, as in Prime Minister Mir-Hussein Musavi's statement that,

> If Kuwait thinks it can help Saddam and still remain safe under the superpowers' flag, it is mistaken. Kuwait is so vulnerable that such arrangements cannot help.[31]

But Iran's strategy also involved indirect pressure aimed at isolating Kuwait within the GCC. Iranian diplomacy towards Oman, the UAE, and Qatar flourished in the spring of 1987, as these countries seemingly expressed their disapproval of Kuwait's actions.[32]

For a while Iran seemed hopeful that the United States would call the whole thing off. Rafsanjani's comment in the wake of the *Stark* incident that '[l]aw-making centres in the U.S. are against [reflagging]' showed his usual sensitivity to American domestic politics, albeit misplaced in this case.[33] It may well be with some hope of fuelling the War Powers debate in the United States that Iranians referred often to America's Lebanon experience and to the equally unhappy 'quagmire' President Reagan was about to enter in the Gulf.[34] Iranian hopes in this regard rose even further after the Venice Summit in early June, which Iranians took to involve a European rejection of US military plans.

Yet by the time of the Venice Summit Iran was itself moving towards isolation, seemingly by choice. When in May British police arrested and – according to the Iranian – beat an Iranian diplomat stationed in Manchester, the Iranians quickly reciprocated, detaining and beating British diplomat Edward Chaplin on 9 May. In the diplomatic crisis that followed the Iranians seemed anxious for a fight. They got one; although diplomatic relations between the two countries were never severed, they were downgraded.[35] Soon thereafter Iran found itself in a similar diplomatic battle with the French over

French efforts to interrogate Iranian diplomats in Europe concerning terrorist attacks in France. In the course of the diplomatic struggle Iranian gunboats attacked a French cargo ship in the Gulf. France and Iran severed relations on 17 July, and shortly thereafter France announced that it would provide naval escorts for tankers starting at roughly the same time that US reflagged tankers began their voyages through the Gulf.[36]

Iran's isolation grew still more in July, when the *USS Bridgeton*, the first of Kuwait's reflagged tankers to make the voyage north, struck a mine north of Bahrain on 24 July. Thereafter the world was treated to the spectacle of US warships meekly following the *Bridgeton*, now a 'minesweeper', as it limped towards Kuwait's harbour. Seemingly adding to its embarrassment, the United States expressed uncertainty about just who laid the mines ('invisible hands', the Iranians retorted), and did not retaliate. Whether what followed was the result of deliberate choice in Tehran or sheer euphoria among Iran's Revolutionary Guards remains unclear, but over the next month mines appeared everywhere in the Gulf, as well as outside the Strait of Hormuz in the Gulf of Oman. Specifically in response to the latter threat, Great Britain finally agreed to send four minesweepers to join its existing Gulf flotilla. France also agreed at this time to send two minesweepers to the Gulf area. In September, Italy, Denmark, and Belgium followed suit. Having made much of Europe's rejection of reflagging at the Venice Summit, the Iranians now had themselves to blame for bringing five European navies more deeply into the Gulf.

The Arab world, too, moved towards a more confrontational stance with Iran, although in this case Iran's complicity in events remains debatable. On 31 July, Saudi police fired on Iranian demonstrators visiting Mecca, killing several hundred. Although specifics in the incident were and remain obscure, the Saudis were able to drum up support among most Arab states for their position that Iranian pilgrims had attempted to storm the Mosque, and that Iranians seemed to understand nothing but force. Saudi and Kuwaiti leaders thus launched a campaign to focus Arab pressure on Iran that would culminate four months later in an Arab League communique from the Amman summit roundly condemning Iranian behaviour, raising the Iran–Iraq War to top priority in the Arab world, and bringing strong pressure to bear on Syria to sever its ties with Iran.

In the wake of Iran's summer débâcles, relative calm returned to the Gulf, largely because Iraq called its tanker war to a halt for most of July and August in order to give Iran time to consider accepting Resolution 598. Significantly, Iranian oil exports quickly rose to 2.2 MBD, and with them rose Iran's income, and evidently its confidence as well. Iranians poked fun at US warships, and at the limited number of convoys the United States had escorted in the wake of the *Bridgeton* incident.[37] They also thanked the United States for helping to protect their oil exports, and called attention to the fact that Iranian warships and minesweepers were also playing a role in securing freedom of navigation in the Gulf.[38]

As calm returned to the Gulf, seriousness and subtlety returned to Iranian strategy. The Iranians made clear that they hoped to avoid a conflict with the United States:

> [W]e do not wish to expand the war, but if a war is imposed on us we will be thoroughly prepared to defend ourselves.[39]

Iran also continued to develop its modest rapprochement with Moscow. Soviet Deputy Foreign Minister Yuli Vorontsov visited Tehran early in August, and in the week after his visit Iran unveiled an economic agreement wherein Iranian oil would be piped to Soviet ports on the Black Sea. Meanwhile, although Iraq reignited the tanker war on 29 August, with major strikes on Iranian export facilities at Kharg, Sirri, and Larak islands, Iranian retaliatory strikes stayed conspicuously clear of US flagships. The mine threat, too, seemed to have disappeared.

None the less, Iranian Revolutionary Guards struck virtually any unprotected ship they could find, including non-US flag vessels doing business with Kuwait.[40] Indeed, total strikes on tankers and commercial shipping reached a new high – 178 strikes by both countries – in 1987.[41] At the same time, Silkworm missiles deployed on Fao began occasionally to fire into Kuwait harbour. The Americans, Iranian spokesmen claimed, had not brought security to the Gulf, and especially to those other GCC states the United States had claimed it would support.

Despite the resumption of the tanker war, optimism generally prevailed at this point that Iran was seriously considering Resolution 598. Tehran received UN Secretary General Perez de Cuellar on 10 September to discuss 'implementation' of the resolution.[42] Noticeably absent from Iranian rhetoric was the traditional strident call for the removal of Saddam Hussein. To be sure, in its place was the call that Iraq be blamed for starting the war, but this could be absorbed within the resolution's suggestion that a commission be established to examine precisely this issue. The Iraqis of course took these signs as an Iranian ploy to buy time while exporting oil at high levels; hence their resumption of strikes on tankers at the end of August. But others felt that, for whatever reasons, Iran was moving closer to a negotiated settlement.

That such a move was difficult within the strictures of Iranian domestic politics, however, could be inferred from events later in September, when Iranian President Ali Khamenei arrived in New York to give his country's formal answer to the UN's call for a ceasefire. Not surprisingly, Khamenei rejected the withdrawal clause of Resolution 598. Beyond this, however, he declared that Iran could live with the resolution, especially if a commission were formed quickly to determine war guilt. To many it sounded like a serious offer.

Yet if Khamenei's purpose was to seriously engage the UN effort, his countrymen in the Gulf were of little help. On the eve of his arrival in New York, US helicopters followed the Iranian landing ship Iran Ajr as it began to lay mines in the northern Gulf. The ship was captured and boarded the next day, and shortly thereafter the world was treated to photographic proof, if any were needed, of Iran's mine laying operations.[43] The incident did not deflect Khamenei from delivering his intended message, although his speech to the General Assembly contained threatening passages provoked by the Iran Ajr's capture.[44] Yet clearly there were those in Iran more interested in fighting the Great Satan than in moving to end the war.[45]

Iran seemed to be moving in two directions at once – towards a more moderate position on ending the war, but also towards a confrontation in the Gulf itself. Whether this was the result of deliberate choice or of Tehran's inability to control its Revolutionary Guard naval forces remains a matter of continuing debate. Whatever its origins, the confrontational direction of Iranian policy was on the whole counterproductive. After a year in which Iran's contacts with the rest of the world had expanded and the leadership had made adroit use of small military victories, Iranians found themselves increasingly isolated, facing not only seven navies in the Gulf but the prospects of an arms embargo. There were many causes behind Iran's predicament, but one of them was Iran's own behaviour.

WHO'S BOXED-IN?

By all rights US strategy was working, albeit after an embarrassing start and partly with Iranian help. Even the *Bridgeton* incident did not seem so embarrassing by the autumn, when it could be argued that in underlying its own hand by not retaliating the United States had allowed Iran to overplay its hand, bringing European navies more deeply into the Gulf. This made the US military presence, aimed initially at supporting the GCC, at least loosely a part of a multinational naval presence in the Gulf that reflected Iran's growing isolation. UN Resolution 598 had been passed, and in a speech to the UN General Assembly on 16 September President Reagan had launched a campaign to pass the Second Resolution. Evidence taken from the Iran Ajr could be expected to strengthen his case.

Finally, neither the War Powers debate the Iranians had hoped for nor the escalating confrontation many Americans feared had occurred. Indeed, in the Iran Ajr operation the United States had exercised a surprising degree of subtlety and sensitivity that effectively reassured critics. The operation had made the point that the United States would not tolerate Iranian mining operations. But it had been run with minimal force; three Iranians were killed and two were lost at sea, but the remaining 26 were returned to Iran soon thereafter. Thus it provided more embarrassment than provocation to Iran. That the crew was returned via Oman, which remained on friendly terms with Iran, suggested a laudable degree of political sensitivity in Washington.

But US military strategy was defined by much more than the Iran Ajr incident, and a broader view of events during this crucial early period of reflagging continued to raise questions about the operation's wisdom. Iranian strikes on unprotected Gulf shipping made a mockery of the stated US mission of 'assisting friendly regional states'. Nor was it entirely clear at the time that the US military presence was exerting the predicted 'moderating' influence on the Iran–Iraq War. MIDEASTFOR was doing nothing more nor less than defending US flagships, eleven of which had once belonged to Kuwait. Technically this was what Kuwait had wanted. Yet Kuwait and the other GCC states continually questioned the utility of doing that and nothing more.

To many – in the government as well as outside it – the US Navy was caught in a quandary. It could defend US flagships, perhaps even retaliate against Iranian naval bases like the very bothersome one on Iran's Farsi island. But limited strikes like this had yet to deter Iran's Revolutionary Guards, hence naval harassment might go on for a long time. Arguably a much larger US strike might deter Iran, but the United States was itself deterred by the risks of such an operation. Most saw the prospect of an American–Iranian war as disadvantageous to the United States, despite the latter's enormous military power. But if the United States feared a war with Iran, then it had to worry about strikes that risked American casualties, since these might create domestic political pressure in the United States for a much larger attack. Meanwhile, strikes against Iran's oil infrastructure might perturb the international oil market, creating a rift between the United States and its allies.

This logic suggested that there was little to do save defend American flagships, which MIDEASTFOR, after a rocky start, seemed fully capable of doing. Saying that, however, merely raised the next problem, which had to do with how one measured success. As many critics pointed out, there were no precise criteria for declaring victory. Reflagging could end only when the tanker war ended. And the Iraqis had already made clear by their actions that the tanker war would not end until the ground war ended.

Indeed, Iraq's role at this point highlighted one of reflagging's most serious problems. Those who criticized reflagging because it left the initiative with Iran missed the fact that Iraq, too, had the initiative. This had become clear on 29 August, when Iraq relaunched its tanker war. Coming at a time when the Security Council was trying hard to interest Iran in Resolution 598, Iraq's move came as an unwelcome surprise; Undersecretary Armacost called the move 'very regrettable, extremely unfortunate'.[46] One state department official put the dilemma squarely:

> The Iraqis can expand the war at any moment, but we cannot translate our presence into bringing the war to an end. We've boxed ourselves into a situation which was initiated by Kuwait, is now driven by Iraq and is ultimately dependent upon Iran.[47]

That the initiative also lay at least partly with Kuwait became clear after 16 October, when a Silkworm missile fired from Iranian-occupied Fao slammed into the side of the *Sea Isle City*, one of Kuwait's eleven reflagged tankers, while the ship waited to unload its cargo in Kuwait's territorial waters. Whatever the ambiguities in the military mission statements published in June, Undersecretary of State Armacost had made clear that the 'GCC states recognize their responsibility for protecting all shipping in their territorial waters'.[48] Yet it quickly became clear that American credibility would be seriously damaged if it stood idly by while Iranians fired on American flagships, whatever their precise location.[49] Thus four days after the *Sea Isle City* was hit American warships destroyed the Rostum offshore oil platform, well south in the Gulf, on grounds that it was being used by Iranian Revolutionary Guards as a communications centre.

Like the seizure of the Iran Ajr, this military operation was well-conceived. To be sure, the Rostum platform had nothing to do with Iran's strike on the *Sea Isle City*, and in this sense was not related to the specific problem that gave rise to the need to retaliate. None the less, it was a limited strike on a target having much to do with Iran's general harassment of Gulf shipping. That the target was not, apparently, a producing oil platform obviated the strike's effects on oil markets. Those on the platform were given time to evacuate before shelling commenced. And the whole operation was couched in rhetoric suggesting that the United States had no desire to escalate.

Moreover, despite warnings from Iranian experts that retaliation might be extremely costly, the operation had the desired deterrent effect.[50] The Iranians seemed as anxious as the Americans to avoid a conflict; perhaps both realized that they were being manipulated, the Americans by Kuwait, Iran by its radicals, into a war neither wanted. Whatever the case, after firing a few more Silkworms in Kuwait's direction, they called a halt to Silkworm strikes from Fao and also to their harassment of US flagships. Not until April 1988 did the United States and Iran again confront each other militarily in the Gulf. If American strategy was 'dependent on Iran', the Iranians in this instance co-operated.

Clearly, however, the United States had been pressured by events and by its Arab friends to move beyond its original mission statement, suggesting that the initiative for defining the US mission lay with Kuwait and the GCC as well as with the United States. Whatever the original agreement with Kuwait and the specifics of the US mission statement, Kuwait, other GCC states, and the United States were essentially negotiating MIDEASTFOR's real mission as events played out in the Gulf.[51] In this case things worked out well for the United States. But Iran's co-operation was not something anyone could have predicted; indeed, in the aftermath of the Iran Ajr affair Iranian rhetoric referred frequently to 'the start of a war by the United States in the Persian Gulf', and Hashemi-Rafsanjani announced the need to redeploy forces to the coast for such an eventuality.[52] In this sense the United States was not so much prescient as lucky. And luck was not the most comforting basis on which to build military strategy in the Gulf.

With victory for reflagging seemingly defined as nothing short of an end to the war, the only escape from the conflicting pressures and worrisome prospects in the Gulf lay along the diplomatic track of US policy. As on the military track, however, here too US policy was producing mixed results. That policy had always been to push for an arms embargo – the Second Resolution – if Iran failed to comply with the ceasefire. Iran had failed to accept UN Resolution 598, yet US diplomats were finding it impossible to manufacture agreement on the Second Resolution. Moscow, not surprisingly, was the chief stumbling block, for understandable reasons.[53] On the one hand, Moscow had been trying for some months to extricate itself from Afghanistan, and could not afford to alienate Iran, which funded major Afghan resistance groups. On the other, Moscow may have hoped to use its diplomatic ties to both belligerents to bring about a ceasefire on its own.[54] Still, Moscow was not alone in stalling. When Shevardnadze introduced a UN proposal calling for a ceasefire and the immediate appointment of a commission to inquire into war guilt, it proved to be popular with several Security Council members. As one UN diplomat admitted, there was no majority for an arms embargo at that time.[55]

US diplomatic prospects rose briefly at the turn of the year, as it became increasingly clear that Iran would not or perhaps could not accept the ceasefire. The western European states had begun informally to staunch the flow of arms to Iran; in particular, on 23 September Great Britain ordered Iran to close its London weapons procurement office, said to have done 'the paper work on an estimated 70 percent of Tehran's worldwide weapons purchases'.[56] And in November the Arab League registered its strong concern with the war at the Amman summit meeting, after which Iraq, Jordan, and Saudi Arabia sent emissaries to Moscow pressing for Soviet acceptance of the Second Resolution. It looked for a moment as if Moscow was boxed-in; it could either accept the resolution or face increasing isolation.

Yet by February the Soviets looked to be no more boxed-in than the Americans. Things might have been different if Iran had run its much-feared winter offensive at Basra, but in fact Iran was unable to mobilize a sufficient force for the effort. Iran's quiescence took some of the urgency out of US diplomacy, while it allowed both Syria and the Soviet Union to take some credit for forestalling the attack. It had been fear of Basra's collapse that had motivated Security Council agreement on Resolution 598, and with that fear abating even US allies like Great Britain – in most Gulf matters the United States' staunch supporter – were tending towards the Soviet position.[57] Meanwhile, in the Gulf itself, Oman's Sultan Qabous, as well as rulers in the UAE and Qatar, were also opposed to the arms embargo.[58]

Ultimately the United States had to relent on the Second Resolution. Secretary of State Shultz travelled to Moscow late in February to discuss the

Second Resolution as well as the impending superpower agreement on Afghanistan. In fact, his discussion focused primarily on Afghanistan; presumably Shevardnadze made clear that his country could not take substantial risks with both Islamic countries along its southern border. If the purpose of the diplomatic track of US policy was to obtain agreement on the Second Resolution, then at this point the diplomatic track collapsed.

Still, if the purpose of US diplomacy was to 'internationalize Operation Staunch', it was more successful than it appeared to be on the surface. The European states began in September to cut the flow of their arms to Iran; the policy was never airtight, but it achieved some success where there had been none before. Interviews suggest that direct Soviet arms transfers to Iran, as well as transfers from Eastern bloc states, declined towards the end of 1987, forcing Iran to depend increasingly on China and North Korea for arms. And after a brief diplomatic flap with China over its sale of Silkworm missiles to Iran, US diplomats were able to cajole that country into partially curbing arms sales to Iran.[59] The United States may have gotten less than it wanted diplomatically, but the Iranians were getting less than they wanted militarily.

Indeed, the United States may have been treated to the best of both worlds. It saw Operation Staunch picked up by other states, including, apparently, the Soviet Union. But it avoided the elaborate formal negotiations that would have been required to impose a formal arms embargo on Iran. Ironically, formal arrangements might well have called for US–Soviet naval co-operation – precisely what the United States had set out to avoid.

Moreover, by the time Shultz visited Moscow relative calm had settled into the Gulf. American convoys ploughed unmolested through the Gulf towards Kuwait. Although Iranian Revolutionary Guards continued to harass unprotected shipping, reflagging was judged a success – even in Kuwait. Thus when Frank Carlucci, replacing Casper Weinberger as Secretary of Defence, visited the Gulf early in January 1988 he announced a reduction in the size of US forces around the Gulf, claiming all the while that the military mission remained unchanged.[60] The allied naval presence was acquiring greater co-ordination, and even the US and Soviet navies co-operated occasionally in finding and destroying Iranian mines.[61] Basra seemed to be out of danger, although the Arab Gulf states continued to worry about an Iranian offensive for some months to come.[62] No one had a clear view of whether or how the Iran–Iraq War would end, but the worrisome crises of 1987 had been weathered safely.

IRAQ'S TURN

The only country unhappy with the situation was Iraq. Basra was out of danger, but Iranian forces, working closely with Kurdish dissidents, had begun a major offensive in the northeast. Worse, international pressure on

Iran seemed to be waning. Iraqis were fond of saying that 'we want the Iranians to attack', implying that they were prepared to extract massive casualties from Iranian forces.[63] They might have said, however, that they needed Iran to attack Basra, since only then would international pressure on Iran continue to mount. From Baghdad, it looked as if Iran had adroitly changed course in a way that threatened once again to leave Iraq on its own.

Facing a similar situation in August 1987, Iraq had taken the initiative by relaunching the tanker war. But the tanker war was temporarily halted at this point because Iraqi anti-ship missiles had come perilously close to US warships early in February.[64] Thus the Iraqis took the initiative this time by launching a new and far more deadly phase in the 'war of the cities'; between late February and April 1988, Iraq fired over 150 missiles at Iran's major cities. The move was virtually risk-free for Iraq. If the missile strikes prompted warlike behaviour from Iran, this would very likely rekindle international support for Iraq and perhaps even lead to conflict between Iran and the United States. If the strikes further undermined morale in Tehran, they would bring Iran closer to the negotiating table or political collapse. As it happened, Iraq's use of Soviet missiles in the 'war of the cities' had the added advantage of driving a wedge between Moscow and Tehran.[65]

At the same time, Iraq also began to make more extensive use of chemical weapons. Early in March the village of Halabja was subjected to a chemical attack that killed hundreds of women and children, presumably to deter Kurdish support to Iran. More often, Iraqi forces used chemicals to blunt Iranian offensive action or to ease the way for their own counterattacks. By early April Iran's northern offensive had clearly failed. Significantly, although individual members of the Security Council publicly disapproved of Iraq's use of chemicals, such was their desire to bring Iran to the negotiating table that they tended to downplay Iraq's behaviour, calling attention instead to Iran's unwillingness to end the war.

With its northern borders relatively secure, Iraq moved its forces southward. On 18 April Iraqi troops launched a surprise attack that recaptured Fao, perhaps the most important piece of territory Iranian forces had ever seized. By June Iraq had amassed an enormous tank force east of Basra and, with Iran apparently unable to do much about it, on 6 June Iraq recaptured territory at Majnoun Island the Iranians had seized in 1984. Although in both cases Iraq's Republican Guards performed with considerable skill, chemical weapons also played a role. Having restored its borders (save for a few points in the northeast), Iraq now launched a series of minor forays into Iran, using either its own forces or those of the Iranian Mujahedeen deployed on Iraqi territory.[66] These seem to have been spoiling attacks designed to pressure Iran; Iraq announced in June that it had no intention of holding Iranian territory.

Iraq could not have predicted precisely how Iran would react to its attacks, yet it is doubtful that the Iraqis could have been much happier with Iran's behaviour during this period. There were sufficient hints of radicalism in Iran's behaviour to renew some of the international pressure that had been abating earlier in the year. The war of words between Khomeini and the Saudis over Iranian participation in the upcoming Hajj reached a crescendo over the spring, prompting the Saudis to sever diplomatic ties with Iran on 26 April. On 15 March Kuwait claimed that a small force of Iranians attacked Kuwait's Bubiyan Island but were chased away. And three weeks later Kuwait again complained when terrorists who had hijacked a Kuwaiti Airline 747 landed in Mashad, Iran, and were apparently given aid and sent on their way by the Iranians. Most important, in mid-April mines once again appeared in the northern Gulf, after a long absence. One hit the *USS Roberts*, prompting a final pro-Iraqi shift in US military strategy that will be discussed in the next section.

Overall, however, Iran seemed to be on the ropes militarily, economically, and politically. Iraq's missiles brought confusion and disarray to Tehran; although the physical damage was not extensive, the government shut down repeatedly as employees joined citizens in leaving the city.[67] Meanwhile, Iranian forces, seemingly taken by surprise at Fao, stood idly by as Iraq massed its tank forces for the final assault on Iran's Majnoun position, and seemed incapable of defending the country should Iraq assume the offensive. Meanwhile, by this time Iraq's bombing raids on tankers and oil infrastructure had ground Iran's economy down to a point where economic crisis seemed just over the horizon and the shortage of consumer goods was undermining civilian morale. In January the Ayatollah Khomeini had sought to relieve these difficulties by giving the government more power, yet the move only increased political problems with conservative clerics and Iran's middle class.[68] Visiting Iran at this time, American journalist and Iranian specialist Robin Wright found morale low, anti-war sentiment high. 'The war that had sustained the revolution,' she concluded, 'had slowly begun to destroy it.'[69]

Perhaps equally important, Iran's international isolation was deepening. In particular, Iran found itself unwilling and unable to play the Soviets off against the United States. It had signalled interest in such a possibility the previous summer, when it announced a series of economic agreements with Moscow. Yet these agreements had produced no visible results. Part of the problem stemmed from Iran's own misgivings about Soviet intentions. As one Iranian official told Robin Wright, 'We are living near a big bear, and it is possible at any moment that this big bear will swallow this little thing [Iran]'.[70] But part of the problem stemmed as well from Moscow's unwillingness to be manipulated. In a sense, Moscow was co-operating with Washington in the Gulf as well as at the United Nations. Ironically, its co-operation was motivated in part by its fear that the US naval build-up, designed to keep the Soviets out of the Gulf, would lead to a permanent, enlarged, US military presence.

THE AMERICAN EMBRACE

Given these circumstances, there was no need for the United States to back Iraqi policy. If the United States had tilted towards Iraq when the country seemed on the verge of defeat, Iraq's spring victories opened the possibility for a US move back towards middle ground between the belligerents – surely where it wanted to be in the long run. Iraq's April victory at Fao, in particular, opened room for diplomacy, since the attack reduced Iraq's need to cling to a strict interpretation of Resolution 598. Meanwhile, Iraqi conduct was hardly something the United States should wish to condone. The use of chemical weapons was especially troubling, the 'war of the cities' only slightly less so. Nor should the United States have wished to see Iraqi pressure produce chaos in Tehran; on this the interests of both superpowers differed from Iraq's.

Yet both tracks of US policy hewed closely to Iraqi policy. With Britain and France, the United States killed a Soviet effort to pass a Security Council resolution calling for an end to the war of the cities. Nor was there any public call from the United States for a more conciliatory Iraqi position after the recapture of Fao, although the 'war of the cities' quietly ended at this point. American officials voiced a general condemnation of chemical weapons, but even state department officials admitted that the United States' (and for that matter West Europe's) opposition to Iraq's use of them was feeble, largely because 'there was too much animus against Iran to allow for effective protests'.[71]

But the more important policy choices were made concerning the military track of American policy. The *USS Roberts* incident came as an embarrassing surprise, since MIDEASTFOR had long-since concluded that the mine threat was under control. After confirming that the mines were newly placed, rather than old mines that had finally broken free and risen to the surface, the United States found itself with no choice but to retaliate.[72] On 18 April US warships struck two offshore oil platforms, one of them (the Sirri platform) responsible for roughly 8 per cent of Iran's oil exports, that served also as Revolutionary Guard command centres in the southern Gulf. There quickly followed a day of intense skirmishing, as the Iranians sent two of their frigates out of port at Bandar Abbas in counter-retaliation, while Revolutionary Guard speedboats attacked an offshore oil platform near the UAE. US warships damaged or sank both frigates, and, after gaining permission from President Reagan himself, eliminated Iran's threat to the oil platform.[73]

The day's battle was taken as a victory for the US Navy, while Defence Secretary Carlucci dubbed Iran's abortive counter-retaliation 'foolhardy'.[74] Iran's military actions may have been the spontaneous decision of ship commanders, but the time that elapsed between the initial US strike and the appearance of Iran's frigates suggests that their deployment was decided in Tehran, where Iran's leaders may have felt the need to retaliate for a US attack on a producing oil platform. After all, US warships were now doing precisely what Iraqi warplanes had been doing for four years. Coming as it did on the same day that Iraq began its attack on Fao, the US strike no doubt was taken in Tehran as evidence of a clear US embrace of Iraqi policy.

The events that followed must have further confirmed that conclusion. Within days the Saudis severed diplomatic ties with Iran. And two weeks later President Reagan announced a minor but none the less significant expansion in the American Navy's mission in the Gulf; henceforth ship captains would have authority to come to the aid of nearby non-US flagships under attack. The 'tilt' towards Iraq had been replaced by an emerging Iraqi-Saudi-US axis aimed at bringing more pressure to bear on Iran.

American officials did not see it quite this way. Iraq's attack on Fao was pure coincidence, they asserted, as was Saudi Arabia's break with Iran. Indeed, the latter resulted from a separate Saudi-Iranian feud that had no specific connection to US military policy in the Gulf. In interviews, US military planners stated that the Sirri platform was chosen as a target for US retaliation partly to make clear that Iran could not hide military forces behind economic assets. They also saw the strike as a way of increasing pressure on Iran, suggesting implicitly that by this time reflagging's mission had expanded considerably from the operation's original purpose. But Sirri's status as a producing platform was not regarded as especially important; real escalation, in their view, would have involved an attack on Iran itself. Meanwhile, US naval commanders in the Gulf were pressing to expand the mission, since crew morale was suffering as they stood by while Iranians attacked neutral ships.[75] And US defence planners saw expanding the mission as a way of 'taking the moral high ground'.

There is some irony in that statement, since a clear line can be drawn from the president's decision to expand the US Navy's mission and the tragic destruction by the *USS Vincennes* of an Iranian airbus on 3 July, in which some 290 Iranian civilians were killed. This is not to say that another US warship might not accidentally have shot down a commercial aircraft had the war continued. Nor is it to quarrel with the Navy's conclusion that the airbus tragedy resulted from crew stress rather than a perverse intention of harming Iranians. But the facts were that the *Vincennes* reversed course to come to the aid of the Danish supertanker Karama Maersk. In the aftermath of that action, Iranian forces in speedboats fired on US helicopters over the Gulf. The *Vincennes* moved to meet that attack, and, partly as a result of the stress of so doing, its crew misidentified the airbus as a military aircraft and fired two anti-aircraft missiles at it.[76] Ultimately the captain of the *Vincennes* fired in defence of his ship. But his ship would not have been in danger had the Navy's mission been confined to defending US flagships.

But the greatest irony is that the airbus tragedy seems to have played a role in finally bringing Iran to the bargaining table. On 18 July Iran accepted Resolution 598. In his letter of acceptance to Secretary General Perez de

Cuellar, Iranian President Ali Khamenei referred specifically to the airbus tragedy, asserting that the war had 'now gained unprecedented dimensions, bringing other countries into the war and even engulfing innocent civilians'.[77] It is plausible that many Iranians believed that the airbus tragedy was a 'premeditated attack', part of a broader plan to pressure Iran. It is equally plausible that even those who understood the airbus incident to be an accident used it both to deflect attention from the failure of the war effort against Iraq and to generate a broader consensus in Tehran concerning the need to end the war. For the Ayatollah Khomeini, in particular, the airbus tragedy may well have come as the last, tragic, straw on the camel's back.[78]

This was sheer luck, however; few American experts expected the Iranian action, and few took it seriously until Khomeini himself endorsed the move a few days after it was announced. Moreover, the *Roberts* incident, the expansion in MIDEASTFOR's mission, and of course the airbus tragedy all resurfaced long-standing doubts in the United States about the wisdom of the military track of US Gulf policy.[79] Fears were raised again about possible Iranian terrorism. Close consultation with key congressional leaders during the April retaliation had finessed the War Powers issue at that time. And Americans generally accepted the fact that the airbus tragedy was an accident. But after a long and happily quiet hiatus reflagging was again controversial; how long could the administration 'stay the course'? Luckily, Iran spared the United States the need to answer that question.

CONCLUSIONS

Those who see reflagging as decisive in bringing Iran to the negotiating table must overlook a great deal else that was pushing Iran in the same direction. Looking outward, Iran's leaders could see only increasing isolation; members of the Security Council, and in particular the superpowers, were clearly set against their war effort. American, Soviet, and European minesweepers in the Gulf were symbols of Iran's isolation, but by themselves could not prevent Iran from harassing ships at a higher rate than ever before. The cost of isolation was better measured in terms of the difficulties Iran confronted in trying to buy arms or to marshall international condemnation of Iraq for using chemical weapons. Looking inward, Iran's leaders could see their revolution in danger not from the US fleet, but from the economic deprivations of Iraq's continuing bombing campaign, and from basic tensions within the revolution itself. War weariness in turn left Iran vulnerable to Iraq's surprisingly successful offensive actions – actions that sooner or later might have taken substantial portions of Iranian territory. Arguably reflagging did not count for much amidst these troubles, and if it counted it was more as a symbol of problems elsewhere.

Ironically, the most plausible argument for reflagging decisiveness evokes the Airbus tragedy, which may well have been the final straw in prompting Khomeini to 'drink the poison' and accept a ceasefire. Clearly, however, this tragedy was neither the result of careful US planning nor a fitting part of a 'model' for other US military actions in the Third World.

Reflagging was never intended to be decisive, of course, nor indeed was it originally intended to pressure Iran. And in terms of the lesser goals attached to it, reflagging must be judged a success. The United States 'stayed the course' in the Gulf, and to Arab states with Lebanon fresh in memory, that was no small accomplishment. Notwithstanding the *Stark* and Airbus tragedies, American military operations overall were run with an impressive degree of political sensitivity. The United States avoided a confrontation with Iran while it contained the urge for more tangible and lasting forms of co-operation with the Arab Gulf states. What it got was renewed credibility and an impressive degree of operational co-operation and experience.

The evidence is more dubious when it comes to the goal of 'keeping the Soviets out of the Gulf'. Reflagging served this purpose in the physical sense of limiting Soviet naval deployments and the associated logistics build-up US military planners feared. That the Soviets none the less and in their own way played a constructive role in bringing the Iranians to the bargaining table was not lost on the Arab Gulf states, however. This may help to improve Moscow's relations with those states, although as only one of several factors, most notable among them the Soviet withdrawal from Afghanistan. Still, the comparison here must be with what might have been, and arguably a larger Soviet naval presence would have set precedents Washington was happy to avoid. At the very least, President Reagan never had to admit publicly that the Soviets were playing a useful role – yet another example of how the need to sustain domestic political support prevented the formulation of a clear and concise statement of what was really going on in the Gulf.

Insofar as it effectively mixed US military operations with a keen sense for regional political dynamics, reflagging should indeed stand as a model for future US military operations in the Third World. Yet if reflagging is to be a model, its troublesome features also deserve consideration. One such feature is the worrisome extent to which pure luck played a role in the operation's success. Reflagging was approved on the basis of assumptions about Iranian behaviour that no one in the United States had a right to make. Iran finally backed away from confronting the United States, but for reasons that were only marginally associated with reflagging *per se*. In a sense the United States entered the Gulf as Iran was beginning a long decline that resulted in a ceasefire in July of 1988. Yet no one could have predicted that decline early in 1987, when the initial American decisions were made.

Indeed, it is relatively easy to take the information available to American policy makers early in 1987 and spin out much grimmer scenarios than what ultimately occurred. Even a partially successful Iranian assault on Basra early in 1988, for example, would have driven a wedge between the United

States and Kuwait, which seems all along to have been expecting more from the United States than its naval forces were able to provide. Or, to take a still more plausible example, what if Iranian Revolutionary Guards had not responded to the *Bridgeton* incident with widespread mining that brought allied navies more deeply into the Gulf? The War Powers debate in the United States, not to mention strategic calculations in Tehran, might easily have played out differently had the US Navy stood alone and isolated in the Gulf. Luck plays a role in any military operation. That occasionally it helps produce success should not blind us to its capacity to induce failure.

The second disturbing lesson from this 'model' US military operation stems from the troubling role others played in shaping it. Iraq exercised a disquieting degree of control over US options. In August 1987 and spring 1988 the United States and Iran were trying to reach some accommodation, only to have the efforts pre-empted by Iraqi military action and the convenient co-operation of Iran's virulent hawks. Iraq also had veto power over UN Resolution 598, in the sense that its refusal to sign the resolution would have left the diplomatic track of US policy stillborn. Despite repeated references to its neutrality, the United States swayed steadily closer to Iraq's position – partly by its own choice, to be sure, but also partly by Iraq's choice.

Nor was Iraq alone in shaping American policy. Unhappy with the limits of reflagging, Kuwait pushed for an expansion of the Navy's mission, with some success. The Navy's operational commanders seemed to be tacitly in league with Kuwait, for their own reasons; watching Iranians attack unescorted ships was having an understandably negative effect on morale, especially in view of the ease with which US warships could take on speedboats. Finally, the president's rhetoric, which never strayed from the grand conception of 'freedom of navigation', no doubt added its own pressures gradually to expand MIDEASTFOR's mission.

In an important sense, reflagging was defined in the doing of it. What Kuwait really wanted, what the United States was willing to give, what would 'work' or 'fail' with the Iranians, and what the Iraqis would allow or seek to prevent – these were worked out over time. This is hardly unique to reflagging. One can see in the early years of American involvement in Vietnam the same kind of negotiations, as the supporter and the supportee mutually determine what 'support' really means. In Vietnam as well as in the Gulf, the superpower that committed military force lost a good deal of leverage; the tail came to wag the dog. Surely the Soviets have already reached a similar conclusion from their experience in Afghanistan.

This suggests that the notion that US forces can be committed only when their deployment is governed by a precise mission statement is either naive or a backhanded attempt to prevent their commitment in the first place. The negotiation of missions is a fact of life for superpowers planning to project their forces beyond their borders. It may be said of reflagging that American policy makers handled these negotiations with laudable care and circumspection. But the role of luck in this case suggests that care and circumspection need not always produce success. If precision is impossible, luck not always good, but commitment none the less essential, it would be advisable to 'start small', as American planners did in this case, in order to leave room for mission expansion without major additional force commitments or symbolic escalation. Notwithstanding the nation's success in reflagging, however, the prior question – is commitment necessary at all? – remains as important as ever.

Notes

1. See, for example, Michael Dunn, 'Hiding our Gulf success?' *Washington Times*, 23 September 1988, p. F1. Dunn argues that the 'US intervention in the Gulf not only worked, it was directly (though not solely) responsible for the end of the bloodiest and longest conventional war since World War II.'
2. On Iranian targeting of Kuwaiti and other GCC shipping, see US House, Committee on Armed Services, *National Security Policy Implications of United States Operations in the Persian Gulf*, Report of the Defense Policy Panel and the Investigations Subcommittee, 100th Cong., 1st Sess., July 1987 (GPO: 1987) p. 8, Figure 3.
3. See ibid., pp. 47–8, and Rupert Pengelley, 'Gulf war intensified: Shipping and oil rigs face increasing threat', *International Defense Review*, 3/1987, pp. 279–80. Shipping executives were sufficiently upset by this turn of events that they approached UN Secretary General Perez de Cuellar in January asking for UN protection of Gulf shipping. See 'Shippers Urge UN Convoy', *Middle East Economic Digest*, 17 January 1987, p. 4.
4. See the interview with Abdul Fattah al-Badr, chairman of the Kuwait Oil Tanker Company, in Milton Viorst, 'A Reporter At Large: Out of the Desert', *New Yorker*, 16 May 1988, p. 49.
5. Except where otherwise noted, precise dates for this and what follows are from Clyde R. Mark, *The Persian Gulf, 1987: A Chronology of Events*, Congressional Research Service Report 88–129F.
6. For the text of both statements, see US Department of State, 'U.S. Policy in the Persian Gulf', Special Report No. 166, July 1987, p. 8. By the time the second statement was made, Iran had deployed and was on the verge of test-firing a Silkworm missile near the Strait of Hormuz. Interviews suggest that most of the administration's military concern, and also its promises to 'ensure the free flow of oil through the Strait of Hormuz', were made with the Silkworms foremost in mind.
7. Tim Carrington and Robert S. Greenberger, 'CIA Says Terror By Iran Is Likely Over Gulf Moves', *Wall Street Journal*, 18 June 1987, p. 5.
8. In April, however, the US Navy was ordered to increase the amount of time spent in the Gulf. Also, the Indian Ocean tour of the carrier USS Kitty Hawk and its task force was extended, and the carrier was ordered to deploy nearer the Gulf. The latter move had more to do with Iran's Silkworm threat, however, than with military requirements for reflagging. For a chronology, see Robert J. Ciarrocchi, *US, Soviet, and Western European Naval Forces in the Persian Gulf Region*, Congressional Research Service Report 87-956F, 8 December 1987, p. 6.

9.   As one admiral put it, 'it would be stretching it to say that the [Joint] Chiefs [of Staff] were in on the [reflagging] decision, or even asked their opinion on it'. As quoted in Bernard E. Trainor, 'U.S. Officers Troubled by Plan to Aid Gulf Shipping', *New York Times*, 29 June 1987, p. A6. DoD officials attended all key interagency meetings leading up to the decision. But operational planners were not consulted until the decision had been made.

10.   Official US statements made this point forcefully. See, for example, the statement by Richard Murphy in Don Oberdorfer, 'U.S. Policy in Gulf Complicates Relations with Soviets, Chinese', *Washington Post*, 31 May 1987, p. A30.

11.   Ciarrocchi, *U.S., Soviet, and Western European Naval Forces in the Persian Gulf Region*, p. CRS–9.

12.   As one State Department official put it, 'We know trying to promote Kuwait is a losing proposition. . . . So we are emphasizing the dangers of a rampant Iran.' As quoted in *Middle East Policy Survey*, no. 179, 26 June 1987, p. 2.

13.   Casper W. Weinberger, *A Report to the Congress on Security Arrangements in the Persian Gulf*, 15 June 1987, p. 16. This remains the most complete and coherent defence department statement on reflagging. In interviews with administration officials conducted early in July, reporters for Middle East Policy Survey found that most rated the conventional threat to convoys as 'low to moderate', but at the moderate end were the Silkworm missiles rather than ambient strikes on convoys as they sailed north through the Gulf. See *Survey* no. 180, 10 July 1987, p. 2.

14.   Murphy stated that he did not think Iran would attack, since doing so would 'add a new dimension' to the Gulf conflict, namely a second war with the United States. Quoted in Tim Carrington and Robert S. Greenberger, 'Pentagon Charts Bigger Role for Navy In Persian Gulf and a Boost in Firepower', *Wall Street Journal*, 26 May 1987, p. 70.

15.   See Weinberger, *A Report to the Congress*, and Department of State, *U.S. Policy in the Persian Gulf*, pp. 10–12.

16.   *U.S. Policy in the Persian Gulf*, p. 11.

17.   *Security Arrangements in the Persian Gulf*, p. 15.

18.   Ibid. It may well be that this statement was more than one of hope, even an attempt to communicate US intentions to Iran, rather than a statement of expectations.

19.   Weinberger, *Security Arrangements in the Persian Gulf*, p. i (emphasis in original).

20.   Only one sentence in the defence department's long statement on US policy suggested a connection between reflagging and Iranian behaviour, and that argued that '[a] firm but unprovocative U.S. policy could encourage an Iranian reevaluation of its foreign policy'. *Security Arrangements in the Persian Gulf*, p. 3.

21.   See Gary Sick, *The Internationalization of the Iran–Iraq War: The Events of 1987*, unpublished paper written for the Center for International and Strategic Affairs, UCLA, 22 April 1988, p. 21.

22.   For the resolution's full text see *New York Times*, 25 September 1987, p. A8.

23.   As suggested by Gary Sick, in *The Internationalization of the Iran–Iraq War*, p. 19.

24.   Interviews with Iraqi officials, in Baghdad, December 1987.

25.   *New York Times*, 25 September 1987, p. A8.

26.   Sick, *The Internationalization of the Iran–Iraq War*, p. 20.

27.   Ibid., p. 25. Mr Armacost made much the same point by stating that the US 'preferences would be for a Western protective regime [in the Gulf] . . . The best

way for the [superpowers] to collaborate in our stated common interest ... is through the work currently being undertaken in the Security Council.' *U.S. Policy in the Persian Gulf*, p. 12.

28.   Gary Sick argues that by late February 1987 Iran's leaders had concluded that the war 'could not be won in a single, decisive battle'. In particular, Sick cites a speech by Revolutionary Guard commander Mohsen Rezai'e in the spring of 1987 stating that Iran had 'put the war's decisive stage behind it last year and has now entered a stage to determine the future of Iraq', with military planners calling for a 'series of limited operations' as well as 'plans to organize, train and arm popular forces inside Iraq'. See, *The Internationalization of the Iran–Iraq War*, pp. 3–4.

29.   *FBIS-South Asia*, (cited **FBIS-SAS**), 4 May 1987, p. 13.

30.   See Mark, *The Persian Gulf, 1987*, pp. CRS–4–5. That Iran soon refrained from further attacks on Soviet shipping – presumably after Moscow quietly threatened action if the attacks did not cease – suggested that Tehran could control its naval forces and also respond to argument or threats. By the time attacks on Soviet shipping stopped, however, Iran had warmed to the Soviets and focused its anger strictly on the United States. Thus it is not clear that US policymakers had a right to take any consolation from May's meagre Soviet–Iranian military confrontation.

31.   *FBIS-SAS*, 7 May 1987, p. 11.

32.   *FBIS-SAS*, 20 May 1987, p. 12, offers Iranian comments in the wake of a four-day visit to Tehran by Omani Defence Minister Yussef al-'Alawi.

33.   See the transcript of his press conference in *FBIS-Near East*, (cited hereafter as FBIS-NES), 4 June 1987, p. S1.

34.   See for example Musavi's 21 May press conference, *FBIS-SAS*, 22 May 1987, p. 11.

35.   Vahe Petrossian, 'Iran: Looking for a Showdown with the "Old Vulture"', *Middle East Economic Digest*, 20 June 1987, p. 12.

36.   Vahe Petrossian, 'Iran takes on France and the US', ibid., 18 July 1987, p. 9; 'Gulf edges deeper into crisis', ibid., 25 July 1987, p. 9; and Paul Lewis, 'Iran Threatening to Cut French Ties', *New York Times*, 17 July 1987, p. A8. The French sent the aircraft carrier Clemanceau and three support ships to the Gulf area, apparently in response to Iran's 13 July strike on a French merchant ship. Mark, *The Persian Gulf*, 1987, p. CRS–10.

37.   See, for example, Rafsanjani's sermon in *FBIS-NES*, 24 August 1987, pp. S-1–S-7.

38.   See, for example, Mohsen Rezai'e's statement in *FBIS-NES*, 25 September 1987, pp. S8–S9.

39.   From Rafsanjani's Friday sermon, in *FBIS-NES*, 24 August 1987, p. S-5.

40.   Twenty ships were hit in the six days after Iraq restarted the tanker war. See John Kifner, '20 Ships Hit in Gulf in Six Days, Raising Fears of Maritime Nations', *New York Times*, 4 September 1987, p. A1. On Kuwait's problem, see Patrick E. Tyler, 'Kuwaiti Crude Oil Fleet Battered by Iran', *Washington Post*, 15 January 1988, p. 25.

41.   Jonathan C. Randal and Patrick E. Tyler, 'Gulf Policy Said to Boost U.S. Credibility', *Washington Post*, 11 January 1988, pp. A1, A18.

42.   David B. Ottaway, 'U.S. Aides See Hope for Gulf Diplomacy', *Washington Post*, 14 September 1987, p. A25.

43.   Richard Halloran, 'U.S. Reports Firing on Iranian Vessel Seen Laying Mines', *New York Times*, 22 September 1987, p. A1, and Halloran, 'Secret U.S. Army Unit Had Role in Raid in Gulf', *New York Times*, 24 September 1987, p. A12.

44.   For the full text of Khamenei's speech, see *FBIS-NES*, 24 September 1987, pp. 34–42.

45. A sense for the political problems these events caused inside Iran can be gained from the fact that some Iranian soldiers 'were apparently so infuriated by the failure to respond to the Iran Ajr attack that they sent a delegation in late September on a long march from the war zone to Khomeini's house in north Tehran to demand action'. Vahe Petrossian, 'Iran's tactical shift heralds Gulf war escalation', *Middle East Economic Digest*, 17 October 1987, p. 20.

46. Elaine Sciolino, 'U.S. Protests New Raids on Iranian Oil Targets and Ships', *New York Times*, 1 September 1987, pp. A1, A6.

47. Another official added, 'We are left to rely on luck, Iraqi restraint and Iranian reluctance to confront superior military power.' Both are quoted anonymously in *Middle East Policy Survey*, No. 183, 11 September 1987, p. 2.

48. Department of State, *U.S. Policy in the Persian Gulf*, p. 12.

49. See Gerald F. Seib, 'U.S. Must Decide if an Attack on Iran Is Worth Enormous , Long-Term Risks', *Wall Street Journal*, 19 October 1987, p. 26.

50. James A. Bill argued that 'If the U.S. gets in the position of killing Iranians, it will take [the Iranians] 35 to 50 years to forget it.' Moreover, Bill continued, '[p]ragmatic leaders ... would be discredited, and more radical leaders would see their stature enhanced', ibid.

51. Shortly after the Sea Isle City strike an Iranian Silkworm missile hit Kuwait's Sea Island oil terminal. The US failure to retaliate in this case apparently 'dealt a severe blow' to 'Kuwait's hopes of a broader U.S. security guarantee'. In such ways, apparently, did the Kuwaitis learn the limits of US military support. See Andrew Gowers, 'U.S. Support bolsters Kuwait's fragile confidence', *Financial Times*, 18 February 1988, p. 3.

52. *FBIS-NES*, 5 October 1987, pp. 57–8.

53. See David K. Shipler, 'Shultz Is Unable to Make Headway on Iran Arms Curb', *New York Times*, 25 September 1987, pp. A1, A8.

54. Several US journalists commented at this point on the advantages of Moscow's position. Karen Elliot House, for example, suggested that among Arabs there was 'a fair degree of unanimity ... that the Soviet Union, not the US, is the superpower positioned to play broker in Mideast quarrels ... [T]he Soviets, while maintaining relations with Iraq, have expanded their influence with Iran, a hat trick no other major power comes close to duplicating.' See her editorial, 'Arabs Look Again to Old Unreliable', *Wall Street Journal*, 8 October 1987. For similar views, see also David K. Shipler, 'U.S. Strategy on Gulf War', *New York Times*, 23 September 1987, p. A15, and Geraldine Brooks, 'Arab World Tale of Two Superpowers: Soviets' Diplomacy Waxes, U.S. Wanes', *Wall Street Journal*, 17 November 1987, p. 34.

55. See Don Oberdorfer, 'Soviets Urge Truce in Iran–Iraq War', *Washington Post*, 24 September 1987, p. 1, and Paul Lewis, 'Council Explores New Path to Truce in Gulf', *New York Times*, 30 September 1987, p. A10.

56. Karen DeYoung, 'Iran's Arms Procurers Ordered Out of London', *Washington Post*, 24 September 1987, p. A27. See also 'Europeans Slow the Flow of Arms to Iran', *Wall Street Journal*, 22 September 1987, p. 28.

57. Great Britain was due to preside over the Security Council in February, and US diplomats hoped for a major push to pass the Second Resolution. They never got it.

58. For Qabous's position, see the interview by Andrew Gowers, 'Arms embargo attack highlights Gulf states' split', *Financial Times*, 8 February 1988, p. 2.

59. Robert S. Greenberger, 'U.S. Retaliates Against Chinese For Sales to Iran', *Wall Street Journal*, 22 October 1987, p. 35.

60. Molly Moore, 'Carlucci, Reagan to Reconsider Size of Gulf Fleet', *Washington Post*, 7 January 1988, p. 1.

61. George C. Wilson, 'Gulf Pact Set by Britain, Italy, France', *Washington Post*,

24 January 1988, p. 1, and Elaine Sciolino, 'U.S. and Soviet, in Gulf, Show Rare Cooperation', *New York Times*, 14 January 1988, p. A11.

62.   Not until April did George B. Crist, commander of the US Central Command, suggest in testimony before the Senate Armed Services Committee that Iran had 'lost so much of its military punch . . . that it is unlikely to be able to launch a . . . major offensive against Iraq in the foreseeable future'. Crist pointed to recruiting problems and also to Iran's inability to replace arms and supplies consumed during the January 1987 Basra offensive, and said that 'Iran was significantly weakened by Iraqi air attacks on its "economic infrastructure"', George C. Wilson, 'Air Attacks, Recruiting Woes Said to Have Weakened Iran', *Washington Post*, 15 April 1988, p. 26.

63.   Patrick E. Tyler, 'Iraq's Missile Attacks Escalate Gulf War', *Washington Post*, 2 March 1988, p. 16.

64.   Two incidents early in February prompted the United States to send a team to Baghdad to discuss rules for 'deconfliction' in the Gulf. Iraq suspended all raids on tankers during and for some time after the team's visit. John H. Cushman, 'U.S. Team To Hold Talks With Iraqis', *New York Times*, 17 February 1988, p. A4.

65.   Iranians demonstrated outside the Soviet Embassy, for example, and for a short time the Iranians also took up a harder line on the Afghanistan settlement. Vahe Petrossian, 'Missile strikes signal Gulf war escalation', *Middle East Economic Digest*, 5 March 1988, p. 11.

66.   On the use of the Mujahedeen, see Bernard E. Trainor, 'Iran Dissidents Enter Gulf War', *New York Times*, 16 May 1988, p. A6.

67.   See Elaine Sciolino, 'Turmoil Is Reported in Iran; Iraqi Air Raids Add to Mood', *New York Times*, 21 April 1988.

68.   See the discussion in Vahe Petrossian, 'Khomeini opens the door for economic reform', *Middle East Economic Digest*, 16 January 1988, p. 10, and Robin Wright, 'A Reporter At Large: Tehran Summer', *The New Yorker*, 5 September 1988, pp. 44, 61.

69.   Wright, *Reporter At Large*, p. 40.

70.   Ibid., p. 71.

71.   From a 'high ranking U.S. official', in *Middle East Policy Survey*, 22 July 1988, no. 205, p. 2.

72.   There is some evidence that the United States was not anxious to retaliate, partly because at that very time Iran had expressed interest in a direct dialogue with the United States. Hopes for a meeting between US and Iranian officials were dashed by the military actions of 18 April. Elaine Sciolino, 'Iran Sought Talks in April, US Says', *New York Times*, 8 July 1988, p. A6.

73.   For a chronology, see 'The Day in Detail: What Happened Where', *Washington Post*, 19 April 1988, p. A22.

74.   George C. Wilson and Molly Moore, 'U.S. Sinks or Cripples 6 Iranian Ships in Gulf Battles', *Washington Post*, 19 April 1988, p. 1.

75.   *Middle East Policy Survey*, no. 199, 29 April 1988, p. 2.

76.   Robin Allen, Stewart Fleming, and Andrew Gowers, 'U.S. downs Iranian airliner with nearly 300 on board', *Financial Times*, 4 July 1988, p. 1.

77.   For the text of Khamenei's letter, see *The Times*, 19 July 1988, p. 9.

78.   As one US official put it, 'The Iranian leadership told its people after the Iran air disaster that the Americans have gone nuts. I think they [the leadership] may have actually believed it.' As quoted in *Middle East Policy Survey*, no. 205, 22 July 1988, p. 2.

79.   See for example, former Navy Secretary James Webb's 'Milo Minderbinder

Would Be Impressed', *Wall Street Journal*, 18 July 1988, p. 18. To his usual criticism of reflagging Webb added that 'the Vincennes was defending a Danish ship from attacks' when it shot down the airbus, and asked rhetorically 'Remember the Danes? They haven't helped us in the Gulf and are sticking to a "no nukes" policy on visits by our Navy.'

12 The Soviet Union and the Iran–Iraq War

Robert S. Litwak

INTRODUCTION

The Iran–Iraq War began within nine months of the USSR's December 1979 invasion of Afghanistan – a move which was widely interpreted in the West as a dangerous extension of Soviet power on the periphery of the Persian Gulf and which prompted a vigorous Western response symbolized by the Carter Doctrine and the creation of the Rapid Deployment Force (RDF, later reconfigured as CENTCOM).[1] Eight years later, as the Gulf War winds down, Soviet forces are being withdrawn from Afghanistan under the terms of the April 1988 Geneva accords. The latter development, which raises interesting questions about how the Soviet leadership now defines security along its southern border, reflects the profound changes in Soviet policies which began following the death of Leonid Brezhnev in November 1982 and which have accelerated with the ascension to power of General Secretary Mikhail Gorbachev in March 1985.[2] In his February 1986 address to the Twenty-Seventh CPSU Party Congress, Gorbachev baldly stated that Soviet foreign policy must be made to serve the ends of the state's ambitious programme of domestic reforms (viz. *perestroika*). The Soviet leadership has called for a more quiescent period in international relations during which the Soviet Union can attempt to rejuvenate its declining socio-economic base. Without the successful implementation of these far-reaching domestic measures, Gorbachev warns that the USSR cannot expect to be a competitive twenty-first-century power.

Soviet policy in the Persian Gulf must be viewed as a subset of the broader policy towards the Third World which has emerged during the post-Brezhnev period. This policy may be seen, in large part, as a reaction to the activist policy of the late Brezhnev period. The late 1970s witnessed unprecedented Soviet involvement in the Third World from Angola to Afghanistan to Southeast Asia – the geographical zone on the Afro-Asian periphery referred to by Zbigniew Brzezinski as the 'arc of crisis'. This involvement, however, was neither cost nor risk-free. The acquisition of additional weak, dependent client states, each requiring annual subventions in the billion dollar range, begged the question as to just how much success the USSR could afford. At the same time, Soviet activism at the expense of Western interests contributed to the demise of detente and the election of the most anti-Soviet

American administration in post-war history. This conjunction of developments led to a reappraisal of Soviet policies in the Third World following the death of Brezhnev; indeed, some manifestations of this reassessment were evident even prior to November 1982.

Under Gorbachev, the Third World has not been a primary foreign policy priority (witness the scant reference to it at the Twenty-Seventh Party Congress). The Gorbachev approach has emphasized three key components: first, a concerted attempt to stabilize, if not lower, the economic maintenance costs of the USSR's existing structure of commitments in the Third World (e.g., Angola, Ethiopia, PDRY, Vietnam); second, the cultivation of major capitalist-oriented Third World states (such as Brazil and Indonesia) which had been largely ignored during the Brezhnev era; and third, efforts to avoid additional entanglements or crises which might adversely affect relations with the United States. In the Persian Gulf, the application of Gorbachev's 'new thinking' has been reflected in moves such as the establishment of diplomatic relations with Oman and the UAE in late 1985 and the reflagging of Kuwaiti tankers in March 1987. These changes are quite striking when one considers that prior to 1985 the Soviet Union, while enjoying diplomatic relations with Kuwait, was identified primarily with the Middle East's most radical states (e.g., Libya and the PDRY) and was essentially shut out of Gulf politics. In greatly expanding Soviet diplomatic options within the region, Gorbachev has effectively escaped the immobility of the Brezhnev era.

Soviet policy during the Iran–Iraq War has been both activist and multidimensional. Moscow has been forced to react to regional domestic developments in the two warring capitals which it could neither very well anticipate nor decisively shape. This type of reactive opportunism has been the hallmark of Soviet Third World policy. At a time when the USSR is mounting the aforementioned diplomatic offensive on the Arabian peninsula, the Iran–Iraq war has provided an additional avenue by which the Soviet Union may stake out what it perceives to be its legitimate role in the region. The central component of this policy has been the attempt to maintain favourable relations with both sides – however contradictory to implement in practice. By demonstrating the utility of Moscow's assistance in the economic and military spheres, the objective has been to increase sensitivity in Tehran and Baghdad to Soviet interests and preferences. As executed by Soviet Deputy Foreign Minister Yuli Vorontsov during his periodic diplomatic shuttles to Iraq and Iran, this Soviet pursuit of respect or deference is noteworthy for its subtlety and long-term perspective. The Kremlin has been careful not to overplay its hand by avoiding excessive, unrealistic requests (e.g., basing rights) and maintaining a low military profile (cf. the Soviet and American naval detachments in the Persian Gulf).

Given the domestic political volatility of both societies, as well as the desire of both leaderships to avoid excessive dependence on any outside power,

Soviet regional specialists (such as those at the Institute of Oriental Studies) do not underestimate the political intractability of the target environment and the consequent difficulties of establishing durable influence relationships with either, let alone both. Soviet offers to mediate the Gulf war, coupled with Moscow's consistent efforts to curtail the Western naval presence, are strongly suggestive of the regional role to which the USSR aspires. In this brief introductory section an attempt has been made to delineate the principle elements of Soviet policy *vis-à-vis* the eight-year Gulf war. Attention will now shift to an assessment of the historical record in order to document the evolution of Soviet policy during this fratricidal conflict – and the broader regional strategy of which it is part.

SOVIET POLICY AND THE GULF WAR, 1980–8

Phase I: 1980–2

The initial Soviet reaction to the outbreak of the Iran–Iraq War in September 1980 must be viewed within the context of Soviet responses to the Iranian revolution – and the perceived opportunities for Soviet policy which were seen to result from it. By all indicators, Soviet analysts, like their Western counterparts, did not anticipate the tumultuous events of 1978–9 which swept the Shah from power. This failure stemmed from at least two sources. The first relates to Marxist-Leninist conceptions of change in the developing world. This worldview, as reflected in policy pronouncements by the top political leadership (e.g., Brezhnev, Suslov, Gromyko, and Ponomarev in 1980) and scholarly writings from the various international institutes of the Soviet Academy of Sciences (e.g., Primakov, Mirsky, Simoniia, *et al.*), would not have led one to believe that the likely successor regime to an authoritarian, modernizing monarch like the Shah would be an Islamic republic. Soviet theory of that period would have predicted, for example, a military coup or resistance from the growing urban proletarian population, but not a mass religiously-based revolution. As a consequence, Soviet analysts since February 1979 have gone through ideological gymnastics trying to explain the Iranian revolution in class terms.[3] A second reason why the Kremlin leadership likely did not expect the outcome of 1979 is their evident belief that the United States would intervene to prevent the ouster of the Shah or that the latter would order the then formidable Iranian military to brutally suppress any domestic uprising.

Once the revolution occurred, the USSR was quick to capitalize on it and attempt to shape its consequences. Moscow pointed to the pluralistic character of the revolutionary opposition and praised the contribution of leftist forces (particularly the role of the Iranian Communist Party, the *Tudeh*). In addition to these exaggerated claims on behalf of Iranian leftist political forces, the Kremlin also suggested that Brezhnev's October 1978 warning against outside interference in Iranian domestic affairs had deterred an American counter-revolutionary intervention. While acknowledging the revolution's 'complex and contradictory nature', Brezhnev praised its 'anti-imperialist' character.[4] Soviet efforts to curry favour with Iran's post-revolutionary regime were complemented by equally assiduous attempts to maintain, and indeed heighten, the tensions in US-Iranian relations. Thus, during the 1979–81 hostage crisis, Moscow warned that Washington was using the crisis as a pretext for increasing its military presence in the region and that American forces constituted a direct military threat to Iran. With respect to the Iran–Iraq War, the Soviet media charged that the CIA had played a significant role in instigating the conflict by channelling misinformation to the Tehran and Baghdad leaderships.

Soviet statements in the wake of the 1979 revolution reflected the dynamic tension between the requirements of border security and ideology which has long existed in the USSR's policy towards its 'southern border' regions.[5] To illustrate this theme, one can contrast the situations facing the Soviet leadership prior to and following the Iranian revolution. Before the overthrow of the Shah, Iran was a stable, predictable neighbour – one which conformed to the norms of international conduct and which in no way posed a challenge to the legitimacy of Soviet rule in Central Asia. While enjoying close relations with the United States (which under the terms of the Nixon Doctrine sought to promote Iran as a regional surrogate), the Shah still developed a pragmatic working relationship with the USSR in the economic and even military spheres. By contrast, post-revolutionary Iran, although ardently anti-Western, has been the antithesis of stability and predictability. Indeed, the theocratic regime's Islamic ideology poses an *ipso facto* challenge to the Kremlin, in a way that the Shah's pro-Western modernizing monarchy never could, by offering an alternative model of legitimate government to the Soviet Central Asian populations. During the immediate post-revolutionary period, Soviet policy makers appeared more impressed by the profound setback to American interests in Iran than to the disturbing new reality on their southern border. This zero-sum perspective (admittedly shared by the Reagan administration) has been characteristic of Soviet policy during the Gulf war.

The outbreak of the war came at a time when Soviet perceptions and policies towards Iran and Iraq were undergoing a reversal of sorts. Iran, long held to be an American surrogate in the region, was now viewed as a strategic opportunity. Conversely, Soviet-Iraqi relations had experienced a significant deterioration in the years following the conclusion of their 1972 Treaty of Friendship. A major dimension of this latter development was Saddam Hussein's attempt, utilizing that country's post-1973 oil wealth, to broaden Iraqi diplomatic contacts with West European states in order to reduce the Ba'th regime's economic and military dependence on the Soviet Union.

During the same period, Moscow and Baghdad found themselves on opposing sides of various regional security questions ranging from Afghanistan to the Horn of Africa. Finally, the late 1970s witnessed the continued brutal suppression of the Iraqi Communist Party. Such was the political context in which Iraqi forces crossed into Iran in September 1980.

The initial Soviet reaction to the conflict was an official declaration of neutrality. While ostensibly evenhanded, in reality, this stance belied an implicit tilt towards Iran given the existence of the Soviet-Iraqi Treaty of Friendship and Baghdad's military dependence on Soviet arms transfers. It remains a matter of contention whether the USSR warned Iran of the imminent Iraqi attack or offered to provide the Tehran regime with arms to prosecute the conflict. The Soviet media did, however, make clear the Kremlin's unqualified displeasure with Saddam Hussein for initiating a war that would drive the moderate Gulf states toward the United States for reassurance and would provide a pretext for the further extension of US military power into the region (e.g., AWACS deployments to Saudi Arabia). Not surprisingly, Iraqi Deputy Prime Minister Tariq Aziz was rebuffed during two low-key visits to Moscow in autumn 1980.[6]

Soviet actions during 1980–1 reflected not only disapproval of Saddam's war, but also a strategic assessment that the USSR should tacitly support the Tehran regime lest the Iraqi military offensive decisively undermine it. These moves included the cessation of direct Soviet arms transfers to Iraq, increased Soviet technical and economic co-operation with Tehran, and Iran's expanded use of Soviet overland transit routes so as to reduce its dependence on the Persian Gulf waterway.[7] In the military sphere, the USSR acquiesced to arms transfers by third parties (notably Syria, Libya and North Korea) to Iran and reportedly concluded an agreement in mid-1980 to train Revolutionary Guards with the objective of making them a more formidable counterweight to the politically suspect regular army. There were further reports in late 1981, vehemently denied in Moscow, of the despatch of Soviet intelligence advisers to Iran in the wake of *Mujaheddin* terror offensive against the leadership of the Islamic Republican Party (e.g., the June 1981 bombing of IRP headquarters).[8]

While registering its disapproval of Hussein's war and bolstering Iran, the Kremlin did not completely forsake Iraq. There was some ambiguity in Soviet policy as some weapons already in the pipeline reportedly reached Iraq and East European governments (e.g., Poland) maintained their existing arms transfer relationship with Baghdad.[9] This dimension of Soviet policy again points to Moscow's effort during the course of the war to maintain favourable (or at least tolerable) relations with both combatants. In Tehran, the perception of an Iraqi military offensive fuelled by a continuing inflow of Soviet arms was a major impediment to the USSR's ability to capitalize on the post-revolutionary turnabout in Iran's foreign policy orientation. An equally important factor circumscribing Moscow's attempted inroads was

the Islamic Republic's own revolutionary ideology and its perceived imperatives. While Soviet assistance was accepted as a pragmatic necessity dictated
by circumstances, Iran's clerical leadership remained highly critical of
specific Soviet policies, notably Afghanistan, and continued to rhetorically
equate the superpowers (e.g., slogans such as 'neither east nor west'). An
additional matter of contention was Iran's unilateral renunciation of the
1921 treaty permitting the Soviet Union to occupy Iranian territory in the
event of a perceived security threat.

Phase II: 1982–4

By mid-1982 two developments – one internal within Iran, the other on the
battlefield – prompted an important re-evaluation of Soviet policy. In the
war, the Iranian military, which had been on the defensive since September
1980, expelled the final contingents of Iraqi forces from the Islamic Republic's territory and crossed the international frontier into Iraq. This decision
was evidently taken after extensive debate within Iran's theocratic leadership
and signified their desire to use the war as a vehicle to topple the Ba'th regime
and extend the Islamic revolution. The Soviet leadership, having refused to
sanction Saddam's war aims, similarly declined to support Khomeini's
maximalist objectives. The USSR emphasized that the return to the territorial status quo ante bellum offered a fresh opportunity to reach a mediated
solution to the conflict. Like the United States, the Kremlin was greatly
concerned about the possibility of an Iranian military victory that would
topple Saddam Hussein and leave Iran the region's dominant power, more
convinced than ever of the efficacy of its revolutionary ideology. To forestall
the possibility of a decisive Iranian military victory and these adverse
political consequences, the Soviet Union stepped up military shipments to an
increasingly desperate Iraqi regime.

On the ground, Iran remained on the offensive during late 1982 and the
first half of 1983. By autumn 1983, however, with Iranian forces threatening
to capture Basra, Iraqi defensive lines stabilized and the land war assumed a
relatively static, attritional character. Following Iran's rejection of multiple
ceasefire proposals, Iraq initiated aerial and naval attacks against Iranian
economic assets as a means of pressuring the Tehran regime into accepting a
mediated resolution. The cutting edge of this Iraqi offensive were French
Super Etendard fighter-bombers equipped with Exocet missiles; their primary target was Kharg Island, Iran's principal oil-exporting facility in the
Persian Gulf. In attacking this complex and Iranian tankers in the northern
Gulf, the Iraqi aim was to reduce Iranian oil revenues and increase insurance
premiums for vessels carrying Iranian crude. Iran's reaction was to threaten
to close the Strait of Hormuz to all shipping – a move which prompted the
Western powers to reinforce their naval contingents in the Persian Gulf and

to reassert their right of free navigation. Moscow, opposing this internationalization of the conflict, again charged that the United States was using the war as pretext for expanding its military presence in the region.

The turnabout in the ground war during 1982–3 and the consequent threat to the Hussein regime was the dominant factor underlying the pronounced shift in Soviet policy. The other key determinant affecting Moscow's actions, of course, was the changing political landscape within Iran itself. By mid-1982, the clerical leadership had effectively eliminated much of its organized secular opposition (notably, the Mujaheddin and Fedayeen). In July 1982, the regime continued this campaign with a series of moves against its sole remaining opponents on the left – the Tudeh. Party activists were purged from government positions and arrested, while the Tudeh newspaper was banned. The denouement of this episode came in February 1983 when the Tudeh's top political leadership, including General Secretary Nuraddin Kianuri, were arrested on charges of spying for the Soviet Union. This move was followed in subsequent months by the formal dissolution of the Tudeh party and the expulsion of eighteen Soviet Embassy officials.[10]

Amidst these developments, Soviet criticism of Iran, previously oblique and generally eschewing direct references to Khomeini, began to be openly voiced. The USSR staunchly denied that arrested Tudeh party members had been Soviet agents. In characteristic language, the Soviet media asked 'who benefits from the crushing of the Tudeh?'[11] Moscow asserted that this campaign of 'judicial murder' against the Tudeh was based upon misinformation provided by the CIA and Mossad, and that this anti-Tudeh crackdown objectively served the interests only of anti-clerical forces both within and outside the Islamic Republic. In a sweeping critique of the Iranian regime, Rostislav Ulyanovsky, then a deputy chief of the Central Committee's Internationl Department, charged that 'the "Islamic Revolution" gave birth to Islamic despotism'.[12] Other Soviet commentaries during mid-1983 charged that the United States had secretly resumed arms sales and that the Iranian regime's anti-Soviet campaign was a prelude to revived relations between Tehran and Washington.[13]

Phase III: 1984–8

Soviet actions – specifically, the marked increase in arms transfers to Iraq and significant reductions in Soviet oil imports from a financially strapped Iran – left the Tehran regime acutely aware of the tangible costs of Moscow's displeasure. Economic pressures and deepened diplomatic isolation stemming from the 'tanker war' prompted a re-evaluation of Iranian policy towards the Soviet Union. Iran's desire for a more moderate dialogue with the USSR was reflected in an exchange of economic delegations in June 1984. A further impetus for improved Soviety–Iranian relations was the US–Iraqi move in November 1984 to restore diplomatic relations. As during the 1979–82 period, the qualified nature of the rapprochement between Moscow and Tehran was evident. While the clerical regime was frustrated in its efforts to affect the quantity or pace of Soviet arms shipments to Iraq, the Soviet leadership bristled at continued Iranian support for the Afghan Mujaheddin.

Despite continuing political differences on a variety of bilateral issues, the 1985–6 period witnessed a significant expansion of Soviet–Iranian economic contacts. In December 1986, a general economic agreement was concluded whose provisions included the resumption of natural gas exports to the USSR via the IGAT-I pipeline.[14] With a clear eye on its political objectives, the Soviet leadership proved adroit in utilizing its economic assets as an instrument of its regional policy. Following Iraq's initiation of the 'war of the cities' in March 1985, for example, Moscow ordered some 1500 of its civilian technicians back to the USSR on the grounds of safety.[15] This move, one which disrupted Iranian power generation and several industrial projects, may well have been a further effort by the Soviet Union to tangibly register its opposition to the Khomeini regime's unwavering commitment to the war effort against Iraq and Tehran's repeated rejection of mediatory efforts.

In December 1985, Iraqi President Saddam Hussein made his first visit to Moscow since the onset of the war in September 1980. A major item on his agenda was reportedly the question of Soviet arms transfers to Iran via third parties such as North Korea, Syria, and Libya.[16] Indeed, by this time the Soviet Union had become, either directly or through surrogates, a major arms supplier to both combatants. Although the Soviet media steadfastly denied that the USSR was providing arms to the Tehran, these weapons are unlikely to have reached Iran without some Soviet foreknowledge or acquiescence. In the case of Iran, Soviet arms, which may now account for as much as 50 per cent of that country's total inventory, have been the mainstay of the Revolutionary Guards, while the regular army (many of whose officers received military training abroad prior to 1979) remains configured primarily with Western equipment. This contrasting pattern of arms dependence could have significant implications in the anticipated post-Khomeini power struggle.

In the case of Iraq, arms have been the dominant currency of its bilateral relationship with the USSR. Just as weapons were withheld to indicate Moscow's displeasure with Saddam Hussein's decision to initiate the war against Iran, so too were arms later provided to prevent the collapse of the Ba'th regime. Likewise, Iraqi attempts to diversify its political and military relationships at Moscow's expense (e.g., the restoration of diplomatic relations with Washington, Western arms purchases, etc.) prompted Soviet criticism and even, reportedly, threats to reduce arms transfers to Iraq while increasing the flow to Iran.[17]

In assessing the politics of Soviet arms transfers to Iran and Iraq, the Soviet Union's provision of surface-to-surface missiles (SSMs) to both combatants offers an illuminating case study of its dynamics. In March 1985, Iraq, utilizing its Soviet SSMs and superior air force, resumed the 'war of cities' as a means of pressuring Iran into peace negotiations. To the Ba'th regime in Baghdad, the Soviet leadership could plausibly claim that it was providing (essentially terror) weapons that might have a real impact on Iranian public attitudes towards the war. However, while providing SSMs to Iraq as part of a war-terminating strategy, the USSR also played an indirect role in the supply of this same category of weapons to Iran. Despite Iraqi protests and Soviet claims that it was not responsible for Libyan and Syrian shipments of SCUD-Bs to Iran, the supply of SSMs to both states continued unabated. The clear message for the Tehran regime was that the Soviet Union would work through its close allies – states, it should be emphasized, who were acting in their own interests – to channel these systems to Iran. This move, while consonant with Moscow's overall goal of fostering and maintaining favourable relations with both combatants, certainly worked against its other objective of ending the war and thereby undercutting the rationale for a continuing Western naval presence in the region.

The dramatic disclosures of November–December 1986 detailing secret US arms transfers to Iran after June 1985 probably served to reinforce Soviet conspiracy thinking about American intentions. These revelations likely triggered renewed Soviet fears that Washington might be able to use arms transfers as a means of reviving its moribund political relationship with Tehran. Given the compatibility of US and Iranian positions on the Afghan war, the possibility of a broader strategic rapprochement (along the lines suggested by Robert McFarlane in his *post hoc* explanation of US arms sales to Iran) could not have been discounted in Moscow. American plans, however, went beyond just the cultivation of Iran. As revealed at the same time, American actions also included the provision of intelligence data to Baghdad to facilitate the Iraqi air war effort. This latter move probably confirmed the worst suspicion of Soviet policy makers – namely that the United States, like the USSR, was striving to develop good, hopefully preferential, relations with both warring parties.

Superpower rivalry for regional influence received fresh impetus in March 1987 when Kuwait sought protection from both Washington and Moscow for its increasingly vulnerable tanker fleet. The request came at a time when Iran's emplacement of Chinese Silkworm missiles near the Strait of Hormuz posed a heightened anti-shipping threat. A hasty American rejection of the Kuwaiti request on legal grounds was followed by a speedy Soviet acceptance. Moscow agreed to lease three tankers to Kuwait, while remaining deliberately vague on the question of military protection. Confronted with the possibility of a protective Soviet naval presence in the Persian Gulf, the Reagan Administration was quick to reconsider its position and agree to reflag Kuwaiti vessels. The US decision to commit substantial naval forces to escort tankers through the Strait was dictated by the desire both to politically counter the limited Soviet deployment and to restore American military credibility in the eyes of the United States' moderate Gulf allies.[18]

The relatively obtrusive nature of the American naval presence in the Persian Gulf created a Soviet political opportunity *vis-à-vis* Iran. Capitalizing on the apparent American tilt towards the Arab side in the Gulf war, Moscow sought ways of improving its relations with the Tehran regime. An Iranian speedboat attack on a Soviet freighter in early May drew strong protests, but no overt response. After a second Soviet vessel struck an Iranian mine, the USSR took the relatively passive step of despatching three additional minesweepers to the Gulf. This pattern of restraint contrasted with the limited American reprisal raids against Iranian economic and military assets in response to similar attacks. In early June, Soviet Deputy Foreign Miniser Yuli Vorontsov announced that the USSR had no intention of increasing the size of its naval force in the Persian Gulf.[19] Later that month, Vorontsov visited the Iranian and Iraqi capitals, and reportedly conveyed a Soviet offer to sponsor bilateral peace talks in Moscow. Western diplomats observed that a major purpose of the Vorontsov mission was to demonstrate that the USSR enjoyed better relations with the two warring states than the United States.

Moscow's central preoccupation during the reflagging episode was the Western naval presence in the Gulf. Soviet commentaries asserted that Washington was, once again, manipulating regional events in order to create a 'pretext' for the further projection of American military power into the war zone. Scant mention was made of those continuing Iranian actions against neutral shipping which had been the immediate precipitant of the augmented naval deployments by the United States, Britain, France and other NATO member states. Indeed, Soviet broadcasts beamed towards Iran claimed that the US naval task force constitued a direct military threat to the Islamic Republic. The US military presence in the Gulf came under further strong criticism during a return visit by Vorontsov to Tehran in August 1987. This meeting yielded additional bilateral economic agreements, including one calling for the construction of additional rail and oil pipeline links between the USSR and Iran.

Given Moscow's comparatively close relation with Tehran, the USSR came under increasing pressure from moderate Arab Gulf states to exert its influence on Iran to end the war. In the United Nations, the Soviet Union voted in mid-July 1987 in favour of resolution 598, which called for an immediate ceasefire and peace negotiations, but refused to support an American-sponsored follow-up resolution imposing an arms embargo on Iran. As a counter to the US diplomatic initiative, in December 1987 the Soviet Union called for the creation of a UN flotilla to replace the large Western naval presence.[20] These manoeuvrings within the UN again underscored the carefully balanced nature of Soviet diplomacy. To Iraq and the Arab Gulf states, Moscow could plausibly argue that it was supporting international efforts to end the war and had indeed launched its own mediatory effort during the 1987 Vorontsov missions. To Iran, the Soviet leadership could take credit both for forestalling a UN-imposed arms embargo and for its efforts to remove the American naval presence. This approach continued during the period between March 1988, when a new round of the 'war of the cities' began, and July 1988, when Iran finally accepted UN resolution 598. While publicly acknowledging that it had supplied SSMs to Iraq, Soviet Foreign Ministry spokesmen denied that they had the range to reach Tehran and asserted that Iraq had not been given permission to modify the missiles to extend their range.[21] Likewise, following the downing of an Iranian airbus by the *USS Vincennes* in early July 1988, the Soviet media asserted that the accident was a natural outgrowth of the US naval presence in the Persian Gulf, charged that Washington was attempting to 'kindle' the Iran–Iraq War, and called once again for the creation of a UN flotilla to replace the Western fleets.[22] Iran's decision two weeks after the airbus incident to accept UN resolution 598 was hailed in the Soviet press as 'a victory for common sense over the senselessness of war'.[23] One Soviet commentator attributed the Iranian move 'to pressures from Speaker Hashemi-Rafsanjani and his "realist faction"'.[24]

CONCLUSIONS

In assessing the Iran–Iraq War from the perspective of Soviet state interests, the outcome, on balance, has been positive. The war, albeit one which the USSR did not welcome, did provide Moscow with an opportunity to expand and further legitimize its regional role through such actions as the chartering of Soviet tankers to Kuwait. The obverse of this policy, of course, has been a concerted effort by the Soviet Union to minimize Western, particularly American, influence in the region. The preferential political relationship which the Soviet Union has enjoyed with the combatants – a status symbolized by the Vorontsov missions to Tehran and Baghdad in 1987 – was a reflection of the degree to which the Soviet Union has developed important shared interests with each in the military and economic spheres (viz., Iraqi dependence on Soviet arms transfers; Iranian reliance on Soviet overland transit rights and technical assistance in various industrial sectors, e.g., power generation).

Soviet mediatory efforts during the Iran–Iraq war are suggestive of the activist regional role to which the USSR has aspired. Western observers speculated that the Soviet Union was hoping to replicate the experience of the Tashkent conference during which Soviet Premier Alexei Kosygin oversaw negotiations to end the 1965 Indo-Pakistani war. This conclusion is no doubt correct, but should be carefully qualified. Unlike the Indo-Pakistani case, in which the Soviet sponsorship role was relatively passive, a

Soviet-mediated settlement of the Iran–Iraq war might have required Moscow to exert considerable pressure on one or both sides to reach an agreement. This possibility, which could have complicated future Soviet dealings with Iran and Iraq, may well have reduced the desirability of playing a mediatory role under these circumstances.

While one should neither overstate the degree of Iraqi and Iranian dependence on the Soviet Union nor its political implications, the USSR has been an important factor in the policy calculations of the two sides during the conflict. Each has sought to exert influence in Moscow to limit Soviet assistance (especially arms transfers) to the other. Both have likewise been made aware of the tangible penalties which Moscow could invoke to register its displeasure. As the region enters the post-war period, a major question which remains is the degree to which these limited influence relationships will persist. The war leaves both combatants weakened and potentially dependent on outside powers for reconstruction assistance and continued arms transfers to maintain a balance of military forces. Under these circumstances, both sides will probably work to develop a differentiated set of relationships to avoid undue dependence on either east or west (to paraphrase the Iranian slogan).

Notwithstanding the relative success of Moscow's policies during the Gulf war, Soviet assessments in the wake of Iran's acceptance of UN resolution 598 have not been overly sanguine about the future course of Soviet-Iranian relations.[25] Iran, for example, has been accused of broadcasting anti-Soviet religious propaganda to the Islamic populations in Soviet Central Asia and Azerbaijan as part of a broader plan to create an 'anti-Soviet Islamic front' involving Turkey and Pakistan. The Tehran regime's unqualified rejection of the April 1988 Geneva accords on Afghanistan and its support of the most militant Afghan Mujahedeen factions is considered consistent with thie view. Although the December 1986 disturbances in Alma–Alta were not religiously inspired, the episode focused renewed attention on the stability of the Soviet Union's southern border regions – publicly acknowledged to be 'a weak spot' – and the potential impact of the 'Islamic revival' on the Soviet Muslim population.[26] A related concern is that the United States in the aftermath of the Iran–Iraq War will be able to revive its strategic links with Iran, possibly using arms transfers as the currency of the relationship.

The ceasefire in the Iran–Iraq War comes at a time when Soviet forces are completing their withdrawal from Afghanistan. As noted at the outset of this chapter, the December 1979 invasion of that adjacent state was taken by many Western analysts, both within and outside government, as an ominous indicator of Soviet intentions towards the Persian Gulf region. What then should one conclude from the withdrawal of the Red Army from Afghanistan? Does it mean that Gorbachev's 'new thinking' signifies a redefinition of Soviet interests along its southern border? The Afghan withdrawal is no doubt a watershed event in Soviet foreign policy, but may indicate less about the USSR's long-term objectives – that is, the kind of security milieu which Moscow seeks to foster – than the means which will be employed to further those objectives. The Afghan War, like the American experience in Vietnam, underscored the limits of military power when employed within the context of a politically intractable conflict. That said, the Soviet experience in Afghanistan, as with the US involvement in Southeast Asia, does not negate the utility of force in international politics. Military power will remain an important component of Soviet policy towards the USSR's southern border regions – if only as a backdrop to the kind of activist diplomacy initiated by Gorbachev.

During the Iran–Iraq War, the United States and Soviet Union shared certain common interests and goals. Both emphasized the dangers of escalation and inadvertent involvement; neither Washington nor Moscow desired to see a decisive victory by either combatant. True, each superpower has continued to pursue essentially a zero-sum approach in the pursuit of unilateral advantage at the other's expense; however, through words and actions, Gorbachev has made clear that he strongly wishes to avoid a repetition of the experience of the late 1970s during which Soviet activism in the Third World was a major factor underlying the demise of detente. The familiar task is that of devising rules of engagement, tacit or otherwise, to keep superpower rivalry in the Third World within acceptable bounds. Within this context, Gorbachev's 'new thinking' emerges less as a means of moving beyond competition than as a means of structuring it.

Notes

1. The author gratefully acknowledges the research assistance of Susan Pratt in the preparation of this chapter.
2. For Western assessments of the changes in Soviet policy since the death of Brezhnev see: Francis Fukuyama, *Moscow's Post-Brezhnev Reassessment of the Third World*, no. R-3337-USDP (Santa Monica, CA: Rand Corporation, February 1986); US House of Representatives, Committee on Foreign Affairs, *The Soviet Union in the Third World, 1980–5: An Imperial Burden or Political Asset?* Report prepared by the Congressional Research Service, Library of Congress (Washington, DC: USGPO, 23 September 1985); and Robert S. Litwak and S. Neil MacFarlane, 'Soviet Activism in the Third World', *Survival* (January–February 1987), pp. 21–39.
3. For a comprehensive analysis of Soviet writings see R. Craig Nation, *Soviet Conceptualizations of the Iranian Revolution*, Carl Beck Papers in Russian and East European Studies, no. 402 (Pittsburgh: University of Pittsburgh, 1985).
4. This characterization was made by Brezhnev in his political report to the Twenty-Sixth CPSU Conference; see *Pravda*, 24 February 1981.
5. For an interesting discussion of this theme see Malcolm Yapp, 'Soviet Relations with the Countries of the Northern Tier' in Adeed Dawisha and Karen Dawisha (eds), *The Soviet Union and the Middle East* (London: Heinemann for the Royal Institute of International Affairs, 1982) pp. 24–44.
6. For a comprehensive discussion of the Soviet policy during the early phase of

the war see Shahram Chubin, *Security in the Persian Gulf: The Role of Outside Powers* (London: Gower for IISS, 1981). At this and other points in this chapter, I would like to acknowledge my debt to Shahram Chubin.

7. Charles Tripp, 'The Soviet Union and the Iran–Iraq War' (paper presented at the conference on 'Soviet Policy in the Third World', University of Arizona, January 1987) p. 7.

8. Aryeh Y. Yodfat, *The Soviet Union and Revolutionary Iran* (London: Croom Helm, 1984) pp. 95–8.

9. This claim was denied by Iraqi officials, including Defence Minister Lt General Khairalla, who maintained in early 1981 that no Soviet arms had reached Iraq since the outbreak of fighting. The USSR evidently did resume limited direct arms shipments (including T-55 and T-72 tanks) following the Israeli raid on the Osiraq nuclear station outside Baghdad.

10. This crackdown on the Tudeh was preceded in mid-1982 by the defection of a KGB operative, Maj. Vladimir Kuzichkin, from the USSR's Tehran Embassy. For an account of this episode see *Far Eastern Economic Review*, 29 December 1983. Subsequent Western press reports indicated that the American and British intelligence services had channelled this information to the Iranians after their debriefing of Kuzichkin.

11. See, for example, text of unattributed broadcast from Moscow in Persian to Iran, 11 June 1983; *FBIS: Soviet Union*, 13 June 1983, p. H2.

12. *Literaturnaya Gazeta*, 22 June 1983; reprinted in *FBIS: Soviet Union*, pp. H1–H8.

13. *Krasnaya Zvezda*, 8 June 1983.

14. For a report on these developmens see Bohdan Nahaylo, 'Moscow and Tehran: Cultivating Mutual Interests Without Budging on Political Differences', *Radio Liberty Research*, RL 47/87, 3 February 1987.

15. Soviet officials denied Iranian claims that the action was taken to create deliberate hardships in Iran. An article in *Izvestia* on 17 July 1985 stated that Soviet technicians would return to the country when 'normal conditions' were re-established.

16. *Washington Post*, 17 December 1985.

17. *Foreign Report*, 4 April 1985; cited in Tripp, op. cit., p. 13.

18. In August 1987, the USSR was reported to have one depot ship, three mine sweepers and three trawlers stationed in the Persian Gulf. By contrast, the United States had some thirty vessels on station, including one aircraft carrier, an amphibious assault ship, a battleship and six cruisers. *Washington Post*, 16 August 1987.

19. For an account of these developments see Bohdan Nahalyo, 'Vorontsov's Visit to Tehran: Preserving the Iranian Connection', *Radio Liberty Research*, RL 222/87, 10 June 1987.

20. *Washington Post*, 16 December 1987.

21. *Washington Post*, 10 March 1988. The *Independent* (London), 22 March 1988 reported that East German technicians had reduced the size of the SCUD-B warhead and added a booster to increase the range of the Iraqi missiles from 220 to 370 miles.

22. See, for example, the report of TASS correspondent Askold Biryukov in *FBIS: Soviet Union*, 13 July 1988, p. 19.

23. Sergey Medvedko, 'Viewpoint: Resolution 598 and the Cup of Poison', *Literaturnaya Gazeta*, 27 July 1988 in *FBIS: Soviet Union*, 27 July 1988, p. 25.

24. Interview with Yuriy Losev, head of the Asia and Africa section of the Soviet Foreign Ministry's journal *International Affairs* in *Tokyo Shimbun*, 5 August 1988; reprinted in *FBIS: Soviet Union*, 11 August 1988, p. 1.

25.   Ibid.
26.   See, for example, the articles by Igor Belyayev in the 13 May and 20 May 1987 issues of *Literaturnaya Gazeta*; summarized in *FBIS: Soviet Union*, 12 June 1987, pp. CC11–CC19.

13 Europe and the Iran–Iraq War

John Chipman

A collective European foreign policy towards any other region has proven difficult to conceive, develop and implement. The requirement to collaborate closely within Europe on economic, juridical and political questions has done little to attenuate natural competitions between European powers for influence and for favour in other areas. This is most notable in the Near East and the Gulf, where the defence of Europe's perceived interests remains driven by national impulses and is beaten into general shape only on matters of broad principle.

West European states may sometimes be able to arrive at common positions concerning the security relationship with the US, and might increasingly have to co-ordinate external economic policies given the moves towards an internal market in 1992. But, in general, the national foreign policies of member states of the European Community are subjects for consultation, but very rarely for co-ordination. The rare examples of trans-regional policies considered in the 1970s (the 'Euro–Arab dialogue') tend to support the argument that Europe is a long way off from being able to present, and defend, *coherent* and *consequential* political goals outside the continent. The enlargement of such institutions as to European Community and the Western European Union only ensures that unity in external policy will remain elusive.

The outbreak of the Iran–Iraq War in the early autumn of 1980 presented special problems for Europeans, and certainly for the few (mainly outside governments) who may have felt that Europe required a collective approach to regional stability in the Gulf. The challenge presented by the war had stark political-military implications given the initial fears that the conflict might not be contained to the region itself, posed potential economic challenges given European dependence on oil and the desire of European commercial enterprises to maintain good relations with petrodollar rich markets, and even more gravely for many, resuscitated an ancient ideological struggle which could conceivably threaten the image of the West in the area. The fall of the Shah and the Iranian Revolution therefore made European chanceries (as well as other Western and certainly Middle Eastern governments) ask themselves whether, like the French or the Russian revolutions, the uprising in Iran would deeply affect both the definition and the practice of international relations, at least in the Middle East, or whether – like countless other

215

succession crises with an ideological cover – it merely affected the nature of domestic order in the country concerned. Would the revolution pose a new Islamic challenge to the West, or was it merely another manifestation of the deep divisions within the Islamic world which would have no wider implications? From the start of the war, a number of common concerns were therefore expressed, but this in no sense led to co-ordinated policy making.

For the Europeans, as for others, the outbreak of the war (which confirmed some of their worst fears) offered the prospect of regional ideological containment and helped to postpone full consideration of what the revolution in Iran might mean for international order. It also intensified the need to assess what short term interests had to be defended in the region and how the form of such defence of national interests would affect the long term positions of the major powers in the area once the war ended. That calculation, in turn, was heavily dependent on guesses – it could rarely have been more than this – of how the war would end. The reality of oil dependency, the desire to pursue basic economic exchanges when possible with both parties, the need to sustain good relations with the smaller Gulf states who came to form the Gulf Co-operation Council (GCC) and the opportunity offered by the war for European powers to sell arms, all mixed with considerations of how best to protect broadly Western interests in the region. Since European states were reluctant to develop a *Gesamtkonzept* to describe their position towards the war and to the region, they were condemned to practice individual *realpolitik* which sometimes had competitive aspects. Until the very end of the war, this meant that in the formation of foreign policy, self-interest tended to triumph over principle.

Retrospectively, one could argue that the resolutely national approach to the conflict followed by European states was to the general benefit of European policy for two broad reasons. First, since some European states sought to develop firm comparative advantages while others adopted a more cautious evenhanded stance, in Europe it was always possible to find an interlocutor to the extent that any of the belligerents wished for one. But the argument that diversity of opinion may sometimes have a political utility would be a weak basis on which to develop future foreign policy strategies. Second, when European states found themselves in agreement: the deployment of naval vessels to the Gulf in 1987, the simultaneous intensification of efforts to bring the war to an end, and the later individual (but still collective in effect) series of decisions to seek a rapprochement with Iran – the impact of such actions was all the more impressive given previous disunity. Yet these three elements were never really part of a *collectively defined* policy. Indeed, proponents of intensified European Political Co-operation (EPC) can find precious few encouraging signs in the history of the European approach to the Iran–Iraq War. On the one issue that perhaps should have inspired a unanimous, principled and co-ordinated response – the use of chemical weapons in the war – European states were largely silent.

Those with historical records in the area (primarily Britain, France, West Germany, Italy), each defined the interests that were engaged in the war slightly differently; pursued particular arms sales policies both to the belligerents and to other states in the region that reflected business interests at least as much as (and sometimes more than) strategic goals, had varying views on the reaction to Iran's violent diplomacy and apparent support for hostage-takers; and kept up commercial links with different countries. When there was an equal threat to their merchant shipping in the area, the European states who decided to deploy to the region agreed to harmonize their activities (and in August 1988 agreed within the WEU to co-ordinate their eventual withdrawal). When the belligerents gave sign that they wished to draw the conflict to a close, Europeans made suitably encouraging noises. But in the main, European states reacted to events throughout the war to defend particular interests, and rarely sought to shape a regional destiny they felt was not susceptible to Western manipulation. A European attitude to the war was never really given form even though during the period of the war the intra-European debates on the need for more coherent defence and foreign policies were conducted with increasing vigour.

DEFINITION OF INTERESTS

It is well to begin with French policy, since more than any other European power France chose to strengthen a comparative advantage in the region based on only recent links. Rather than hedge her bets on future outcomes, as did a number of other European states, France became firmly tied to one belligerent and determined to do what could be done to prevent the spread of Islamic fundamentalism. Without displacing traditionally strong British positions in Iraq, since the mid 1970s France had increased her activity in the area, transferring helicopters in 1974, signing an economic co-operation agreement in 1976, transferring Mirage F1's in 1978 and, throughout this period, helping to build the nuclear reactor eventually destroyed by Israel in 1981. By the time Mitterrand came to power in May 1981, Iraq owed France some 15 billion francs, and like all large creditors in similar circumstance France was therefore obliged to continue to assist Iraq or risk losing all.[1] Grafted on to this economic imperative was a strategic goal elaborated mainly by politicians, namely preventing the Islamic revolution from spreading further west, and particularly towards such Maghreb states as Tunisia on which France's Mediterranean policy had long depended. The perception that France needed to play a balancing role in the Gulf soon came to override other considerations. Arms transfers, particularly the lease of five *Super Etendards* to Iraq in 1983 (returned in 1985) were intended to ensure that Iran always felt under pressure of attack from Iraq either on her shipping or oil installations. While France had no ambition (nor the capacity) to pursue a full fledged containment policy towards Iran, she more than any other Western power openly committed herself to a particular strategic analysis of the war. The fact that France also gave refuge to some of the earlier Iranian refugees after the first phase of the revolution, and was later sometimes perceived to be offering succour to counter-revolutionary elements put France in a very exposed position *vis-à-vis* Iran. The need to deal with the adverse effects of the tacit alliance with Iraq occupied much of French foreign policy, and was a consistenly central issue in domestic politics, between 1985 and 1988.

The primacy of good relations with Iraq was a persistent feature in French diplomacy even when a ceasefire was in the offing. In May 1988 the French government lifted its embargo on oil purchases from Iran and later, in mid-June, pledged to renew diplomatic relations, but care was still taken to keep the pace of economic *rapprochement* slow so as not to harm the existing oil trade with Baghdad and upset a partner whose goodwill France had carefully cultivated for over a decade and a half. The widely reported remark made in May 1983 by Iraqi Foreign Minister Tarik Aziz to the effect that once the war was over and the Iraqi oil industry had recovered its normal capacity, Iraq would favour those who co-operated with us in our time of difficulty, was carefully noted in France and reflected the subtle hold that Iraq held on French economic sensibilities.[2] While it would be an exaggeration to argue that France's relative dependence on Middle East and particularly Iraqi oil supplies *determined* its political-military assessments (which centred on a conviction that an Iranian military victory would produce havoc in the Arab world), economic considerations and the need to maintain good relations with Iraq were always present in French calculations. More than any other European country French leaders were subliminally affected by Iraqi declarations about the geopolitical interests that were at play in the conflict. In July 1984, Mitterrand told journalists in the presence of King Hussein of Jordan that 'France does not wish to be the enemy of Iran or of anyone else ... [but] ... she does not want ... the age old equilibrium between Persians and Arabs to be broken.'[3] The spectre of Persian expansionism was the one fearful image on which Iraq could draw in soliciting support from the smaller Gulf states, and it also helped to seduce France into Iraqi quarters.

As an oil producer, the United Kingdom had no obvious strategic vulnerability that conditioned her response to the outbreak of the war. The United Kingdom therefore had the luxury, at least initially, of seeing her interests more plainly as retaining decent relations, to the extent that the policies of either belligerent allowed, with both Iran and Iraq. The Western conventional wisdom which came to be accepted after the first year or so of the war, that Iraq could not win the war, and Iran could not lose it, had some of its strongest believers in Whitehall. While equally catastrophic outcomes were feared no matter which side won, there was a deep-seated conviction that neither would. The United Kingdom's strong relations with the small sheikdoms in the Gulf perhaps made her especially sensitive to some of their fears about an Iraqi victory, but just as the GCC tried to maintain some lines of communication with Iran, the United Kingdom did all she reasonably could to retain a capacity for dialogue with Khomeini's revolutionary regime. The fact that the UK had had very close links with the Shah's regime (including an active policy of military transfers) hardly endeared the new regime to the UK, but Whitehall still made efforts to keep some contact. Even in 1987 and early 1988, when Anglo-Iranian relations were at their worst, and despite the UK's traditional attachment to perfect reciprocity on matters relating to diplomatic protocol, Iran was allowed to retain a diplomatic mission in London even though British representation in Tehran was reduced to an interests section.

A declaratory policy of neutrality in the war was in part a fruit of the realization that the United Kingdom was not in a position to play a balancing role in the region either diplomatically or militarily. The UK's 'colonial' history with Iraq (perceived as the important oil power) made for sometimes awkward contemporary relations, and the difficulty of dealing with the revolutionary government in Tehran (clearly seen as the more vital geopolitical force) offered substantial impediments to the most imaginative diplomacy. Even if the Iranian leadership might from time to time have proclaimed its suspicion that the UK was still playing a 'Great Game' in the area, there was a profound realization in the UK that only defensive foreign policy goals could be pursued, and that any attempt to shape events would be at best embarrassing and at worst counterproductive. The UK was respected by both belligerents, but had little or no influence.

For virtually the whole length of the war there was also a perception in the UK that no other outside power could easily affect outcomes in the war. It was clear that the United States, vilified as the Great Satan by Iran, would have at best limited leverage in that country. The Reagan Administration, while maintaining the *officially* neutral stance of the Carter government, also sought to develop better relations with Iraq and some recognition by that country of US positions in the region. Secretary of State Alexander Haig hoped that Iraq could be wooed into some sort of anti-Soviet strategic view.[4] These goals of American policy, which were very modest, did not lend themselves to collaborative effort with the UK. As in all matters, consultation between the UK and the US was considerable, but the Gulf War did not offer opportunities for the 'special relationship' to be reconfigured for the region. For most of the war, the UK was especially sceptical of American suggestions that certain Western interests in the Gulf might have to be protected by the use of military force, and in concert with many other NATO allies was critical of some of the more grandiose plans developed for the possible use of a Rapid Deployment Force (RDF) in the Gulf. The UK, like other European powers, did not wish the US ever to draw down forces in Europe to meet usually ill-defined Gulf contingencies, nor did she relish the prospect of having to compensate 'in-area' in the event of a possible deployment of US forces from Europe. Thus UK policy from the start was centred on preserving through diplomacy minimal British interests in the region. The mission of the Armilla Patrol in the Gulf from 1980 was humbly defined as accompanying, within certain limits, British merchant traffic in the Gulf region. This naval policy would become more active only when the changing nature of the threat to shipping in the Gulf forced a UK response. Equally, UK diplomacy became more intense when changes in the international political climate produced an environment conducive to multilateral diplomacy at the UN where the UK's position on the Security Council meant that it could shape the politics of war termination.

If the UK's strategic calculations were not affected much by the specific interpretations and concerns of the US, though both agreed on many issues, it was also little worried by the prospect (which more easily animated the leadership in France) of increased Soviet influence in the Gulf. The USSR's alliance with Iraq was considered in the UK more apparent than real. The late 1970s had seen strains between the two countries (the 1978 execution of twenty-one Communists in Iraq for subversion, the Iraqi decision to reduce the number of Iraqis receiving military training in the Soviet Union, disputes about military and economic co-operation), and the eventual Soviet decision to repair relations with Iraq in late 1979 was taken largely in the context of deteriorating relations with Iran, despite the Soviet Union's initial praise to the Iranian revolution.[5] While noting Moscow's later improvement of relations with Iraq, and the continued attempts to court Iran (whenever the latter's strong anti-Soviet rhetoric permitted it), most observers in the UK felt that the Soviet Union's leverage in the war was minimal. There was therefore no urgent need to seek to offset any growth of Soviet influence, as this was seen to be low with little chances of improvement.

The political calculation that little could be done by Western powers to affect the conflict and that the Soviet Union could not easily take advantage of it for its own ends, led to an unassuming military policy. The government made a decision not to sell lethal arms to either side. Some British companies might well have treaded close to this definition (a number of spare parts were sold), but the UK was never affected by the sort of arms-to-Iran scandal that touched at one point or another Sweden, West Germany, France, Portugal, The Netherlands, Italy or Spain.[6] The UK's arms sales effort during the war was directed much more to the Gulf states, and particularly to Saudi Arabia, than to the principals in the conflict and this gave the UK the twin political advantage of being able honestly to claim neutrality while making a positive contribution to the confidence, stability and strength of the small states in the region with whom the UK had long established links. The commitment to ensure that British merchant shipping be afforded reasonable protection in an international waterway was reflected in the decision to mount the Armilla Patrol in 1980 to accompany commercial vessels. This activity became more important after 1984 when attacks on shipping intensified. The deployment was sufficiently discreet that when in the autumn of 1987 there emerged a major intra-Western debate on the utility of sending military force to the Gulf given the heightened threat, few knew that the UK had for a long period already deployed to the region. As argued below, the UK's eventual decision to add minehunters and minesweepers to the region was taken once a specific mine threat was seen to exist, and not as a result of a larger geopolitical calculation.

While willing to accept whatever benefits might accrue from the fact that many American congressmen approved of the UK's decision (and that of other Europeans) to support American policy in the Gulf, like other European states, the UK was at pains within the limits imposed by her close relationship to the US to stress the independence of her military activity. The United Kingdom, like France, became more active in the diplomacy surrounding the conflict when there emerged an urgent need to deal with deteriorating relations with Iran and a more complex military situation in the Gulf. But these two major European powers never sought to co-ordinate policies with each other and were often at odds both on how to deal with hostage-taking and on how, within the UN Security Council, to best exert pressure on the belligerents to bring the war to an end.

While France and the United Kingdom could at least pretend to roles in the region (even if minor) given their historical links, no other European power sought to do much more than ensure that national positions were as insulated as possible from the turbulence caused by the war. In fact, for most European countries, the war had virtually no effect on oil supplies or on their own attempts to retain or to build on their existing markets in the region, though markets for products other than arms for the two belligerents were naturally small. Many of the smaller European countries, particularly the Scandinavians and the Dutch procure most of their oil supplies from the North Sea and therefore did not see themselves as economically at risk from the war. Those who were more dependent, like the Greeks and the Spaniards, were able in any case to receive all the oil they needed. some of the smaller European powers may have liked, as on all intra-European matters, for strong European Community positions to emerge on the conflict, but found that even drafting language on terrorism and hostage-taking, or on the use of chemical weapons in the war, was difficult because of the distinct national perspectives and diplomatic interests that the larger powers brought to Brussels. Consistent with previously established views, the smaller powers also expressed a preference for the war to be settled through the multilateral mechanisms of the UN, a plea which began to look realistic only when, in early 1988, the five permanent members of the UN simultaneously, and with roughly equal levels of concern, felt the need to press firmly ahead for a ceasefire.

West Germany and Italy, while retaining very low diplomatic profiles over the war, did have more interests, largely commercial in nature, to defend and advance than did the smaller European powers, but had neither the will nor the capacity to take a front line approach to the conflict. Both countries early on declared their neutrality. For Italy, this meant that its previously solid economic relations with Iraq were put under pressure, as a result of the non-delivery of 11 warships ordered in 1980 as part of a 1.1 billion dollar contract awarded to Fincantieri. While export licences were granted for all 11 in 1981, these later lapsed because of the Italian government's decision to ban military exports to both combatants. Iraq as a consequence refused to make repayments on its 2 billion dollar debt to Italy.[7] Italian companies maintained large construction projects in the country led by a large number of Italian workers. Italian relations with the country throughout the war were cordial and clearly the presence of many Italians in Iran was an important fact which militated against Italy taking a high diplomatic profile in the region.[8] Italian businesses were able to operate with both belligerents, and one company, Saipem, had a 100 million dollar contract to build the northern sector of a 320 kilometre pipeline to carry Iranian crude oil to export terminals midway down the Gulf Coast, and also led a multinational consortium to build the second stage of an Iraqi pipeline through Saudi Arabia.[9] During the war, Italian diplomacy was largely successful in maintaining the strict neutrality reflected in the commercial practices of Italian business.

West Germany was also able to sustain an evenhanded approach, but perhaps more than any other European power was concerned to maintain constant diplomatic relations with the regime in Iran and strong commercial relations. West Germany's goal was to keep a very low key approach and maintain acceptability in both states. However, it is clear West Germany had particular links to Iran. When a West German hostage, Alfred Cordes was released from captivity in Beirut in September 1988, Foreign Minister Hans-Dietrich Genscher noted that this was a triumph for Bonn's quiet diplomacy and a result of Germany's ability to keep channels open to Iran. Genscher had visited the Islamic Republic in July 1984 and described Western attempts to isolate the country as 'one of the biggest mistakes made by Western powers'.[10] In November 1987 he visited Baghdad and rescheduled over 2 billion dollars of credits owed by Iraq. By the summer of 1988 Genscher was the only European foreign minister who was listened to in both capitals, and he used this position to try – discreetly – to convince both parties to scale down military activities and move towards a ceasefire. Once the ceasefire was in place, West German relations with Iran intensified with a visit by Genscher to Iran in November 1988. While a carefully crafted evenhanded policy continued to be cultivated, it was evident that West Germany was particularly keen not to offend Iran, as symbolized by West Germany's refusal of a visa to the young Shah of Iran during his European tour in December 1988.

EUROPEAN INSTITUTIONS AND CRISIS DIPLOMACY

The very distinct national positions and interests of the West European states towards the two belligerents and the war itself made it especially awkward to harmonize European official attitudes and indeed no serious effort was even made to do so. The dilemma of how to preserve individual policies seen as advantageous while cultivating common European views was never overcome. The organs of European Political Co-operation were active during the whole war, and near the end helped to reinforce diplomatically the urgency felt throughout Europe for a peace settlement. But national approaches to certain problems made it difficult to fashion a general European foreign policy on the war. This was particularly evident on the issue of negotiation by European states with Shi'ite hostage-takers in Lebanon which often affected policies previously established *vis-à-vis* Iran. Officially the European Community adopted the principle that there should be no negotiation for hostages. The United Kingdom stuck most resolutely to this policy and had the luxury of considerable public support for a firm stand. Arguing that dealing with hostage-takers only encouraged them to believe that their crime paid and thus raised the relative value of British citizens in dangerous areas of the Middle East, the UK opposed all forms of negotiation. The French government, which was perhaps subject to more public pressure to negotiate, was willing to deal with Tehran over hostages believed to be held by Shi'a groups in the Lebanon. Such negotiations became more frequent after Jacques Chirac became prime minister in 1986, and were an important feature in the immediate period before the May 1988 presidential elections when Chirac worked hard for the release of French hostages in the hope that this would give him an electoral success. France's policy on negotiation with kidnappers, viewed in London as too cynical by half, angered the United Kingdom and seemed also to undercut a basic consensus established at the Community level. It also provided a perhaps salutary lesson on the limits to foreign policy co-ordination in Europe.

While European leaders meeting at the Community level did their best to develop common positions, or at least common attitudes of mind, on terrorism and violent diplomacy, any deep consensus was frustrated by the special problems some countries confronted in their diplomatic relations with the belligerents, particularly Iran. In 1987 both Britain and France had serious diplomatic rows with Iran over which the Community had virtually no influence. In the case of Britain, a crisis was sparked in July 1987 by the arrest of Iran's vice-consul in Manchester for theft which resulted in the retaliatory seizure of the UK head of chancery. Eventually the crisis was resolved through the expulsion of both, and a year later relations were improved once the two countries had agreed on compensation for damage previously made to the respective embassies in the two capitals. This paved the way (after Iran had agreed to UN Resolution 598) for the eventual re-establishment of a diplomatic mission in Tehran at the end of 1988; these relations were, nevertheless, severed again in the spring of 1989 following the Rushdie affair.

France, also in mid-1987, engaged in a lengthy battle with Iran, later referred to as the *guerre des ambassades*, after it wished to interrogate an Iranian 'interpreter' at the Paris Embassy (Wahid Gordji) over terrorist acts that had taken place in Paris the previous September. French police eventually felt it necessary to surround the Iranian Embassy in Paris and the Iranians then did the same to the French Embassy in Tehran. By the early autumn Paris announced that it was sending the aircraft carrier *Clemenceau* to the region, whose only mission could have been to 'show resolve', and indicate the seriousness of Paris' concern. By 30 November 1987 this crisis was ended when Gordji was exchanged in Karachi for captured French consul Paul Torre. This was interpreted by many as a violation of the EC's policy not to make deals on questions concerning terrorism. During the crisis, and indeed later, Iran insisted that relations could only improve once France agreed to repay the 2 billion dollars it owed Iran, put an end to the activities of Iranian opposition groups in France, and stopped selling arms to Iraq. While in later dealing with Iran, France offered Tehran some satisfaction on the first two of these demands, she was never willing to sacrifice good relations with Iraq for slightly better ones with Iran.

The experiences of France and the UK in dealing with Iran, and the equally individualistic policies of a number of other European states, offer proof of the difficulty of developing common European policies of consequence on any extra-European activity. Particularly in the Gulf, any common policy would be hostage to the degree of exposure of one of the EC member states to the ire of one of the two parties. Since European states had asymmetrical interests, different levels of influence and variable political, economic and even military agendas, a common policy *on any issue* was difficult both to draft and to enforce.

In this context the ability of a number of European states to harmonize policies relating to the naval deployment in the Gulf beginning in autumn 1987 is all the more remarkable. The capacity of the member states of the WEU to consult on this policy and even co-ordinate some of their activity was all the more important given a previous record of disunity. This was possible because the various European states who agreed to consult on their activities in the Gulf waters all accepted a common definition of the threat, perceived a common sense of vulnerability, and were able to agree on a common response. By the autumn of 1987, after the US had begun to deploy warships in the Gulf following her decision to reflag Kuwaiti vessels, it was generally agreed that the threat to shipping, and particularly the threat from mines, had increased. The UK felt it was in her *national* interest to add a minesweeping and minehunting capacity to her existing military assets in the Gulf. France took the same decision. Eventually so did Italy and Belgium;

and the Netherlands, which later collaborated very closely with the United Kingdom in the area, also added ships. West Germany, feeling that its constitution prevented deployment of military power beyond the NATO area, nevertheless sent four ships to the Mediterranean (much to the satisfaction of the Navy who welcomed the opportunity to sail outside of the Baltic and the North Sea) to compensate for the draw down of other NATO ships from the Western Mediterranean. Luxembourg, which has no ships, nevertheless helped pay for the operation.

Thus all WEU member states participated in some way in the deployment policy. Italy, Belgium and the Netherlands probably would not have deployed were it not for the useful political cover offered by the WEU. While France and Italy pursued more independent policies than did the other three deploying states, all agreed to consult within the WEU framework. As a result it was possible for European states deploying to the Gulf in 1987 to arrange for communication to take place easily between ministers, naval points of contact in capitals, and commanders at sea. Regular meetings of WEU naval experts took place in London to discuss the evolving threat. Despite this, it is doubtful that very much co-ordinated thinking took place on questions such as common responses to shipping under attack. Rules of engagement were still strictly national. Still, efforts were always made at the public level to display a general unity of purpose by the WEU. When in late summer 1988 some of the opposition parties in some of the deploying countries argued that there should be a reduction of assets in the Gulf, the WEU member states agreed that any withdrawal should be coherent and take place only after consultation. Deploying countries agreed that should the ceasefire between the belligerents hold, they would stay on to clear some of the estimated 2000 mines in the Shatt-al-Arab and the Northern Gulf area.

Politically, this co-ordinated European action was possible because it could be justified as a contribution to international order: maintaining the freedom of navigation within an international waterway. While *de facto* this meant a tilt in favour of Iraq, diplomatically it was still possible to argue that the policy was intended to be neutral. Operationally, the fact that the deployment was *naval* also meant that there was never any question of breach of territorial sovereignty though of course port visits had to take place, and by invitation there was some mine clearing done in territorial waters. This display of a general European interest in the security of the Gulf additionally had the advantage of focusing international attention on a conflict much of the world had learned to live with.

Much of the diplomacy in the UN was still in its early stages when the deployment began, but the policy considerations that the deployment had inspired in European capitals led to intensification of the efforts to bring the war to an end. The fact that European governments had made certain military commitments which they did not wish to be open-ended helped to concentrate minds on ways to arrange a ceasefire or at least to make the conduct of the war more difficult. The United Kingdom perhaps did most to press for a consensus within the Security Council, seeking in August and September 1987, in collaboration with the United States, to arrange a mandatory arms embargo on the belligerents. By January 1988 the UK was forced to accept a draft text which singled out Iran for failure to comply with the July 1987 ceasefire resolution. Both Washington and Paris preferred that sanctions, if any, be applied only against Iran, while the UK would have liked a more evenhanded approach. The Soviet Union and China, which had had little difficulty the previous year in approving Resolution 598, dragged their feet on the arms embargo draft, worried that it represented a tilt in favour of Iraq which would make mediation by the UN difficult. But although these various deliberations did not result in a formal resolution, the diplomatic momentum thus established probably had the net effect of putting added pressure on Iran to accept the earlier and more important Resolution 598.

EUROPE AND POST-WAR RELATIONS IN THE GULF

The interest of European states in the war deepened in 1987 and 1988 owing to their naval deployment in the Gulf and their later need to develop policies within the UN. Once the ceasefire was accepted in the Gulf, diplomatic efforts were concentrated on normalization of relations with the two parties to the conflict. As UN-led discussions began in August 1988 in an attempt to translate the ceasefire into a durable political settlement, European companies also began to plan for a possible role in a reconstruction effort. The official aim of European governments, like the private ambition of European companies, was to return, if not to a status quo ante bellum, at least to a post-war order which was susceptible to rational calculation and practical planning. The physical eccentricities of the Shatt-al-Arab and the political interest it inspires, will be only one of many obstacles to the establishment of an order in the Gulf which would allow for a true return to business as usual. In any case, whatever order is established, or whatever form of anarchy prevails, individual European states will continue to pursue national interests that will reflect a common European view only on some issues, and that probably more by accident than by design. Each will seek to retain and build on the special comparative advantages they may have gained with the area. During the war, West Germany was particularly successful in preserving and even cultivating links with Iran without injuring its position of neutrality. France, which never pretended to neutrality, was nevertheless successful in quickly re-establishing good relations with Iran once the ceasefire was accepted. The United Kingdom, despite some ups and downs, was also in a position, once the ceasefire began to take effect, to begin to build balanced relations with both Iran and Iraq, something which Italy had been able to maintain throughout the war. The smaller European countries, to the degree that their political systems and economic energies allow, will be able, slowly to build better relations with both Iran and Iraq. No European country, nor any group acting together, will wish or be able to shape events in the region, but the experience of European states in the war suggests that Europe's general image in the Gulf will emerge as stronger in relation to the perceptions held by local states of the US, than was the case on the eve of the war.

In general, European governments were able, while pursuing a clearly Western political strategy in the region, to distinguish themselves from the US. They made separate, if not radically different, definitions of Western interests in the region, and by their policies demonstrated that Western interpretations on Gulf events were variable. The deployment of European naval power to the Gulf, while short of a totally co-ordinated or centrally directed effort, had the net effect of improving the status of a number of European states with many GCC members, including the two most important: Saudi Arabia and Kuwait. Through their need to deal with these states (for on-shore facilities, and to consult generally on policy), the European and Gulf states concerned were able better to appreciate each others' perspectives on the regional situation. If in the first year of the war the Europeans generally were most agitated by the question of oil supplies, later, when this was clearly no longer a problem, it was possible for some of them to build a relationship with the Gulf states which reflected broader mutual concerns. As for post-war relations with the two belligerents, European states will seek to advance their diplomatic and commercial interests individually – conditioned and affected in part by attitudes struck during the war, and in part by reactions to emerging developments in the area. Perhaps more than in the past – but not much more – the behaviour of the two powers will colour attitudes. Iraqi policy towards the Kurds or Iranian support of extreme Shi'ite groups could affect the speed of rapprochement pursued by European and other powers. In the long run, a number of states will likely perceive that the importance of Iran is such that it should not remain even in self-imposed isolation. But none of this will be a result of decisions taken in Brussels; nor will Brussels machinery help in harmonizing policies which no European state will consider to be importantly advanced by making them the object of collective attention. While European states might see some advantage in making declarations of principle on Middle Eastern questions – perhaps primarily on the Arab–Israel dispute – in the Gulf, Europeans will choose resolutely to muddle through on their own.

Notes

1. See Ralph King, *Irak–Iran: la guerre paralysée* (Paris: Editions Bosquet 1987) p. 108, an expanded and updated version of his earlier 'The Iran–Iraq War: The Political Implications', *Adelphi Papers* 219 (Summer 1987). Shahram

Chubin, 'La France et le Golfe: opportunisme ou continuité', *Politique Etrangère*, April 1983, pp. 879–87; and Jose Garcon, 'La France et le conflit Iran–Iraq', *Politique Etrangère*, February 1987, pp. 357–66.

2. See Paul Gallis, 'The NATO Allies and the Persian Gulf', in Christopher Coker (ed), *The United States, Western Europe and Military Intervention Overseas*, RUSI Defence Studies Series (London: Macmillan, 1987), p. 42.

3. Ibid., p. 45.

4. See M.S. El Azhary, 'The Attitudes of the Superpowers Towards the Gulf War', *International Affairs*, vol. 59, no. 4 (Autumn 1983), p. 615.

5. Ibid., p. 616.

6. For a survey see George Russell, 'Everybody's Doing It', *Time* 16 (March 1987), p. 33.

7. See 'Italy Special Report', *Middle East Economic Digest*, July 1988, p. 16.

8. See Gallis, *The NATO Allies*, p. 43.

9. *Italy Special Report*, ibid., p. 3.

10. See 'How Bonn Got Iran Off the Hook', *The Middle East*, December 1988, pp. 20–22.

Part IV

The Economics of War

14 Economic Implications for the Region and World Oil Market

Eliyahu Kanovsky

Analyses of the Iran–Iraq War have focused mainly on its political, strategic, and military ramifications. This chapter will focus on the war's impact on the economies of the belligerent countries, on other Middle Eastern economies, and on world oil markets.

ECONOMIC DEVELOPMENTS IN IRAQ DURING THE 1970s

Iraq's economy was booming during the 1970s, with (real) gross domestic product (GDP) rising by an annual average rate of 15–16 per cent between 1972 and 1979. The boom continued until the outbreak of hostilities in September 1980. In fact these figures tend to understate the magnitude of the boom after oil prices rose very sharply in 1973–4 and, even more so in 1979–80. Since the precipitous rise in oil prices greatly exceeded the rise in the prices of goods imported by Iraq, its international terms of trade were far more favourable, and the growth in gross national income was far more rapid than that of gross national product. Oil export revenues – the source of Iraq's prosperity – rose from one billion dollars in 1972 to $21 billion in 1979 and $26 billion in 1980, as a whole. During the months preceding the war, oil revenues were flowing into the country at an annual rate of about $33 billion. The volume of oil exports had risen from 1.4 million barrels per day (MBD) in 1972 to 3.2 MBD in 1979 and continued at that rate during the first eight months of 1980.[1] Iraq was building up its oil production capacity and fully exploiting the escalation in oil prices.

It is noteworthy that during periods of glut in the 1970s (i.e., when spot market prices were lower than those set by OPEC), such as in 1975 and again in 1978, the Iraqis were amongst those OPEC members offering discounts. Thus, in 1975, Iraqi oil production rose 14.7 per cent while for the rest of OPEC (as a whole) there was a decline of 13.1 per cent. Again in 1978 Iraqi oil production rose 8.9 per cent, while for the rest of OPEC there was a decline of 5.6 per cent. The rise in Iraqi exports while those of its rivals in OPEC were declining, was due to heavy discounting by the Iraqis. Plans announced before the war were for an expansion of capacity to five MBD by 1985.[2] Peak production before hostilities was 3.5 MBD.

Aside from its huge oil potential, Iraq possesses an abundance of other natural resources including cultivatable land and plentiful water supplies as well as large deposits of phosphates and sulphur. Ambitious development plans announced during the 1970s called for a more intensive exploitation of these resources, through high rates of investment especially in industry and agriculture. Large investments in infrastructure (roads and railroads, water, electric power, etc.) would underpin the expansion of the economy. The goal was to utilize the expanding stream of oil revenues to finance overall development in order to reduce the country's overwhelming dependence on oil. Agricultural and industrial expansion would provide import substitutes as well as more non-oil exports.

Government spending increased very sharply during the 1970s, but while actual military and current civilian expenditures equalled or exceeded the announced budgets, investment spending lagged far behind goals. None the less, overall government spending rose precipitously from a mere $1.4 billion in fiscal 1972/3 to $16.1 billion in 1979 and $20.9 billion in the following year.[3] The escalation in public spending was financed solely by the above-mentioned rise in oil revenues. However, despite far higher levels of public expenditures they lagged behind the influx of oil revenues. The small fiscal deficit in 1972/3 ($243 million) was replaced by large surpluses, especially in the years immediately following the oil shocks of 1973/4 and 1979/80. The budgetary surplus in 1974 was $1.8 billion; in 1980, $9.1 billion.

The rise in public expenditures was inevitably followed by a major increase in imports. Civilian commodity imports rose from $0.7 billion in 1972 to $4.2 billion in 1975 and $13.9 billion in 1980. Military expenditures are understated in the Iraqi official accounts and figures for the importation of military hardware are not disclosed. Estimates of the US Arms Control and Disarmament Agency suggest that military spending (including both local military expenditures and payments for arms imports) rose very sharply from $0.7 billion in 1972 to $6.4 billion in 1979 and $11.2 billion in 1980. Arms imports rose from $140 million in 1972 to an annual average of $2.1 billion in 1978–80.

The goal of the planners to reduce the country's dependence on oil was not realized; quite the contrary. Estimates of the US Department of Agriculture indicate that Iraqi farm production per capita in 1977–9 was about the same as in 1969–71 (annual averages). However, since personal incomes were rising rapidly (fuelled by the oil boom), agricultural imports rose very sharply from $214 million in 1972 to $1.4 billion in 1979 and $2.0 billion in 1980. Official Iraqi sources suggest that industrial production (excluding crude oil output) rose at an average annual rate of 11 per cent between 1972 and 1980. However, other sources suggest that the public sector firms – which dominated industry – were generally inefficient and poorly managed.[4] In terms of both government finance and the balance of payments, Iraq's dependence on oil was not only overwhelming but increasing during the 1970s. In 1972 oil accounted for 55 per cent of government revenues; in 1979–80, over 90 per cent. Non-oil exports which accounted for 8 per cent of Iraq's commodity exports in 1972, were less than 1 per cent of total exports in 1979–80.

In short, at the eve of the war, Iraq's economy was prospering, fuelled by the world oil boom. Despite massive military spending, as well as large-scale civilian outlays, it accumulated an estimated $35 billion in foreign exchange reserves.[5] Its foreign debt was miniscule.

THE WAR'S IMPACT ON THE ECONOMY OF IRAQ

By far the most severe blow to the economy of Iraq was Iran's successful closure of the Persian Gulf – soon after hostilities began – to Iraqi oil exports, as well as imports. Until 1975 Iraq's main oil export outlet had been via the pipeline through Syria. As a result of disputes over transit dues, this pipeline was closed in 1976. But, between 1974 and 1976 the Iraqis had built an internal north-south pipeline, and a much smaller pipeline through Turkey, and could therefore resist Syrian demands for still higher transit dues. Subsequently the Syrians lowered their demands and in the spring of 1979 the Iraqis resumed shipments through Syria, but in far smaller quantities. The closure of the Gulf to Iraqi oil shipments since September 1980, again put the Iraqis at the mercy of Syria. In 1981 the Syrians permitted limited Iraqi exports through their pipeline. But in the spring of 1982 the Iranians persuaded the Syrians to close their pipeline by offering them, in lieu of Iraqi transit dues, a million tons of oil per annum as a grant, and an additional five million tons per annum at discounted prices and on easy credit terms. This left the Iraqis with but one outlet, the pipeline through Turkey with a capacity (at that time) of 650 thousand barrels per day (TBD). In other words, Iraqi oil exports in 1982 were but one fifth of their pre-war volume.

Moreover, oil prices which had peaked in the spring of 1981, were beginning to decline. Iraqi oil revenues which had been over $30 billion during the year preceding the war were down to about $10 billion per annum in 1981–3.

The Iraqi authorities, in the initial phases of the war, believed that hostilities would be short-lived, and, that they would soon be victorious. Until 1982 their policy was what might be described as 'guns and butter'. Public spending, both military and civilian, continued to rise, despite the very sharp fall in revenues. Total government spending which had risen sharply from $7.4 billion in 1976 to almost $21 billion in 1980 rose even more

Table 14.1   Iraq – selected economic indicators

Iraq	1972	1973	1974	1975	1976	1977	1978
Oil production (thousands of barrels per day)	1465	2020	1970	2260	2415	2350	2560
Oil exports (thousands of barrels per day)	1436	1926	1850	2059	2241	2167	2384
Domestic oil consumption (thousands of barrels per day)	–	–	–	–	–	–	150
Total commodity exports (millions of dollars)	1108	1955	6601	8297	9272	9649	11 061
of which oil exports (millions of dollars)	1022	1836	6506	8176	9114	9505	10850
Sales from neutral zone (millions of dollars)	–	–	–	–	–	–	–
Total civilian imports (millions of dollars)	705	894	2371	4214	3470	3899	4213
of which Agricultural imports (millions of dollars)	214	224	704	777	617	4775	1043
Military imports (millions of dollars)	140	625	625	750	1000	1400	2100
Ratio of military expenditures to GNP (%)	14.9	25.5	21.6	17.4	17.2	18.1	19.2
Balance of payments – balance on current account – (billions of dollars)	0.5	0.8	2.6	2.7	2.5	3.0	5.2
Foreign exchange reserves – end-of-year (billions of dollars)	0.6	1.3	3.0	2.5	4.4	6.7	8.0
Foreign debt – end-of-year (billions of dollars)	–	–	0.4	0.4	0.4	1.0	1.1
Population (millions)	10.07	10.41	10.77	11.12	11.51	12.03	12.41
Armed forces (thousands)	105	105	110	155	190	140	362
Official exchange rate – US dollars per Iraqi dinar (annual average)	3.0039	3.3064	3.3862	3.3862	3.3862	3.3862	3.3862
Consumer price index (1975 = 100)	80.8	84.7	91.3	100	112.8	134.1	144.3
Change in consumer price index (%)	5.2	4.8	7.8	9.5	12.8	9.1	7.6
Change in real gross domestic product (%)	2.9	9.1	6.1	18.4	18.0	19.6	10–18
Index of real gross domestic product (1972 = 100)	100	109.1	115.8	137.6	162.4	194.2	223.3
Index of agricultural production (1976–8 = 100)	99	82	87	78	95	98	107
Index of agricultural production per capita (1976–8 = 100)	118	94	96	83	97	98	103
Index of industrial production (1962 = 100)	191.5	207.0	221.7	263.3	324.9	362.8	399.1
Change in index of industrial production (%)	8.2	8.1	7.1	18.8	23.4	11.7	10.0

Sources and Notes: [1]There was a dearth of official Iraqi data even before the war, and fewer are available since the war which began in 1980.
[2]Oil production figures are from the *BP Statistical Review of World Energy*, various issues.
[3]Data for oil exports and domestic oil consumption are from the Economist Intelligence Unit (EIU) reports.
[4]Figures for commodity exports, including oil export revenues and from the Neutral Zone, are from the International Monetary Fund *International Financial Statistics* and from *Middle East Economic Digest* (MEED), various issues. Revenues from the Neutral Zone refer to the sales of oil from the Neutral Zone, jointly owned by Saudi Arabia and Kuwait, on behalf of Iraq.
[5]Civilian Commodity import figures are from *International Financial Statistics*.
[6]Estimates of agricultural imports and of Iraqi agricultural production are from US Department of Agriculture *Middle East and North African-Situation and Outlook Reports*, April 1987, and earlier issues.
[7]The estimates for military imports, the number of men in the armed forces, and the ratio of military expenditures to GNP are from the US Arms Control and Disarmament Agency *World Military Expenditures and Arms Transfers 1986* April 1987, and earlier issues.
[8]The estimates for the balance on current account refer to exports of goods and services plus minus imports of

1979	1980	1981	1982	1983	1984	1985	1986	1987
3475	2645	895	1010	1105	1225	1440	1725	2110 Est.
3275	2459	746	861	787	917	1155	1465	1700 Est.
184	189	205	203	250	234	256	275	300
21431	26278	10530	10250	9785	11440	10579	6765	11500
21289	26136	10388	10100	9650	11242	10285	6465	11158 Est.
		4000	4000	3175	3175	2901	1315	1800 Est.
7179	13942	20735	21534	12166	11078	10556	10190	11000
1383	1988	1996	2535	2857	3085	2858	2712	
2300	1900	3800	4600	5800	7700	2100	5000	
14.9	22.5	45.1	44.8	44.3	42.5			
10.4	13.0	-12.7	-19.1	-7.6	-4.7	-3.7	-3.5	0.8
20.0	30.0	20.0	6.0	3.0	1.5	1.0	1.0	1.0
1.0	2.5	10.3	19.9	26.4	55.0	65.0	75.0	80.0
12.82	13.24	13.67	14.11	14.70	15.20	15.70	16.21	16.30
444	430	392	404	434	788			
3.3862	3.3862	3.3862	3.3513	3.2169	3.2169	3.2169	3.2169	3.2169
163.4	191.9	232.2	301.9	392.5	569.1	711.4	995.9	1237.9
13.2	17.4 Decline	21.0 Decline	30.0 Decline	30.0 Decline	45.0 Decline	40.0 Decline	40.0 Decline	30.0
24	5	35–44	3–5	7–15	8	10–14	8–22	2
276.9	263.1	171.0	164.2	146.1	134.4	118.3	100.6	102.6
106	100	92	101	103	104	130	138	
99	90	80	85	84	82	99	102	
468.8	499.3	451.8						
17.5	6.5	-9.5						

goods and services plus or minus transfers. The estimates are from *International Financial Statistics* for earlier years and from EIU for later years. The figures for the 1980s apparently exclude all or most military imports. Estimates of foreign exchange reserves are from the same sources. Estimates of foreign debt are from EIU, and include so-called loans from Iraq's Arab supporters, mainly Saudi Arabia and Kuwait. Iraq's 'real' debt was probably $40–50 billion at the end of 1987, including debts on account of arms purchases.
[9] The figures for the official exchange rate and for population are from *International Financial Statistics*. It should be noted that the black or free market rate of exchange is far lower.
[10] The estimates for the consumer price index and the real changes in gross domestic product are from *International Financial Statistics* for earlier years and from EIU for later years. These figures must be viewed as no more than broad estimates. The range shown for changes in real gross domestic product in the 1980s reflects estimates given by various sources. The index of gross domestic product is based on the mid-points of these estimates. The index of industrial production includes oil refining, but excludes crude oil production. I have not seen more recent figures.
[11] 1987 figures are estimates.

strongly to $30.5 billion in 1981, dropping slightly to $29.5 billion in 1982. But oil revenues had dropped sharply, and huge fiscal deficits emerged. The total deficits for the three years 1981–3, were a whopping $42 billion.

Increased government spending was soon reflected in growing imports. Civilian commodity imports which had risen from $4.2 billion in 1978 (i.e., before the second oil shock) to $13.9 billion in 1980, rose to $20.7 billion in 1980 and a new peak of $21.5 billion in 1982. Moreover, the closure of the Gulf compelled the Iraqis to utilize circuitous and more costly routes through Jordan, Turkey, and the Arab countries in the Gulf for their imports.

An additional burden on the balance of payments since the war has been the large number of foreign workers 'imported' from Egypt and other countries. The universal military draft, extended for so many years, is a severe burden on the economy. Labour shortages, both quantitative and qualitative, are pervasive. The International Institute for Strategic Studies estimated that Iraq's armed forces numbered one million in 1987 – aside from reserves.[6] This would imply that over one fourth of adult males aged 18–64) was in the armed forces.[7]

There are widely varying estimates as to the number of killed, wounded and captured, but they certainly number in the hundreds of thousands. The severe manpower strain has been alleviated, in part, by a higher female labour force participation rate, but mainly by bringing in large numbers of foreign workers, primarily Egyptians. One estimate published in 1985, suggested that there were as many as two million Egyptians working in Iraq.[8] Another estimate (published in early 1986) suggested that there were two million foreign workers in the country, aside from an equal number of family dependants.[9] Other sources estimated 1.5 million foreign workers, mainly Egyptians and Sudanese.[10] The remittances sent home by these workers were about $4 billion annually.[11] Subsequently the Iraqis, pressed by their balance of payments problems, sharply restricted the amounts of foreign currency which these workers could remit to their home countries. The restrictions reduced the number of foreign workers and in subsequent years remittances declined significantly.[12] An estimate, published in 1988, suggested that the number of Egyptians working in Iraq was 1.7 million 'even after departure of many because of limits of foreign currency remittances'.[13] An estimate published in 1988, suggested that remittances had declined to $1.2 billion in 1987.[14] A decline of that magnitude appears to be implausible. However, it may very well be that a much larger share of remittances was being channelled through the black market.

Military imports which had risen to $2.1 billion per annum in 1978–80 – were far higher in subsequent years. According to the US Arms Control and Disarmament Agency, arms imports averaged $4 billion per annum in 1980–3. An estimate published by the US Congressional Research Service suggested that Iraqi arms imports in 1980–3 were even higher, averaging $5 billion per annum, and rose to $5.8 billion per annum in 1984–7.[15]

The huge pre-war balance of payments surpluses (the current account) were replaced by even larger deficits, $12.7 billion in 1981 and $19.1 billion in 1982. There is a strong presumption that the reported deficits do not include all or most arms imports which were paid for by Iraq's rich Arab neighbours and by Soviet long-term credits, as well as credits from other arms suppliers, especially France. The austerity programme which began in 1982 reduced the balance of payments deficits in subsequent years.

The large 'kitty' of $35 billion in foreign exchange reserves, plus very generous financial aid from Saudi Arabia and Kuwait, and the feeling that victory was in sight, apparently made the Iraqi leadership feel complacent during the first two years of the war. But in 1982, the authorities came to the realization that the war may well go on for several years, and they implemented a sharp reversal in economic policy, in favour of austerity. Imports deemed non-essential were restricted or banned. New contracts (mainly awarded to foreign firms) for construction, which had risen strongly in 1980 and in 1981, were sharply restricted.

Budgetary data are unavailable for more recent years, but (civilian) import data (derived from those published by Iraq's trading partners) show a sharp drop from a peak of $21.5 billion in 1982, to $12.2 billion in 1983, and $10–11 billion per annum in 1984–7. Foreign reserves had dropped precipitously from $35 billion before the war to $3 billion at the end of 1983, and, despite austerity, declined further to one billion dollars in the following year.

Official data on the magnitude of Arab financial aid are not available. Unofficial estimates vary widely. One report (December 1982) suggested that Arab aid had reached $50 billion by the end of 1982, of which about $30 billion was from Saudi Arabia, $15 billion from Kuwait, and the balance from the United Arab Emirates and Qatar.[16] Another report (1988) suggested far lower figures: $50–60 billion until the end of 1987 (including oil sales from the Neutral Zone on behalf of Iraq).[17] It may very well be that the lower estimate excludes Arab payments to the Soviet Union, and possibly to other arms suppliers, on behalf of Iraq.[18] Sales of oil from the Neutral Zone (jointly owned by Saudi Arabia and Kuwait) on behalf of Iraq, began in 1981 and have continued since that time. However, with the sharp drop in oil prices, their value diminished from about $4 billion in 1981 and in 1982 to about $1.8 billion in 1987. What is clear is that though Saudi Arabia and Kuwait continue to provide financial aid to Iraq, its magnitude has most probably diminished. The Saudis, in particular, have been incurring large deficits – both budgetary and balance of payments – since 1983, and their own financial reserves have been drastically reduced. Their fear of Iran impels them to aid Iraq, but their ability to do so has been severely curtailed.

Aside from the austerity programme, the new economic strategy consisted of three elements: a) increasing export capacity by building or expanding oil pipelines; b) extensive external borrowing to finance civilian and military imports, and c) more belatedly, measures to improve efficiency and productivity of the domestic economy.

As noted above, following the closure of the pipeline through Syria in the spring of 1982, the Iraqis were left with the pipeline through Turkey with a capacity of 650 TBD. The Iraqis soon expanded its capacity to one MBD. In 1985 a pipeline through Saudi Arabia, with a capacity of 500 TBD became operational, and in the fall of 1987 an additional pipeline through Turkey was completed with a capacity of 500 TBD. In addition a large fleet of trucks was operating, transporting crude and some refined oil products for export through Turkey and Jordan. Iraq's oil exports (over and above domestic oil consumption estimated at about 300 TBD) had risen sharply from about 800 TBD in 1981–3 to about 2.1 MBD in the first quarter of 1988.[19] But, the expanding volume of exports was, more or less offset by declining oil prices, with revenues remaining at about the $10–11 billion level between 1981 and 1985. 1986 was a disastrous year for oil exporters. Despite increased volume, oil revenues dropped sharply to less than $7 billion. There was a recovery in 1987, both due to higher prices – as compared with 1986 – and the increased volume of sales, with oil revenues rising to about $11 billion. Barring a strong decline in prices, oil revenues will be still higher in 1988. However, it is important to note that even if oil prices do not drop sharply, Iraqi oil revenues in 1988 will be less than half of what they had been before the war, even when measured in nominal dollars (i.e., not corrected for dollar inflation).

The Iraqi authorities appear to be making determined efforts to further expand their oil production and export capacity. A small 70 TBD pipeline to Turkey is scheduled for completion in 1988, and another far larger pipeline through Saudi Arabia with a capacity of 1.15 MBD is scheduled for completion during the latter months of 1989. In other words by the end of 1989 Iraq's exports should reach 3.2 MBD, approximating their pre-war peak levels.[20]

The Minister of Oil made a number of announcements in 1987 and in 1988, claiming that his country's oil reserves are far larger than had been estimated in earlier years, and are second only to those of Saudi Arabia. He stated that production capacity was being expanded from the current 4 MBD by at least another 0.5 MBD. He announced plans for a major increase in drilling for new oil wells, as well as the development of some new oil fields.[21] A new pipeline for natural gas to Kuwait, completed in 1987, should also enhance export revenues by about $500 million annually.[22] Clearly the exigencies of war, and its enormous costs have impelled the Iraqi authorities to exploit their huge oil reserves to the maximum, and if price discounting and ignoring OPEC quotas are necessary, the Iraq authorities have no hesitations. This was their practice during the 1970s under far less compelling circumstances.

Foreign indebtedness which was a miniscule $2.5 billion in 1980 (when oil revenues were over $30 billion per annum), rose very sharply in subsequent years. The precipitous decline in oil revenues, while military expenditures climbed, was offset only in part by Arab financial aid, and by the utilization of foreign exchange reserves accumulated before the war. The Iraqi authorities are very secretive about the magnitude of the debt, in particular the debt owed to arms suppliers. Unofficial estimates of Iraq's external indebtedness vary widely. One report estimates that the foreign civilian debt was $25–30 billion at the end of 1987. This excludes so-called loans from Saudi Arabia and Kuwait, and also excludes debts to the Soviet Union and others on account of arms supplies.[23] Iraq has been pressing its suppliers, military and civilian, for long-term credits, and most often, when payment is due it demands a 'rescheduling' of the debt. The creditors have little choice. The Iraqis dismiss the so-called debt to the Arab oil states as being no more than disguised gifts.[24] According to the above-mentioned study of the US Congressional Research Service, total Iraqi arms imports in 1980–7 were $43.5 billion, of which $20.3 billion were from the Soviet Union; $4.2 billion from China; $5.7 billion from other communist countries; $10.3 billion from Western Europe, of which France was the leading supplier; and $3.1 billion from other countries. Brazil has become an important arms supplier. These purchases were financed, in part, by payments to the arms suppliers by Iraq in oil shipments; in part, by payments in cash or in oil by Iraq's Arab supporters, and in part, by extended credits. As for the civilian debt the creditors include France, West Germany, Japan, the US (mainly agricultural products); and some poorer countries including Turkey, Jordan, India, Brazil and others. Excluding the nominal loans from Iraq's Arab financial supporters, Iraq's external debt, on account of civilian and military purchases were probably $40–50 billion at the end of 1987. At the same time, foreign exchange reserves dwindled from $35 billion before the war to about one billion dollars at the end of 1987. The war has been very costly in economic as well as human terms.

One of the possibly longer-term benefits from the war has been the recent drive to alter the structure of the economy in favour of more private enterprise and more efficiency in the public sector. The change in policy need not have been stimulated by the war, but, in reality, it was dire need which overcame the resistance to change which is endemic in the large and dominant public sector. After Saddam Hussein became president in 1979 there was a partial reversal of the socialist policies which had been dominant in the 1960s and 1970s. In the farm sector the number of collectives and cooperatives was sharply reduced and the private sector was allocated a far larger share of loans from the state-owned Agricultural Bank, and also received a larger share of farm subsidies. During the 1980s many wealthy urban Iraqis invested in agriculture, and others turned to farming, especially fruits and vegetables, on a part-time basis, in order to supplement their incomes. However, Ba'th party officials, resisted moves to weaken the public sector.[25]

In 1987 the president announced and began to implement a major change in policy. The principle features of the new economic policy were: Selling state lands and collective farms, as well as some state enterprises in the urban sector, to private enterprise; shaking up the bureaucracy; introducing incentives for productivity and efficiency in state-owned enterprises; a greater emphasis on quality; and new labour laws which made it easier for managers in the public sector to hire and fire in accordance with performance and need.[26] The government announced in 1987 that all public sector poultry, dairy, and other agricultural enterprises were to be sold to the private sector, as well as supermarkets, gas stations, and some smaller factories. In other cases the authorities were advocating joint public-private enterprises.[27] As important as these measures may be in the longer run, their importance should not be overemphasized. Even if all the announced reforms are implemented – and there is strong resistence in the bureaucracy and in the dominant Ba'th party – the state will still retain its preponderant role in the economy. The only foreign private investment permitted is by citizens of other Arab States, and they do not appear to exhibit any great enthusiasm for investment in Iraq.[28]

All in all the situation as it appears in mid-1988 is that there has been an improvement in the economy, led by the upturn in oil revenues, and barring a significant decline in oil prices, oil revenues should rise again towards the end of 1989 when the new pipeline through Saudi Arabia is scheduled to open. At the same time continued high-level military outlays and large-scale mobilization is bleeding the economy. In many ways the Iran–Iraq War has become a war of attrition, economic as well as military.

THE IRANIAN ECONOMY BEFORE THE ISLAMIC REVOLUTION

Following unprecedented period of boom, oil production, the wellspring of prosperity, rose moderately from 5.1 MBD in 1972 to 5.7 MBD in 1977, but the sharp rise in oil prices raised revenues from $4 billion in 1972 to $24.3 billion in 1977. There were large-scale investments in modern industry, agriculture, the infrastructure, as well as massive military outlays. Industrial production rose by an annual average rate of 15 per cent, and agriculture by 4.6 per cent per annum. The gross domestic product rose by about 8 per cent per annum, but incomes increased far more rapidly. Civilian commodity imports (both for consumption and investment) rose sharply from $2.4 billion in 1972 to $14.6 billion in 1977. Despite the fact that farm production per capita rose, expanding incomes raised demand far more rapidly. Agricultural imports rose from less than $400 million in 1972 to $1.9 billion in 1977. Outlays on arms imports rose from $525 million in 1972 to $2.6 billion in 1977. None the less, despite massive spending – including waste and corruption – foreign exchange reserves rose strongly from $760 million in 1972 to $10.8 billion in 1977. The oil-led boom created a situation of labour shortages, inducing the importation of some foreign labour (especially unskilled labour from Afghanistan), as well as the return of many Iranians who had migrated in earlier periods. However, social dislocations and discontent, and growing inflation, strengthened revolutionary forces.

THE KHOMEINI REVOLUTION

During the course of 1978 revolutionary forces were becoming increasingly powerful and disruptive, and in the last quarter of the year they progressively shut down oil installations. In December oil exports ceased. Iran, under the Shah, had been the world's second largest oil exporter during the 1970s (following Saudi Arabia), and the panic which seized world oil markets was unprecedented. Prices rose from $12–13 per barrel in 1978 to $30–37 per barrel in the summer of 1980, plus additional so-called premiums and surcharges (over and above prices set by OPEC), demanded by many oil exporters. The new regime which assumed power in February 1979, resumed oil exports but at levels significantly lower than under the Shah. In April–June 1979 production averaged 3.9 MBD, as compared with 5.7 MBD in 1977 and the first nine months of 1978.[29] However, internal turmoil in Iran, the loss of many technical and managerial personnel (executions, arrests, dismissals, and migration) steadily reduced even this lower level of production. During the three months preceding the war (June–August 1980) production was a mere 1.4 MBD. Oil exports (i.e., after deducting domestic consumption) during the latter period were one MBD, as compared with over 5 MBD under the Shah.

The turmoil in the country during the last months of the Shah's regime and the first year and a half of the revolutionary regime (i.e., before the war with Iraq), affected the whole economy, including agriculture, industry and other sectors. Tens of thousands fled the country, especially many of the more educated, more skilled and managerial personnel. Many of the wealthy, whose property was taken over by the new regime, or was in danger of expropriation, fled. There are no reliable figures as to the magnitude of the exodus, as well as the number executed or arrested by the new regime, or the flight of capital, but, there is little doubt that these developments had a strong negative long-term impact on the economy. Investment and private consumption turned down strongly. Between 1977 and 1979 there was a massive decline of 19 per cent in gross domestic product, according to official figures, and a further sharp drop of 15 per cent in 1980 – in part due to the war which began in September of that year.

THE WAR'S IMPACT ON THE ECONOMY OF IRAN

In sharp contrast with Iraq which was in the midst of an unprecedented boom when it initiated hostilities, Iran's economy was in the throes of rapid deterioration. There is little doubt that this was one of the factors the Iraqi leadership took into account in assessing the overall strength of Iran and the decision to attack. Iranian oil production, which had reached a very low level during the months preceding the war, 1.4 MBD, receded slightly to 1.3 MBD in 1981. Despite high oil prices, revenues declined from $19 billion in 1979 to $13 billion in 1980 and $12 billion in 1981. Between 1974 and 1978 annual oil revenues (when prices were a mere $10–12 per barrel) had been between $20 and $24 billion. In addition to the dire need to revive the economy, the new regime was now burdened with the mounting costs of the war. Before the war the revolutionary regime had cut back sharply on military spending from $14.2 billion in 1978 (under the Shah) to $7.5 billion in 1980. Arms imports were cut back even more strongly from $2.3 billion in 1976–8 (annual average) to a low of $470 million in 1980. The war forced the regime to raise military outlays, both local spending and arms imports. The sharp decline in revenues combined with increased military spending resulted in large balance of payment deficits (the current account). Foreign exchange reserves, inherited from the previous regime, dropped from $14.6 billion in 1979, to about one billion dollars at the end of 1981. The authorities decided on a major expansion of oil production and exports.

Production rose sharply in 1982 to 2.4 MBD, almost double the previous year's level (though far below the pre-revolutionary rate of production), and remained at that level in 1983. Oil revenues rose strongly from $12 billion in 1981 to $19 billion in 1982 and again in 1983. This permitted the authorities to liberalize import restrictions. The (relative) influx of raw materials, machinery, and spare parts, stimulated a revival in industrial and agricultural production, and in the economy, as a whole. In 1983 (real) gross domestic product was about 30 per cent higher than in 1981, according to official estimates. Even if the official figures tend to exaggerate (by underestimating inflation), there is little doubt that the economic upturn was substantial. Despite a higher level of both military and civilian imports, the balance of payments (the current account) was positive, and foreign exchange reserves rose from $1.1 billion at the end of 1981 to $5.3 billion a year later.[30]

Since 1984 the Iraqis focused much more strongly on economic warfare, in particular, by bombing oil installations and tankers carrying Iranian oil to their buyers. By and large the Iranians have proved to be rather resourceful. One Westerner who travelled through the southern oil region in 1986 stated that Iranian technicians were 'performing miracles' in repairing damaged oil facilities.[31] None the less oil production fell from 2.5 MBD in 1983 to 2.2 MBD in 1984 and again in 1985. Moreover, this occurred while oil prices were drifting downward. Oil export revenues fell sharply to $12–13 billion per annum in 1984–5 as compared with $19 billion per annum in each of the previous two years. In fact real income from oil fell far more steeply since the Iranians had to compensate oil buyers for the far higher costs of insurance and transport from the war zone – an estimated two to three dollars per barrel.[32] Moreover, heavy damage to refineries compelled the Iranians to import large quantities of refined oil products. Reports published in early 1988 stated that these amounted to 300 TBD. Total domestic consumption of refined oil products was an estimated 700 TBD. Gasoline was rationed, and there were shortages of oil for heating.[33]

1986 was a disastrous year for the economy. Iraqi bombings reduced production to 1.9 MBD (as compared with 2.2 MBD in the previous year) while world oil prices plummeted. Oil revenues fell sharply to $6.6 billion, half of the previous year's level. After deducting the costs of war insurance for cargos from Iran, net revenues were miniscule. Oil production revived in 1987, averaging 2.3 MBD, and prices were higher than in 1986, though far lower than in 1985 and in earlier years. Oil revenues were as estimated $9.5 billion, far higher than gross receipts of $6.6 billion in 1986, but far below the $13 billion level in 1985, let alone the $19–20 billion level in 1982 and 1983. Non-oil exports rose significantly in 1987 to about one billion dollars (as compared with less than one half billion dollars per annum in previous years), but this was meagre compensation for very low oil revenues. Intensified Iraqi bombings reduced Iranian oil production in the first quarter of 1988 to less than 2 MBD[34] and, in view of the soft oil prices prevailing in the first half of 1988, the prospects for revenues in 1988 were poor. Civilian commodity imports which had peaked at $18 billion in 1983, were reduced very sharply in the following years to $10–11 billion per annum in 1985–7. Excepting factories engaged in military production and other sectors with very high priority (such as oil), industry and other sectors were faced with severe shortages of raw materials, spare parts, and machinery, and their production declined. There was some improvement in the performance of agriculture in 1985–7, and agricultural imports declined from a peak of $3.9 billion in 1982 to $2.5 billion in 1986. The reduction was partly due to lower international prices of farm commodities. In most sectors of the economy there were serious problems. Gross domestic product in 1987 was 12 per cent lower than in 1983–4, which had been a post-revolutionary peak. The balance of payments (the current account) which was in surplus in 1982 and 1983, was in deficit in 1984–7.

The economic deterioration exhibits itself in many ways. Unofficial estimates are that inflation reached 40–50 per cent in 1987 and in early 1988. The official exchange rate in February 1988 was about 68 Iranian riyals to the US dollar; but in the black market it was over 1000. Unemployment is widespread and increasing. The poorer classes, avowedly favoured by the regime, were worse off than before the revolution.[35] The salaries of civil servants have not risen since the revolution and rising inflation has eroded their living standards significantly.[36] Even according to official estimates the consumer price index in 1985 was 2.7 times that of 1978, and prices have climbed even more rapidly in 1986–8. Despite the high level of mobilization, unemployment was officially estimated in 1986 at 3.8 million, 28.6 per cent of

Table 14.2   Iran – selected economic indicators

Iran	1972	1973	1974	1975	1976	1977	1978	1979	1980	1981	1982	1983	1984	1985	1986	1987
Oil production (thousands of barrels per day)	5050	5895	6060	5385	5920	5705	5275	3175	1480	1325	2410	2465	2195	2215	1885	2270
Domestic oil consumption (thousands of barrels per day)				352					512	618	719	871	723	735	724	
Oil export (thousands of barrels per day)				5032					952	809	1718	1816	1579	1607	1464	
Oil exports revenues (millions of dollars)	3636	5617	20904	19633	22923	23600	21684	19185	13300	12053	19200	19225	12300	13100	6600 Est.	9500 Est.
Total commodity exports (millions of dollars)	4038	6207	21571	20211	23507	24260	22101	19976	14106	12597	19430	19512	12531	13380	7000	10500
Total commodity imports (millions of dollars)	2409	3393	5433	10343	12894	14645	13549	9738	12246	12499	11955	18320	15370	11635	10521	Est. 10500
of which agricultural imports (millions of dollars)	393	433	1271	2011	1478	1862	2235	2128	2775	3473	3900	3500	3570	3280	2480	
Military imports (millions of dollars)	525	525	1000	1200	2000	2600	2200	1700	470	1000	1500	875	2200	800		
Balance of payments – balance on current account – (millions of dollars)	–388	154	12267	4707	7660	2816	104	11968	–2438	–3446	5733	358	–414	–750	–4500	–400
Foreign exchange reserves – end-of-year (millions of dollars)	760	976	7652	7556	7447	10824	10907	14561	9617	1102	5287					
Gold reserves – end-of-year (thousands of ounces)	3743	3743	3738	3738	3738	3779	3820	3903	4932	6057	5923					
Consumer price index (1980=100)	33.5	36.8	42.0	47.4	52.8	67.1	75.0	82.9	100	124.2	147.4	176.5	198.6	238.3	309.8	418.2
Change in consumer price index (%)	6.3	9.6	14.1	12.9	11.4	27.1	11.8	10.5	20.6	24.2	18.7	19.7	12.5	20.0	30.0	35.0
Index of real gross domestic product (1972=100)	100	111.8	120.5	122.0	144.3	148.4	125.4	120.4	100.8	103.6	119.3	134.1	134.2	132.2	121.6	118.6
Change in real gross domestic product (%)	16.9	11.8	7.8	1.2	18.3	2.8	–14.5	–4.0	–16.3	2.8	15.2	12.4	0.1	–1.5	–8.0	–2.5

Index of agricultural production (1976–8 = 100)	70	76	84	92	100	96	104	99	88	89	96	95	94	104	113
Index of agricultural production per capita (1976–8 = 100)	81	85	91	98	103	96	101	93	81	79	83	80	76	82	86
Index of real private consumption per capita (1972 = 100)		100	111.4	133.5	135.7	157.9	174.5	160.9	144.3	137.3	144.8	142.7	146.2	141.6	124.6
Index of real wage rates (1980 = 100)		26.9	31.0	35.5	44.3	55.5	56.8	66.5	89.0	100	87.4	80.7	78.6	80.0	75.7
Ratio of gross domestic fixed capital formation to gross domestic product (%)		24.3	21.9	17.1	28.4	33.8	30.1	30.7	18.7	16.7	18.9	17.5	21.4	19.2	16.6
Index of gross domestic fixed capital formation in constant prices (1972 = 100)		100	118.6	138.7	242.3	353.4	340.5	292.6	180.1	160.5	147.0	156.2	212.5	193.3	161.5
Ratio of military expenditures to gross national product (%)		8.9	8.3	13.8	17.6	15.6	11.9	16.6	8.2	6.6	6.8	6.7	5.2	7.2	
Population (millions)		30.41	31.23	32.50	33.38	33.66	34.57	36.11	37.20	38.35	39.54	40.78	42.07	43.41	45.91
Armed forces (thousands)		265	285	310	385	420	350	350	415	305	260	240	240	335	

Sources and Notes: [1]Oil production figures are from the *BP Statistical Review of World Energy.*

[2]Estimates of Domestic Oil Consumption are from the Economic Intelligence Unit (EIU) reports (various issues)

[3]Oil Export volumes and revenues are reported in the International Monetary Fund *International Financial Statistics* (IFS), various issues, and for more recent years are from EIU reports.

[4]Commodity Export and Imports are from IFS, various issues, and for more recent years from, unofficial estimates published by EIU and *Middle East Economic Digest* (MEED).

[5]Estimates of agricultural imports, and of agricultural production are from US Department of Agriculture *Middle East and North Africa–Situation and Outlook Report,* various issues.

[6]Estimates of military imports, the ratio of military expenditures to GNP, and the size of the armed forces, are from US Arms Control and Disarmament Agency *World Military Expenditures and Arms Transfers, 1986* Washington D.C., 1987, and earlier issues. There is a strong reason to assume that these figures are underestimated. The size of the armed forces obviously excludes the irregular forces.

[7]The estimates for the current account in the balance of payments (exports of goods and services minus the imports of goods and services, plus or minus transfers) are from official sources as reported in IFS, except for more recent years which are from EIU. The figures for foreign exchange reserves and for gold reserves are form IFS.

[8]The estimates of the consumer price index are from official sources, as reported in IFS, except for more recent years which are unofficial estimates reported by EIU.

[9]The index of real gross domestic product was calculated from official data, in constant prices, as reported in IFS, except for more recent years, which represent unofficial estimates reported in EIU.

[10]The index of real private consumption per capita, and the index of real wage rates, were calculated from official data as published in IFS. The latter represents wage rates in what are described as larger manufacturing establishments.

[11]The ratio of gross domestic fixed capital formation (investments) to gross domestic product was calculated from official data, in current prices, as reported in IFS.

[12]The official national accounts, as reported in IFS, give estimates of investment in current prices only. I have used the official wholesale price index as the deflator.

[13]The population estimates are those reported in IFS. There is reason to believe that these are underestimated, probably excluding most of the refugees, mainly from Afghanistan, and some from Iran, who fled to Iran in the 1980s.

[14]The data for 1987 are provisional estimates, and, in some cases this is true of 1985 and 1986 figures, as well.

the labour force. The number of unemployed had gone up from about 3 million in 1984 to 3.8 million in 1986.[37] In view of the continued economic deterioration, the number of unemployed has surely risen to even more calamitous dimensions since 1986.

One sector which receives high priority, and has prospered, is the local arms industry. Foreign observers in Iran report that the Iranians are 'masters of invention and innovation [and that the country] provides its requirements in small arms, machine guns and recoilless rifles [and] half the country's ammunition needs'. They were reported to have test-piloted a fighter plane modelled on the F5.[38] Officials claim that the country is self-sufficient in mortars, shells, anti-tank grenade launchers, as well as small arms and ammunition. They assert that they are producing medium-range radar, specialized radios, pilotless aircraft, helicopters, speedboats, and cargo boats. They also state that in addition to the state-owned military industries about 12,000 private workshops are engaged, mainly as subcontractors, in the production of war-related equipment. While civilian industries are starved for resources, and produce far below capacity, these factories and workshops are working overtime, often in three shifts.[39] However, despite expanding local military production the importation of arms rose very sharply from less than one billion dollars in 1980–3 to two billion dollars in 1984–7 (annual averages), acording to official US estimates.[40] These figures do not include the importation of machinery, raw materials and spare parts for Iran's military industries. None the less, Iranian arms purchases abroad are far lower than those of Iraq because of the lack of major arms suppliers, because of local military production, and because they apparently have relied on their numerical superiority to offset Iraq's use of more sophisticated military equipment.

The allocation of scarce resources to the military industries and to the war effort, at a time when foreign exchange earnings have reached low levels, has adversely affected the economy as a whole. Iraqi air raids have destroyed or damaged oil refineries, petrochemical plants and electric power stations, causing frequent blackouts which further hamper industrial and other productive activities, as well as the overall welfare of the population. Shortages of refined oil products and of chemicals, aggravate economic problems, and rebuilding or repairing the damaged plants adds to the scarcity of already scarce resources.

Unlike the Iraqis who have greatly expanded their oil export capacity since 1983, the Iranians have done little in that regard. In 1985 there were reports of negotiations with Turkey regarding the construction of an oil and gas pipeline through that country for export to Europe.[41] But no action was taken. There were also reports of talks with the Soviets to utilize the gas pipeline through their country (built during the Shah's time) for exports. Here, too, no action was taken. In early 1988 it was reported that construction had started on a pipeline with a 600 TBD capacity, from the oil fields further north, to Taheri in the central Gulf. It was reportedly scheduled for completion by the end of 1988. Presumably it was expected to provide a safer terminal for oil, as compared with the then heavily-bombarded Kharg Island.[42] However, even if completed on schedule, the small increment in oil revenues would be very far from sufficient to reverse the economic downtrend.

THE WAR'S IMPACT ON WORLD OIL MARKETS

Iranian–Iraqi Oil Production

Following the very sharp run-up in prices in the wake of the Iranian Revolution, prices began to soften in the spring of 1980. The war which began in September of that year, temporarily reversed the downtrend. Prices peaked in the spring of 1981, and the downward trend resumed – despite the war – until the price collapse during the first half of 1986. The new OPEC agreements announced in the summer of 1986 raised prices to $17–18 per barrel (as compared with $26–28 per barrel in 1985), but the oil glut continues and prices have been softening.

It is axiomatic that increases in world oil supplies tend to put downward pressure on prices, and the opposite is true when supplies are reduced. During the first years of the war, Iraqi exports were reduced very sharply – as noted above. However, the war compelled Iraq to seek alternative routes and the expansion of its pipelines through Turkey and Saudi Arabia, raised its exports from 0.7 MBD in 1981 to 2.2. MBD in 1988. The completion of the new pipeline through Saudi Arabia towards the end of 1989 should raise Iraqi exports by at least another one MBD, putting additional downward pressure on oil prices. As noted above, Iraq ignored OPEC prices in the 1970s, and is even more likely to do so under the exigencies of war and enormous foreign debts.

Iranian production had declined to very low levels during the first year and a half of the revolutionary regime, with exports dropping to about one MBD, as compared with over 5 MBD under the Shah. The war, and its financing, compelled with Iranians to bend every effort to raise production, and exports rose to about 2 MBD in 1982 and 1983. In 1983 the Iranian oil ministry announced that its near-term goal was to raise exports by another one MBD.[43] However, despite valiant efforts by the Iranians to repair damages and maintain or raise their oil exports, Iraqi bombings succeeded in holding down Iranian output to lower levels in subsequent years. It should be emphasized that it was not OPEC quotas which kept Iran at or below its assigned production ceiling. OPEC quotas and prices are ignored by the Iranians when it suits them, just as they are ignored by Iraq. This is, of course, also true of other OPEC members not burdened by huge military expenditures. If, indeed, the Iranians complete their internal pipeline towards the end of 1988, their exports will again rise.

The net effect of the war has been to lower supplies in the first years of the war, and to raise them in subsequent years. This is especially true of Iraqi oil exports.

The War's Impact on the Neighbouring Arab Countries

The war's economic impact on the neighbouring countries expresses itself both in their need to support Iraq (especially Saudi Arabia and Kuwait), and their drive to strengthen their own military forces. No official figures are available, but Arab financial support for Iraq has probably been in the range of $40–60 billion since the war began, and, according to some estimates, even higher with about two thirds from Saudi Arabia and most of the balance from Kuwait. This has had a powerful impact, especially on Saudi Arabia. Saudi oil revenues in fiscal year 1980/1 and again in 1981/2 peaked at $96–7 billion. By 1987 they had declined precipitously to $16 billion. Though the Saudi authorities have reduced expenditures, these have been far from sufficient. Instead of huge fiscal surpluses they have been incurring large fiscal deficits in every year since 1982/3. The fiscal deficits were soon translated into large balance of payments deficits in every year since 1983. Central bank financial reserves – accumulated in the boom years – have been drastically reduced in order to cover deficits. Under these circumstances the Saudi authorities have little choice but to increase oil exports. The Iran–Iraq War was not the only factor, but it greatly aggravated Saudi Arabia's financial woes, which, in turn, persuaded the authorities to abandon their swing role in OPEC since 1985.

The fear of Iran has been a major determinant of the high level of military spending by the Saudis and their neighbours. Saudi military expenditures (as announced in their budgets), were about $15 billion per annum in 1985–7, the equivalent of about 22 per cent of the gross national product. Few countries, not at war, have allocated anywhere near that ratio to the military.[44] Unofficial reports indicate that there are also off-budgetary allocations to the military and that financial aid to Iraq is also excluded from the budgetary reports.

Saudi arms imports, as well as financial support for Iraq's military imports are paid for, in part, by oil shipments to the arms exporters (i.e., barter trade). The drive to purchase more and more sophisticated, and highly expensive military equipment is typical of other countries in the region also motivated, in large measure, by their fear of Iran. There is only one way for them to finance these expenditures – by selling more oil.

The Greatly Diminished Importance of the Strait of Hormuz

Passage of oil through the Persian Gulf was once considered 'the West's lifeline'. The figures show, that, if, indeed, this had been the case, its importance has greatly diminished. In 1978 oil tankers through the Strait of Hormuz carried 19.6 MBD. By 1985 this had been reduced drastically to 6.4 MBD.[45] The sharp decline was due to many factors including many new oil discoveries outside the Persian Gulf. Another factor was the Iran–Iraq War which compelled Iraq to seek alternative outlets by building pipelines through Turkey and Saudi Arabia. The Saudis have also built an internal east–west pipeline with a capacity of 3.2 MBD, and are planning to expand it to close to 5 MBD. This was built mainly for insurance – in case the Strait of Hormuz is closed. The planned expansion of the Saudi pipeline means that even if the Saudis increase their production by as much as one MBD above its 1987 level, they could, if necessary, completely avoid the Strait of Hormuz for their oil exports. As noted earlier, the Iraqis are currently buidling another pipeline through Saudi Arabia with a capacity of over one MBD. It was the Iran–Iraq War which stimulated the construction of these pipelines.

The longer term impact of these pipelines on world oil markets is to keep prices from skyrocketing should disruptive political-military developments occur in the region such as the Islamic revolution in Iran in 1979. It was fear, rather than global oil shortages, which accounted for the massive speculative buying and skyrocketing prices in 1979 and for a short while after the Iran–Iraq War began. The existence of alternative routes for oil, as well as unused capacity in oil-producing countries outside the Gulf, should do much to reduce such speculative fever in the future.

LONGER-TERM IMPACT ON OIL-MARKETS

I have expressed the view, in various studies, that, for many reasons, oil prices, in the long run, are likely to remain depressed, and probably decline, at least when measured in constant dollars.[46] This does not preclude fluctuations arising from wars, revolutions, etc., but these fluctuations are likely to be far milder than what was witnessed in 1979–80. One of the major factors which will tend to depress prices in the long run is the Iran–Iraq War and its aftermath.

In July 1988 Iran announced its acceptance of the UN ceasefire resolution. If, indeed, the ceasefire will evolve into a more durable solution, this would have a major impact on oil markets, and on the economies of other countries in the region. What is abundantly clear is that:

1. Both countries have huge oil and gas resources. Iraq's oil reserves are believed to be second only to those of Saudi Arabia and Iran's natural gas

resources are second only to those of the Soviet Union. Iran also has vast underutilized oil resources, even if they are not as large as those of Iraq.

2. Both countries have suffered from massive destruction of their civilian economies, especially Iran. But even Iraq which until 1985, had been relatively immune to Iranian attacks on its civilian economy, suffered from massive destruction of its second largest city, Basra.

3. Both countries have neglected their infrastructure since the war and huge sums will be required for reconstruction as well as for long-delayed development plans. Though Iran's economy is far more diversified than that of Iraq, both countries are overwhelmingly dependent on their oil resources to finance large-scale imports of machinery and equipment for reconstruction and development, as well as spare parts and raw materials needed to raise domestic production. Iraq has the additional burden of a massive foreign debt which it has, for the most part, been 'rolling over'. With the end of the war the creditors will be pressing for payment.

The combined production of Iran and Iraq in 1987 was about 4.5 MBD, about half of their peak production in the 1970s. I would anticipate that Iraq, especially, whose oil facilities have been, for the most part, immune to Iranian attacks, will bend every effort to raise its production and exports as rapidly as possible. The opening of the Gulf to Iraqi exports would enable it to increase oil exports by about 1.5 MBD within about a year after hostilities come to an end, and far more in subsequent years as production capacity is expanded. Iran will, most probably, follow suit. Both countries will demand that other OPEC members reduce their quotas to 'make room' for their production, and will, most likely, be ignored. I have stated, in earlier studies (1983)[47] that the Iran–Iraq War is like the 'Sword of Damocles' hanging over the world oil markets. If anything, the sword has become far more threatening for the oil exporters.

It appears likely that Saudi and Kuwait financial aid to Iraq will cease, or at least be reduced sharply, and to that extent, the end of the war will bring some financial relief to those countries. It is far less certain that there will be a significant cutback in their military expenditures. The conservative Gulf countries fear both Iran and Iraq, even if their fear of Iran and its revolutionary ideology is greater. Reports from these countries frequently noted that their leaders hoped for a stalemate, not an Iraqi victory, despite their Arab sympathies. These hopes appear to have been realized.

On the other hand, whatever 'savings' these countries gain from the end of the war – in particular aid to Iraq – may well be offset by the deepening of the oil glut, and depressed prices which would ensue as a consequence of far higher Iraqi and Iranian production. In the unlikely event that they and other OPEC members agree to significantly lower quotas, to make room for increased Iranian and Iraqi production (and that OPEC members adhere to their quotas), their revenues would drop from their already very low levels.

From the past eight years the Gulf states have lived in fear that the war would engulf them. The end of hostilities will certainly bring a sense of relief. But for those countries in the region overwhelmingly dependent on oil revenues for their very survival – of which Saudi Arabia is a prime example – the aftermath of the Iran–Iraq War may be almost as burdensome, from an economic and financial point of view, as the war itself. Diminished expenditures (aid to Iraq) may well be offset by lower oil revenues. On the other hand, the world's oil-importing countries both the rich industrialized countries and the poor less developed countries will breathe a sigh of relief. Lower oil prices should help to stimulate economic growth, reduce inflationary pressures and interest rates, and aid their balance of payments.

Notes

1. See Statistical Appendix. Sources cited in the Footnotes are other than those found in the Statistical Appendix.
2. *Economist*, 16 October 1982, p. 58; *BP Statistical Review of World Energy*, various issues.
3. The figures in dollars are based on the official exchange rate of the Iraqi dinar.
4. See, for example, Economist Intelligence Unit (EIU), *Country Profile – Iraq, 1988–89*.
5. US Department of Agriculture, *Middle East and North Africa Situation and Outlook Report*, April 1986, p. 7.
6. International Institute for Strategic Studies, *The Military Balance 1987–1988*, p. 100.
7. I have based this estimate on the age and sex structure of Iraq in 1986 as reported in EIU *Country Report 1988–89*, p. 8, and population estimates for 1987 as reported by the International Monetary Fund *International Financial Statistics*, May 1988, p. 286.
8. *The Middle East*, September 1985, p. 8.
9. *EIU Iraq*, no. 1, 1986, p. 10.
10. *Economist*, 15 March 1986, pp. 53–4.
11. *Middle East Review*, 1984, p. 128.
12. *Middle East Economic Digest* (MEED), 19 April 1986, p. 16.
13. *Economist*, 13 February 1988, pp. 57–78.
14. *MidEast Markets*, 7 March 1988, p. 12.
15. R. F. Grimmet, *Trends in Conventional Arms Transfer to the Third World by Major Suppliers 1980–87* (Washington D.C.: Congressional Research Service, 1988).
16. *Business Week*, 6 December 1982, p. 45.
17. *EIU – Country Profile, Iraq 1988–89*, p. 38.
18. *Middle East Review*, 1984, p. 121.
19. *Petroleum Economist*, June 1988, p. 220.
20. *MEED*, 26 September 1987, p. 26; *EIU – Country Report – Iraq*, no. 1, 1988, p. 12.
21. Ibid., *MidEast Markets*, 13 June 1988, p. 15.
22. *MEED*, 21 March 1987, p. 8.
23. *MidEast Markets*, 7 March 1988, p. 12.

24.   *MEED*, 27 June 1987, pp. 44–5.
25.   Robert Springborg, 'Infitah, Agrarian Reform, and Elite Consolidation in Contemporary Iraq', *The Middle East Journal*, Winter 1986, pp. 36–43.
26.   *EIU Country Report – Iraq*, no. 4, 1987, p. 9.
27.   *MidEast Markets*, 7 March 1988, p. 12; *Gulf States Newsletter*, 27 June 1988, pp. 6–7.
28.   *MidEast Markets*, 13 June 1988, p. 15.
29.   *Petroleum Economist*, various issues.
30.   See International Monetary Fund, *International Financial Statistics*, various issues.
31.   *MEED*, 13 December 1986, p. 43.
32.   *Gulf States Newsletter*, 11 January 1088, pp. 8–11.
33.   *MidEast Markets*, 22 February 1988, p. 6.
34.   *Petroleum Economist*, June 1988, p. 220.
35.   *Economist*, 2 April 1988, pp. 45–6.
36.   *MEED*, 13 December 1986, p. 4.
37.   *EIU Country Profile – Iran*, 1988–9, p. 22.
38.   *The Middle East*, April 1988, p. 18.
39.   *MEED*, 27 February 1988, p. 9; 2 January 1988, p. 12; 2 May 1987, p. 11.
40.   *MidEast Markets*, 13 June 1988, p. 12.
41.   *Economist*, 2 February 1985, p. 47.
42.   *MEED*, 12 March 1988, p. 34.
43.   *MEED*, 7 January 1982, p. 22; *An Nahar Arab Report and Memo*, 15 November 1982, p. 21.
44.   For sources and details see my study 'Saudi Arabia's Dismal Economic Future: Regional and Global Implications' in I. Rabinovich and H. Shaked (eds), *Middle East Contemporary Survey*, vol. IX (Tel-Aviv University: The Dayan Center for Middle East and African Studies, 1987) pp. 278–339.
45.   *Wall Street Journal*, 21 April 1987, p. 6.
46.   See my above-mentioned study of Saudi Arabia. Also see my study *Another Oil Shock in the 1990s? A Dissenting View* (Washington D.C.: The Washington Institute for Near East Policy, January 1987).
47.   *The Iran–Iraq War: Its Economic Implications* (Tel-Aviv University: The Dayan Centre for Middle Eastern and African Studies, May 1983) p. 18.

Part V

Strategic and Military Implications

15 A Military-Strategic Overview

Chaim Herzog

The Gulf War between Iran and Iraq, which lasted almost eight years, is undoubtedly one of the bloodiest conflicts which has raged anywhere since the end of the Second World War and, indeed, it ranks as one of the longest wars in this century.

The Iraqis started the war in 1980 in the hope of gaining a quick victory over a neighbour weakened by the overthrow of the Shah. But they discovered within a matter of months the truth of a famous dictum: 'Never attack a revolution.'

During 1987–8 it became clear that the final victory promised annually by the Iranians was improbable. An exhausted tie was the result the rest of the world wanted. This futile war cost somewhere between one and one-and-a-half million casualties, and came to a conclusion as it did along roughly the same line along a 730 miles front from Turkey to the Persian Gulf, on which it started.

I doubt that it will be a war which will be studied by military historians for its strategic lessons or battle field accomplishments. One of the documents that I read recently described the war as a 'delicate balance of incompetence', and as an illustration of the failure to apply most of the classic principles of war from the adoption of realistic war aims to the conduct of the war itself. But since military failure no less than success contributes to the development of military knowledge, obviously the lessons of this war with its very broad implications, particularly for the Near and Middle East, cannot be over-looked.

In analysing the origins of the war one cannot ignore the longstanding ethnic rivalry between the Arabs and the Persians and the rivalry between opposing versions of Islamic practices by the Sunnis and the Shi'ites. Persia was converted to Islam after the Arab conquest in the seventh century. In the sixteenth century Iran adopted the Shi'ite version of Islam and its official religion and thus became the centre of Shi'ism.

Thus, with 85 per cent of its population Shi'ite, Iran stood out from the rest of the Muslim world which was mainly Sunni and its influence on Shi'ite communities in their countries was significant. The differences between these two Muslim sects are not only concerned with the question of the Prophet Muhammad's successor; they also tend to be separated by political and economic conditions. In the Arab world of today only Iraq and Bahrain have a majority of Shi'ites although, paradoxically enough, the Iraqi leaders are all Sunni.

During the period which produced modern Iran, its successive leaders tried, particularly through the arts and architecture, to give their country a distinct cultural identity, which would set it apart from the rest of the Middle East.

The advent of both Iranian and Arab Nationalism in the twentieth century helped to drive Iran and Iraq even further apart. At the end of the 1960s Iraq adopted a policy of pan-Arabism combined with an increasingly secular outlook just as the Shah of Iran was embarking on an ambitious programme to promote his interests in the area.

I was a witness to the obsession of the late Shah of Iran with power. For I was personally directly involved in the special relations which developed between Israel and Iran and became closer and more involved as the years passed, indeed, until the Khomeini Revolution. On repeated occasions I heard from the Shah in the early 1960s a clear unequivocal enunciation of his resolution to make Iran the dominant military power in the Gulf, with a view to creating an Iranian zone of influence in West Asia.

When the British withdrew from the Gulf in 1971 the Shah reacted by intensifying Iran's military growth on which he had already embarked in the 1960s. His policy was supported by the US and Britain, both of which saw the advantages of stengthening Iran, thus guaranteeing the stability of the Gulf. The Shah's military purchases as his appetite grew, became an important economic consideration for the Western powers. By the time of Khomeini's Revolution Iran's arms purchases in the preceding decade surpassed some 20 billion dollars' worth.

The beginning of the Shah's policy of regional assertiveness coincided with the advent to power of the present Iraqi regime. The Iranian drive for regional hegemony was not ignored by Iraq. Since its accession to power in 1968, the present Iraqi Ba'th regime found itself forced to respond again and again to challenges posed by Iran. Iraq began to focus on the extention of its ground and air forces. The nature of the military purchases and developments in Iraq at this period indicate an understanding by its leaders of its basic inferiority in relation to Iran. The 'mix' of the Iraqi purchases reflected its essential defensive posture, with its preoccupation with domestic affairs and the need to deter its two hereditary enemies – Syria and Iran. We must remember too that during the 1970s Iraq's ground forces were concerned both with the Kurdish Revolution in the North and the stability of the regime.

Iraqi forces crossed the Iranian frontier in strength in September 1980. One of the grievances announced by the Iraqi leader Saddam Hussein a week later was the question of the sovereignty over the Shatt-al-Arab. This dispute about the control of the stretch of water running from the confluence of the Tigris and Euphrates rivers to the Gulf dates from the period of the Ottoman and Persian Empires. The various agreements reached in the nineteenth century were the basis of Iraq's claim as successor to the Ottoman Empire to the Shatt-al-Arab. Despite the fact that these treaties upheld the principle of unrestricted navigation on the Shatt by ships of all nations, Iran had never been satisfied with the status quo. Iran was concerned because of the growing economic importance of the ports of Abadan and Khorramshahr and the shipping traffic to them. Disputes continued, especially during the period of General Qassem after the overthrow of King Faisal. The continued open Iranian support for the Kurdish Revolt in Northern Iraq finally forced Baghdad to give in to Iran's claims.

In 1975 Saddam Hussein, then Vice President of Iraq, was obliged to sign the Algiers Agreement whereby Iran cut off aid to the Kurds in Iraq in return for the regulation of the frontier along the Shatt. Thus the sovereignty in the Shatt was divided, with the line of deepest water replacing the eastern bank as the international boundary. This agreement, incidentally, represented a deep personal humiliation for Saddam Hussein, who became President in 1979 and he, undoubtedly, harboured a strong desire to avenge this setback.

However, it is most unlikely that given the military predominance of Iran and its relations with the US and the major Western Powers, Saddam Hussein's desire for revenge would have materialized and would have driven him to attack the Shah's Iran. The catalyst was provided by the triumph of the new Islamic regime in Iran in February 1979. Khomeini's accession to power in Iran brought about a major change in the political atmosphere. The Islamic regime in Iran questioned the legitimacy of traditional rulers as well as that of the Iraqi Ba'th. Khomeini appealed to the Shi'ites of the Gulf. He attacked the Ba'th regime in Iraq. The seriousness of this attack was underlined by Iraq's demography. Some 60 per cent of Iraqi Muslims are Shi'ites, as opposed to some 20 per cent Sunnis. This ethno-religious composition made Iraq extremely vulnerable. To this, one must add the complications created by the Kurdish Revolution which forced the Iraqis to sign the Algiers Agreement.

Indeed, in 1980 Saddam Hussein publicly aired his fears that Iraq might disintegrate into separate Sunni, Shi'ite and Kurdish communities. Khomeini for his part had an account to settle with Saddam Hussein, who had expelled him from Iraq after an exile of 14 years, at the Shah's request.

The war of words in 1980 became more intense, with Ayatollah Khomeini calling for the Ba'th regime to be consigned to the 'dustbin of history'. As the situation became very intense, more frequent and heavier border clashes were reported during the summer. The Iraqis maintained that the war began in early September when Iraq was forced to reply to Iran's shelling. An analysis of the developments, however, indicates that the war broke out when Iraq invaded Iran. It was clear that Saddam Hussein came to the conclusion that it would be wise on his part to take advantage of what appeared to be a moment of Iran's weakness following the purge of its armed forces and the deterioration of its equipment and to pre-empt a possible future intervention by a militarily reorganized Iran.

It is fair to conclude that the Iran–Iraq War was, to quote a contemporary Iranian commentator, a direct outcome of the Islamic Revolution, both in terms of the threat it posed to Iraq and the opportunity it presented.

The Iraqi attack took place at what seemed from the military point of view to have been a particularly opportune period in the developments in Iran. The revolution had thrown the Iranian armed forces into total disarray. Khomeini's regime emasculated and purged them and had established the Revolutionary Guard Militia, Pasdaran, as a counter weight to the military. In the first phase the senior ranks which included many of my former colleagues and friends were decimated. Some 85 senior officers were executed and hundreds more (including Major Generals and most Brigadier Generals) were imprisoned or forced to retire.

The purges continued until by the outbreak of war in 1980 some 12,000 had been purged, 10,000 of them from the army. Thus the Iranian army lost over half of its officers in the ranks of Major to Colonel. The airforce reportedly lost half of its pilots and 15–20 per cent of its officers, NCOs and technicians. In addition about half of the regular servicemen deserted and many more were killed during and after the revolution. Those who survived the purges are supervised by 'spiritual guidance officers', just as post-purge Red Army line officers were supervised by political commissars.

Many fighting formations were dissolved or fell apart. By the outbreak of the war it was a reasonable assumption on the part of the Iraqis to estimate that the Iranian armed forces were inferior to the Iraqi army. The Iranian army was down from 285,000 to around 150,000, whereas the Iraqi army stood at 200,000. Indeed, it was estimated at the time that the 12 Iraqi divisions faced 6 under strength Iranian divisions. The operational strength and ability of the Iraqi army was estimated to be far superior to that of the Iranian forces. While Iraq could deploy almost all of its major weapons systems (2750 tanks, 2500 AFV and some 920 artillery pieces) Iran could hardly deploy half of its 1735 tanks, 1700 AFV and 1000 artillery pieces.

The Iranian airforce was unable to fly more than half its aircraft, with key avionics removed from most of Iran's F14, F4 and F5 following the departure of the American advisers. The Iraqi airforce on the other hand, had modernized and attained a high level of serviceability. Only at sea was Iran's pre-1979 superiority maintained.

Numbers are, however, not everything. One cannot discount the problem of the quality of military leadership, combat experience, training and command and control. Blinded by its own numerical strength, Iraq ignored its basic deficiencies as well as Iran's qualities. The Ba'th regime over the years went to extraordinary lengths to strengthen its grip on the armed forces. It naturally led to a situation where Sunni and Takriti affiliation were the most important criteria for military promotion. Saddam Hussein's near relatives were prominent in the military leadership. Indeed, in both countries the military leadership was selected and promoted not according to professional criteria but rather because of its loyalty to the regime. Both countries, even at the time of the Shah, had great difficulty in maintaining the advanced major weapons systems which they had acquired. Six Iranian brigades had been rotated in the suppression of the Dhofari Rebellion from 1972–5 in Oman. They did not particularly distinguish themselves.

On the other hand, Iraq's combat experience in the October War in 1973 was no more impressive. The armoured division that arrived at the Golan Front ten days after the war began, was ambushed by Israeli forces and lost some 100 tanks within a very short period of time.

But in the Gulf War Iraq did have a central command in that Saddam Hussein controlled the war from the Revolutionary Command Council (RCC) where each of the war services was represented. Iran, on the other hand, at the outbreak of the war, had no central command and control system which could co-ordinate the execution of its war strategy and suffered from a power struggle between the Revolutionary Guard Corps and the armed forces.

Iraq began the war on 22 September 1980 with a large scale air attack on ten military airfields in Iran, intended to destroy the Iranian air force on the ground. This failed, but five Iraqi divisions crossed the border the next day and began to advance into Iran. Within a week Saddam Hussein announced (in his 'Address to the Nation' on 28 September) that Iraq's territorial aims had been attained and that his country was willing to cease hostilities and to negotiate a settlement. This declaration, which reflected Iraq's limited strategy, was founded on apparently solid gains.

The Pasdaran bore the brunt of halting the Iraqi advance; the Iranian army deployed only one armoured division in the whole of Khuzestan (around Ahwaz), while the majority of its units were deployed in the hinterland and the north (along the Soviet border and in Kurdistan). According to President Bani Sadr, the absence of the army from the southern war theatre was premeditated, designed to give it more time to recover from the purges. In the long run this consideration proved to be prudent and enabled the army, which did not suffer heavy casualties during the invasion, to preserve its strength and to move to the offensive in 1981. But this would seem to be the wisdom of hindsight; in the short run, Iran's total lack of co-ordination prevented it from putting up an effective defence and accounted for the initial Iraqi successes. Contrary to common belief, the fervour and determination of the Pasdaran generally proved insufficient to halt the Iraqi army in open terrain. It was only in urban warfare (especially in the fighting for Khorramshahr) that the Pasdaran came into their own and made a significant operational impact. Their determination and the defensive advantages of built-up areas caused great problems for the advancing Iraqi forces, which seemed most unwilling to accept the casualties inevitably caused by street fighting. Long-range bombardment could not dislodge the Pasdaran from the rubble of Khorramshahr, only infantry on foot could do that, and for weeks the Iraqis were reluctant to face this prospect. Incidentally, casualties in the Battle of Khorramshahr along exceeded the total of all the casualties sustained by Israel and the Arab armies together in all the Arab-Israeli wars.

To compensate for its weakness on the ground, Iran rapidly escalated the conflict by extending it to Iraqi cities and strategic targets. As early as 24 September, the Iranian navy attacked Basra and, destroyed two oil terminals near the port of Fao. The Iranian air force struck at a variety of strategic targets within Iraq, including oil facilities in Mosul and Kirkuk, dams on the Zab river, petrochemical plants near Basra and Zubair and the nuclear reactor near Baghdad. By 1 October, Baghdad itself had been subjected to eight air raids. Despite the low level of damage caused by these raids, Iraq retaliated with a series of strikes against Iranian targets, such as the oil complex on Kharg Island, but this did not cause Iran to desist. Soon both sides were involved in widespread strategic exchanges.

Within a fortnight the war turned from a limited dynamic war into a general static one. This escalation was a direct result of the Iranian war strategy which sought to strike at Iraq's weak points by extending the theatre of war to the rear. The shift from a dynamic to a static compaign, on the other hand, was a deliberate Iraqi move. Having swept aside the Pasdaran and occupied the territories assigned as the objectives, Iraq seemed quite satisfied with its strategic position and showed no appetite for further territorial gains; thus, for example, the Iraqi army stopped its advance in front of Ahwaz and Susangerd and made no attempts to occupy them. Although Saddam Hussein did not announce Iraq's resort to a defensive strategy until 7 December 1980, the strategy from mid-October onwards, and particularly after the fall of Khorramshahr (24–5 October 1980), was in effect one of static war which aimed at retaining captured territories rather than attempting further advances. Thereafter, the two armies remained more or less locked in a typical static war for about eight months. Very few ground operations were mounted by either side.

As noted earlier, Saddam Hussein's strategy was one of a limited war. But limited wars have a habit of not remaining very limited. The Soviet invasion of Afghanistan, the United States intervention in Vietnam, President Sadat's crossing of the Suez Canal in 1973, the Israeli intervention in Lebanon in 1982, and many other examples come to mind.

The invasion of Iran was carried out by some five divisions, approximately half the Iraqi army. The Iraqi war plan was for three simultaneous thrusts along a front of some 400 miles. The main axis of attack involving the bulk of the forces was made in Khuzestan, the armoured thrust aimed at separating the Shatt-al-Arab from the rest of Iran and establishing a territorial security belt along the Southern frontier. The operations in the central (Mehran-

Qasr-e-Shirin) and far Northern (Penjevin) fronts were no more than secondary and supportive efforts designed to secure Iraq against an Iranian counter-attack. The occupation of Qasr-e-Shirin which dominated the traditional Tehran–Kermanshah–Baghdad invasion route was intended to protect Baghdad situated only 80 miles from the frontier. The operations on the Northern front aimed at establishing strong defence positions opposite Suleimaniyah to protect the Kirkuk oil complex.

Iran's initial war strategy, on the other hand, was for general war. Recognizing its military inferiority, its response was a determined resistance within and around the border towns and reliance on strategic depth to contain the invading forces. At the same time, Iran was quick to carry the war to the Iraqi rear by initiating air and naval raids on Iraqi strategic targets within less than 24 hours of the outbreak of hostilities.

From 1981 onwards, however, Iraq began to lose its strategic advantage. Iran carried out several successful local attacks with its infantry, and relieved Abadan which had been under siege. Baghdad then switched to a defensive strategy. The situation at the front remained virtually at a stalemate until May 1982 when the Iraqi troops were pushed back almost to the frontier. Once it had liberated its territory Iran did not confine its efforts to maintaining military pressure on Hussein. Instead, Iranian spokesmen placed more and more emphasis on the need to invade Iraq, which they viewed as a step on the path to 'liberate Jerusalem'. At the end of the year Iran crossed the border and opened up new fronts in Iraqi territory in the direction of Basra in the south and Mandali in the north, as well as in the central zone. It did not, however, succeed in winning a single decisive victory. In 1983 three limited offensives enabled Iran to make some gains, particularly in the north, and the Iranian infantry launched massive frontal attacks on the Iraqi lines. However, the delivery of five French Super Etendard fighters armed with Exocet missiles strengthened Iraq's air force, which not only attacked strategic and economic targets in the heart of Iran but also opened fire on merchant shipping and oil tankers in the Persian Gulf. It also attacked Iran's main oil terminal on Kharg Island. Unlike Iran, which had never stopped exporting its oil by sea, Iraq had been forced shortly after the beginning of the war to rely on overland pipelands for its exports.

The following year a series of Iranian offensives on the southern and central fronts resulted in the capture of important strategic objectives including almost all the oilfields on the Majnoun islands north of Basra. While both sides were stepping up their attacks in the Persian Gulf, Iraq had begun to bomb population centres in Iran, in a prelude to what would become known as 'the war of the cities'. Meantime Iraq began to use chemical weapons in cynical defiance of international accords and norms.

In 1985 Iran launched an offensive on its southern front, north of Basra, which involved heavy loss of life. Iranian troops also fought in the north, in the mountainous area of Kurdistan. Air raids in the Persian Gulf were increasing. By that date, more than 300 tankers sailing under the flags of various nations had been attacked by one or the other of the belligerents. Iraq's air offensive was designed to compensate for its disadvantages on land and to weaken Iran by reducing its capacity both to produce oil and to export it. The principal targets for Iraqi air attacks in the Gulf were oil terminals and complexes, oilfields and tankers which were either Iranian or chartered by Iran. Iran's naval attacks, on the other hand were principally directed at ships which it suspected of delivering arms to Iraq.

It was the crossing of the Shatt-al-Arab by Iranian forces, in 1986, however, followed by the capture of the port of Fao, which was of great strategic importance, for this two-pronged attack opened the route to Basra, Iraq's second most important city, and ultimately to Baghdad. Meanwhile the war of the cities continued and was especially effective against the Iranian population.

In January 1987 an Iranian offensive known as Operation 'Karbala 5' was launched against the Iraqi lines east of Basra, apparently with the object of either capturing or encircling that city. After six weeks of violent fighting Iran gave up this attempt which had, however, enabled it to occupy territory in the area of Shalamcheh and some islands in the Shatt-al-Arab.

A large part of the world's oil supply passes through the Persian Gulf, which is an area of major strategic importance. In 1987 the United States deployed additional air and naval forces in the Gulf in order to facilitate navigation there. Following Iraq's attack on the frigate *USS Stark*, in May 1987, and in response to several requests from Kuwait, Washington undertook to provide an escort of warships for eleven Kuwaiti tankers which were already registered under the US flag. Shortly before this the Soviet Union had lent Kuwait several Soviet tankers. Italy, France, Great Britain and the Netherlands backed up the United States by also deploying warships and minesweepers in the area. The fact that Iran had missile launching pads near the Strait of Hormuz, at the entrance to the Gulf, was a particular source of concern to the Americans. In addition Tehran had stepped up the naval war by making greater use of fast patrol boats armed with missiles and grenade launchers. These developments led to several encounters in the Gulf between Iran's forces and those of the United States.

The war in the Gulf is fraught with paradoxes and this applies equally to the way in which hostilities developed. Since 1981 Iraq had proposed a ceasefire on several occasions, and as the years passed these proposals were accompanied by fewer and fewer conditions. Baghdad appealed to the UN and to other organizations to act as mediators. Iran, on the other hand, made any ceasefire conditional on the payment of billions of dollars in reparations, and also insisted on the removal of Iraq's president, Saddam Hussein. Iraq's determination to end the war did not prevent it, however, from resorting to tactics with serious consequences from several points of view. These included its use of chemical weapons and its attacks on Iranian cities as well as on the shipping in the Gulf.

The turning point in the war occurred at the outset of 1987 with the Iranian failure to capture Basra. Khomeini's main purpose was to bring about the downfall of Saddam Hussein. The Iranians believed that the fall of Basra would inevitably bring about his downfall.

Now, however, they were defending their own country and after the experience gained in years of fighting, the Iraqi forces improved. They built effective fortifications based on the natural obstacles on the ground. They made good use of their superiority in fire-power, artillery, tanks and attack helicopters, and perfected the rapid movement of reinforcements to weak spots in their defences. Tens of thousands of young *Basij* volunteer Iranian militia, endowed with an overdose of religious fervour but lacking military training, lost their lives as they stormed the Iraqi defences. For the first time officers in the Iranian forces began to talk about 'the lost war'.

On the other hand the success at Basra proved Saddam Hussein's ability to maintain his power and to control a complex military situation, moving over ultimately to an all-out attack. Side by side with the improvement in the military showing of Iraq and the leadership of Saddam Hussein, the internal front in Iran began to falter. The defeats and military débâcles which Iran suffered both from the Iraqis and at the hands of the Americans in the Gulf, wore down the fanatic motivation of the Iranians and enabled the Iraqis to move over to a major attack last April.

Iranian confidence eroded. Despite the apparent religious fanatic determination of the Iranian population to follow its Imam, Iranian morale broke. This was brought about by a realization by much of the Iranian population that the war was an orgy of senseless blood-letting without any end in sight, certainly as long as Khomeini lived. The failure to take Basra despite Iranian human-wave assaults was followed by the Iraqi counterattack. Iraq's air superiority enabling it to attack civilian targets began to have its effects. Iraq's success in extending the range of the Soviet made Scud surface-to-surface missiles to approximately 500–600 kilometres, enabled the Iraqis to attack Iranian cities.

Between February and April 1988 in yet another war of cities, Iraq launched 160 missile attacks on urban areas in Iran terrifying the civilian population. Following the missile attack on Tehran an estimated one-and-a-half million people fled the city of 8 million population. This coupled with the fear that the missiles, might be armed with poison gas, increased the panic. Iraq increased its use of chemical weapons and the world was shocked in March 1988 by the published results of Iraq's chemical weapons attack on Halabja which severely demoralized Iranian troops. The employment of chemical weapons and the publishing of its effects on the human body had its effect too on the nation morale in Iran. It affected directly the spirit of volunteering and the normal contingent of 300,000 *Basij* volunteers attached to Iran's Revolutionary Guard, the Pasdaran, fell off by one third.

The lack of cohesion in the Iranian armed forces becan to have its effects as defeat followed defeat. The Iraqi army demonstrated superior training, organization and morale. Unlike the fearful and uncertain Iranian regulars who were purged, spied upon and saddled with military incompetent 'spiritual guidance officers' the Iraqi army had the full and enthusiastic support of its government. Saddam Hussein appeared in public only in army uniform. Quantitatively Iraq more than doubled the army's first-line man-power from less then 200,000 when the war began to almost a half a million.

As defeat followed defeat the Pasdaran's lack of military experience and lack of discipline contrasted sharply with the by now smoothly oiled Iraqi war machine, making use of chemical weapons. The defeat of the Pasdaran at Fao was a rude awakening for the Iranian Command.

An analysis of Iran's failure during this current war cannot be complete without taking into account the economic aspects. During the war the oil production of both countries dropped considerably, but evened out to roughly half the pre-war production. Iraq managed to recover to a certain extent by increasing its pipeline capacity through Turkey. Furthermore, these oil production facilities were not seriously damaged by the attacks of a very weak Iranian airforce. Iraq's airforce which on the other hand had continued to improve by experience and by the acquisition of additional aircraft used its air superiority to good effect against the Iranian oil pumping and oil loading facilities. The direct involvement of the US and other Western countries prevented Iran from effective retaliation measures against oil tanker traffic.

In 1988 Iran went from defeat to defeat. Fao in April, Majnoun in May, Shalamche and Mehran in June, Dehloran in July, emphasized to the leadership in Tehran the gradual military decline which had occurred since the major battle of *Karbala 5* in January 1987. At the beginning of June 1988, following the Fao and Majnoun defeats, Khomeini obviously saw the writing on the wall and with it the danger to the Revolution. He appointed Ali-Akbar Hashemi-Rafsanjani, the Speaker of Iran's Parliament, to be acting Commander-in-Chief of the Armed Forces. Rafsanjani, a political pragma-tist, displeased the more extreme Islamic Fundamentalists by his pragmatism during the war, as for instance in connection with the alleged negotiations which led to the Irangate affair. It is clear from his public statements at the time that he appreciated the scope of Iran's basic problems. Unlike Iraq, which had a regular supply of arms and equipment from the USSR and later from the French, not to mention, incidentally, over a billion dollars worth of military purchases from Egypt, Iran had to shop around the arms' markets of the world. This, in turn, created a very difficult logistic problem for the Iranians, having to adapt themselves to various types of weapons which were bought not because of the logistic convenience of Iran, but because of their availability on the market. The US Government decided at a certain stage in

1987 to block Iran's sources of arms and mounted a diplomatic offensive in the various capitals of the world, in countries which were suspected of being suppliers of arms to Iran. Gradually this so-called 'Operation Staunch' began to have its effect. Rafsanjani and many other leaders in Iran became increasingly desperate and concerned by their country's isolation from the rest of the world. Accordingly they mounted a major effort to mend Iran's fences in different parts of the world. In June, after the freeing of the French hostages in Lebanon, Iran resumed normal relations with Paris. In July, diplomatic relations with Canada were resumed.

Iran's attack on neutral shipping in the Gulf indicated that Tehran had been counting on the US and the Soviet Union to neutralize each other in the Persian Gulf. Khomeini's extreme policy of isolation led to an increased ideological hostility towards Iran's theocracy on the part of the Soviet Union. In April 1988 Gennadi Gerasimov, seen as the chief spokesman for the Soviet leader Mikhail Gorbachev, said when discussing Soviet policy in the Persian Gulf: 'We now have something which we haven't had for a very long time: a Soviet–American dialogue, not just on disarmament but on all the issues. This includes regional conflicts. There are many problems made more difficult by our rivalry that we can solve together.'

The Iranians must surely have been aware of the fact that the Soviet Union did not condemn the attack by the US on the Iranian oil platforms and ships in April. They were well aware of the fact that the USSR was Iraq's main arms' supplier and that it provided all the surface-to-surface missiles that had been employed against Tehran. There were reports indicating that some of the chemical munitions used on Iraq's Soviet-made guns and rocket launchers could well be Soviet equipment. There was widespread suspicion that Iraqi planes that had bombed Iranian targets along the Caspian Sea near the Soviet border in 1987 refuelled in the Soviet Union. However accurate these reports might or might not have been, it was reasonable for the sober element in the Iranian leadership to assume that the two major powers might be moving towards a concensus on the question of Iran. Rafsanjani obviously saw the situation in all its stark reality. He was facing an Iraqi army of a million troops – one of the largest in the world – with eight years of continuous battle experience and an appreciable edge in tanks, training and aircraft. War weariness was obviously gripping Iran, and military enlistment had dropped sharply. The resolve of the US and the allies to keep the oil shipping lanes open in the Gulf was evident to all. Iran was isolated from the rest of the world. Rafsanjani understood that he must bring the war to an end and that the only one capable of so doing in Iran was Khomeini. While reports of Khomeini's impending death have proved to be erroneous in the past, it was quite clear that he was neither getting younger nor healthier. It was obvious to Rafsanjani and his supporters that Khomeini's departure will almost certainly open a period of political turmoil in Iran, with prolonged jockeying for position by among others, Rafsanjani and Ayatollah Hussein

Montazeri, Khomeini's designated successor. The Iranian leaders realized that Khomeini alone possessed the power to extricate his country and, incidentally, his Revolution, from the war. It was vital for Khomeini to move now, for after his death there could well be nobody with the authority to do so. The proverbial straw that may well have given Rafsanjani his chance was the accidental US shooting down of an Iranian Jet liner on 3 July with the loss of 290 lives. This tragic incident gave to moderate political figures in Tehran a chance to argue the futility of continuing the war which they insisted the US would never permit Iraq to lose. The US Navy was protecting the Gulf shipping from Iranian attacks. The US forces had attacked Iranian oil platforms and ships in the Gulf. The US was accused of providing military intelligence to Iraq.

In mid July a meeting of leaders which included Ahmead Khomeini, the Ayatollah's eldest son took place. The meeting was reportedly marked by much recrimination but it decided to recommend to the Imam to agree to a ceasefire. In his broadcast to the Iranians on 20 July, Ayatollah Khomeini offered no pretence that Iran had achieved a victory. He called his decision to accept Resolution 598 'more deadly than taking poison'.

Thus, to all intents and purposes, ended this futile war. It is early to evaluate the possible train of events in Iran as apparently a policy based on irrational ideological revolution has made way for a rational approach based on national interests. In Iraq, too, burdened with a 50 billion dollar debt and facing a long period of recovery, questions will bound to be asked about Saddam Hussein's misreading of the post-Revolutionary confusion in Iran, which brought about a futile war with its horrendous cost in life and resources. Sooner or later, when the cheering dies down, even Saddam Hussein may have to answer many embarrassing questions.

This war came as a rude reminder to the world that even at the end of the twentieth-century violent conflicts based on religious fanaticism are not a phenomenon of the past.

Furthermore, this is a war worthy of a place of honour in Barbara Tuchman's March of Folly. It will be cited as a classic example of the power of an individual's blind dogmatism in totalitarian states to lead a people towards disaster and thereby to change history. This occurrence could well repeat itself especially in the prevailing instability presided over by autocratic regimes in the Middle East.

Iraq, and also Iran, created and maintained two of the largest armies in the world in the field of battle for a period of eight years. This is no small achievement in the Middle East in terms of military experience and potential, Israel cannot and dare not ignore it. However, it seems that from a short term point of view, both countries will continue to be more preoccupied one with the other, with a major reconstruction effort and with internal developments as the scope of one of history's major blunders in our area sinks in with all the consequences that are liable to develop therefrom.

I would hesitate to prognosticate at this junction except to say that we could well be witnesses to major developments in both countries with all that this implies. Somebody is bound to present a demand for an accounting of the tragic massacres and destruction which have gone on for eight years because of the obstinacy of two stubborn men. It is early to draw all the conclusions and lessons. They are not necessarily in the field of military science. It is clear that each army, but more especially in the case of Iraq, as it was driven on the defensive in order to protect its own soil and to fight off an invasion, fought more resolutely than in other circumstances. Not all Iranians support Ayatollah Khomeini's Revolution but most seemed willing to fight off the invasion. Iraq's Shi'ite Muslims have quarrels with President Saddam Hussein's predominantly Sunni regime, but most became loyal Arabs when they had to fight a Persian enemy. Khomeini in Tehran and Saddam Hussein in Baghdad face an identical question: How long will these loyalties last once the war is over?

Obviously Iraq's greatest mistake was to open only a limited war and to stop and try to negotiate once they had made their first advance. Their army was doing well, the enemy was disorganized, the cost of giving the Iranians time to mobilize more young men was eight years more fighting.

A thought about air power. The Iraqi pilots have thousands of hours of flying time. They did not have to face a serious airforce nor a serious anti-aircraft system. But they did mount long-range attacks reaching a distance of 1000 km., hit their target, refuelled in the air and returned safely. Few airforces in the Middle East are capable of carrying out such attacks. On the other hand one cannot avoid noting that Iran never had air superiority anywhere but until the last year of the war almost always won.

The exceptionally mild international reaction to the use of chemical weapons by the Iraqis, is alarming. Who could have dreamt that the world would stand by almost mute, and in fact by doing nothing, acquiesce in a ruthless use of poison gas by two Third World countries? The taboo has been broken and every army facing the possibility of war must now take into consideration that the international accords barring the use of chemical weapons in war are apparently of little binding value.

However, it seems that the main lesson for all countries to note is that the standing in the world of a country engaged in a military struggle is a vital element not only politically, but also economically and therefore militarily. What brought Iran to agree to a ceasefire was its isolation internationally. No country can afford to become isolated while at the same time maintaining a strong military posture. The nations of the world are interdependent, and a major element in any middle and small nation's military capability must of necessity be based on its international economic and political standing. The Gulf War proved that this must be a major and vital consideration in the defence of any country.

Furthermore, one cannot ignore a new element which has begun to have its effects on many of the conflicts in the world today. Most conflicts thrived when they took place against the background of the hostility and rivalry between the two major powers. But as we in Israel are aware from the days of our struggle for independence, nothing can stand in the way of a consensus between the two great powers. This truism is amply demonstrated by what is happening now in the Gulf. It is a lesson that must not be overlooked.

In conclusion, suffice it to say that while, as pointed out at the outset, from a pure battlefield point of view there is little to learn from this senseless, dreadful conflict, which was such a tragic mistake from start to finish, the broader implications are of vital interest to everybody. They deserve a most thorough analysis and study, so that all can learn from them in the hope that such ghastly and tragic errors will not recur.

16 The Arms Race after the Iran–Iraq War

Geoffrey Kemp

INTRODUCTION

Will the end of the Iran–Iraq War and a Soviet withdrawal from Afghanistan herald a new era of co-operation among Middle East adversaries? Or will the hiatus in these conflicts lead to a new and possibly more deadly arms race with important strategic consequences for all the major players in the region? The thrust of this essay is that the arms race will intensify unless two things happen: the United States and the Soviet decide to put some ceilings on high-tech weapons proliferation to the region; some progress is made to resolve the bitter and longstanding conflicts of the region.

When wars end Ministries of Defence try to discover the lessons learned and apply them to their plans for fighting the next war. Many of the lessons from the Iran–Iraq War will stimulate demand for new generations of weapons and revised procedures for war preparation including training, mobilization, use of reserves, and war-fighting strategies. Unless regional 'peace' is accompanied by harmony and trust, latent hostility between former adversaries will ensure that defence preparedness remains a priority item. Iran and Iraq themselves are unlikely to risk taking unilateral steps to reduce their arsenals. The contrary is more likely; both sides will rearm.

Other Middle East countries have been strongly influenced by the war and have learned their own lessons. The most talked about example is that chemical weapons and counter city bombardment with surface-to-surface missiles can have a decisive psychological impact on the outcome of a war. But there are other strategic lessons. A unique coalition of Arab countries worked together to deny Iran victory and were able to sustain a massive war effort for over eight years. Without the respective financial, political and logistical support of the GCC countries, Jordan and Egypt, it is doubtful whether Iraq could have withstood the onslaughts of Khomeini's armies. The most troublesome, but, as yet rarely discussed lesson is that while most of the world has greeted the end of the war with relief, many in the region have emerged from this experience with a jaundiced view of the high morale tone the West has adopted on the use of chemical warfare and the spread of missile technology.

If there is to be any co-operation to limit the proliferation of new military technologies there must first be greater awareness of the positions of the

269

regional powers and what their leaders are thinking about arms control, the conditions for conflict resolution, and Western homilies over the evils of modern warfare.

To better understand the emerging strategic environment it is useful to recall the reasons why there was such concern about the Iran–Iraq War, and what effect the ceasefire will have on the Gulf countries and the super powers as they contemplate their security needs. This will be followed by an overview of the arms race in late 1988 and how likely it is that arms control measures will succeed.

SUPPOSE IRAN HAD WON?

Since 1982 it had been conventional wisdom that an Iranian defeat of Iraq would have had more serious consequences for Western interests than an Iraqi victory. A Khomeini victory would have given an enormous shot in the arm to the variant of Islamic fundamentalism he had been preaching and exporting to Muslim countries. A new 'domino theory' presumed that a collapse in Iraq would quickly lead to Iranian hegemony, if not direct control, over Kuwait, Saudi Arabia and the remaining GCC countries. Such a political upheaval would have posed direct and ominous threats for Jordan, Syria and Lebanon and would eventually be felt by Israel and Egypt. To the north the Soviet Union would have had to reassess the vulnerability of its own Muslim population to the influence of Khomeinism. To the east, Pakistan, already favourably disposed towards some of Khomeini's ideas, would have fallen more and more under a strident Islamic banner. This would have then posed a strategic challenge to India, which, in its own worst case analysis, talks about a 'sea of militant Islam' from Turkey to Indonesia. This could have threatened India's internal cohesion by encouraging separatist tendencies among its own 122 million Muslims. India, already fighting the Sikh insurgency in the Punjab, feared that an Iranian victory would undermine its secular status.

An Iranian victory and the spread of radical Islam could have meant higher oil prices because OPEC would be an Iranian controlled institution. This could have led to the use of the oil weapon in a way we have not seen since the mid-1970s. If Iran and its surrogates had controlled oil prices, a shift in the world balance of power would have occurred.

In short, it is not difficult to come up with a string of scenarios as to why, from many points of view, an Iranian victory was to be fiercely resisted.

Whether or not all, or any, of these events would have taken place had Basra fallen and Saddam Hussein been toppled, remains an open question. Almost certainly, the sequence of events would have been more muddled and ambiguous; there is no guarantee that the Gulf countries would have collapsed. Their resilience to Iran in the past two years has been one of the more interesting wildcards of the war. Similarly it is not clear that the appeal of Khomeinism would have overridden the dislike of Iran and Iranians in much of the Arab world; Iran has had little success wooing the Iraqi Shi'ites even when an Iranian victory seemed most plausible.

Nevertheless, very few, if any, Western analysts have come up with 'good' scenarios stemming from an Iranian victory. Fears of the 'bad' scenarios were used to justify the actions taken by the Western countries, the Soviet Union and the Gulf Arab countries to stop Khomeini.

Fears of an Iraqi victory did not raise global temperatures as much. No one believed Iraq wanted to occupy Iran and spread the gospel of the Ba'th party. But, if Saddam Hussein had won the war decisively in the early years, it would have put Iraq in an overpowering position in the Gulf which would have posed strategic problems for the Gulf countries and Jordan and, ultimately for Syria and Israel.

The Iranian threat was considered the more serious threat because of the ideology of the revolution and Iran's geopolitical importance. These factors remain as true today as they did before and during the war.

WHAT FOLLOWS THE CEASEFIRE?

No one expects a peace agreement between Iran and Iraq in the near future, but what does the end of the fighting mean for the strategic dynamics of the Middle East and beyond?

Since the summer of 1982, when the Iranians finally took the offensive following the Iraqi invasion in 1980, Khomeini seemed determined to keep fighting. He believed the catharsis of war would sustain the revolution. By early summer of 1988 a dramatic reassessment occurred; continuing the war could destroy the revolution. Six years of killing had resulted in hundreds of thousands of martyrs and the enmity of the world. By mid-1988, the efforts of the external powers and the GCC countries gave Iraq with enough military and economic support to defeat the Iranians.

Iraq will not be easy to deal with in its post-war mood. However, given its large foreign debt, small war-weary population and long delayed ambitions to restore economic growth, it will be susceptible to some forms of inter-Arab and international pressure. Neither Iran nor Iraq will be able to sweep their mutual animosity under the carpet after such bitter confrontation. Rather, one can expect both to retain a healthy scepticism of each other's intents and, for this reason, maintain significant military forces on, or near, the front line. Both sides will have to assume that at some point in the future they may have to fight again.

From the perspective of regional stability a preferred outcome would be that both countries come to realize the futility of further military confrontation and actively seek ways to establish a working relationship. But this may be expecting too much. Short of such an achievement, the best outcome would be that the two countries while retaining a vigilance along the border, gradually turn their focus on their internal problems and attempt to rebuild their shattered and stagnant economies. This will require that they both establish better relations with their neighbours, as they gradually build up their economic base through increased oil sales, having first rebuilt their oil infrastructure and logistical systems.

Each country will have to cope with new problems. Aside from worrying about the security of its eastern flank, Iraq's most overwhelming concern is its $30 billion debt, mainly to the Arab world. Since defence spending will remain high as long as peace is unobtainable, getting Iraq launched on reconstruction may take a long time. But if Iraq is able to rechannel its energies to the problems of economic growth, it will have little incentive to bully its smaller Arab neighbours and antagonize the United States by reverting to its pre-war hostility to Israel. Iraq has already been made aware of the power of international opprobrium following its use of gas against Kurdish dissidents.

The Mid-East country that has a lot to worry about is Syria, whose leadership supported Khomeini. Indeed, following the ceasefire Iraq decided to intervene with arms and money in Lebanon and back Syria's most intransigent enemies. One irony was that the end of the Iran–Iraq War made a settlement in Lebanon more difficult. The failure of Lebanon to elect a president in September 1988 was in large part due to Syrian suspicions about Iraqi involvement in Lebanon.

Iran's internal situation is more volatile and complicated because of the abrupt and startling change in Iranian policy and the fragile health of Khomeini and the ongoing succession struggle. The key question is whether preoccupation with domestic concerns will encourage more moderate Iranian policies abroad. While Iran will always play a predominant role in the Gulf because of its size and geography, its capacity to influence its neighbours based on its Islamic credentials is an open question. The test cases will be its future relations with Lebanon's Shi'ite radicals, particularly Hizballah, who have depended so heavily on Iran for financial and military support, and its relations with the Gulf Arab countries, especially Kuwait and Saudi Arabia, which have been so badly damaged. By the end of 1988 there were signs that Iranian influence in Lebanon was already on the wane and Hizballah were increasingly described as 'home grown'.

Iran, too, has major economic reconstruction to do. Pumping more oil is the obvious way to raise the money to reinvest in the country and rechannel energies and skills away from the war front. However, most observers believe there will be no quick demobilization. This suggests that economic recovery will be slow and suffer from many bottlenecks.

The role of the various factions in the Iranian military and the revolutionary guards will be important in event of a succession crisis. Will the military be blamed for the losses at the front? Or could some strong nationalist army officer claim that Iran was 'stabbed in the back' by treachery in Tehran? One lesson of history is clear; when armies lose wars domestic turmoil often follows.

Another key element in the emerging strategic equation is how Iran will rebuild its depleted military inventories. Will it try to emphasize its self-sufficiency and self-reliance and deliberately not seek help from outside, or will it attempt to improve its fragile, shattered relations with most of the world by offering new trade arrangements?

The behaviour of other countries who have suffered from arms embargoes in times of crisis suggests that memories linger on. After the 1965 Indo-Pakistan war, during which the US and UK imposed an arms embargo, both countries turned to other sources and emphasized self-sufficiency. However, given the relatively primitive state of Iran's armaments infrastructure, it cannot meet its own needs against a highly-armed and sophisticated Iraq unless it turns to outside sources. Only the Soviet Union could provide massive military assistance on a short-term basis. Other countries might be prepared to sell, although this will clearly be a contentious issue amongst the main supplier nations. The most dangerous possibility will be that Iran, having learned the lesson of isolation, will proceed steadily and covertly to consider ways to re-establish its military predominance or certainly to balance anything Iraq might do. The possibility of a resurrection of Iranian and Iraqi nuclear capabilities cannot be ruled out, though this would have to be a long-term programme in view of the extreme technical difficulties involved.

The Gulf States

While the Gulf States have welcomed the ceasefire, all remain nervous about their futures. Though their resilience and unity these past eight years has been surprising in view of the predictions that they would collapse like dominoes, none of the Gulf states can stand up to the military strength of either Iran or Iraq. If either Iraq or Iran try to re-establish greater dominance over the Gulf countries, historic tensions are bound to surface once more.

How much influence will the United States now have with the GCC countries and Iraq? The US commitment to reflag the Kuwaiti ships in the summer of 1987 and build up the biggest flotilla of American naval power since the Korean war stemmed from the disastrous fall-out from the Iran–Contra affair which, for many Arabs, was the third in a series of events that weakened American credibility. (The first event being the weak-kneed American response when the Shah was in trouble; the second, the unilateral pull-out of Lebanon in 1984 undercutting Amin Gemayel's credibility.) In the short run, the United States has probably redeemed its credibility in the

Gulf because it was prepared to use force against Iran and the Western European allies, albeit initially reluctantly, joined in a successful operation.

However, now the Arab Gulf countries face a major question mark concerning their own security arrangements. The GCC can make a strong case for re-equipping their military forces with the more sophisticated systems, particularly air defence, in view of the overweening power and presence of Iran and Iraq. One can anticipate the steady but growing demand by the GCC countries for advanced military training and technology. Here the United States faces a growing dilemma in view of the decision of Saudi Arabia to seek diversified supplies and not rely on the United States as its primary provider. The Saudi decision to turn to China for missiles and to Britain for advanced fighters, helicopters and warships, is a new trend. Kuwait has threatened to go to the Soviet Union for aircraft if it cannot get American F-18s and Maverick missiles. Other Gulf countries may follow suit.

New generation Soviet and European equipment, while perhaps not as good in certain categories of American equivalents, is nevertheless highly sophisticated. The Mig-29, for instance, is considered a match for the F-16, or at least the Indians think so. Keeping close US ties with the GCC countries is in American interests. And yet the opposition in Congress to US arms sales to the GCC has made it difficult for any administration to guarantee to GCC countries that they will have uninterrupted supplies of American equipment.

From a strategic standpoint America's unreliability as a supplier may not be in Israel's long-term interests either. Israel's security in the region is linked to American presence, influence and, ultimately, power. The more American power is diminished, the less assured Israel must be of American credibility and support in a time of crisis. While no one underestimates the dangers to Israel of F-16 and F-15 aircraft, and Maverick missiles appearing in Saudi Arabia, or for that matter Jordan, the fact is the American controls on spare parts, training and deployments are likely to be much more vigorously enforced than equipment coming from Europe or the Soviet Union.

A debate on Israel's relations with the Arab Gulf countries is long overdue and has been hidden in the closet on Capitol Hill as well as in Jerusalem. An early resolution of US–Israeli differences on this question is desirable. Public brawls concerning US arms sales to the Arabs are in no one's interests.

Superpower Relations and the Gulf War

Unlike recent Arab–Israeli wars and conflict in North Africa, which has pitted Soviet-backed adversaries against US friends and allies, the super-powers had a very strange relationship during the war. Since they were not directly threatened, neither had a compelling interest to end it, even though both saw benefits in preventing an Iranian victory. The result has been that, although neither superpower will admit it, both have been 'allied' in helping Iraq for the last five years. The Soviet Union provided massive quantities of arms; the United States provided a massive military presence in the Gulf, was generally supportive of the Iraqi position in the UN and other diplomatic circles, and enforced the arms embargo against Iran (which, with the exception of Colonel North's caper, was successful).

There is much evidence that the superpowers have made a deliberate effort to tolerate each other. Soviet criticism of American military actions, including the attack on Iranian oil platforms in April 1988 and the shooting down of the Iran airbus, was exceptionally mild. Similarly the rhetoric of the Reagan Administration concerning the Soviet threat to the Gulf diminished greatly over the past year, especially since the Geneva agreements on Afghanistan. The Iranians have persisted in viewing both superpowers as devils incarnate. Iranian alienation of both superpowers may well have been the most serious mistake of the Khomeini regime.

This trend has not alleviated longer-term American and Soviet fears of each other despite the friendly overtures of Mr Gorbachev and the anticipated Soviet withdrawal from Afghanistan. Americans still worry about potential Soviet inroads into Iraq, and particularly Iran. The Soviets are concerned about the 'success' of the American military presence and worry that it will remain there. Both countries have an interest in seeing the other not establish strong positions in the region now that the war is over. They also have a common interest in seeing a relatively stable balance of power between Iraq and Iran.

The United States and the Soviet Union are now engaged in wide-ranging bilateral discussions on conflict resolution including the dynamics of regional conflict and proliferation of non-nuclear weapons. Whether this dialogue will continue and be successful remains to be seen, but co-operation between the superpowers in resolving first Afghanistan, and now the Gulf confrontation, raise the possibility that they may work together on the third, and probably most difficult conflict, the Arab–Israeli question.

Until the outbreak of the Intifada in December 1987 the Arab world was preoccupied with the Iran–Iraq War. Now that the war is over attention has focused even more sharply on the Palestinian issue, which remains unresolved and highly visible. The dramatic events of November and December 1988 which led to US dialogue with the PLO has changed the political map in several ways. Since the Soviet Union is believed to have played an important role in persuading Arafat to adopt a more moderate public posture, it is increasingly difficult to see how the Soviet Union can be denied a role in the peace process.

THE ARMS RACE AND ITS CONTROL

The proliferation of high technology military items to the Middle East and South Asia has received a great deal of attention in the past year. Four events have prompted this publicity: the *effective* use of chemical weapons and surface-to-surface missiles (SSMs) by Iraq; the purchase of long range Chinese SSMs by Saudi Arabia; reliable reports that Libya and Syria are developing chemical warfare capabilities in addition to their continuing interest in procuring more surfact-to-surface missiles; and Israel's successful launching of a research satellite in September 1988 which conclusively demonstrates the sophistication of its own missile programmes.

While these examples have attracted most of the publicity, the extent of this proliferation is much deeper and includes an impressive array of other new military technologies. Nevertheless, chemical weapons and surface-to-surface missile warfare are two unique features of the Iran–Iraq War. Many of the chemicals were of Second or even First World War vintage. The missiles used – modified Scud-B's, Silkworms, and Frogs – were first generation tactical missiles, inaccurate and less effective than new generations already in production. Here the linkage between the Iran–Iraq experience and a potential Syria–Israel war is important. With more accurate SS-21s, with the Lance and Jericho series, with chemical submunitions and nuclear capabilities, an all-out war between Syria and Israel has horrendous implications for the region, the superpowers and the world. The lessons have been learned in other countries too. A list of those developing missile capabilities runs the gambit from Libya to India and indicates the dimensions of the problem. Thus, one outcome of the war must be to re-examine the dynamics of the arms race throughout the region, the arms transfer process itself, and whether limitations on certain technologies can be imposed.

There is nothing new about a build-up of sophisticated arms in the Middle East. In the mid-1950s Soviet military assistance to Egypt and Syria heralded direct Soviet involvement in the region and was one of the contributing causes of the 1956 Arab–Israeli War. In the 1960s the influx of supersonic jet fighters and first generation missiles, including SSMs and the use of chemical weapons by Egypt in Yemen, was a front page item before the 1967 Arab–Israeli War. The 1967 war intensified the demand for high technology and at the time of the 1973 war, much publicity was given to the presumed revolutionary impact of precision guided munitions on the modern battlefield. The tank and manned aircraft were thought to be on the verge of obsolescence and a new era of warfare had dawned. But this was not to be. By the time of the 1982 Israeli invasion of Lebanon and the military clashes with Syria that occurred in the early days of the war, it became clear, especially in the air battle, that electronic warfare was the cutting edge technology that had most dramatic impact on the engagements. Also, during the mid 1970s, a great deal of attention and analysis was devoted to the extraordinary arms purchases by the Shah of Iran and the impact this was having on regional security and domestic harmony.

Given this background, it is important to approach the current interest in the subject with a sense of what is new, what is important, and what, in the way of arms control, is practical. If not, these serious and highly complicated issues will be overwhelmed by the 'motherhood factor' as politicians jump on the band wagon of 'stopping the missile race', 'banning chemical weapons' and putting pressure on governments to 'act responsibly' in the context of arms and technology transfers to the region.

Like most complex phenomena of international relations, the Middle East arms race and its impact on regional conflict generate different perspectives as to what to do about it. While experts, by and large, agree that there is something inherently troubling about the unregulated spread of advanced military technology into an area beset with traditional sources of conflict, there is little agreement as to what the realistic policy alternatives are for both the supplier and recipient countries.

Indeed, efforts to control the process will fail unless certain realities are faced. The first reality is that it is not at all clear the Arab countries, Iran and others in the Third World share Western and Israeli disgust over the use of chemical weapons, which, in part, is based on horrific historical experiences. But more important, many countries in the Near East and South Asia express a profound irritation at what they perceive to be selective Western outrage over the use of chemicals. They believe that the United States, having failed to prevent India, Pakistan and Israel from building nuclear weapons is now trying to deny them the very weapons that provide some sort of counter balance to nuclear devices. Consider, for instance, the views of Mamdouh Ateya, the former head of Egypt's chemical warfare department. He acknowledges that the ultimate Arab goal must be to build nuclear weapons 'but until we can catch up with Israel, there must be an urgent deterrent which should go beyond conventional weapons ... a chemical and biological Arab force could provide a temporary protective umbrella until we can achieve nuclear parity with Israel'.[1]

This viewpoint is so widely held in the Arab world and elsewhere that multilateral efforts to restrict chemicals and surface-to-surface missiles, are likely to fail unless some provisions are also made for limitations on combat aircraft and nuclear weapons. Hence, Israel's nuclear programme would probably have to be part of any comprehensive agreement on arms control. But since it is unrealistic to suppose any Israeli government will give up the nuclear option in the absence of fully fledged and iron-clad peace treaties and security arrangements with its neighbours, comprehensive arms control prior to a peace settlement is not on the cards.

So what can be done? Practical steps to limit the effectiveness of chemical attacks can be taken. For example the development of anti-ballistic missile systems by the United States and Israel can certainly provide some deterrent to Syria's SSM capability. But here again it must be accepted that an ATBM can no more be considered a 'defensive' system than the provision of Hawk missiles to Jordan in the 1970s was seen as 'defensive' by the Israeli military planners. Distinctions between offensive and defensive systems in the Mideast (or anywhere else for that matter) require highly complicated analyses of overall force postures and military strategies. However in the absence of any controls on chemical proliferation the US and Israel are quite right to press ahead with ATBM development. In fact if the Arrow concept works, it may be preferable to encourage other countries to invest in ATBMs rather than SSMs. In short, similar logic for Middle East arms control to that discussed in the context of Nato–Warsaw Pact relationships may be necessary.

Another problem is that multinational efforts to restrict weapons from external supplies come up against the fact that some regional countries, notably Egypt, India, and Israel, have better indigenous capabilities than others. Therefore, unless these factors are taken into account, asymmetries will persist and it will be difficult to achieve an arms balance that will be remotely acceptable to the more radical states who are committed to resolving regional conflicts with military power.

In the short run the most promising avenue for controlling the most dangerous components of the arms race would be superpower co-operation. If the United States and the Soviet Union decided that it were in their interests to restrict, or limit, certain categories of weapons and could agree on means of verification and implementation, this would have a powerful impact on other suppliers. It wouldn't stop maverick suppliers but it would put great pressures on the Europeans and probably the Chinese to conform. But while this is an intriguing possibility, it does raise once more the problem of the linkage between nuclear and chemical weapons and missile and aircraft proliferation. The Soviet Union has a good record on conforming to the edicts of the NPT – some would say it has been more thorough in this matter than the US – but it is the leading supplier of SSMs worldwide. The Soviet Union has reasons to worry about both nuclear and SSM proliferation in view of its geographic proximity to the most likely candidates for nuclear or chemical armed missiles.

An interim deal could be one that linked Israel's deployment of long range missiles that could hit the Soviet Union with Soviet supplies of missiles to Syria and Libya. While it is unlikely the Soviet would stop *all* deliveries of SSMs for this arrangement, it might be prepared to limit the numbers and quality to the point where there was less threat of a counterforce first strike against Israel.

CONCLUSION

The control of the Middle East arms race will be one of the top priorities of the incoming US administration. Whether it will be possible to do any more than draw attention to the problem remains to be seen. The pressures on all states in the region to rearm and requip forces are strong. To expect unilateral arms limitation is unrealistic. Multilateral arms control will only happen if either the US and Soviet Union work out a tough agreement and enforce it; or if there is a reduction of regional tension through active and effective peacemaking.

Note

1. *Reuters*, 27 July 1988, 'Egyptian says Arabs should acquire Chemical Weapons'.

17 Escalation in the Iran–Iraq War

Philip A. G. Sabin

The word 'escalation' has only been in common use for some thirty years, but it has become such a commonplace term that it is now employed to signify virtually any kind of rise or growth, be it in the intensity of an armed conflict or in more mundane items such as house prices. This dilution of the concept is regrettable, because the word initially arose as a particularly vivid descripion of how a conflict could increase in intensity through an inherent upward dynamic, much as passengers are carried upward on an escalator without any deliberate effort on their own part. However, the broadening of the concept reflects more than just sloppy usage; it stems also from the development of rival strategic theories suggesting that an antagonist may master and control the 'escalation' of a conflict to its own advantage.[1]

This latter idea has caught on sufficiently to make the word 'escalate' into a transitive as well as an intransitive verb, and has given rise to such additional concepts as 'escalation dominance' and the bizarrely mixed metaphor of an 'escalation ladder'.[2] The battle of theories over escalation has been played out primarily in the United States, and has taken the form of abstruse debates about the likely controllability of limited nuclear war as well as bitter practical disagreements over US policy in Vietnam.[3] So far, however, there has been very little discussion of the dynamics of escalation in conflicts between Third World states themselves, in circumstances where the super-powers neither intervene directly nor stand squarely behind their opposing local clients.

Neglect of this aspect of the issue is not difficult to understand. Analysts in the industrialized world naturally have a more pressing interest in conflicts in which their own countries are or might become directly involved. There have not so far *been* very many Third World conflicts entirely independent of the East–West confrontation; the Arab–Israeli War of 1973, for example, rapidly escalated into a superpower crisis. Furthermore, given the relatively limited and finite military capabilities of Third World states, escalation in conflicts between them may be considered less 'analytically interesting' than in the superpower confrontation where both sides are inhibited from all-out conflict by their possession of overwhelming destructive power.

Today, however, these arguments are increasingly losing their force. With the decline of the Cold War and the rise of post-colonialist tensions among industrializing states, more and more wars in the Third World are governed by their own intrinsic dynamics independent of the ideological confrontation between East and West. The proliferation of increasingly sophisticated military hardware, including nuclear and chemical weapons, to Third World states is giving them impressive escalatory potential of their own, even without superpower intervention. This growth in the potential destructiveness of warfare in the industrializing world makes it harder for developed nations to ignore such conflicts, even though they will have less and less say over their course and outcome.

This chapter, therefore, will examine the dynamics of escalation in one particularly striking Third World conflict – the eight-year war between Iran and Iraq. Its object will be to assess how far that conflict vindicates or challenges particular established theories about escalation, and whether it highlights any major gaps in current theory as developed for conflicts involving the superpowers. The overall aim will be to allow a better analytical understanding of conflict escalation between Third World states, in the hope that this may increase the chances of controlling such conflicts in the future.

In one way, the Iran–Iraq War offers an ideal case study, thanks to the wide range of 'escalations' which occurred during its course. The land fighting intensified from border clashes in mid-1980 to full scale combined arms warfare, including the use of chemical weapons. Air and naval attacks spread from strikes against military targets to concerted campaigns against economic targets such as oil tankers and to coercive bombardment of civilians in the 'war of the cities'. The war also escalated in international terms, with sporadic Iranian strikes against the Gulf States and with the recent involvement of naval forces from the two superpowers and various West European countries in protecting shipping in the Gulf.

A less satisfactory aspect of the Iran–Iraq War as a case study for assessing escalation dynamics is the limited availability of reliable evidence concerning decision-making in either capital. However, there is enough material in the form of interviews, speeches and so on to give a fairly good indication of both belligerents' perceptions, and what the two states actually *did* often provides a powerful indication of their underlying thought processes. The lack of formal cabinet records thus does not represent a crippling handicap.

The question of what actually constitutes an 'escalation' is particularly difficult in the context of the Iran–Iraq War, because of the peculiar character of that conflict. From one point of view, many of the important 'thresholds' had been broken within days or weeks of the Iraqi invasion, with cities and oil installations being bombed, and even an Iranian raid on Kuwait.[4] From another point of view, however, the essentially static character of most of the war meant that almost any belligerent action by either side, be it an air raid or a land offensive, constituted an 'escalation' from the accustomed routine of entrenched stalemate. The term was even used in connection with the employment of a new weapon in an established role, such as the Iraqi use of Super Etendard of Tupolev-16 bombers against Iranian oil tankers.[5]

Richard Smoke's solution to the general problem of defining escalation is to describe it as the crossing of a natural 'saliency' whose significance is recognized by all parties to the conflict,[6] but this criterion is rather difficult to apply in the case of the Iran–Iraq War because of our lack of conclusive information about policy makers' perceptions. A more analytically useful approach is to focus on the issue of what criteria matter most in escalation dynamics; it is this question which will be used as the basis for the forthcoming analysis, with particular 'escalatory' events being discussed as and when required, regardless of whether they meet some arbitrary definitional criterion.

Two definitional issues nevertheless need to be addressed at the outset. The first is whether the actual outbreak of the war should be considered under the heading of 'escalation'. Although the origins of the Iran–Iraq War have already received detailed scrutiny from a large number of scholars, it seems artificial to exclude the issue entirely here. Not only was the Iraqi invasion of September 1980 undoubtedly the most significant 'escalation' of the entire war, but it also came after months of 'escalating' tensions and hostilities between the two countries. This latter pattern has been echoed in many other Third World conflicts, and it is worth at least a brief examination here.

The second definitional issue is whether to discuss 'de-escalation' as well as 'escalation'. De-escalation has received almost no analytic scrutiny in the past, except in the limited context of war termination.[7] Despite this lack of attention to the issue, the re-imposition of limits on the scale of the fighting without an overall ceasefire was striking feature of the Iran–Iraq War, with a large number of more or less durable truces in particular activities such as city bombardment. Such de-escalations will therefore be considered here in order to obtain a balanced picture of the forces making for expansion and for restraint in the war as a whole.

The following analysis will proceed by discussing various different issues from current Western escalation theory, and by relating each to the experience of events in the Iran–Iraq War. In each case, the object will be to assess whether certain theories have proved more applicable than others, and whether there are particular dimensions which the theories entirely fail to capture. The chapter will then conclude by identifying those issues which deserve greater attention when considering escalation in the specific circumstances of regional conflict in the industrializing world.

IS ESCALATION DELIBERATE OR UNCONTROLLED?

As already noted, the central dispute over escalation is whether the appropriate image is of a ladder or an escalator – that is to say, whether the participants have any choice in the intensification of the conflict. The foremost theorist associated with the image of uncontrolled escalation is Thomas Schelling, who compared crisis and limited conflict to a slippery slope on which the antagonists would engage not in a test of strength but in a 'competition in risk taking', with victory going to whoever was prepared to take a greater chance of sliding (and dragging his opponent) into disaster.[8]

Literally uncontrolled escalation is often anticipated in *nuclear* war due to the likely disruption of command links,[9] but it does not seem to have been a feature of the war between Iran and Iraq. There were certainly a number of unintended military actions during that conflict, but if anything they seem to have prompted *de*-escalation rather than triggering an expansion of hostilities. The accidental Iraqi attack on *USS Stark* in May 1987 led to a temporary lull in Iraqi air raids, and the same happened in early 1988 after further US complaints regarding incidents involving American warships and undisciplined Iraqi pilots.[10] The potentially much more serious incident in July 1988 when the *USS Vincennes* unintentionally shot down an Iranian airliner, far from triggering enraged Iranian retaliation, seems to have been one of the factors which persuaded Iran to accept the United Nations ceasefire resolution a fortnight later.[11]

Some of the various rounds of bombardment of civilians by the two antagonists may have been sparked by 'collateral damage' caused by inaccurate attacks aimed at military or economic targets, but it is hard to argue that the decision makers were unaware of this risk, particularly when using missiles whose inherent inaccuracy made their ostensible targets of 'Air Force headquarters' and the like merely a flimsy public relations excuse for attacks on non-combatants. When leaders on both sides decided that attacks on civilians were no longer in their interest, they were able to control and restrain them by outside-sponsored or even unilaterally declared ceasefires. This contrasts strikingly with the experience in some previous conflicts such as the Second World War, when attempts by the Germans to de-escalate the air war were not even recognized by their British opponents.[12]

A more sophisticated theory of 'loss of control' points to the passions aroused when war begins, and to the escalation of the stakes as losses mount and as the fighting threatens wider interests or opens unexpected opportunities. As in the First World War, states may find themselves 'locked in' to a conflict which has become wholly disproportionate to the original objectives, even without losing control of their individual actions. This type of uncontrolled escalation has obvious echoes in the Iran–Iraq War, with Iran's determination to pursue the conflict being fuelled by revolutionary fervour and by the growing need to justify the sacrifice of so many Iranian lives. It was this which led Iran to continue the war for six years at enormous cost after recapturing virtually all its territory, and which caused Ayatalloh Khomeini to describe his eventual decision to accept a ceasefire as 'like drinking poison'.[13]

Nevertheless, one should not exaggerate the extent to which passion overruled rationality during the Iran–Iraq conflict. The war had certain advantages for the Iranian regime in buttressing the revolution and justifying purges of political opponents; also, despite the military stalemate, it looked for a long time as if Iran might eventually win. The religious fanaticism so chillingly evident on the battlefield or in demonstrations in Tehran did not lead the Iranians to abandon all restraint in the strategic conduct of war, and it was the Iraqis who took the lead in most of the escalations which occurred. Similarly, Iranian policy towards hostilities in the Gulf was strikingly circumspect, with revolutionary zeal being outweighed by a hard-headed awareness of the superiority of American power and by reluctance to divert resources from the main conflict with Iraq.[14]

The fact that Iraq and Iran maintained diplomatic missions in each other's capitals almost throughout the war is a telling illustration of their determination to keep the conflict under firm political control.[15] It is true that any war is likely to develop in ways unforeseen at the outset, and Saddam Hussein in particular must have been horrified at the consequences of his 'limited' strike of September 1980.[16] Nevertheless, the fact that the escalation of the conflict resulted almost exclusively from deliberate and rationally intelligible decisions by one regime or the other means that the war as a whole seems to fit in somewhat better with a 'deliberate' than with an 'uncontrolled' model of escalation dynamics.

DO STATES ESCALATE TO ACHIEVE VICTORY OR TO AVOID DEFEAT?

Clausewitz's precept that 'all war tends to the absolute' raises the question of whether a stronger motive for this 'natural' escalatory tendency is fear of being defeated or frustration at being blocked in one's quest for victory.[17] These two motives are obviously not mutually exclusive, and represent rather the ends of a spectrum running through the intermediate position of wishing simply to stop and disengage from a stalemated war such as Korea or Vietnam. However, it is useful to try to assess at what points along this spectrum escalatory pressures tend to be strongest.

The Iraqi invasion of September 1980 might at first seem an instance in which escalation was prompted by ambition, in the form of Iraqi hopes for a more favourable settlement of certain border issues than they had been forced to accept in 1975, under pressure from the Shah's more powerful Iran. However, an even stronger motive for the invasion appears to have been the Ba'th regime's concern about its long-term survival in the face of revolutionary Iran's efforts at propaganda and subversion (possibly including the attempted assassination of the Iraqi deputy premier in April 1980).[18] The exact balance of Iraq's motives remains obscure, but the outbreak of the war does seem to have represented more defensive than offensive escalation.

Most later escalations of the war also appear to have been aimed more at avoiding defeat than at achieving victory. Iran took the lead in launching countervalue attacks immediately after the Iraqi invasion, and prosecuted the land war with vigour rather than accepting the limited defeat which Saddam Hussein had hoped to impose. Similarly, most Iraqi escalations against Iranian economic or military targets in the later stages of the war were strongly linked to Iranian land offensives, and were explicitly aimed at persuading Iran to cease its attacks and accept a ceasefire.

Several other escalations during the war also seem to have involved primarily defensive motives. The Gulf states gave financial and other aid to Iraq as a means of containing the Iranian revolution, and in fear that if Iraq were to be defeated their own turn would come next.[19] Likewise, the Iraqis used chemical weapons initially as a last resort device to forestall Iranian breakthroughs, a fact which may have made it harder for NATO nations to issue an uncompromising condemnation given their own dependence on escalation to *nuclear* strikes in such a circumstance.

This pattern of defensive escalation was not an absolute one, however. Iran's attacks into Iraq after mid-1982 could themselves be described as an escalation, and they were aimed at achieving 'victory' through the overthrow of Saddam Hussein and the extraction of reparations, not to speak of the more ambitious objectives which many feared Iran to possess. Iraq, for its part, came to use chemical weapons for more than last resort defensive purposes, as in its recapture of the strategic Majnoun islands in March 1984 and in its final offensive in Kurdistan in July 1988 after Iran had already agreed to the UN ceasefire.[20]

Even in those more numerous instances where the losing side took the lead in escalation, its decision may have been prompted by other military or strategic factors (to be discussed below) as well as by its fear of defeat. However, as will also be discussed below, desire for a ceasefire may in some circumstances lead a state to escalate simply in order to make the conflict more dangerous and hence force the superpowers to intervene. On balance, therefore, it is probably reasonable to conclude that it was fear rather than ambition which did more to prompt qualitative escalation during the Iran–Iraq War.

IS ESCALATION GOVERNED BY RESOLVE OR MILITARY SUPERIORITY?

One of the bitterest controversies in current Western strategic theory concerns the political importance of nuclear superiority. Some contend that theoretical advantages such as a Soviet ability to destroy American land-based missiles in a first strike could demoralize the US president and embolden Soviet leaders in a future crisis. Others argue that such calculations are irrelevant in a situation of mutual 'overkill' capabilities, and that what would matter in a crisis is which side had stronger *interests* at stake.[21]

With conventional forces, the spectre of mutual annihilation does not apply, but it remains of great interest whether a more important determinant of escalation is strength of will or military superiority in the area concerned. The Iran–Iraq War provides a particularly interesting case study in this regard, because it took the form of a contest between Iraqi technology and Iranian fanaticism. A fairly clear picture emerges from this confrontation, which is that military superiority was usually decisive in deciding whether or not an escalation was launched, but that the balance of resolve was crucial to whether or not it was sustained.

This is illustrated both by Iraq's initial invasion and by that country's later recourse to the bombardment of civilian targets. Iraq seems to have been tempted to invade by the military 'window of opportunity' created by the disarray of the normally stronger Iranian armed forces in the wake of the 1979 revolution. However, Saddam was most reluctant to incur large casualties lest this jeopardize the stability of his regime; this led him to avoid costly attacks on cities in the initial invasion, to seek a ceasefire almost immediately, and to abandon his gains and pull his forces back to static defence lines in Iraqi territory in June 1982. Similarly, Iraq's growing superiority in air power increasingly tempted it to bombard Iranian cities to try to force a ceasefire, but the high morale of the Iranians and the disturbing effects of their artillery and missile responses against Iraqi civilians usually encouraged Saddam to back down once several raids had been carried out.

Iran's conduct offers a mirror image of this pattern, and bolsters the idea of military superiority being decisive in initiating escalation but morale being decisive in sustaining it. Iran began land offensives into Iraq at a time when it seemed to have won superiority in the ground war; later events showed that the Iraqi defences had stabilized, but Iranian fanaticism meant that the attacks were sustained for six bloody years. In the Gulf, on the other hand, Iran took great care not to get into an all-out confrontation with the United States; military realities overrode revolutionary fervour in the initial escalation decisions. Iran's escalation of the air and naval war immediately after the Iraqi invasion also fits the pattern, given Iranian superiority in these arms at that time; the escalation could not be sustained because combat losses and maintenance and manpower problems meant that a continued air effort was a practical impossibility.[22]

This last point highlights a very important issue which is often neglected in traditional escalation theory, namely that the *means* of escalation may be a fragile or wasting asset, especially for a Third World state without reliable sources of resupply and other necessary outside assistance. This can cut both ways – on the one hand, Iraq seems to have held its air force back at certain times as a last resort weapon against the long-threatened Iranian 'final offensive', but on the other hand, one motive for attacking economic and civilian targets appears to have been that they were less well defended than military ones, and hence would impose less attrition on scarce air force assets.[23] However, loss of precious aircraft and pilots was probably one of the main factors encouraging the various truces in the bombing campaigns, as were similar resource considerations affecting the later exchanges of costly and inaccurate one-shot missiles.

A more widely recognized characteristic of escalation in conventional conflicts is that it may not be decisive in influencing the situation on the ground, as illustrated by the failure of the successive American bombing campaigns against North Vietnam.[24] The Iran–Iraq War offers a less clear-cut lesson in this regard, since although neither side's attacks on oil targets succeeded in crippling the other's economy (thanks in part to the surplus oil and tanker capacity resulting from the world oil glut),[25] Iraq's bombing of civilian targets does seem to have contributed substantially to the eventual erosion of Iranian morale. Bombing alone, however, was not sufficient, and it was not until Iraq regained the initiative on the battlefield itself, starting with its recapture of Fao in April 1988, that Iran was impelled to accept a ceasefire.[26]

One should not assume that the patterns displayed during the Iran–Iraq War can necessarily be generalized to other Third World conflicts. In 1973, for example, the Israelis were wrong-footed by assuming that the Arabs would not attack because of their military inferiority, when in fact other considerations swayed this particular escalation decision.[27] However, as with the Israeli invasion of Lebanon in 1982, the Iran–Iraq conflict does highlight the risk of escalations taking place because of military 'superiorities' which are subsequently found to be far from decisive in the overall outcome.

HOW IMPORTANT IN ESCALATION ARE STRATEGIC ASYMMETRIES?

One may identify three different patterns of escalation – *unilateral* (where one side escalates without drawing a response), *reciprocal* (where a response occurs and then the conflict stabilizes at the new level), and *open-ended* (where escalation proceeds through a series of alternating upward steps by the two antagonists). A crucial determinant of which pattern occurs is the degree of strategic asymmetry between the two sides. If one side is clearly dominant, it may escalate unilaterally with virtual impunity; if both have roughly equivalent capabilities and vulnerabilities, the chances are that they will fight under matching and reciprocal limits; but if large strategic asymmetries exist, there is a risk of open-ended escalation through alternating but dissimilar upward steps.

Escalation theories as developed for the nuclear confrontation between East and West tend to neglect this issue of strategic asymmetries and to focus on symmetrical escalatory 'rungs' such as 'counterforce with city-avoidance'.[28] In conventional warfare, however, strategic asymmetries between the two antagonists may have a profound effect on how the conflict develops. As Richard Smoke put it, 'In most real conflicts the potential escalation sequence is more like a ladder that has been bent and twisted out of shape, with all sorts of extras and odd protuberances added on, which vitally affect how the conflict does or does not climb it.'[29]

Several instances of escalation during the Iran–Iraq War appear to have been prompted in part by strategic asymmetries which made it difficult for the opponent to respond in kind. Iraq's use of chemical weapons was encouraged by Iran's lack of defensive or retaliatory capabilities and by the much greater susceptibility of Iran's manpower-intensive tactics to this particular countermeasure.[30] Iran decided to attack Iraqi oil exports through the Gulf at the start of the war because of their glaring vulnerability to disruption, whereas when Iraq achieved air superiority and redirected its oil exports through land pipelines, it launched its own 'tanker war' in 1984. Three years later, rather than confronting the United States Navy in direct air or naval engagements, Iran took advantage of the lack of Western minesweeping capability and resorted to mine warfare against the US convoys.

Often, these exploitations of strategic asymmetries provoked a dissimilar response, as predicted by the model of open-ended escalation. Iraq's strategy of launching air raids in response to Iranian land offensives is the most obvious example, but there were other lesser instances also. In October 1987, for instance, Iran responded to a long-distance Iraqi air raid on five tankers in the Strait of Hormuz by firing two missiles at Baghdad.[31] Even Iran's more usual response of attacking other Gulf tankers was more than just a matching action, since not only were the tankers flying neutral flags (as were many of Iraq's targets), but they were also heading for ostensibly 'neutral' ports on the southern shore of the Gulf; in July 1987, this led to a further asymmetric escalation as US warships began to protect Kuwaiti shipping.

However, there was usually a strong preference where possible for *reciprocal* responses to escalation (though not necessarily using the same military means – Iran regularly used missiles and artillery to reply to Iraqi air raids). When such symmetrical responses were not available, the antagonists sometimes refrained from retaliation rather than carrying out a dissimilar action of their own. Iran, for example, countered Iraqi use of chemical weapons merely by trying to improve its defensive preparations and to arouse world opinion against Iraq's actions (in both of which endeavours it had only limited success).[32] Similarly, the Western response to the mining of its vessels in the Gulf in July and August 1987 was limited to the passive measure of dispatching minesweepers to the area, until an 'appropriate' active response became available in September with the capture of an Iranian minelayer.[33]

The many strategic asymmetries between Iran and Iraq thus did not have quite as escalatory an effect on the conflict as might have been anticipated, because the antagonists were often hesitant and careful about engaging in dissimilar retaliatory actions. It was not until seven years after the start of the war, and three years after Iraq started serious attacks on tankers, that the conflict finally spiralled into direct clashes between Iran and the United States over freedom of navigation in the Gulf. Nevertheless, the Iran–Iraq War illustrates the crucial role played by strategic asymmetries in tempting unilateral escalatory moves and in denying the possibility of neat, reciprocal limits on the fighting.

HOW IMPORTANT IN ESCALATION ARE WELL-DEFINED 'THRESHOLDS'?

A key concept in escalation theory this that of clear 'thresholds' within which each side may limit its belligerent acts in a way which will be immediately apparent to the opposing side. Thomas Schelling wrote that such thresholds should ideally be 'qualitative and not matters of degree – distinctive, finite, discrete, simple, natural and obvious'.[34] The thresholds observed need not necessarily by symmetrical between the two sides, but unless clear thresholds exist, it may be difficult to maintain limits on one's own military effort or to convince the opponent that a particular escalation is intended to go only so far and no further.

The clearest thresholds involve the non-use of certain distinctive weapons, the restriction of operations to a certain geographical area or type of target, and the non-involvement of certain nations. All three of these types of threshold played a part during the Iran–Iraq War, but none of them did so in the all-or-nothing manner which escalation theory tends to envisage. Instead of being solid but brittle, the thresholds proved surprisingly elastic, permitting the conflict to slide across them but retaining considerable restraining force even after they had been repeatedly violated by the antagonists.

No threshold proved clear-cut enough to withstand gradual erosion through a series of ambiguous events. The principle of not targeting civilians, for example, was undermined by the proximity of inhabited areas to the battlefront, and Iraq regularly justified its air or missile attacks on cities as retaliation for the casualties caused by Iranian artillery in front-line cities such as Basra. Even the seemingly unambiguous threshold of non-use of chemical weapons was finessed by the Iraqis through an initial use of non-lethal tear gas in the summer of 1982.[35] An important factor in compromising potential thresholds was the propaganda and disinformation spread by the antagonists, which often made it very hard to know what had really occurred.

The threshold between peace and war proved particularly vulnerable to erosion and ambiguity. Iraq's invasion of 22 September 1980 came after months of escalating tension, subversion and border clashes, and Iraq itself dated the start of the war to the artillery exchanges of 4 September. 'Neutral' Gulf states such as Saudi Arabia and Kuwait gave substantial assistance to the Iraqi war effort, prompting Iran to make periodic punitive strikes against their oil tankers and other facilities; they remained officially at peace, however, and even continued to trade with Iran. The clashes between Iran and the United States in the last year of the conflict also took place within an ambiguous contect of 'no peace, no war', very similar to that which had developed between the USA and Libya in 1986.

The other side of the coin from this erosion of thresholds was that, even after they had been breached, they were rarely entirely ignored. Sometimes escalation was reversed and the threshold re-established by tacit or explicit ceasefires. At other times, the antagonists continued to show restraint in the *intensity* of their operations, rather than pursuing all-out campaigns in the new area. It was this combination of restraint and de-escalation which kept the war limited, and not any inviolability of the thresholds per se.

De-escalation often occurred through one side declaring a unilateral halt to a particular activity such as attacks on civilians, provided the other side reciprocated. Alternatively, the pattern of strike and counter-strike might simply stop, as happened after the various episodes of US–Iran conflict in 1987–8. The additional possibility of restraint in the intensity with which operations were conducted was particularly evident in Iranian attacks on the Gulf states and in Iraqi use of chemical weapons; although both increased in intensity as the conflict continued, they remained at a lower level then the belligerents were theoretically capable of sustaining.

Outside pressure seems to have been one reason for this readiness for de-escalation and restraint. Both Iran and Iraq depended on outside suppliers for their war materials, and it would have been counterproductive for them to appear too trigger-happy or to offend world opinion too gratuitously through concerted terror bombing or poison gas attack. Iraq's allies in the southern Gulf seem to have exerted a restraining influence of their own on Iraq's 'tanker war', since they did not want to suffer Iranian reprisals or trigger an American intervention which would jeopardize their delicately balanced attempts to remain independent.[36]

A more powerful influence for restraint appears to have been the judgement that the benefits of further attacks were outweighed by the costs associated with likely enemy retaliation. There was often a close linkage between the attacks made by the two sides, with a pattern of 'tit for tat' reprisals instead of two independent strategic campaigns. This meant that escalation often acquired an episodic rather than a sustained character, with particularly escalatory incidents appearing as exceptions to the established rules rather than changing the rules altogether.

The tit-for-tat regime rested on a delicate mixture of retaliation and restraint. Where no counter-action was taken there was a temptation for further unilateral escalation, as with the gradual expansion of Iraq's use of chemical weapons. If attacks were reciprocated, on the other hand, then since the antagonists often disagreed over who had fired the first shot, one of them at some stage had to forego retaliation in order to break the cycle of mutual reprisals. It sometimes took a bitter series of air raids and missile exchanges before this point was reached, but although the ideal of restraint became weaker and weaker as the war progressed, it never quite collapsed altogether.

The Iran–Iraq War thus suggests that clear qualitative thresholds may not be quite as critical in channelling and containing escalation as might have been thought. Even the clearest threshold is vulnerable to ambiguity, yet may continue to exercise some restraining influence despite successive violations. As other recent experience in the Middle East confirms, acts of violence may be episodic rather than sustained, and do not necessarily change the rules for good.[37] This highlights the importance of the balance between policies of retaliation and restraint in determining whether escalation may be brought under control in each particular case.

SHOULD THE SUPERPOWERS GET INVOLVED OR LEAVE WELL ALONE?

Ever since the crises in Iran and Afghanistan at the end of the 1970s, the Persian Gulf has been seen as the most likely flashpoint for a nuclear confrontation between the superpowers. This has highlighted a perennial dilemma in American foreign policy, namely whether the best way to avoid war is to stand aside from regional disputes or to get involved in order to manage them safely. The experience of the First and Second World Wars illustrated the dangers of the isolationist solution, but interventionism could bring the problems of its own, as the United States discovered in Vietnam.

Despite the new international assertiveness of the United States and the creation of a Rapid Deployment Force for operations in the Persian Gulf region,[38] the Iran–Iraq War did not provoke rapid superpower intervention as had the 1973 Arab–Israeli War. This was partly because the world recession made oil exports from the Persian Gulf less sensitive than they had been during the 1970s, but mainly because neither superpower stood firmly behind either of the antagonists. The Iranian revolution broke the alignment between Iran and the United States and brought overtures of friendship from the Soviet Union, which disapproved of the Iraqi invasion because of the risk that it might allow a US 'return' to the region. Both superpowers were thus at odds with their erstwhile clients at the outset of the war, and they soon agreed to stand aside from the conflict.

The drawback of this detachment was that the superpowers lost both the leverage and the compelling incentive to bring about a ceasefire. The war continued, and when Iraq began to face defeat it was prompted to escalate the conflict partly in order to *make* the superpowers stop the war. Just as one reason for President Sadat's attack on Israel in 1973 was to shock the United States into doing something to settle the issue of the occupied territories, so a major reason why Saddam Hussein launched the 'tanker war' in 1984 was that he *wished* to provoke Iranian reprisals against the shipping of the Gulf states. This, he hoped, would either bring the United States into the war against Iran or would create sufficient international pressure to compel the ceasefire which Iraq desired.

Iran, the Gulf states and the USA itself were all understandably reluctant to fall in with this plan, but the Iranians were eventually provoked into sufficient reprisals to make Kuwait appeal for superpower protection. The Kuwaitis overcame US reluctance to be dragged in by playing on superpower rivalry and threatening to invite Soviet intervention instead. Fortunately, both superpowers had now gravitated against Iran for refusing to end this increasingly dangerous conflict, and direct US involvement did not go far before the combined pressure of the major powers impelled the antagonists to reach a ceasefire. The Iran–Iraq War thus suggested that both competitive intervention and mutual detachment on the part of the superpowers pose their own escalatory risks in regional conflicts, and that the safest way to control such conflicts lies in great power collaboration.

Another unsurprising lesson of the war was that outside arms supplies tend on balance to encourage escalation, as with the shipments of aircraft and missiles such as the Super Etendard and Exocet which enabled Iraq to launch its 'tanker war'. Creating an arms 'balance' between the two sides does not necessarily deter them from using those arms, especially if a conflict is already in progress, as witness the prolonged exchanges of Soviet-made Scud missiles in the final year of the war. Nor is it easy to control a conflict by supplying more arms to the 'peaceable' side, since roles may easily be reversed – Iraq started out as the aggressor, but Iran then regained predominance and took the lead in prosecuting the war, until the arms balance once more swung in favour of Iraq at which point that country itself became reluctant to accept the ceasefire it had once so urgently demanded.

The prolongation of the war for almost eight years despite the lack of consistent superpower support for either belligerent showed how difficult it is to control the flow of arms to modern regional conflicts now that arms suppliers have become so widespread. Nations such as China and Israel were prompted by commercial and political motives to assist the Iranians, and the superpowers themselves were tempted to supply arms in order to maintain influence with the belligerents in the future, as illustrated by Moscow's shipments to both sides and by the US 'Iran–Contra' scandal in 1986.[39] Despite all the difficulties, however, the international efforts in the final year of the war to use arms sanctions as a way of ending the conflict *do* seem to have been a major factor in finally persuading Iran to accept the UN ceasefire resolution.[40]

Many escalations occurred during the Iran–Iraq War, but what did *not* happen was the spiral into superpower confrontation and nuclear war which many in the early 1980s thought might develop in this sensitive region. This was avoided partly because the USA and USSR did not have as starkly opposed interests as in previous regional crises, but partly also because the superpower leaders were just as aware of the risks as were the alarmists, and adopted deliberately cautious policies precisely to avoid such an escalatory spiral. The tragedy for the region was that this caution translated itself initially into a 'hands-off' attitude which allowed the conflict to continue for eight bloody years; only when superpower detente re-emerged with the advent of Mikhail Gorbachev was it possible to take a more active approach to ending the war.

CONCLUSIONS

The Iran–Iraq War should not be treated as typical of regional conflicts in the industrializing world; to do so would be to ignore major differences which may create quite dissimilar conflict dynamics in other areas or at other times. Nevertheless, the war does throw important light on certain basic theoretical issues concerning the escalation process, as it applies in conflicts in the Third World. In this particular regional struggle, the following patterns were apparent:

—Although the war developed in ways unforeseen by either belligerent, individual escalations tended to occur in a deliberate rather than an uncontrolled manner.
—Most escalations during the war were initiated by the losing side, in an attempt to reverse the situation on the battlefield, to wear down the opponent's resolve, or to start an escalatory spiral which would force the superpowers to impose a ceasefire.
—Initial escalation decisions tended to be governed by the military balance in the field concerned, but morale and resolve were paramount in determining whether the escalation was sustained.
—Strategic asymmetries between the belligerents were important in tempting unilateral escalatory acts, though they did not immediately produce open-ended escalatory spirals.
—Conflict thresholds proved elastic rather than brittle, being vulnerable to

erosion and ambiguity but retaining some restraining effect even after repeated violations.
—Mutual detachment on the part of the superpowers avoided an East–West confrontation, but allowed the conflict to drag on until its escalation prompted a more active international peace initiative.

These patterns from one particular conflict should not be treated as general principles which may be applied without modification elsewhere, but should be incorporated into an escalation theory which can be used to assess each conflict on a case-by-case basis. Such a theory needs to bare especially in mind the fact that traditional military considerations such as force levels and attrition rates may be much more influential in shaping escalation in Third World conflicts than they are given credit for in current nuclear theory. Finally, the Iran–Iraq War highlights the need to pay more attention to the dynamics of de-escalation, which may be just as crucial in conflict control as the escalation process itself.

Notes

1. See Lawrence Freedman, 'On the Tiger's Back: The Development of the Concept of Escalation' in Roman Kolkowicz (ed) *The Logic of Nuclear Terror* (Boston: Allen & Unwin, 1987).
2. See Herman Kahn, *On Escalation: Metaphors and Scenarios* (New York: Praeger, 1965).
3. The post-Vietnam reflections of an early US theorist of limited war are found in Robert Osgood, *Limited War Revisited* (Boulder, CO: Westview, 1979).
4. In November 1980 and June 1981 Iran bombed the Kuwaiti border town of Abdali on the border with Iraq.
5. See *Financial Times*, 28 March 1984, and *The Independent*, 16 February 1988.
6. See Richard Smoke, *War: Controlling Escalation* (Cambridge MA: Harvard University Press, 1977) pp. 32–4.
7. One of the few discussions of de-escalation is in ch. XII of Kahn, *On Escalaion*. On war termination see Fred Ikle, *Every War Must End* (New York: Columbia University Press, 1971).
8. See Thomas Schelling, *Arms and Influence* (New Haven: Yale University Press, 1966).
9. See, for example, Desmond Ball, *Can Nuclear War be Controlled?*, Adelphi Paper 169 (London: The International Institute for Strategic Studies, 1981).
10. See, *International Herald Tribune*, 11 August 1987, and the *Financial Times*, 1 March 1988. Although the US Navy increased its involvement in the Gulf immediately after the attack on the *Stark*, this move was already in preparation, and was directed more against Iran than against Iraq.
11. See, *The Independent*, 19 July 1988.
12. See George Quester, 'Bargaining and Bombing during World War II in Europe', *World Politics*, April 1963.
13. See, 'Message from Khomeini Calls Ceasefire "Bitter"', *Daily Telegraph*, 21 July 1988.
14. Contrast this with Germany's disastrous readiness to take on new enemies such as the Soviet Union and the United States during the two world wars.

15. See *The Times*, 3 October 1987.
16. The misconceived nature of Saddam's attempt to fight a brief, limited war against a revolutionary state is well brought out in Efraim Karsh, 'Military Power and Foreign Policy Goals: The Iran–Iraq War Revisited', *International Affairs*, vol. 64, no. 1 (Winter 1987/8) pp. 83–95.
17. Clausewitz's attitude to limited and absolute war is a complex subject, a good short discussion of which is found in Michael Howard, *Clausewitz* (Oxford: Oxford University Press, 1983) ch. 4.
18. On the causes of the war see Efraim Karsh, *The Iran–Iraq War: A Military Analysis*, Adelphi Paper 220 (London: The International Institute for Strategic Studies, 1987) ch. I.
19. See Gerd Nonneman, *Iraq, the Gulf States and the War* (London: Itacha, 1986).
20. See W. Andrew Terrill, 'Chemical Weapons in the Gulf War', *Strategic Review*, Spring 1986, and *The Independent*, 23 July 1988.
21. A valiant attempt to resolve this theoretical dispute using the experience of past nuclear crises is Richard Betts's book *Nuclear Blackmail and Nuclear Balance* (Washington D.C.: Brookings, 1987).
22. On all these military issues see Efraim Karsh, *The Iran–Iraq War: A Military Analysis*.
23. See Anthony Tucker, 'The Gulf Air War', *Armed Forces*, June 1987.
24. A good discussion of the problems involved is Alexander George's work *The Limits of Coercive Diplomacy* (Boston: Little, Brown & Co., 1971).
25. See Anthony Cordesman, *The Iran–Iraq War and Western Security, 1984–87* (London: RUSI & Jane's, 1987) pp. 46–53.
26. See, *The Independent*, 27 May 1988.
27. See Michael Handel, *Perception, Deception and Surprise: The Case of the Yom Kippur War* (Jerusalem: Hebrew University, 1976).
28. See Kahn, *On Escalation*.
29. Smoke, *War*, p. 252.
30. The Iraqis repeatedly compared the masses of Iranian infantry to swarms of 'flies' which had to be exterminated.
31. See, *Middle East Economic Digest*, 17 October 1987.
32. Iraq repeatedly denied using chemical weapons, and claimed that Iran was using them itself. Not until a few days before the ceasefire did a UN report finally vindicate the Iranian position. See *The Independent*, 2 August 1988.
33. See *The Times*, 23 September 1987.
34. Schelling, *Arms and Influence*, p. 138.
35. Terrill, *Chemical Weapons*.
36. Nonneman, *Iraq*.
37. See, for example, Tim Zimmerman, 'The American Bombing of Libya: A Success for Coercive Diplomacy?', *Survival*, May/June 1987, and Alex von Dornoch, 'Iran's Violent Diplomacy', *Survival*, May/June 1988.
38. See Charles Kupchan, *The Persian Gulf and the West*, (Boston: Allen & Unwin, 1987).
39. On the Soviet dimension, see Robert Litwak's chapter in this volume.
40. See *The Independent*, 22 July 1988.

Select Bibliography

Books

Adbulghani, Jasim M., *Iraq and Iran: The Years of Crisis* (London: Croom Helm, 1984).

Amin, S., *The Iran–Iraq War: Legal Implications* (London: Butterworth, 1982).

Axelgard, Frederick W. (ed.), *Iraq in Transition: A Political, Economic and Strategic Perspective* (Boulder, Colorado: Westview, 1986).

Bakhash, Shaul, *The Reign of the Ayatollahs* (New York: Basic Books, 1984).

Benard, Cheryl and Khalilzad, Zalmay, *The Government of God: Iran's Islamic Republic* (New York: Columbia University Press, 1984).

Chubin, Shahram and Tripp, Charles, *Iran and Iraq at War* (London: I. B. Tauris, 1988).

Cole, Juan R. I. and Keddie, R. Nikki (eds), *Shi'ism and Social Protest* (New Haven: Yale University Press, 1986).

Cordesman, Anthony H. *The Gulf and the Search for Strategic Stability* (Boulder, Colorado: Westview Press, 1984).

Cordesman, Anthony H. *The Iran–Iraq War and Western Security 1984–1987* (London: Jane's Publishing Co. for RUSI, 1987).

Grumman, Stephen R. *The Iran-Iraq War: Islam Embattled*, The Washington Papers vol. 10, no. 92 (New York: Praeger, 1982).

Heller, Mark., *The Iran–Iraq War: Implications for Third Parties*, JCSS Paper No. 23 (Tel-Aviv University, 1984).

Helms, C. M., *Iraq–Eastern Flank of the Arab World* (Washington, DC: Brookings Institution, 1984).

Hickman, William F., *Ravaged and Reborn: The Iranian Army*, 1982 Staff Paper (Washington, DC: Brookings Institution, 1982).

Hiro, Dilip, *Iran Under the Ayatollahs* (London: Routledge & Kegan Paul, 1985).

Ismael, Tareq, *Iraq and Iran: The Roots of the Conflict* (Syracuse University Press, 1982).

Kanovsky, Eliyahu, *The Iran–Iraq War: Its Economic Implications* (Tel-Aviv: Shiloah Center, Tel-Aviv University, 1983).

Karsh, Efraim, *The Iran–Iraq War: A Military Analysis*, Adelphi Paper 220 (London: International Institute for Strategic Studies, 1987).

Khadduri, Majid, *The Gulf War* (New York: Oxford University Press, 1988).

King, Ralph, *The Iran–Iraq War: The Political Implications*, Adelphi Paper 219 (London: International Institute for Strategic Studies, 1987).

Kramer, Martin (ed.), *Shi'ism, Resistance and Revolution* (Boulder, Colorado: Westview, 1987).

Litwak, Robert., *Sources of Interstate Conflict: Security in the Persian Gulf-2* (London: Gower for IISS, 1981).

Marr, P., *The History of Modern Iraq* (Boulder, Colorado: Westview, 1985).

Naff, Thomas (ed.), *Gulf Security and the Iran–Iraq War* (Washington, DC: National Defense University Press, 1985).

Nonneman, G., *Iraq, the Gulf States and the War* (London: Ithaca Press, 1986).

O'Ballance, Edgar, *The Gulf War* (London: Brassey's, 1988).

Ramazani, R. K., *Revolutionary Iran: Challenge and Response in the Middle East* (Baltimore: Johns Hopkins University Press, 1986).

Taheri, Amir, *The Spirit of Allah: Khomeini and the Islamic Revolution* (London: Hutchinson, 1985).
Tahir-Kehli, S. & Ayubi, S., *The Iran–Iraq War: New Weapons, Old Conflicts* (New York: Praeger, 1983).
Yodfat, Aryeh H., *The Soviet Union and Revolutionary Iran* (London: Croom Helm, 1984).

Articles

Anthony, John Duke, 'The Gulf Cooperation Council', *Orbis*, 28, Fall, 1984.
Baram, Amazia, 'Saddam Hussein: a Political Profile', *Jerusalem Quarterly*, 17, 1980.
——'Qawmiyya and Wataniyya in Ba'thi Iraq', *Middle Eastern Studies*, 19/2, 1983.
——'Mesopotamian Identity in Ba'thi Iraq', *Middle Eastern Studies*, 19/4, 1983.
Batatu, H., 'Iraq's Underground Shi'i Movements', *Middle East Journal*, 35, 1981.
Bill, James, 'Resurgent Islam in the Persian Gulf', *Foreign Affairs*, 63/1, Fall 1984.
Chubin, S., 'Israel and the Iran–Iraq War', *International Defense Review*, 3, 1985.
——'Reflections on the Gulf War', *Survival*, July/August 1986.
——'Hedging in the Gulf: Soviets Arm Both Sides', *International Defense Review*, 20/6, June 1987.
——'The Conduct of Military Operations', *Politique Etrangere*, 2, 1987.
——'Iran and its Neighbours: The Impact of the Gulf War', *Conflict Studies*, 204, 1987.
Cohen, Eliot, 'Distant Battles: Modern War in the Third World', *International Security*, 10/4, Spring 1986.
Cottam, Richard, 'Regional Implications of the Gulf War: Iran, Motives behind Foreign Policy', *Survival*, November/December 1986.
Dawisha, Adeed I., 'Iraq and the Arab World: the Gulf War and After', *The World Today*, May 1981.
——'Iraq: The West's Opportunity', *Foreign Policy*, 41, Winter 1980/81.
Farhang, Mansour, 'The Iran–Iraq War: The Feud, the Tragedy and the Spoils', *World Policy Journal*, Fall 1985.
Farley, J., 'The Gulf War and the Littoral States', *The World Today*, July 1984.
Heller, Mark, 'The War Strategy of Iran', *Middle East Review*, 19/4, Summer 1987.
Hunter, Shireen, 'After the Ayatollah', *Foreign Policy*, 66, Spring 1987.
Karsh, Efraim, 'Military Power and Foreign Policy Goals: The Iran–Iraq War Revisited, *International Affairs*, 64/2, Winter 1987–8.
——'Military Lessons of the Iran–Iraq War', *Orbis*, 33, Spring 1989.
Karsh, Efraim and King, Ralph, 'The Gulf War at the Crossroads', *The World Today*, 42, October 1986.
McNaugher, Thomas L., 'The Iran–Iraq War: Slouching Towards Catastrophe?', *Middle East Review* 19/4, Summer 1987.
Maddy-Weitzmann, Bruce, 'Islam and Arabism: The Iraq–Iran War', *Washington Quarterly*, 5/4, Autumn 1982.
Mylroie, Laurie, 'The Baghdad Alternative', *Orbis*, 32/2, Spring 1988.
Olson, William J., 'The Gulf War: Peace in our Times?', *Parameters*, 16, Winter 1986.
Parsons, Anthony, 'The Iranian Revolution', *Middle East Review*, 20/3, Spring 1988.
Precht, Henry, 'Ayatollah Realpolitik', *Foreign Policy*, 70, Spring 1988.
Razi, Gholam H., 'The Effectiveness of Resort to Military Force: The Case of Iran and Iraq', *Conflict Quarterly*, 5, Summer 1985.
Sciolino, Elaine, 'Iran's Durable Revolution', *Foreign Affairs*, 61/4, Spring 1983.

Segal, David, 'The Iran–Iraq War: A Military Analysis', *Foreign Affairs*, 66, Summer 1988.

Sick, Gary, 'Iran's Quest for Superpower Status', *Foreign Affairs*, 65/4, Spring 1987.

Staudenmaier, William O., 'Military Policy and Strategy in the Gulf War', *Parameters*, 12, June 1982.

Tripp, Charles, 'Iraq – Ambitions Checked', *Survival*, November/December 1986.

Viorst, Milton, 'Iraq at War', *Foreign Affairs*, 65/2, Winter 1986/7.

Wright C., 'Iraq: New Power in the Middle East', *Foreign Affairs*, 58/2, 1979.

——'Implications of the Iraq–Iran War', *Foreign Affairs*, 59/2, 1980/1.

——'Religion and Strategy in the Iraq–Iran War', *Third World Quarterly*, 7/4 October, 1985.

Index

Index